AS LONG AS THERE IS RESISTANCE,
THERE IS HOPE

AS LONG AS THERE IS RESISTANCE, THERE IS HOPE

ESSAYS ON

the Hong Kong freedom struggle in the post-Umbrella Movement era, 2014-2018

KONG TSUNG-GAN

Published in the United States by Pema Press

Print: ISBN: 978-0-9972385-5-6
Ebook: ISBN: 978-0-9972385-6-3

CONTENTS

PREFACE

In 2017, I published a comprehensive account of the Umbrella Movement, *Umbrella: A Political Tale from Hong Kong.* This book picks up where that one left off.

The essays collected here chronicle, as a group, Hong Kong's political trajectory since the 2014 Umbrella Movement. Even as I wrote and published each one, I had that in mind: I wanted the essays to document a history, to act as signposts. This post-Umbrella period, coming after the struggle for genuine universal suffrage and the defeat of fake suffrage in mid-2015, represents a distinct historical era.

And what defines that era? In a nutshell, it is the story, on the one hand, of resistance and the struggle for self-determination, and, on the other, of unprecedented mainlandization, imposition, infringements of rights and persecution. It is the story of competing political visions: freedom, democracy and human rights versus authoritarianism.

That is not only a Hong Kong story. It is the story of our age. Perhaps no other issue will determine our future as human beings as much as the global battle between democracy and authoritarianism. HK is on the front line.

Since the Umbrella Movement, many new initiatives and ideas have arisen from within the pro-democracy movement. New groups have been formed, new causes espoused, new objectives articulated. Most noteworthy have been localism—in short, the assertion of a separate HK identity—and advocacy of self-determination and independence.

These new objectives have created tensions between, broadly, two sides in the movement.

The one side continues to regard the Basic Law as authoritative and to insist upon a "high degree of autonomy" within the People's Republic of China and the realization of genuine universal suffrage. This position is not new; it pre-dated the Umbrella Movement and provided the foundation of the pro-democracy movement for many years. Those holding it are often referred to as moderates or traditional pan-democrats.

The other side sees the Communist Party's refusal in 2014 to allow genuine universal suffrage as per its obligations in the Basic Law and international law as irrevocably breaking the implicit contract between the Party and HK people, according to which HK people would (grudgingly) accept both PRC sovereignty over HK and the Basic Law (though HK people had no say in determining either) in exchange for the Party (grudgingly) allowing real autonomy and democracy. The 2014 refusal shows there is no realistic prospect of genuine universal suffrage ever being realized under Communist Party rule, and therefore, the objective of the freedom struggle must be more fundamental, self-determination or even independence.

Indeed, these developments have recently lead me to conclude that the term "Hong Kong freedom struggle" is more accurate than "pro-democracy movement", a term I have used up to now, for the reason stated above: It's not just democracy that's being demanded now; the political status of Hong Kong has become a matter of contention, much to the wrath of the Communist Party, though no one is more responsible for this state of affairs than it is. Hardline imposition may snuff out one problem but has a tendency of creating new problems that may be even more difficult to contain.

Back in the Umbrella Movement, most demonstrators disavowed the term "revolution". They said that rather than calling for the overthrow of the system, all they were demanding was that the Party fulfill a constitutional obligation; they wanted the Party to abide by the terms of the existing system. In a sense, that was a conservative demand, though if the Party had allowed genuine suffrage, it would indeed have had far-reaching implications for HK, leading to great change in governance and society. Now that the Party has refused to meet that conservative demand, HK is arguably entering a more revolutionary period with an increasing number of people refusing to accept Party rule and demanding respect for the right of HK people to determine their own political future, especially after 2047 when the 50-year "one country, two systems" arrangement is set to expire.

Leaving nothing to chance, the Party is doing whatever it can to nip these post-Umbrella sprouts in the bud. Its rule is becoming more draconian, arbitrary and oppressive. It has been responsible for the abduction of an HK bookseller and a mainland tycoon in HK and their transport across the border to detention on the mainland. It interpreted the Basic Law, compelling the HK High Court to disqualify six democratically elected pro-democracy Legislative Council members, thus compromising the only free and fair elections that existed in HK. It promulgated a People's Republic of China anthem law on the mainland which it then inserted into the Basic Law, requiring the HK government to criminalize "insulting" the anthem. Acting on the Party's behalf, the HK government took the unprecedented action of barring nine candidates from running for Legco on political grounds, further damaging the integrity of HK's only free and fair elections. The HK government has also prosecuted dozens of pro-democracy leaders and hundreds of activists. And, for the first time ever, it has recently banned a political party. The High Court has handed down the heaviest sentences ever for both nonviolent protest-related offenses (though these were later overturned or reduced) and violent protest-related offenses, the latter having to do with the February 2016 police-protester clashes. It has also issued harsher sentencing guidelines for nonviolent protest-related offenses. Meanwhile, the Party has stepped up efforts to mainlandize Hong Kong, integrate it with the mainland through mega-infrastructure projects and the Greater Bay Area plan, and gain tighter control over sectors of society that had previously been the most resistant to interference, such as the judiciary and universities.

Many of these episodes and incidents are discussed in the essays in this book.

I sometimes wonder if I don't spend more time chronicling the slow death of a city than the freedom struggle. HK is a case study in a place under relentless attack, and in that sense, it is also a litmus test of the willingness of the free world to stand up for the values of democracy, freedom and human rights. People's Republic of China sovereignty over HK—agreed by the powers that be while excluding those whom it most directly affects, the people of HK, from the decision-making—does not give the Party the right to do whatever it wishes, to infringe upon agreed autonomy, to abuse and restrict rights, to refuse to fulfill promises and legal obligations. And yet that's just what it's done while the world's watched.

Given that the world hasn't done much more about Syria, where millions have been killed and displaced, inaction on HK is no surprise. But at least in the case of Syria, statements have been made by governmental authorities that clearly describe what has happened there as war crimes and human rights abuses on a massive scale. Here, in HK, all we want is some acknowledgement by the United Kingdom, the United States and the European Union that "one country, two systems" is not working; in fact, is fast disappearing, and it is the fault of the Party. Instead, we get mildly expressed concerns coupled with complacent conclusions that, all in all, "one country, two systems" continues to function well. The cynicism of the exercise, the willful insistence on seeing but not saying, reflects poorly on the ability of the global system to deal with conflict and injustice.

Of course, Hong Kong is hardly the only place under the shadow of authoritarianism these days, and we should not forget to regard its situation within a global context. While China is by far the biggest, most powerful dictatorship, Russia has been under the grip of a strongman for years, and there has been substantial democratic deterioration in a wide range of countries, Turkey, the Philippines and Venezuela being among those most frequently mentioned. The United States and India have governments that regularly undermine democratic norms; the same goes for Hungary and Poland in Europe. The Arab Spring failed in every country but Tunisia. The hoped-for democratic transition in Burma is apparently stalled, Thailand is still under military dictatorship; in fact, most of Southeast Asia is ruled by one kind of tyranny or another, Indonesia and Malaysia being the only bright spots there. Central Asia is a democratic no-man's-land. Iran and Vietnam have been authoritarian for decades. And even promising democracies like Brazil and South Africa are going off the rails, undermined by kleptocracy. Surveying that record, it's no surprise that no country in the world, except maybe Taiwan, has firmly stood up for HK.

In the absence of any but the most anodyne international response, the Communist Party keeps pushing and pushing. How far will it have to go before there is a substantial reaction? The invasion of Taiwan, perhaps? And at that point, won't it be too late? In the face of the Party's aggressive militarization of the South China Sea, its draconian crackdown in Tibet, its detention of upwards of a million Turkic Muslims in political re-education camps in Xinjiang, its vehement denial of the basic human right of universal suffrage and relentless attacks on civil liberties in HK, and its continued attempts to undermine Taiwan, the rest of the world has made little more than a peep. Its silence encourages a bully, and not any old bully but one who is implacably hostile to the values of democracy, freedom and human rights that (should) underpin the international order.

What are the people of HK to make of their abandonment by the international community? Well, seems to be the phlegmatic response, at least we know where we stand. It's up to us and us alone, with the solidarity of our many non-governmental allies around the world. At least, I thought as I wrote these essays, the free world can't turn around later and say it didn't see it coming. Small consolation, that.

I had never actually planned to write about HK. In the summer of 2014, I was working for one of the pro-democracy organizations pushing for the introduction of genuine universal suffrage. In particular, I was liaising with the international media. This brought me into contact with foreign reporters, which, in turn, made it clear to me just what a poor job we were doing at getting our message out to the rest of the world. That provided the motivation to write the first essay, "Hong Kong's Power of the Powerless (or Hong Kong's Last Stand)", published in *openDemocracy* in July. It is the only pre-Umbrella Movement piece in the collection. That summer in HK felt pressurized: You felt something had to give, and the essay was meant to sound the alarm.

When the Umbrella Movement ended in December 2014, I saw that it needed to be documented. While it had received widespread media coverage, it was, as hard news journalism tends to be, piecemeal and lacked the requisite analysis and context. Anyone living under Party rule confronts the fact that the regime systematically lies about its history, and this propaganda is central to the maintenance of its monopoly on power. To chronicle what happened, to say, simply, "This is how it was," becomes, under such circumstances, an act of resistance. And so the book on the Umbrella Movement came about.

Before the Umbrella Movement, the international media largely regarded HK as a place where finance and business happened and not much else. As a result of the movement, foreign coverage increased dramatically, and although it declined in the aftermath, there is still more international reporting on HK politics now than before. The coverage has been, for the most part, solid if perhaps somewhat superficial, with limitations in conveying the complexity and nuances, and so I gradually found myself writing more on HK affairs.

Just as I had not originally intended to write about HK, I hadn't planned the pieces I ended up writing to be so long either. I wondered, Who wants to read long pieces about HK? I still wonder that. I wanted to show what things looked like from the inside, from a pro-democracy point of view obviously, and think about what was happening in an extended and serious way. There is much writing of this kind about bigger, "more important" places, so why not HK? These essays' implicit assertion is that what's going on in HK matters, not just for HK people but for the rest of the world, and should be treated seriously. I wanted to know in this kind of serious way about freedom struggles elsewhere in the world, and I hoped people elsewhere wanted to know the same about HK. It was also important to situate the HK freedom struggle in an international context, to compare it to other freedom struggles, both past and contemporaneous, and to regard what was happening in HK as part of the global struggle between democracy and authoritarianism.

The collection houses 28 essays in total: in addition to the one mentioned above from before the Umbrella Movement in 2014, eight from 2015, two from 2016 (I was working on the book then), eight from 2017, and nine from 2018. The essays are published here as they originally appeared, with only minor changes—corrections of errors and a bit of tidying up of the language. There is some repetition between essays since each was originally written as a stand-alone piece and needed to provide necessary context, but I let that stand. Those reading the essays from beginning to end can skim over the repetitions. Those skipping around in the collection won't recognize them as such and might even find them useful.

Most of the essays that appear in this book were originally published in *Hong Kong Free Press*. Many thanks to Tom Grundy for that. Thanks also to En Liang Khong of *openDemocracy* and Yaxue Cao of *China Change* for publishing some of the articles.

A word about the front cover: The image is abstracted from what had been Lennon Wall, days after the end of the Umbrella Movement. During the Admiralty occupation, the wall was covered with multi-colored post-it notes, on which tens of thousands of ordinary people had written their hopes and dreams for HK. All those colors, representing all those hopes and dreams, made for a striking sight. Before the police moved in to clear the occupation site on 11 December 2014, volunteers carefully removed all of the Post-It notes and stored them, hoping to exhibit them once again, both online and in the non-virtual world. After the occupation, the wall returned to what it had been before, bare grey concrete flanking government headquarters, a fitting symbol of the stark contrast between the vibrancy of citizens demanding their basic human right to genuine universal suffrage and the deadness of authoritarian imposition. Signs banning posting were posted, and police vigilantly patrolled the area. A few days later, someone left an umbrella made of masking tape on the wall, and in the early hours of 23 December, a 14-year-old girl ventured up to it and drew two flowers in chalk, one on each side of the masking tape umbrella. For this, she was arrested. Though she was not charged with a crime, she was held against her will in a children's home, and the police attempted to separate her from her father's legal guardianship. She was one of two minors, the other a boy, who were removed from their parents' custody in retaliation for their participation in the movement. An eruption of popular outrage caused the authorities to relent: When the cases were brought to court, the government did not actively oppose the legal representatives of the children and their families who fought for custody. The girl, who to this day is anonymous, is known throughout HK as Chalk Girl. Her story is symbolic of the post-Umbrella attempts by the Communist Party and HK government to crush the young people in the forefront of the freedom struggle. The vast majority of HK young people wants democracy and detests Party interference. The Party has persecuted those who dare to speak out and targeted youth in particular for stepped-up "educational" initiatives. Much of HK's future rides on how young people respond to the smothering of their desire for freedom; essentially what the Party is trying to do is kill our future. The masking tape umbrella is at once a symbol of the fading hope of the Umbrella Movement and its haunting legacy, affecting just about every aspect of the city, its politics and its spirit. The bare grey concrete wall outside government headquarters seems impenetrable, but the wall and the power that hides behind it are always there for the taking. Thanks to HK designer Kaitlin Chan for painstakingly recreating the image.

Lastly, a word about the collection's title, *As long as there is resistance, there is hope.* It is not meant to be uplifting or inspirational but conditional, with as much stress on "as long as" as on any other part of the assertion. It is a kind of warning: If HK people continue to resist, there is hope, but if they don't, well, then, perhaps there is none. It is also an implicit reprimand to the pessimism that has pervaded HK in the post-Umbrella era, as it situates power in the hands of the people: As long they continue to resist, it will be very difficult if not impossible for the Communist Party to entirely have its way. Yes, things often look bleak, and there is plenty of evidence to support a pessimistic view, but ultimately, it is a matter of what HK people decide to do. The intent of the Party's actions since 2014 is to kill hope, to give people the sense that there is no way out, no alternative to Party rule, to instill not only pessimism but fatalism, a sense of powerlessness and resignation. Only if the Party can extinguish hope will it have the captive population it desires. It wants people to lose faith in themselves and relinquish their power to the Party. This is in the DNA of dictatorship. At times such as these, a people needs to find within itself the courage and strength to persevere, especially as the Party does whatever it can to divide people from one another. I honestly don't know whether HK people will continue to resist in sufficient numbers, let alone turn their attention, as they need to do, toward finding a way to the positive goal of self-determination. But if we recognize the immense effort HK people have made over the course of the past twenty years and more, if we recognize that when HK was at its most imperiled, in 2003 and 2014 in particular but also at many other times down through the years, they have stood up in their millions—as a percentage of the population, perhaps larger than anywhere else in the world over the same period of time, then that track record alone gives some ground for hope.

As I wrote these essays over the last four years, the words of Frederick Douglass, former slave and abolitionist, spoken in 1857, eight years before the end of slavery, hovered like a shadow over the page, and as I went out onto the street, there they were as well, echoing in my ears, and now that my words are written, his words flicker just beneath the surface: "The whole history of the progress of human liberty shows that all concessions yet made to her august claims, have been born of earnest struggle.... If there is no struggle there is no progress. Those who profess to favor freedom and yet deprecate agitation, are men who want crops without plowing up the ground, they want rain without thunder and lightening. They want the ocean without the awful roar of its many waters.... Power concedes nothing without a demand. It never did and it never will. Find out just what any people will quietly submit to and you have found out the exact measure of injustice and wrong which will be imposed upon them, and these will continue till they are resisted with either words or blows, or with both. The limits of tyrants are prescribed by the endurance of those whom they oppress." The Communist Party is continually pushing to find out just what HK people will submit to, just how much oppression they will endure, just what the limits of its tyranny may be. The answer remains to be seen. Will HK people finally succeed in writing their own history, or will it be imposed upon them, their mouths sealed shut?

As long as there is resistance, there is hope.

A NOTE ON TERMS

"Hong Kong" and "HK" are used interchangeably.

People from Hong Kong are referred to as "Hong Kong people" or "HK people". This goes against English general usage, which prefers "Hongkongese" or "Hongkongers", two terms I've never liked, mostly because they sound terrible and feel imposed, objectifying the people described rather than issuing from them. My preferred term, "Hong Kong people", may sound a little awkward, at least at first. It is a direct translation from the Chinese 香港人, and is how HK people refer to themselves in their own language. In Cantonese, the language in which I always hear 香港人 in my mind's ear and the native spoken language of 90 percent of HK people, the term stirs a patriotic feeling and sounds like a term of endearment, even when it is used to disparage the people to whom it refers. The term also includes the word "people", and I assert that Hong Kong people are indeed a people according to international law and therefore have the right of self-determination, as all "peoples" do.

HK people are not referred to as "Chinese" because the question of whether or not they are Chinese, and if so, in what sense, is a complex matter requiring some discussion. Especially since the Umbrella Movement, it is also a matter of political contestation.

"China" and "Chinese" refer to mainland China, the China under direct Communist Party rule. "People's Republic of China" refers to the same entity. Again, the question of whether or not Hong Kong should belong to that entity is increasingly a matter of political contestation, and many of those involved in the Hong Kong freedom struggle insist on making a distinction between Hong Kong and China.

The government of China is referred to most frequently as "the Communist Party" or "the Party" or, in earlier essays, "the Partystate". People unfamiliar with China who are used to conceiving of the state and the government as two separate entities may initially be somewhat confused because even though, technically, that distinction does exist in the People's Republic of China, in practice, there is virtually no distinction, or, at any rate, to the extent that there is, Party always trumps state, and the Party is entirely above and outside of the law. Indeed, the military of China (officially referred to as the People's Liberation Army although in recent decades it has done more to suppress and kill the people than liberate them) answers directly to the Party, not to the state. In this sense, the PRC is not a "normal" country. At points, specific organs of the state making decisions about HK are referred to by name, such as the National People's Congress Standing Committee. It should be understood that all such organs are directly controlled by the Communist Party and are in no way independent of the Party. Such formally state organs are for all practical purposes indistinguishable from the Party. The term "the Communist Party" or simply "the Party" is frequently used in reference to the Party, the state, and state organs.

The Hong Kong government is essentially a puppet of the Communist Party. The leader of the Hong Kong government, the Chief Executive, is selected by a group of about 1,200 electors constituted so as to ensure that they serve the will of the Party. The CE is then appointed by the central government, ie, the Party. In other words, the process is thoroughly rigged to determine the outcome the Party preordains. The Hong Kong government does not reflect the will of the people in any formal sense, for example by being elected by the people according to principles of genuine universal suffrage, and therefore is primarily accountable to the Party and only secondarily, if at all and even then in only a vague, informal sense, to the people of HK. The 2014 Umbrella Movement came about to protest this acutely unjust and deeply entrenched state of affairs. In the following essays, the somewhat cumbersome phrase, "the Communist Party and Hong Kong government" is used when in fact the terms could often be collapsed to simply "the Party". In the same sense, when the term "Hong Kong government" is employed, it should be understood that the government is acting on behalf of the Party unless otherwise stated.

TIMELINE

Milestones of the Hong Kong freedom struggle in the post-Umbrella Movement era, 2014-2018

28 September to 15 December 2014

Umbrella Movement, consisting of street occupations of three city hubs, Admiralty, Causeway Bay and Mong Kok for a total of 79 days, opposing restrictions on universal suffrage imposed by the Chinese government and calling for full and genuine universal suffrage.

18 June 2015

Fake suffrage proposal defeated: The Hong Kong government's fake suffrage proposal, following the restrictions imposed by the Chinese government, is defeated in the Legislative Council, where pro-democracy Legco members make up more than one-third of the total number of members and therefore have veto power on constitutional amendments.

30 December 2015

Bookseller abductions: Bookseller Lee Bo is abducted from Hong Kong and detained in the mainland. He is one of five who ran a bookstore in Hong Kong detained by mainland authorities; another, Gui Minhai, was abducted from Thailand. The cross-border abductions cause great alarm regarding the Communist Party's infringement of Hong Kong's autonomy and the prospect of Hong Kong citizens being abducted by the Communist Party and brought to the mainland. On 28 January 2017, mainland tycoon Xiao Jianhua is abducted from a luxury hotel in Hong Kong and brought to the mainland.

8 to 9 February 2016

Mong Kok police-protester clashes: Nightlong clashes between police and protesters take place in Mong Kok on the first day of Chinese New Year, precipitated by a crackdown on unlicensed street vendors. The Hong Kong government and police immediately label the violence a "riot".

4 September 2016

New candidates win Legislative Council elections: Localist and self-determinationist groups, all but one formed in the aftermath of the Umbrella Movement, win six seats and nearly 20 percent of the vote in Legislative Council elections, a development that alarms the Communist Party, which regards such groups as "separatists".

7 November 2016

NPCSC Basic Law interpretation; Legco disqualifications: The National People's Congress Standing Committee interprets Article 104 of Hong Kong's Basic Law, opening the door to Hong Kong government efforts to disqualify democratically elected pro-democracy Legislative Council members. Over the coming months, six will be disqualified.

27 March 2017

Umbrella Movement 9 arrested; prosecutions of pro-democracy leaders: Over two years after the end of the Umbrella Movement, nine pro-democracy leaders are charged with "inciting public nuisance", the Hong Kong government essentially blaming them for starting the street occupations in September 2014. By the end of 2018, the Hong Kong government has brought altogether 48 legal cases against 32 pro-democracy leaders, effectively using prosecutions to crack down on the pro-democracy movement.

4 November 2017

Criminalization of "insult" of national anthem: On 1 October, the National People's Congress passes a new national anthem law which includes criminalization of "insulting" the anthem, and on this date, inserts the mainland law into Annex III of Hong Kong's Basic Law, requiring the Hong Kong government to pass a law in Hong Kong criminalizing "insult" to the anthem. Prior to this, it has become common practice for fans of Hong Kong's national football team to boo the anthem at football matches. The Hong Kong government plans to introduce legislation criminalizing "insult" in early 2019.

27 January 2018

Candidates barred from running for Legco on political grounds: Agnes Chow is banned from running in a Legislative Council by-election to replace her Demosistō party fellow Nathan Law, who was disqualified after having been democratically elected in September 2016. The grounds for barring Chow are that she belongs to a party that advocates self-determination, which, according to the Communist Party and Hong Kong government, is against the Basic Law, even though Law was allowed to run in 2016. Chow is one of altogether nine candidates prohibited from running for Legco, six in 2016 and three in 2018.

31 January 2018

Nobel Peace Prize nomination: A bi-partisan group of U.S. lawmakers nominates Joshua Wong, Alex Chow, Nathan Law and the Umbrella Movement for the Nobel Peace Prize.

6 February 2018

Prison sentences overturned, but stricter sentencing guidelines upheld: The prison sentences of Joshua Wong, Nathan Law and Alex Chow for occupying Civic Square in the lead-up to the Umbrella Movement on 26 September 2014 are overturned by the Court of Final Appeal, but stricter sentencing guidelines imposed by the Court of Appeal are upheld. The guidelines recommend heavier sentences for those convicted of protest-related crimes in cases where there may be some violence involved, even if the defendant himself is neither charged with nor convicted of a violent crime. Many fear the guidelines will lead to the imprisonment of more protesters in the future.

11 June 2018

Edward Leung and other Mong Kok 'rioters' receive heavy sentences: Former Hong Kong Indigenous leader Edward Leung is sentenced to six years in prison after having been convicted of "riot" and other crimes related to his participation in the violence between police and protesters in Mong Kok at Chinese New Year in 2016. In all so far, 25 defendants in relation to the police-protester clashes have been convicted and sentenced to over 71 years in prison. Leung's is by far the longest prison sentence of altogether 14 given to political opposition leaders since the Umbrella Movement.

14 June 2018

Mainland authorities to enforce mainland law in HK: The rigged Legislative Council passes the so-called "co-location" bill which will allow mainland officials to enforce mainland law at the terminus of the new express rail link between Hong Kong and the mainland. This will be the first time mainland law enforcement officials operate in Hong Kong, in direct contravention of the Basic Law which stipulates that no mainland laws shall apply in Hong Kong except those relating to defense, foreign affairs and other matters outside of the limits of the city's autonomy. Any exceptions must be listed in Annex III before they can be applied. Despite this, the National People's Congress approved co-location at the end of 2017. Legco's approval is the last step in the process. The co-location arrangement comes into effect at midnight on 4 September with the handing over of jurisdiction from Hong Kong to mainland authorities. On 14 December, the High Court rules that co-location is consistent with the Basic Law. The Hong Kong Bar Association has clearly stated that co-location is unconstitutional for the reasons stated above, and it is considered by many to be a gross infringement on Hong Kong's autonomy.

24 September 2018

Hong Kong government bans Hong Kong National Party, on grounds of "national security or public safety, public order or the protection of the rights and freedoms of others" under never-before-used Article 8 of the Societies Ordinance. This is the first time the government has outlawed a political group.

5 October 2018

Victor Mallet, Asia Editor of the Financial Times, is expelled from Hong Kong. The Hong Kong government refuses to renew his visa, usually a routine matter, though he has lived in Hong Kong for seven years. It also refuses to explain why, saying it never comments on individual immigration cases. Just about everyone suspects the measure was taken in retaliation for Mallet hosting a talk by Andy Chan, chair of Hong Kong National Party, in Mallet's capacity as vice-chair of the Foreign Correspondents Club of Hong Kong. This is the first time the Hong Kong government has expelled a journalist on political grounds, mirroring actions regularly taken by the mainland government. The incident is considered a precedent-setting sign of the deterioration of freedom of expression and of the press in Hong Kong.

12 October 2018

Lau Siu-lai is barred from running for the Legislative Council in a by-election to fill the seat from which she was expelled over her oath-taking in October 2016. She becomes the tenth potential candidate arbitrarily barred on political grounds by a Returning Officer of the Electoral Affairs Commission, who serves an administrative role with neither the authority nor expertise to make political decisions. The decision is final and non-appealable. As in the cases of Edward Leung and Demosistō (Nathan Law and Agnes Chow), it is a sign of moving goalposts, as all were once allowed to run but then not. As in Agnes' case, the decision apparently has to do with Lau's advocacy of self-determination, which the Party and Hong Kong government say is "against the Basic Law" even though Basic Law Article 39 states Hong Kong is party to the ICCPR and ICESCR and Hong Kong people are entitled to the rights therein, including Article 1 of both, the right of self-determination. To many, the only free and fair elections Hong Kong once had, for the Legco geographical constituencies, have been irrevocably compromised.

Hong Kong's Power of the Powerless (or Hong Kong's Last Stand)

July 2014

The post-totalitarian system touches people at every step, but it does so with its ideological gloves on. This is why life in the system is so thoroughly permeated with hypocrisy and lies: government by bureaucracy is called popular government; the working class is enslaved in the name of the working class; the complete degradation of the individual is presented as his ultimate liberation; depriving people of information is called making it available; the use of power to manipulate is called the public control of power, and the arbitrary abuse of power is called observing the legal code; the repression of culture is called its development; the expansion of imperial influence is presented as support for the oppressed; the lack of free expression becomes the highest form of freedom; farcical elections become the highest form of democracy; banning independent thought becomes the most scientific of world views; military occupation becomes fraternal assistance. Because the regime is captive to its own lies, it must falsify everything. It falsifies the past. It falsifies the present, and it falsifies the future. It falsifies statistics. It pretends not to possess an omnipotent and unprincipled police apparatus. It pretends to respect human rights. It pretends to persecute no one. It pretends to fear nothing. It pretends to pretend nothing.....

People who live in the post-totalitarian system know only too well that the question of whether one or several political parties are in power, and how these parties define and label themselves, is of far less importance than the question of whether or not it is possible to live like a human being.

— from "The Power of the Powerless", Vaclav Havel

> *. . . freedom is never voluntarily given by the oppressor; it must be demanded by the oppressed.... Oppressed people cannot remain oppressed forever. The yearning for freedom eventually manifests itself.*
>
> — from "Letter from Birmingham City Jail", Martin Luther King, Jr.

> *I thought: hope cannot be said to exist, nor can it be said not to exist. It is just like roads across the earth. For actually the earth had no roads to begin with, but when many men pass one way, a road is made.*
>
> —Lu Xun

1. Who are we? How did we get to be this way?

In any freedom struggle, much of the struggle is between not only the oppressed and their oppressor but between the oppressed themselves, some of whom side with the oppressor, and *within* each of the oppressed, who in struggling against their oppressor also struggle against the voices within themselves that tell them to unconditionally obey authority or that there must be something wrong with them if they have such a grievance against "the way things are", or that even if there is something wrong, it is utterly futile to fight it. The fault lines are many. Such is the case in the Hong Kong freedom struggle. This is the result of Hong Kong's history as a colony and an immigrant society.

In the entirety of its modern history, from the start of British colonial rule in 1842 up to today (when Hong Kong is essentially under a new colonial rule of the Chinese Communist Party), Hong Kong has always been a colony and never been a democracy. Like the rest of China, it has no democratic tradition. Much of the current freedom struggle involves building the democratic culture Hong Kong has never had from the ground up. Creating culture, changing culture is by no means an overnight process. It takes time. The question is, Does Hong Kong have the time it takes? (More about that question in a moment.)

The process of democratic cultural change involves people transforming themselves from subjects ruled by others—which Hong Kong people have always been—to citizens who rule themselves. This means changing the way we see ourselves. It does not mean, in the first instance, the subjects ask the ruler for citizenship rights, for the ruler will not freely grant them. It means the subjects refuse to any longer act as subjects and instead act as citizens, demanding their full rights as citizens, demanding ownership of the society that is rightfully ours, taking our fate into our own hands. In the midst of the struggle for genuine universal suffrage in Hong Kong, this is what is occurring. (But again, does Hong Kong have the time it takes?)

Gandhi had the concept of "swaraj" or self-rule. He certainly meant this politically, in the sense of India casting off British colonial rule and ruling itself, but he said that in order for political self-rule to differ substantially from colonial rule, Indians had to undergo the intellectual, psychological and spiritual transformation of ruling themselves as individuals, as communities. They had to stop being subjects and start being citizens, they had to take responsibility for their own lives and their own society, and not allow people far away to make decisions for them. This is what is occurring in Hong Kong.

But again, do we have time? For at the same time that this cultural transformation of citizenship and democracy is occurring, there is another very powerful transformation, orchestrated by the CCP: the at-times seemingly inexorable assimilation of Hong Kong into a mainland governed by a dictatorial regime. Hong Kong is in the process of being swallowed whole.

Which side will win, democratization or assimilation? On whose side is time? Living in Hong Kong these days, we hear the clock ticking very loudly.

Hong Kong has not only been ruled as a colony for the entirety of its modern existence. It is also an immigrant society par excellence. Almost every Hong Kong person (or her parents or grandparents) came here from somewhere else within the last century. The vast majority came from the mainland. Modern-day Hong Kong was created by people seeking refuge from the poverty, chaos, terror, regime-inflicted famine, tyranny, persecution and rights abuses of the society whose rulers now colonize us. These immigrants (our parents and grandparents) built the city we see before us every day, but in spite of that, they never saw it as theirs, they never had a sense of ownership. As immigrants, their lot was to keep their nose to the grindstone and work hard to materially improve their own lives, to give their children greater opportunities—the typical immigrant's dream.

Our parents' and grandparents' reward for building the city is a miserable retirement with no pension since Hong Kong has no public pension or social security system. (And don't you dare mention the Mandatory Provident Fund in the same breath as pension or social security!) One in three elderly people in Hong Kong lives in poverty. That's the thanks they get for building the city. A common sight on Hong Kong streets is old people half bent over pushing trolleys loaded with cardboard they've collected for recycling, slaving away 'til the day they die.

Their children are different. We were born in Hong Kong. We identify with Hong Kong. It is our place, our society. We have a sense of ownership the older generations lacked. But we also notice that though we have this sense of ownership, we most definitely don't own this place, our home. Our home is owned by others far away. Their Hong Kong minions, fully beholden to them, administrate on their behalf, not unlike the old British Governor. We experience this state of affairs as an affront to our sense of justice. We feel our powerlessness as we walk about the city every day and see it changing before our eyes, usually in ways of which we do not approve. But we have no say.

In all of our history, nobody—not the British and not the CCP—has ever bothered to ask Hong Kong people what we want. Hong Kong was simply handed by the UK over to China like a gift box with its people rattling about inside. (Us! Yes, us! Hello, we're in here! This is starting to sound like *Horton Hears a Who*—"Boil that dust speck, boil that dust speck," the evil kangaroos chant.) And "handover", yes, what an amazing metaphor: Here you go! Seven million people in a nice tidy box, just as you please! In these days when the UK has neglected to so much as utter a peep about the CCP's implementation of its end game for Hong Kong (oh, sorry, there was a peep, a very faint peep—what did you say? Oh, yes, something about genuine choice mumble mumble trade agreements mumble mumble), it is astounding to remember that Britain resumed negotiations with the CCP over the handover only seven weeks after the Tiananmen massacre in 1989. Seven weeks. At that time, Hong Kong people were terrified at the prospect of being "handed over", and anyone who was sufficiently wealthy and connected was scrambling to procure foreign passports for himself and his family. But Britain was apparently blithe. Oh, everything should work out o.k. in the end, give or take a massacre or two. (And since then it's repeated the self-hypnotizing mantra, Everything's working out o.k.) And now the CCP thinks it can go on indefinitely ignoring the desires of Hong Kong people for full universal suffrage, all the way to 2047 when the window dressing of "one-country-two-systems" will be dismantled, revealing the iron fist. Of course, at this rate, by that time, Hong Kong will be so fully assimilated into the mainland that there will be virtually no difference between it and any other mainland city. Or so the CCP's game plan goes. Which is why they're so furious with Hong Kong people for maybe having a different idea. The CCP perceives us as attempting to thwart its plan. If the people are an impediment, change the people.

Only within this historical context can one understand what is happening now. What the freedom struggle in its current manifestation is all about is Hong Kong people saying, Hey, no one's ever bothered to ask us what we want, and you still don't want to hear it, but we demand that you hear it. And we are demanding firmly but rationally, "with love and peace", having already made substantial concessions you don't seem to recognize. It's maddening to hear the word "radical" employed pejoratively by Hong Kong media and government and pro-CCP groups to refer to pro-democracy groups threatening nonviolent direct action if the CCP fails to keep its promise, fails to fulfill its legal obligation of genuine universal suffrage. "Radical" in the Hong Kong context would mean refusing to recognize the legitimacy of the Hong Kong Basic Law because it was never in any way approved by the Hong Kong people (indeed, it was never so much as put to the Hong Kong people for approval). And a "radical" of this sort would be right to do so: The Basic Law does not have the legitimacy that would be conferred upon it by constitutional referendum; it has never been formally recognized by the people it concerns as legitimate. But all pro-democracy groups accept the Basic Law, however unjust the process that brought it about, however unjust many parts of it may be. If you keep in mind this crucial concession we have already made, all pro-democracy groups in Hong Kong are eminently "moderate". Perhaps far too moderate. If anything, Hong Kong people have been far too patient for far too long, far too willing to work within a system that is rigged against us. Now we're saying, *Enough! We've had enough!*

But will saying, *We've had enough!* be enough? I suspect not. In terms of 'real power' (the only kind the CCP recognizes and takes seriously), what do we Hong Kong people have going for us? Not much, I'm afraid. Perhaps only the power of the powerless, whatever that's worth.

2. HK in light of Gandhi and MLK (and '89)

Before looking at why nonviolent direct action (often referred to by the less satisfactory term, civil disobedience) is perhaps the only hope for Hong Kong, let's put things in perspective and compare the nonviolent direct action movement for genuine universal suffrage in Hong Kong to famous historical antecedents elsewhere.

Gandhi and Indians knew it was just a matter of time. They could wait out the Brits. At the end of the day, there were just so many more Indians than British administrators and resources that if the Indians refused to cooperate, British rule was unsustainable. The Indians had superior numbers on their side. Hong Kong obviously doesn't. There are 7 million Hong Kong people, and 1 billion mainlanders (or, maybe more to the point, 86 million Chinese Communist Party members). These days, Hong Kong people feel almost inundated by the number of mainland visitors. The number of mainland immigrants per year is about 63,000. One cannot help but think that part of the CCP's end game for Hong Kong involves the mainlandization of Hong Kong's population, much as in Tibet and Xinjiang, a process very different from the type of immigration from the mainland that occurred in the mid-twentieth century.

MLK and the US civil rights movement had as their allies consistently favorable federal court decisions as well as the goodwill and sense of justice of a significant number of fellow citizens in a relatively democratic country where black people were a minority of about 10 percent of the population. Then, to top it all off, President Lyndon Baines Johnson, a southerner from the state of Texas, "got religion" and the mountain was moved. The Hong Kong judiciary will not play a decisive role in the democracy struggle. Formally, its highest authority is the National People's Congress Standing Committee, the very same big gorilla standing in the way of genuine universal suffrage. (The CCP has never been big on separation of powers or checks and balances; maybe the SC should be renamed the Standing-in-the-Way Committee.) The most we can hope for from the Hong Kong judiciary is that it manages to maintain its current modicum of independence. We don't have the democracy the US had, so the popular will is not reflected in formal political power, and the ruling party, the CCP, is determined, through its United Front work, to clandestinely set the Hong Kong population against each other—to divide us against ourselves, a typical colonial ploy. On top of this, the prospect of a Hong Kong Chief Executive, appointed as he is by the CCP, "getting religion" à la LBJ is remote, to put it mildly.

Even in the case of the nonviolent direct action movements in India and the US, which are today widely regarded as successful, it is important to remember that it took them literally decades to achieve success, and for years, both of these movements appeared to be going nowhere. It took dei ex machina— that is to say, circumstances not within their control (for India, the toll of World War II on Britain; for the US civil rights movement, LBJ)—to put them over the hump.

Then, of course, there are the massive 1989 pro-democracy demonstrations in China, whose fate, twenty-five years on, is still almost too horrible for me to regard directly, without blinking or closing my eyes. June 4 casts a long long shadow of sadness and horror on Hong Kong, and we cannot contemplate a nonviolent direct action campaign on CCP-ruled territory without, in the back of our minds, the prospect, however remote, of PLA tanks rolling through the streets.

The Chinese demonstrations of '89 failed just as the Soviet Communist empire was in the process of collapsing, but it's actually China's '89 demonstrations that are the rule and the collapse of the Soviet Empire the exception: Successful nonviolent direct action movements are quite rare. They happen, yes indeed they do, and they give tremendous cause for hope, but most of the time, most nonviolent direct action movements fail. That is the simple truth. Just as most political movements fail.

(For a good counter-argument, see *Why Civil Resistance Works: The Strategic Logic of Nonviolent Conflict* by Erica Chenoweth and Maria Stephan. Gene Sharp's classic *From Dictatorship to Democracy* is also there, available free online—give a copy to a friend!)

So where does that leave us here in Hong Kong? What do we have going for us? If India had numbers and the civil rights movement had the courts and widespread support in a democratic country, who are our allies?

The Hong Kong business community? It is to laugh! If you ever were under the illusion they might be secret democracy lovers, the anti-Occupy Central movement has definitely put paid to that. Local chambers of commerce, foreign chambers of commerce, multinational accounting firms, local businesses, mainland-owned businesses, the list goes on and on. They're lining up to get in thick with the big bully across the border. They know on which side their bread is buttered (or think they do).

The Hong Kong media? There are lots of great journalists and reporters in Hong Kong, but they're not the ones with the power. With precious few exceptions, Hong Kong media leadership is either outright hostile or indifferent. There is the explicitly pro-CCP media (actually very small in terms of audience) and then the media that believe it's commercial suicide to be pro-democracy (because those very same businesses which are de facto pro-dictatorship will withhold advertising, as even big international banks like HSBC and Standard Chartered have done with *Apple Daily*, the only pro-democracy publication with any substantial market share).

Foreign governments? *Gee, it sure would be nice if there were genuine choice!* is about as much as we can expect from the US and the UK. (The EU isn't even as "radical" as that. It just says it's "monitoring the situation", with a very serious look on its face). As Hamlet said, *Words words words....* (Or, as my daughter says, *Blah blah blah....*)

International media? The international media has actually been pretty amazing over the past few months. It's gone from basically thinking nothing ever happens in Hong Kong that's worth covering except business and finance and that everything is pretty much hunky-dory with "one country, two systems" to educating itself quickly and reporting with striking accuracy and insight. But how far is that going to take us? First of all, international media attention is fickle and fleeting. Secondly, what comes to mind is a recent conversation with a journalist from a major international newspaper. I thanked him for his great article on Occupy Central, for getting the word out there about what's going on in Hong Kong. He laughed and said, *No one cares about Hong Kong at home. In fact, the average guy doesn't even know what's going on here.* There's some nice bracing perspective to snap you back to reality. The international media have very limited influence on foreign governments, especially as regards a place like Hong Kong which foreign ministries file as a minor matter under "China policy".

So the Hong Kong democracy movement has no real allies to speak of that would help to leverage the situation in our favor. It is rare for nonviolent direct action movements to succeed without powerful allies or other forms of leverage. The anti-Occupy Central campaign is largely an artificial crock, but it is important insofar as it has made the most powerful forces in Hong Kong society formally declare themselves for the oppressor.

It's just we ourselves and us. Power of the powerless. Thanks, Havel—lotta good it will do us. But then again, as Mandela said, *It seems impossible until it is done.* He just failed to add, *Of course, most things never get done.* (And therefore, remain impossible.)

Oh, yes, I almost forgot: We have truth, justice and international law on our side, none of which, unfortunately, have much power here. But just so you know!

3. What we're up against

On top of this bleak prognosis, pit the Hong Kong democracy movement against the CCP, the biggest, wealthiest, and most powerful political organization in the world, which just happens to be dictatorial as well.

The CCP's end game for Hong Kong is full assimilation. According to the "one country, two systems" agreement, this is not scheduled to occur until 2047, but in fact, it has been steadily and gradually and often invisibly but increasingly palpably happening ever since the 1997 handover, if not before. The CCP seeks to fully control Hong Kong and govern it for all intents and purposes just like any other mainland city. Politically speaking, what this means is that it wishes to implement an electoral system that mirrors the "elections" on the mainland. Yes, they do have "elections" on the mainland. They differ slightly from elections elsewhere in that the result is predetermined from above, always in favor of the ruling power. This is what the CCP wishes to see in Hong Kong. There would be a small variation from the mainland in that the CCP would allow the Hong Kong electorate to "choose" between Puppet A and Puppet B, but all that means is legitimizing a charade. (Very few of my Hong Kong friends understand the expression, "putting lipstick on a pig"—doesn't translate well into Cantonese!—but that's what we're talking about here.)

The CCP seems to have been a bit startled that a rather large number of Hong Kong people don't like its plan. It had thought it had sufficiently tranquillized us, divided us, bought us off. But no matter: It has still other means. In the topsy-turvy world of Hong Kong politics, the ruling party of the country to which Hong Kong belongs is underground. That's right: The CCP has no legal presence anywhere in Hong Kong (then again, it's not legally registered in the mainland either, for it is above the law). There is no Hong Kong branch of the CCP (unless it is secret), but the CCP is everywhere, most obviously through its control of the Hong Kong government, but also through its alliance with Hong Kong tycoons and chambers of commerce as well as through an elaborate system of front organizations. Unfortunately, there has been almost no recent journalistic investigation into this murky world or how it works (that would be a juicy story indeed, but the HK mainstream media is too compromised and scared and the international media doesn't have the attention or see the importance).

For starters, the CCP essentially created the DAB (I can never remember what it stands for—oh, yes, the Democratic Alliance for the Betterment and

Progress of Hong Kong, "democratic" here employed in the same sense as the Democratic People's Republic Of Korea). The DAB has become, both in terms of number of elected representatives to District Councils and the Legislative Council (Hong Kong's pseudo-legislature) and in terms of funding and number of permanent offices open around the city, the biggest political party in Hong Kong. I presume the CCP, whether directly or indirectly, is also the main funder of the DAB, though since there is no political party law in Hong Kong (political parties are registered under the Companies Ordinance—that's right, legally, they're companies) or law regulating funding of political parties, there is no legal requirement that parties reveal the source of their funding. The CCP has also played a major role in the founding and support of pro-business parties such as the Liberal Party and (once that proved to be a miserable failure) Regina Ip's New People's Party (Regina Ip being the former Hong Kong government Secretary for Security who in 2003, only six years after the handover, tried to force down Hong Kong's throat draconian security legislation that would have brought Hong Kong in line with mainland security laws and restricted a number of civil liberties, then once we beat that down, resigned, went to Stanford to launder herself, and magically reappeared with a new political party and think tank a couple years later). The CCP also has its own unions and community organizations and has very close relations with so-called patriotic associations, usually named after the part of China that the members originally came from (such as the Longyan Association after Longyan, Fujian Province, which recently gained some notoriety for offering members top dollar—HK$400—to participate in the anti-Occupy Central rally).

After the CCP was taken aback (or enraged) by the enormous number of people (792,808) participating in the June 20 to 29 Occupy Central referendum on genuine universal suffrage and the annual July 1 democracy march (half a million) (July 1, by the way, is the date of the handover, which just happens to also be the anniversary of the founding of the CCP—yes, Hong Kong's "return to the motherland" was the CCP's birthday present to itself—how perverse can you get?), the CCP mobilized this United Front more brazenly than ever before. It created out of nothing the "Alliance for Peace and Democracy" (one of the great misnamed organizations in the world, "democracy" here again in the sense of the Democratic People's Republic of Korea) to carry out an anti-Occupy Central petition campaign. All pro-CCP elements in the city, from top government leaders to business leaders to political parties to patriotic associations to unions and community organizations have dutifully pledged their allegiance. Being clandestine by nature, usually the United Front is more comfortable working in the shadows, and it's a sign of just how nervous the CCP has become that it is wielding its clout so openly. If anything, the campaign has shown the true extent and depth of the CCP's infiltration of Hong Kong society. But that wasn't enough for the CCP's Leninist rage for control. It has almost certainly been behind a number of cyberattacks on pro-democracy groups and media as well as smear campaigns targeting a number of pro-democracy leaders. Its methods have shown just how important it is to oppose further CCP influence and infiltration in the city by standing up for genuine universal suffrage, the promise made to Hong Kong in the Basic Law in the form of a clear legal obligation, the promise the CCP appears dead set on breaking. What it wants is our complete and full capitulation.

It knows the 20 to 30 percent of the population who firmly demand genuine universal suffrage and actively participate in the pro-democracy movement will not back down. And it knows it's got 20 to 30 percent of the population in its pocket. It wants those people in the middle—most of whom would choose genuine universal suffrage if they felt they could—to back down, to give in, to give up, to gulp and say, Well, ok, maybe this fake democracy is not so bad after all; at any rate, it isn't worth standing up to the CCP over.

It's unclear whether this current anti-democracy onslaught of propaganda and intimidation will succeed. It could backfire as these people reveal more than ever before how nasty, brutish and clownish they are. The people in the middle may look at them and ask themselves, Eegads, Do we want *them* to run our city?!

But whatever the results of this spectacular barrage (I often feel I am hiding under one of those old tin garbage can covers with a steady rain of rocks pouring down on me), it is pretty clear that the CCP thinks that in the long run, it's got Hong Kong check-mated. It may be right.

But it may be wrong. It's a victim of its own success: It has so artificialized and falsified large swathes of Hong Kong society, creating a "movement" out of thin air, that it doesn't know what it has on its own hands, it can't tell false from true, and therefore can never quite be sure what it's up against. Thus, its consternation that rather than rolling over and surrendering at sight of the White Paper, Hong Kong people were provoked to stand up in larger numbers than ever before. As it peers into the hall of mirrors which is the Hong Kong created by its falsification, all it can see is an infinite number of reflections of itself. (What a scary thought!)

On top of that, its victories, whatever they may be, are by definition Pyrrhic, since it must destroy so much in order to succeed. If the CCP has its way, Hong Kong will clearly be a much worse place for the vast majority. Of course, it probably just doesn't care—control is of the utmost importance; everything else is of secondary priority.

But it's constant work to maintain a monopoly on power through coercion and deception. The old people, some of whom are the Party's only possible "popular base" to speak of in Hong Kong (if, by popular base, we mean the generally apolitical folks who enjoy attending the DAB's complementary banquets and seafood excursions and can be shuffled out to vote or sign any old petition put under their noses), will die. The young people are already entirely alienated from your bullying ways. You might succeed in co-opting them in middle age, but you have nothing to buy them off with now: low social mobility, low-paying and thankless jobs, unaffordable housing, marriage and children financially out of reach, no power to change anything for the better, all-around low quality of life getting worse by the day. Thanks a lot, CCP!

Still, can't you hear that clock is ticking? Or is that just the beating of our hearts pounding ever harder? Time is not on our side; it's on the side of the adversary.

4. Why nonviolent direction action is probably the only option left, however futile it may prove to be

Which is why nonviolent direct action is necessary. Or not so much necessary as the only real option left, the only chance. We've tried everything else, to no avail. Hong Kong people are too patient, too deferential, too willing to "eat sorrow" and consider our misfortunes our own fault. We have that colonial, authoritarian reflex deep inside of us, to defer to power, to give power the benefit of the doubt, to think of ourselves as inferior, unworthy, and if we can't make it, then it's down to our own personal failings. As said, much of the struggle is with this side of our own selves. And because of our better nature (which is also our worse), we've put up with a postponed promise (not to mention a defied legal obligation since, legally speaking, the Hong Kong government is illegitimate because not elected by universal suffrage as stipulated in the Basic Law, where Hong Kong, as party to the International Covenant on Civil and Political Rights, is also legally obliged to comply with the ICCPR, including

Article 25, and since universal suffrage—one-person-one-vote and the right to run and be elected—is a political right, the concept of "progressive realization" or "gradual and orderly progress" does not obtain—it is a right that must be realized immediately; thus, we're in the amazing situation of our own government according to our own pseudo-constitution being illegal) for seventeen years, and as we all know, justice delayed is justice denied. We've put up with an obviously rigged system, which the CCP has tried to stack even more against us, moving the goalposts with its NPCSC add-ons to the Basic Law (if you don't know about these, don't worry; all you need to know is one way the CCP prevents progress is by making everything so damn complicated it's like being bound up in knotted twine—it's all you can do to move your little finger), and we've tried to work within the system. To no avail. You'd think the CCP would at least throw the dog a bone to encourage the dog to delude itself into thinking that it had something to gain from working within the system, but to do so would have been to transgress its authoritarian impulse. This dog is under no illusions: We have nothing to gain from working within the system.

So what are the calculations of this nonviolent direct action campaign?

The thinking goes like this: If the CCP manages to ram through mainland-style "elections", it will cement in place a precedent from which there's no return short of full-on revolution. It is the first brick in the wall of formal mainlandization of the political system. It would really be a huge accomplishment, especially if achieved right under the noses of the Hong Kong people. And the pro-democracy cause would essentially be sunk.

As long as the pro-democracy groups stay united (a big if, considering the Democratic Party broke ranks and compromised the last time around, sinking us even further in the muck of the detested Legco functional constituencies—see above for the knotted-twine policy), the CCP won't be able to do this. The CCP is currently trying to trick so-called 'moderates' on the pro-democracy side into going along with its "pocket it first" ploy—take a bit of "improvement" now and more "improvements" can be made later. But this ain't improvement, mister; it's your grave.

For the pro-democracy side, no electoral reform would be better than fake universal suffrage. (This view flies in the face of the proliferating screamers who say, Oo oo oo, if we don't take scraps this time, there might be nothing next time.)

No electoral reform is also the CCP's second option (after mainland-style "elections"), for then it can blame Hong Kong people for failing to reach "consensus" and thereby simply postpone its promise even longer, claiming that "gradual and orderly progress" is not occurring, through no fault of its own, of course—those people in Hong Kong just can't seem to get their act together!

And genuine universal suffrage, what are the chances of that? Only a truly starry-eyed idealist could believe that we will bring it about through nonviolent direct action, only someone who doesn't grasp what the CCP's all about.

So what's the point of nonviolent direct action, then, if it stands so little chance of achieving its declared aim? (Of course, historically, in the short term, most forms of nonviolent direct action stood little chance of achieving their aim. They were not the first choice but a last resort for people with little to no access to formal political power.)

The point is, first of all, to draw a line in the sand: You can't steamroller us.

Secondly, the only thing the CCP understands or will even take into consideration is power. Working within the system in Hong Kong, pro-democracy groups have no power, so the CCP doesn't take them seriously. Stepping outside of the system and presenting the prospect of an occupation of the central business district changes the equation and forces the CCP to take heretofore unthreatening little gadflies seriously. (And if you don't believe that, how do you explain the gigantic fit it's throwing right now?)

Thirdly, it draws the attention of Hong Kong people who might otherwise be checked out (a depressingly large number, but then, considering most Hong Kong people spend long days just trying to make ends meet, unsurprising) and the rest of the world to the gravity of the situation here. Both groups have paid more attention than ever before.

Fourthly, if it is successful (a big if), it will force the CCP to react. Exactly how it reacts, of course, is an open question. The very worst scenario is that it sends in the PLA. That seems farfetched, but the People's Liberation Army liberating people from their lives seemed equally far-fetched to many demonstrators in Beijing in 1989. More likely is that it will be compelled to devise a face-saving compromise or climb-down. It doesn't want to look too ruthless with the rest of the world watching (even if they won't do much). By rest of the world, we also mean Taiwan. Taiwanese are watching what the CCP is doing in Hong Kong with great wariness.

And fifthly, you never know what will happen. And at this point, there's little to lose.

Some will disagree with that. They will say that Occupy Central risks provoking the CCP into taking more drastic actions in Hong Kong than it otherwise would. Like what, exactly? Almost nothing that it isn't otherwise already considering, short of sending in the tanks. For that reason, I don't think the nonviolent direct action freedom struggle is acting irresponsibly or toying with Hong Kong's future. One cannot predict or determine every aspect of the future, especially when it comes to politics. It is simply unknown, but the actions we take can't make it worse than now, or worse than it would otherwise be if the CCP gets its way.

And lastly, if the pro-democracy movement stands firm (a big if), it will be difficult for the CCP to implement anything smoothly here, short of sending in the tanks. It could, of course, all collapse like a house of cards. Pro-democracy groups must stay united.

Sometimes I wonder (and I am one of them), Do they really understand what this is about? Do they really understand that this is Hong Kong's Last Stand? We are stronger than ever but infinitely fragile. Unlike the CCP, we leave too much to chance: Will people really turn out to occupy Central when the time comes? We hope so; the referendum and July 1 march were encouraging, but we don't really know. And it's a big leap from voting online or marching a few hours to dedicating yourself to a sit-in: Can you take time off work? Can you afford to be arrested? Which is why so much depends on the young people, not only because they are amongst the most passionate and dedicated and least likely to be tricked into false compromises, but because they don't have jobs and don't have to support a family.

I spoke of what's happening in Hong Kong as the development of a culture of democracy and citizenship, as a psychological shift from being subjects to citizens. But Occupy Central is a high-risk gamble, for if it fails, especially if it fails spectacularly rather than nobly, it risks sealing the fate of the pro-democracy movement.

If you can think of a better strategy, let us know, please! None of our trenchant critics, of whom there are quite a few, have managed to yet—generally, they're much better at criticizing than proposing. (And here, I mean *strategy*, not tactics. We have stumbled often and badly already, and perhaps it is ironically a sign of the movement's strength that we haven't yet done ourselves in. We need help on tactics too. But on strategy, I can't think of better than nonviolent direct action, given our limited options.)

If nothing else, it is important to show we are citizens, not subjects, and refuse to be treated as subjects.

5. And if it fails, if *we* fail? Begin to begin

I think of how demonstrations just seem to burst out of nowhere in other places, and I have to laugh: Ours must be the least spontaneous nonviolent direct action movement ever—in existence for eighteen months without ever yet having taken nonviolent direct action! Then again, when you think that for a decade and more, some of the biggest demonstrations for democracy in the world have taken place here in Hong Kong, without hardly anyone noticing, least of all, it seems, our own government, then it looks different: Occupy Central is the logical conclusion of trying by almost every other means conceivable for a decade and more.

Anytime you ask the leaders of the nonviolent direct action movement, they will tell you that the very last thing they want to do is take nonviolent direct action! Sometimes I think we will have to drag our own leaders kicking and screaming to the sit-in. The most powerful political organization in the world, the country's ruling party, is clandestine in Hong Kong, and the most striking characteristic of the city's nonviolent direct action movement thus far is its reluctance to take nonviolent direct action. Too funny. You couldn't make this stuff up. Sounds like a Murakami story.

And if it fails, if *we* fail, what happens next? The CCP has its way. Hong Kong is changed irrevocably. The pace of mainlandization will be stepped up. More mainland immigrants will arrive. More mainland visitors will come. The already fragile walls between the CCP and the media, business and the Hong Kong government will all but disappear. Who knows about the judiciary, but it's hard to imagine it won't be affected. The demographics of Hong Kong will change substantially. To put it simply, anyone who can get out, will. Most of the population is trapped and will continue to be a source of captive, exploited labor. Inequality—Hong Kong is already the most unequal developed society in the world—will be exacerbated. Hong Kong will suffer brain drain. Many of the people already making money in Hong Kong will stay, but the educated classes will begin looking for opportunities elsewhere as it becomes harder and harder to go against the grain, as opportunities here lessen, as the general environment becomes ever more hostile, as it becomes more and more thankless to be a Hong Kong person with ideas and a willingness to contribute. People are already looking for the exit. As I say, most people are trapped, with no other options, so the exit-seekers are a minority, but in terms of what they have to contribute to the society, the impact of their exit would be great.

This is why we must realize the power of our powerlessness. It is our own society that's up for grabs. It really is Hong Kong's Last Stand. It's a point at which people have to make difficult decisions between their own immediate short-term interests and the long-term interests of society. Even if, in the long run, the two coincide, in the short run they often seem to diverge. One can often ask oneself, Why bother? What's the point? There's little chance of success. The situation is already so bad. I could probably be enjoying myself more doing something else. And there are so many Hong Kong people who just don't seem to get it—why bang my head against the wall? Why waste my time?

I can't convince myself (or you, or you) with one simple answer. The only answer I have goes something like this: Because—to return to the point at which I started—the struggle for democracy, for a just and fair society in Hong Kong, is also the struggle for my own soul. In a sense, it is an end in itself, regardless of the result, which lies beyond my control. Or to put it another way, it beats sleepwalking to my doom. And though focused on this small place, this struggle is part of much larger struggle, a global struggle. Because at the end of the day, there has to be more to this world than ill-gotten gain and illegitimate power. Because Hong Kong, as so many places in the world, hangs in the balance: Will Hong Kong and the world become more like the CCP-ruled mainland over the course of this still-young century, or will China become rights-respecting and democratic? Are we entering a new era in which authoritarian rule will dominate much of the globe, or will the world become increasingly democratic? I don't know. Much is uncertain. So much is beyond my control.

Havel wrote his long essay (much much longer than this one), "The Power of the Powerless" in 1978. At the time, he believed Czechoslovakia was so deep in the Communist deep freeze that it didn't even make sense to begin talking about taking political action. What he meant by 'the power of the powerless' was that even in very repressive situations, we have a choice. We can choose to live freely in each and every detail of our lives. We can choose to act as if we live in a free society, and perhaps by doing so, we begin to transform ourselves and the society ever so slightly. It begins, by the accumulation of our actions, to be a freer society because we are in the process of liberating ourselves.

The difference in circumstances between Czechoslovakia circa 1979 and Hong Kong circa 2014 couldn't be greater. Havel's strategy was essentially to wait out the repression—Communist dictatorship, the thinking went, couldn't warp the society any more than it already had—and while doing so, exercise (and exorcise) the spirit to prepare for when the time was ripe for political action. In Hong Kong, the time is ripe now. We have everything to lose by waiting, and who knows what we stand to gain by acting. The room for maneuver narrow, the chances slim, let's begin to act freely. Let's begin.

I don't know if we will win this time, or next time, or the next, or the next, but we (Hong Kong people, Chinese, human beings) will win.

Or so I think on better days....

Some thoughts on the Hong Kong anti-parallel trade demonstrations

March 13, 2015

I've been trying to think my way through the anti-parallel trade demonstrations. My opinions have oscillated. The demonstrations have provoked a wide range of views on the pro-democracy side.

Some say they represent a new strain or phase of the movement. These people say that traditional demonstrations à la Civil Human Rights Front's Victoria-Park-to-Central marches have proven ineffectual and new methods need to be employed, methods these recent demonstrations are developing as they evolve. They say the HK government is so unresponsive and anti-democratic that the only way of having any effect on it is to really push hard and embarrass it. Otherwise, it's simply intransigent. They say these demonstrations have been successful in tapping into popular resentment at the mainlandization of HK and thereby embarrassing not only the HK government but also the Partystate into at least speaking as if they are going to do something to compensate for their obvious neglect if not facilitation of the over-running of parts of HK with mainlanders and what amounts to illegal activity. In addition, the demonstrations address what has arguably been a blind side of the pro-democracy movement, socioeconomic issues, which for many HK people are much more urgent in their everyday lives than genuine universal suffrage.

Others say the anti-parallel trade demonstrations are providing the perfect opportunity for the anti-democrats of HK to tar and feather the pro-democracy movement with charges of "radicalism" and "violence", charges they've trotted out ad nauseam in the past but which have never really stuck because the movement has more often than not appeared reasonable and peaceful. I've spoken with many "ordinary" (ie, generally apolitical) people who have vague sympathy for the pro-democracy movement (ie, they passively support it) and who have been shocked at video images of what appear to them to be demonstrators harassing and verbally abusing parallel traders and shopkeepers involved in parallel trading. The critics of the demonstrations say we should not condone behavior on our side that we abhor when blue ribbons engage in it. They say the demonstrations can't do the pro-democracy movement any good and may harm it. They know that the pro-democracy movement and the anti-parallel trade protests are not the same thing, though they may overlap, but they're afraid that "ordinary" HK people won't be able to distinguish between the two, especially when HK government propaganda (as well as much of the media, the pro-Partystaters, and the police) encourages people to equate them. They say principles of nonviolence must be strictly adhered to, and that includes not verbally abusing or acting aggressively towards others.

Before I go any further, I must thank all of the people who've been facebooking and tweeting the demos. Mainstream media coverage has been inadequate and often misleading, and the facebookers and tweeters have provided much needed perspective and information. More than ever, opinion in HK is divided between those who rely on the mainstream media for their news and people who get it from social media. And I should note that I haven't attended an anti-parallel trade demonstration, not for lack of desire but due to parental duties.

My own reaction has been mixed. On the one hand, it's rah-rah, sock it to 'em, let's show these people (ie, the police, the HK government)! But I wonder if that's to do with my desperation for something, anything to happen to further the cause. On the other hand, I've felt uneasy, and at times I've not been quite sure what that unease is about—am I simply getting more conservative as I get older?!

But I think my unease is related to the fact that the target of much of the demonstrations' ire has been the little guy, the parallel trader. However obnoxious some parallel traders might be, however much their huge influx has damaged the quality of life of some parts of HK, and despite the fact that many engage in what strictly speaking is illegal activity, most parallel traders are people just trying to scratch a living at the margins of society. In that sense, they're not much different from many HK people. They have an impact on HK not by intention but by their sheer numbers.

The parallel traders as individuals are not the true culprits here. Parallel trade is one piece of the big picture of the mainlandization of HK, and it's the Partystate and the HK government which are responsible for that. We should at the very least thank the demonstrators for putting the focus on mainlandization, one of the top problems facing HK. The manifestations of mainlandization are wide-ranging:

- The fake universal suffrage that the Partystate wants to foist on HK would cement mainlandization in terms of **formal politics and governance**.

- In addition to that, we've got the many **United Front operations** ranging from obvious ones like the DAB and the pro-Partystate political establishment to the FTU and the many "patriotic" and neighborhood organizations as well the infiltration of many sectors of society.

- Then there's **the media and the police** which at times appear to pretty much have gone over to the dark side. (The judiciary and the education sectors have been the ones that up to now have best withstood mainlandization pressures, and that is why they are coming under increasing attack.)

- There are **the infrastructure mega-projects** such as the high-speed rail link and the Macau-Zhuhai-HK bridge tying HK physically closer to the mainland.

- And then there's the changing **demographics** of HK, the mainlandization of the population. As the government itself says in its recent Population Policy report, "new arrivals under the OWP [one-way permit] Scheme will continue to be the major source of our population growth", and since 2003, 828,000 mainlanders have settled in HK—63,000 a year.

- And then there's the **economy**: At the high end, you've got mainland money swamping HK, buying up properties and companies, and various mainland businesses—many either Partystate-owned or closely allied with the Partystate—taking over ever more of the economy, gradually elbowing even some HK tycoons out of the way. At the low end, there are the tourists and the parallel traders.

So the parallel traders are the bottom-feeders of mainlandization. Targeting them seems like attacking the most vulnerable in order to get at the most powerful. I get that parallel trade is one of the most visible and obvious forms of mainlandization, but of all the forms we have to worry about, it's far from the most insidious or damaging.

The problem with the demonstrations, then, is that they in effect attack the little guy for what is really the fault of the big guy, and not only that, they distort perspective on the much larger issue of mainlandization by focusing on one small aspect of it, blowing parallel trade out of proportion while the really big fish go about their business of swallowing HK whole.

But here we face a conundrum: how to get at the big guy, a government that is utterly impervious to popular opinion and refuses to address the myriad problems that HK people confront in their everyday lives?

One of the reasons I've been encouraged by the emergence of supposedly more "radical" groups is that other groups simply haven't done that much of late. The established pro-democracy political parties are really quite a conservative force and play largely a defensive role. Hopefully, they can be counted on to defeat fake universal suffrage (though I will worry right up to the last moment, given the Democratic Party's capitulation last time around), and within their realm in the Legislative Council, they are doing what they can. But traditional pro-democracy political organizations, whether parties or NGOs, in HK have been inadequate at organizing, mobilizing, strategic planning and execution, and coordination. HKFS, Scholarism and students in general came along with the Umbrella Revolution, and their emergence is hugely positive, but since the end of the occupations, they've been relatively quiet, understandably exhausted and having to attend to the rest of their lives which were put on hold for months during the occupations.

In his recent interview comparing the Sunflower and Umbrella Movements, Ian Rowen says that a key difference between the two was the centralization of Sunflower versus the loose organization of Umbrella. He said the latter was clearly a disadvantage when it came to developing strategy and taking concerted action, but it can also be seen as a sign of maturity that the movement didn't have to rely on a few key actors. I agree with that, but it's easy, in the midst of it all, to become exasperated with our frequent inability to get our act together when it comes to strategic collaborative action. We have to remember we're up against the Partystate, one of the most centralized and powerful political forces in the world, not to mention the HK government and police, which are well-funded and well-organized, and whose members get paid for what they do. What chance do we stand if we're not well-organized ourselves? I like the idea of everyone doing their bit, and here the anti-parallel trade groups are stepping up and doing theirs, but on the other hand, I fear their emergence also points to our continuing weakness when it comes to strategizing and coordinating.

Their emergence also challenges a central tenet of the more moderate or mainstream parts of the movement: Whatever you do, you've got to track close to public opinion. That view is understandable: You've got to reach out to people and invite them to join, broaden your appeal, not alienate them. The thinking is that the middle 50 percent of HK people are conservative by nature, could go one way or the other, and will shun you if you're perceived as "radical", whereas you stand a good chance of getting their support if you appear "rational". But there are several problems with the tenet. The first is "public opinion" is illusory. Yes, it can be measured to some extent by opinion polls. But it can also be actively shaped. And that has to do with leadership. Few freedom movements sit back and say, Well, let's just wait until public opinion is firmly behind us, especially given that in less-than-democratic societies such as ours, public opinion is distorted. They say, this is what we believe in, and we're going to go out and shape public opinion. I recall well when, after the NPCSC decision, all the air seemed to go out of Occupy Central, to the point where its plan was to, well, yes, occupy Central, but, hey, we don't want to disturb anybody or disrupt any activity, so we'll plan it on a national holiday when much of Central will be shut down anyway; that way, we won't offend anybody. That was tracking of public opinion taken to absurd lengths, and it's also the reason why Occupy Central failed to appeal beyond a core group. Thank whomever the students came along! Something that many of the groups that have emerged since last summer have going for them is they say, We're going to be out in front, we're going to take the lead on this. That doesn't mean ignoring public opinion (after all, there's pretty strong public opinion against parallel trade, which is why the HK government has been so embarrassed at being so negligent about it). It means that sometimes you go out in front and encourage others to follow, or even that you are willing to sacrifice your popularity if it advances the cause.

Lastly, the anti-parallel trade demonstrations have focused on a socioeconomic issue, and socioeconomic issues are ones that most of the pro-democracy spectrum has traditionally not provided strong leadership on. This goes way back to parties like the Democratic and Civic Parties being founded by lawyers and other professionals and having little to no base in the grassroots. I was encouraged when League of Social Democrats first emerged because that's what HK needs—a strong commitment to both democracy and social justice in order to oppose oligarchic control of the economy. But LSD opted far too much for street politics and throwing bananas in Legco, which is o.k. for starters but can only take you so far and has basically brought LSD to a dead end. LSD's promise was that it could reach out to the public housing estates and appeal to people there. Up to now, the huge Achilles heel of the pro-democracy movement is that it's ceded huge swathes of HK territory to the well-funded DAB. It needs to have a strong and consistent presence in those communities to tell people the reason they're getting screwed—that their lack of access to meaningful political participation is the main reason for the worst income inequality in the world, low wages, exorbitant property prices, poor labor protections and working conditions (no mandatory overtime pay, no standard working hours law, poor parental leave laws, no child care provision unless you can afford to hire someone from a faraway land to leave her own children and come look after yours, no law to enforce the right to collective bargaining guaranteed in international law) is that the political system and the economy are controlled by a tiny number of elites intent on milking them for all they're worth—it's not for nothing that HK ranks #1 on *The Economist's* crony capitalism index. But up to now, no one in the pro-democracy movement has effectively made that argument to the people who need to hear it.

So it's great these anti-parallel trade groups are focusing on a socioeconomic issue that impacts people in their daily lives. I'm just not sure it's the most pressing one for HK as a whole. In this sense, the solidarity with hawkers shown in Sham Shui Po and Mong Kok around Chinese New Year is perhaps what there needs to be more of. And would it be possible for the anti-parallel trade groups to shift their focus slightly from parallel trade to mainlandization more generally?

As much as anything else, the anti-parallel trade demonstrations have shown that the traditional weaknesses of the pro-democracy movement—organization, mobilization, coordination and strategic planning—persist in the post-occupation era, despite the fact that various groups have expressed their intention to do "community work". Yes, there should be plenty of room for initiative, spontaneity, improvisation, feeling our way along as we go—many successes come of just such approaches—, but we have to remember that since we don't have economic or political power, our main leverage is people power, and the power of numbers doesn't amount to much in the end if it's not maximized by organization, mobilization, coordination and strategic planning. And while the demonstrations may have helped to develop some new techniques of demonstrations, they also point to the limitations of street action in general if it doesn't occur on a solid foundation of community organization and strong democratic presence in the most socioeconomically disadvantaged areas of HK.

Six months after the Umbrella Movement began, where is the HK pro-democracy movement at?

March 27, 2015

This Saturday, March 28 is the six-month anniversary of the beginning of Occupy HK. For all its strengths and gains, the HK pro-democracy movement suffers from the same weaknesses as before: insufficient organization and coordination, poor strategizing, lack of mass mobilization, and limited fundraising capabilities.

We HK citizens live in a double reality.

On the one hand, the Umbrella Revolution occupations of Admiralty, Mong Kok and Causeway Bay, lasting from September 28 to December 15, 2014, changed nothing. The Partystate and HK government did not budge an inch. The demonstrations appear to have had little measurable effect on public opinion, at least according to opinion polls.

On the other hand, the occupations changed everything. HK is not the place it was before. *Varsity* magazine, in its March 18 edition, refers to a "civic awakening".[1] That is most surely an accurate characterization, at least of a portion of the population. In particular, 80 to 90 percent of people under 30 are fed up with the status quo, distrust the Partystate and HK government, and demand genuine universal suffrage. This is the generation the regime will have to contend with for years to come. It is a foundation of permanent resistance.

More than three months after the end of the occupations, a visitor walking the streets of HK on any given day could be forgiven for thinking this is a normal place. Just below the surface, this seemingly prosperous, stable society is in perpetual political crisis.

The occupations succeeded in consolidating the view that fake electoral reform would be much worse than no reform at all and would be a step on the way to sealing HK's doom amongst about half the population. A poll commissioned by the Alliance for True Democracy showed last week that 41 percent see the National People's Congress decision of August 31, which essentially set off the occupations, as "tantamount to turning the popular vote in 2017 into a fake universal suffrage", while only 21 percent disagreed with that statement.

But if indeed the Partystate and HK government's fake universal suffrage is rejected by the Legislative Council, then 18 years after the handover in 1997, HK will still be stuck in political limbo, and stuck with a political system which is not only unfair in a strictly legal sense (Basic Law Article 39→ International Covenant on Civil and Political Rights Article 25) but also just so happens to be highly dysfunctional. That's the uncertain ground upon which the unsuspecting visitor walks, the uncertain ground we HK citizens tread every day.

Given this critical situation, some observers have remarked at how quiet things have become since the occupations ended on December 15. But this is a misperception. We're in a holding pattern at the moment. The ball is in the Partystate and HK government's court, as they prepare to table the bill on fake electoral reform in the Legislative Council. The pro-democracy movement is simply waiting for the 27 Legco pan-democrats to block its passage, and the only suspense is whether the Partystate and HK government will at the last moment dangle some temptation to bolt in front of so-called "moderate" pan-dems, and whether they will bolt, as the Democracy Party did last time around. In addition, the misperception equates lack of mass demonstrations with lack of anything happening.

In fact, one of the most striking things about this post-occupation period is the sheer variety and proliferation of pro-democracy initiatives. Concurrently, many pro-democracy activists question the efficacy of mass demonstrations, whether of the one-day July 1 march variety or even the occupations. Below is a brief and incomplete overview of some of the initiatives.

New groups have been set up that have their origin and inspiration in the occupations

Professional groups

- *Progressive Lawyers Group*

  . . . grew out of frustrations with especially the Law Society but also the HK Bar Association due to their lack of aggression in addressing issues of democracy, rights and law. With a well-written, strongly worded sample letter, they've organized a submissions campaign to the second round of fake public consultation on fake electoral reform. They've also run a campaign to get the HK government to stop running its political advertisements which are in contravention of the HK law against broadcasts of political ads.

- *HK Finance Monitor 2047*
  Formerly the Occupy Central finance and banking sector concern group, it published an open letter to Xi Jinping in the *Wall Street Journal*, calling on him to introduce genuine universal suffrage in HK as well as to respect the Basic Law limitations on the actions of the Central Government vis-à-vis HK and not infringe the "one country, two systems" policy.

- *Médicins Inspirés*
  Pro-democracy doctors who succeeded in getting the Legco Medical Functional Constituency representative, one of the swing voters, to say he would vote against fake electoral reform

Youth groups

- *Umbrella Blossom*
  Former volunteers for Occupy Central who now advocate genuine universal suffrage at street stalls and have plans to run for District Council seats

- *Youngspiration*
  . . . plans to run for District Council seats; right now, says it will contest eight seats

- *HK Indigenous*
  . . . stands up for the rights, traditions and culture of HK people; has been involved in anti-parallel trade protests and Chinese New Year actions in solidarity with street hawkers against draconian HK government laws that threaten to wipe them out

New actions have been taken

- *Scholarism*'s on-going citizenship classrooms keep popping up around the city

- Out-going president of the University of Hong Kong Student Union *Yvonne Leung* filed an application for judicial review of the hardline NPCSC 31 August decision for transgressing constitutional limitations on its actions

- The hanging of 我要真普選 ("I want real universal suffrage") banners and other banners and art with similar messages all over the city

On-going and new street demonstrations

- Continuing *small-scale occupations* of Admiralty and British High Commission (the number of tents in Admiralty has grown from 78 in mid-December to 147 on 24 March)

- *Civil Human Rights Front*'s annual January 1 march, held this year on February 1 (though notable mostly for the lower than hoped-for turn-out)

- *Gao Wu* "shopping trips" in Mong Kok, which have shown extraordinary staying power, turning out virtually every night since the occupations ended on 15 December

- *Anti-parallel trade protests* in Yuen Long, Sha Tin and Tuen Mun that have excited a lot of media attention and debate and actually pressured the HK government and Partystate into at least talking as if they might do something about the problem of parallel trade negatively affecting people's daily lives (not to mention its questionable legality)

In formal politics, pan-dems in Legco have....

- reiterated their vow to block passage of the fake electoral reform bill

- called for a full independent investigation of and accountability for the policing of the occupations

- called for an independent investigation of Chief Executive CY Leung for corruption in connection with the shady DTZ/UGL affair

- blocked and slowed down HK government initiatives, especially through the pivotal Finance Committee, basically torpedoing government plans for a new technology bureau.

The message is: No business as usual as long as the HK government refuses to face the people on the issue of genuine universal suffrage. It's forced the HK government into contortions to try to make progress on its agenda, circumventing Legco with its self-financing plan for a third airport runway, bundling the finance appropriation request to increase the number of Police Tactical Unit officers into the overall budget so as to avoid scrutiny. In doing so, the HK government has appeared more anti-democratic than ever.

Then there is the **burgeoning independent news and commentary scene on the internet**, including groups that pre-date the occupations such as SocRec and InMedia and groups that grew in prominence parallel to the occupations such as Stand News and Passion Times. This is in addition to the many individual citizen journalists who have made substantial contributions in reporting many issues and events largely absent from mainstream media.

So there's a lot going on, and this is most surely a far from exhaustive list of initiatives and activities. (Apologies to those not mentioned here.) The same inspiring qualities demonstrated in the occupations have been present in the post-occupation period: tenacity, wit, humor, resilience, heart, soul, creativity, ingenuity, fortitude, perseverance, hope, optimism, positivity. And the sheer number of initiatives and activities is all the more impressive considering just how exhausting the occupations were, physically, psychologically, spiritually. Equally encouraging is that a whole host of new actors have emerged from the shadows to lead, while some of the faces that featured most prominently in the occupations have taken a backseat (presumably to recover and get on with the rest of their lives put on hold during the occupations). This is hopefully a sign that amongst the young generation, there are many people to take up the baton. Everyone realizes the fight for genuine universal suffrage and genuine autonomy is long and hard. We need to pace ourselves, and we need new people to take over when those in the forefront get tired.

This is all for the good, and one of the positive effects of the occupations has been to strengthen what has been a rather weak civil society. I applaud the people taking these initiatives, and I'm grateful to them, but as a whole, the initiatives can seem a little piecemeal and uncoordinated, taken in too great isolation from one another.

At this point, we should be asking ourselves: What do they all amount to? Where are we at? Is the pro-democracy movement consolidating its gains? Is it using this period before the defeat of the HK government's fake electoral reform bill in Legco to strengthen itself?

For all the initiatives, no one has really stepped up to provide leadership in addressing **weaknesses that have dogged the HK pro-democracy movement down through the years, including during the occupations**. What are those weaknesses? Simply put:

- *poor organization and coordination*
- *poor mobilization and outreach*
- *limited fundraising capabilities*
- *insufficient strategizing*
- *lack of mass mobilization*

Of course, these are all related to one another.

Ian Rowen compares Taiwan's Sunflower Movement with Occupy HK and sees the latter's decentralized structures as a sign of maturity. Rowen refers to the fact that the occupations had no leader; the people were the leader; it was and is a true people's movement that takes orders from nobody. When the tear gas went off on September 28, HKFS and Occupy Central both asked people to go home, but instead of going home, they stayed, occupied, and spread out to other parts of the city. From that moment on, the occupations were a broadbased, decentralized people's movement.

I agree with him, and also agree that's a great strength, but distinct disadvantages come with it. Letting a hundred flowers bloom is all fine and well, but if we're allies, how are we collaborating, and toward what end? What objective and strategy unite our efforts? Are strategy and actions aligned? Are actions chosen to further progress to the overarching objective? How do we know that they're all not just trickling out into the sand? To a great extent, we can't know, because HK is a place where the future is highly uncertain, but we should still be asking ourselves these questions as a movement and using them to help plot a united course.

Many of the civil society initiatives both during and since the occupations have been in response to the limitations of the formal pro-democracy political parties which have traditionally provided leadership. They decided long ago to mainly work within the established system, even though it is rigged against them. They have failed to grow and reach out beyond their bases. They have failed to fundraise effectively. They have been decisively outflanked by pro-Partystate parties in District Council elections, and they have even fared more poorly than they really should in Legco elections, considering the number of people in Hong Kong who want democracy. Overall, they have failed to get their message out effectively, failed to broaden their base of support, and failed to reach out to large segments of the HK electorate. They have been too tentative and cautious (or, alternatively, resorted to antics such as throwing bananas at government officials—great the first few times, but tiresome when repeated ad infinitum). It's telling that in the lead-up to the occupations, the new group Occupy Central with Love and Peace took over the lead in the struggle for universal suffrage from the pro-democracy political parties.

But while it's encouraging that ever more people realize that we cannot achieve our objectives solely by working within a rigged political system and that methods such as civil disobedience are necessary, in other ways, the new initiatives have simply replicated some of the failings of the traditional pan-democratic political parties.

We need a **coordinating body** to help the different parts of the pro-democracy movement collaborate towards common ends. The movement needs to remain loose and decentralized enough to continue to promote diversity, initiative and innovation, but there need to be much greater communication and discussion of common ends and how to reach them. Such a body, meeting perhaps once a month, could also discuss gaps in the movement and how to address them. Just to give a single concrete example: There have been numerous initiatives to contest District Council elections, but it seems as if the different groups are hardly talking or even aware of one another. This is surely an area where an overall, agreed and coordinated strategy is needed. Through the summer, major voter registration drives should take place, in which as many pro-democracy groups as possible are involved.

In the wake of the occupations, many groups have recognized the need to "go out to the community". The movement needs to reach out and broaden its support base. This is a very important recognition, but the gap between recognition and action is great. This is where our weaknesses as political organizers are most clearly shown. And again, strategy is lacking: in "going out to the community", what end do we hope to achieve? can we quantify it and measure our progress? Finally, and perhaps most importantly, the problem with the idea of "going out to the community" is it sounds like we're missionaries out to convert. Rather than going out to the community, we must **be the community**.

What this means is that rather than outsiders going to Shun Tin Public Housing Estate and setting up a stand, people who live in Shun Tin are actively recruited to set up their own 我要真普選 ("I want real universal suffrage") committee. The committee then is responsible for holding activities on the estate to promote discussion and understanding of genuine universal suffrage and for getting people involved in the struggle. People at Shun Tin (or any other public housing estate or neighborhood, for that matter) are much more likely to listen to and identify with their neighbors than with outsiders coming in proselytizing. The goal should be to have **an 我要真普選 committee in every HK public housing estate and neighborhood**. These would be true anchors in the community and help to deepen and widen the base of the movement. And with 我要真普選 committees in every neighborhood in HK, all of the city could be better mobilized to participate in various activities, events and initiatives. For example, the six-month anniversary of the beginning of the occupations is this weekend. The committees could call on people to congregate in their neighborhoods and then march to one of the occupation sites where the whole city would congregate. Or the committees can take the lead in getting out the vote for District Council elections.

This would also help to overcome one of the biggest and best propaganda messages of the Partystate — that HK is a "divided society". The Partystate puts a lot of effort into dividing HK. It knows it can't openly win the debate on universal suffrage, so instead it seeks to create the impression that HK is divided. The logic is, well, if one side says this and another says this, then in the end there's no real truth and we can just settle for what we (the Partystate) want. It's a tactic of relativization. In fact, most people, if they could, would prefer genuine universal suffrage, but the pro-democracy movement doesn't reach out enough to tap into and cultivate this sentiment. There's not so much a "divided society" as the illusion of a divided society. The real division is between the Partystate and HK government on the one hand and the HK people fighting for their basic human right to genuine universal suffrage on the other. The Partystate and HK government enlist front organizations, pro-Partystate political parties, tycoons and all the rest to create the illusion of a divided society. Polls and surveys ask questions like, should Legco vote for an NPCSC-decision-based electoral reform package? But that question should be preceded by another that would act as a baseline: If you could have genuine universal suffrage (one-person one-vote, with full rights to run for and be elected to office), would you want it? Then, at least, you could compare what people really want to what some are willing to settle for. By having a standing and constant presence in all of HK, we can defeat the myth of the "divided society".

Right now, HK suffers from Thomas Frank's "What's the matter with Kansas?" complex. Frank sought to understand why voters in Kansas voted Republican even though to do so was against their socioeconomic interests. In the same way, many people in HK public housing estates vote DAB, and the DAB has a strong presence in these estates. 我要真普選 committees would help people to see that the Partystate, the HK government, the DAB are opposed to their socioeconomic interests, to see how grossly unequal HK is, and to see that there is a causal relation between genuine universal suffrage and socioeconomic justice.

The most recent survey from the HKU Public Opinion Programme shows 61 percent of those interviewed perceive HK's distribution of wealth to be "unreasonable", while only 25 percent see it as "reasonable". There is growing awareness of the gross inequality of HK's social and economic systems. Surely the pro-democracy movement can do a better job of tapping into that.

We must **think much more strategically as a movement**. If genuine universal suffrage is our goal, how do we get there? If indeed the fake universal suffrage bill is defeated in Legco, what's the next step, and the next? What should we be aiming for a year down the road, two years, five, ten? And how does what we're doing now fit into that plan, that vision? Certain individuals are discussing such questions, but it's not something you hear much discussion of in the wider movement or in many groups, organizations or parties.

Benny Tai is such a moderate guy (woefully so, in some people's opinion) that the radicalism of some of his thinking is overlooked. After the NPCSC decision of August 31 and before the occupations began on September 28, he spoke of the beginning of an "era of resistance". He said that in 2017, the pro-democracy movement could hold its own referendum for Chief Executive parallel to the sham official election. He spoke of the pro-democracy movement gradually developing a parallel society, a traditional strategy of long-term civil disobedience movements. I happen to like the idea of the parallel society, but whether you like it or not, it's this sort of longer-term strategic thinking we need to be engaging in as a movement. If this is a long-term era of resistance, as I and many others believe it is, then we have to be planning for the long term. We need to coherently theorize, flesh out and realize the era of resistance. The movement can't subsist on the bursts of emotion and energy that sustained the occupations; some supporting structures need to be formalized that will allow it to adaptively perpetuate itself over time without ossifying.

The movement's power will always be the people. It will never have as much money as the Partystate, the HK government and the pro-Partystate tycoons, but that doesn't mean it shouldn't **get better at fundraising**, something the pro-democracy movement has traditionally been quite poor at. (When it was revealed that the Democratic Party was mostly funded by Jimmy Lai, more than anything else it was embarrassing: surely, they have to be better at raising money than that, I thought.) During the occupations, pro-Partystaters made many baseless allegations that the movement was receiving foreign funding. They had no evidence; their reasoning was deductive: The thinking went, how could they otherwise possibly afford all those supplies? Well, we could afford all of those supplies thanks to the support of HK people, who happen to have quite a lot of money after all. But how are we tapping into that potential financial support now; what should we be tapping into it for?

Just to give an example: Earlier in the article, I mentioned that there are a lot of great initiatives in online pro-democracy media, but, hey, most people in HK, excluding young people, get their news from TVB or some free print newspaper they pick up on their way to the MTR. What if the pro-democracy movement had its own free print newspaper that was distributed outside MTR stations? (The Partystate-backed *Wen Wei Po* and *Ta Kung Pao* already do this in many areas of the city.) We have to do a better job of fighting the propaganda war. You need money for that, but if we wanted to, we could surely raise it, no? Individual groups can be responsible for their own fund-raising, but isn't there a need to consider movement-wide fundraising as well, especially for projects such as a pro-democracy free newspaper that need more resources than any individual group can afford?

These are just a few ideas to address the movement weaknesses itemized above. I know there are many other ideas out there because I've heard them. If people are our main resource, we need to tap into their great ideas. HK is a society that is strongly influenced by four types of culture—corporate, colonial, communist and traditional Chinese—the quadruple whammy of the four Cs. What all four have in common is that they're authoritarian and hierarchical. The Partystate vision for HK is that it will remain a hierarchical place and will become more authoritarian. This is what we're fighting, but over the years, I've noticed the tendency in many pro-democracy groups to steep hierarchy and exclusivity. Often, these groups have been quite bad at listening to their own members. This is a tendency that, given the influence of the wider cultural context, is understandable, but one that must be resisted. **If we want democracy, we must act democratically.** In acting democratically, we realize democracy in the here and now and this improves our ability to fight for it. Only by acting democratically can we maximize our strength—people, and utilize their ideas to the fullest. As much as we have to resist the Partystate, we have to resist the little authoritarian in each of us as well. One of the most beautiful things about the occupations was that, in fighting for a certain vision of the society HK could be, we realized it there at the occupation sites. Just witnessing that gave tremendous hope: yes, it can be done because we're doing it now. That's the way the movement needs to be run.

This essay has discussed the pro-democracy movement as if in a vacuum. But the fact is, as we work on improving the movement, **Partystate-driven mainlandization is advancing at a rapid pace**. The Partystate believes that time is on its side and that the occupations will eventually be seen, if at all, as a mere blip in the rearview mirror. The Partystate and HK government have decided to simply ignore the pro-democracy movement; full speed ahead with their plan for the Partystate to consolidate control over HK! Since the end of the occupations, the Partystate and HK government have been very busy, especially with attacks on education, one of the areas of HK society that up to now has best withstood the pressure to mainlandize. One last thing we must get much better at: understanding what the Partystate is up to and finding ways to effectively counter and neutralize its efforts. Because while we're fighting for democracy, they're mainlandizing, and the question is, as ever, which side will win in the end.

Herman Melville said, *The Past is the textbook of tyrants; the Future is the Bible of the Free.* I'd like to think so, but it's by no means certain who will write the future. We need to be strategically savvy, resourceful, organized, effective, and both diverse and united to break out of the textbook of the tyrants and write our own bible of the free.

The metamorphosis of an old friend and the birth of the era of resistance

April 2, 2015

She visited the other day. It was the first time I'd seen her since we shared a tent at the Admiralty occupation.

She manages to come and see me at least twice a year. She's really good that way. A very loyal friend. She's been doing this for years, ever since we were in secondary school together. After months of not having any contact, out of the blue she'll say, *I'm coming this weekend.* And then she shows up.

During this past visit, she talked about her life. When I see her together with other secondary school friends, she hardly says anything. She's so quiet, meek even. But when we're alone, just the two of us, she opens up. She talked of her frustrations, the ups and downs of her life, mostly the downs. Then she said something I didn't quite catch. Or, I heard it but thought I must have heard it wrong.

What did you say? I asked.

I've come to the point where I think it is justifiable to use violence against the government.

How does a person like her get to the point of saying something like that? I wondered. And I wondered if, in answering that question, I'd be saying a lot about Hong Kong, about where Hong Kong's at, about Hong Kong people.

Just for the record, I don't agree with her. I think violence of most every kind is morally wrong and strategically a bad idea. But I didn't say anything in response to her because I knew she wasn't really making an argument for using violence. The statement was a direct extension of her rage at the state of affairs in Hong Kong and her blame of the government for it.

Back in secondary, I could never have imagined she'd say such a thing, nor in the many years afterwards either. Neither she nor any of our other secondary schoolfriends. We're a tight-knit grip. We've all gone our own ways in life. Most all of us live in HK, but like she and I, we only see each other maybe a couple of times a year. But we always make sure we do. We stay in touch. We see our lives change.

But I was always the different one, the political one. They never wanted to talk politics. Whenever they heard of my political involvements, they smiled as if they found them entertaining but not much else. They were apolitical. They just weren't that interested. They were too busy making lives for themselves. That's pretty typical of my generation.

Every now and then, they would say things that just made me shake my head and wonder what in the world I had in common with them, apart from having gone to secondary school together. One of them became an English teacher and ended up teaching at the very secondary school we went to (a good, solid Band 1 government school). She told me about a student she'd punished recently for wearing red socks.

Why did you punish him? I asked.

Because it's against the rules, she said, *you can't wear red socks with your uniform. And he insisted. He was stubborn. Even after I asked him not to, he continued. I had no choice.*

So what? I said. *What's the big deal?*

What if everyone just decided what color socks to wear?

So what? I said. *Maybe it would be better that way.*

But we didn't get to do it, she said, *and they shouldn't either.*

What a weird argument, I thought, the revenge of the old on the young: we didn't get to do it, so why should you? The very definition of anti-progressive. An attitude perhaps all too pervasive amongst older HK people. According to that logic, how could you ever make anything better?

Otherwise, my secondary school friends were pretty typical HK: live and let live. They didn't really care what other people did; it was fine with them. They weren't interested in political or social issues. They didn't see how their daily lives fit into the big picture, or the impact the big picture had on them. They bought the old dogma that your life was what you made of it: If you were a failure (as defined economically), it was your own fault; if you were a success (as defined economically), it was down to your effort and intelligence.

Things changed in summer 2014. I can mark the exact moment: it was the publication of the Partystate's White Paper on Hong Kong on June 10. That really woke HK people up. It woke my friends up. You could almost hear the collective gulp. My secondary school friends don't have foreign passports. They don't have foreign connections. They, like most HK people, are stuck here. They began to feel the long shadow of the Partystate looming over them. Initially, I first noticed the change in their Facebook comments: *I'm really worried now, what are we going to do?. . . We have to stand up for HK. . . . We can't accept this, we must do something. . . .* I would see the comments and think, Could that person really be the person I know? I could never have imagined her saying such a thing before.

Still, it wasn't as if they did much about it. It's hard to go from having zero political consciousness to becoming politically involved. With most people, it doesn't happen overnight. Most of my secondary school friends have pretty good jobs earning pretty good money and work very long hours. They don't have a lot of time for other things like politics. They haven't exactly "made it"—most of the single ones still live with their parents and can't afford their own home—but they're not the losers of society either.

My meek, quiet friend who believes violence against the government is justifiable works in theater. She's a stage manager. It's been a solid job, but she hoped for more. Her dream had been to go to London to study theater. After secondary school, she worked and worked and saved and saved in order to be able to afford it, and she realized the dream. For much of her time in London, she had so little money that she ate poorly and often went hungry. But she was in London. At the end of her studies, she wanted to stay in London and get experience in the theater world. She didn't rule out coming back to HK one day, but she didn't want to right away. Her parents, who lived in a public housing estate, had other ideas. They told her it was time to come home and start supporting them. I told her she was out of her mind to do so; she should stay in London. But she listened to her parents, not to me. Again, the revenge of the old on the young. Or, to put it another way, the way lack of a universal pension system or other effective social welfare system for older people leaves one in three living in poverty and puts undo burden on their children, narrowing their opportunities, economic and other. I was struck, too, at the hold her parents had over her, a psychological hold; to me, it seemed as if she was being held hostage, even as I recognized this as a very common HK phenomenon. I thought they were unreasonable and unfair. But they did need the money. And of course, ever since she returned, she's been living with her parents in the same apartment in the same public housing estate where she grew up, a hostage indefinitely.

She got a job in the theater she's worked in for years and eventually got promoted to stage manager. Recently, she quit and got a new job at the West Kowloon Cultural District, working with a group of theater people who liaise with architects to design a theater for the district. She said there is pessimism the theater will ever be built, but she's happy to have the opportunity to work with smart and cosmopolitan people who know their stuff and are full of ideas. So, work-wise, things are actually looking up for her, which is why I was all the more surprised to hear her justification of violence.

I'd run into her during the occupations and mentioned I had a tent at Admiralty.

Could I join you? she asked.

Yes, of course! I said.

And she did, at least once a week, usually on the weekend, in spite of her busy work schedule. She would come there late at night after work and stay into the next day. Even then, we didn't really talk politics that much. She just wanted to be there and thought it was the right thing to do. Some of our other secondary school friends came as well. In the course of a few months, how much things had changed!

But it's a leap from participating in the nonviolent occupations to saying violence against the government is justified. I don't even know how much she really meant it. But three things strike me about the statement: First, that someone like her would say it, not someone clearly branded as "radical" by the establishment. Second, that her personal frustrations find outlet in political expression because she sees the ways the unjust political system works to oppress people. Third, the vehemence and conviction in what she said: She might very well change her mind about violence against the government being justified, but it's hard to imagine her changing her mind now about the basic injustice of the system in which we live and her opposition to it.

Thus, the "era of resistance" is born: A very large portion of the population is dead set against greater Partystate influence or greater mainlandization and ready to fight for our basic political rights.

Or am I overstating the case? My friend is just one person, but I've heard many similarly formerly apolitical HK people say similar things.

The lesson the Partystate seems to have learned from the occupations is that it needs to step up propaganda, especially targeting young people. Will it succeed?

Several months from now, a couple of years from now, will the occupations just seem like once upon a time in a place far far away? Or will we look back on them as the beginning of the era of resistance, the beginning of the formation of a political consciousness amongst the formerly apolitical, the beginning of Hong Kong people demanding to take their political fate into their own hands?

A lot depends on what we do, on what happens, from here on out.

For now, I'm striding hand in hand into the future with my secondary school friend.

What would it take to succeed? The HK pro-democracy movement through the lens of nonviolent civil resistance theory and in global context

April 10, 2015

The other day, while making dinner, I was listening to BBC Hard Talk interviewing Benny Tai.[1] Stephen Sackur's questions were exasperatingly facile, and Benny's answers were far too mild. He was willing to concede Sackur's simplistic points without much qualification. At one point, the interviewer said (I paraphrase), You invoke Martin Luther King and Gandhi, but isn't it the hard fact of the matter that they won and you lost, they succeeded and you failed? *C'mon, Benneeeee!* I shouted while chopping vegetables. *Nail it!* But he didn't. Once again, he gave some forgettable mealy-mouthed response. Poor Benny! I wouldn't have done any better in his place. Ingeniously sparkling repartee is much more easily thought than spoken. And the interview made me reflect how complicated and confusing the situation in HK can seem from afar, how difficult it is to communicate to people elsewhere exactly what's going on in HK. But still.... While cooking, I composed answers in my head. Here they are.

Failed?! The HK pro-democracy movement has failed?! You gotta be kidding! First of all, we alerted the whole world to the situation in HK, and now everyone's watching. Otherwise, I wouldn't even be here talking with you, Mr Sackur. Secondly, we awakened the political conscience of many in HK and gave them courage to resist. We initiated an era of resistance that will be on-going, and considering especially how many young people are involved, perhaps even for years and decades to come. The Communist Party is going to have to contend with that resistance into the foreseeable future. Thirdly, we put our foot down, drew a line in the sand, consolidating support for blocking the fake universal suffrage the CCP is trying to ram through the Legislative Council. Fourthly, if you are going to say we failed, then you must say the CCP has failed as well. They wanted to sneak fake universal suffrage by under the noses of the HK people and the world. Now, that will not happen. We have the power to block it in the Legislative Council. We have forestalled the worst—which is in itself a victory—while fighting for a positive outcome, and all of us know achieving that positive outcome entails long-term struggle. So, at most, rather than saying we failed, it would be more accurate to say there's a stalemate; neither side has the power to realize its desire without resort to brute force, and there are few if any times in the history of CCP rule in China that that can be said.

I would go on: But really, to answer your question more directly, Mr Sackur: Don't you know how long it took Gandhi and MLK to succeed? Gandhi returned to India in 1915, and independence was achieved in 1947. He struggled for 32 years, and when independence was achieved, he thought he had failed because it also meant partition and the attendant mass communal violence which resulted in the deaths of hundreds of thousands. He considered his accomplishment a tragedy. In the case of MLK, the Montgomery Bus Boycott was in 1955. The Civil Rights Act was passed in 1964, the Voting Rights Acts in 1965. But starting in those very years, race riots occurred across US cities into the early seventies. Recent shootings of black men by white police and the mass incarceration of black men show there's still some way to go for true racial equality. So, hey, justice is a long time coming, man, and definitive, pure victories are few and far between along the way. By the yardsticks of MLK and Gandhi, there is still some way to go until one can present convincing evidence that we have failed. Everyone in the HK pro-democracy movement knows this is a long-term struggle and perseverance is key. And we've been very busy since the end of the occupations in December. If you haven't already, Mr Sackur, please read my article, "Six months after the Umbrella Movement began, where is the HK pro-democracy movement at?"

Still, I thank you for posing the question, for it's worth asking what could bring about "success" in the sense that you mean, namely, getting the Partystate to honor its legal obligation under the Basic Law and the International Covenant on Civil and Political Rights to implement genuine universal suffrage in HK. I mean, we're not talkin' revolution here, just trying to get the Partystate to subordinate itself to the law. (Then again, I guess that would be a kind of revolution.)

Back in October, not long after the occupations started, Erica Chenoweth was asked this question.[2] She is co-author of one of the best books on nonviolent civil resistance, *Why Civil Resistance Works: The Strategic Logic of Nonviolent Conflict*. She's not an expert on HK, but she knows a lot about what works and doesn't, globally and historically. Chenoweth said that if everything went right—a big if— HK stood at best a 50–50 chance of success. She emphasized four factors that generally determine the success of nonviolent resistance:

1. **The size and diversity of the movement:** how many people are involved in the movement and whether they're broadly representative of different groups and social classes?

2. **Staying power**: can they keep protests going, avoiding both fatigue and repression?

3. **Diversity of tactics**: do they not just protest but also use strategies such as mass boycotts and strikes?

4. **Co-option of opposing elites**: does the movement create divisions inside the leadership class of the government and society that they're opposing?

Chenoweth said that the HK pro-democracy movement appeared to be doing rather well in terms of the first three but not the last, and she identified co-option of elites as perhaps the crucial factor.

That seemed a fair analysis at the time, and six months later, it still does.

To take a quick inventory:

Size and diversity of the movement

Here, you could say the pro-democracy movement had initial success but has hit a wall. The *size of the movement* is arguably larger than ever, but it is not significantly growing. In stalling, the Partystate won itself time to fight back, to implement its divide-and-rule tactics. There is still a significant sector of the population that is either opposed to or apathetic about the movement's aims. Compared to many other movements, you could argue that the size is proportionately large enough. About 20 percent of non-minors in a population of 7.2 million have been actively involved in the movement, and something like two-thirds support the cause. But from other perspectives (such as the fact that the size of the Communist Party alone is more than ten times the size of the whole HK population), you could say that the pro-democracy movement's failure to continue to grow in numbers is a serious impediment and will continue to be.

The movement is also reasonably *diverse*. While the occupations were often characterized as a student movement or a student-led movement, a *Ming Pao* survey conducted at the occupation sites in October found that only 26 percent of those surveyed were students. A wide range of people was involved in the occupations and is involved in the pro-democracy movement more generally. 80 to 90 percent of young people generally support it. There is strong support amongst many professional groups, especially lawyers, teachers and social workers. But here, too, the movement has hit something of a wall because it has made relatively few inroads into the public housing estates and more generally, lower income groups, which comprise around half of the population. Again, under other conditions, this might not be such an impediment, but in HK, it is.

Staying power

The pro-democracy movement has already been around for decades. The occupations in three key nodes of the city lasted for an impressive 79 days. Since the occupations, many other initiatives have been taken. And the pro-democracy movement doesn't look like it's going to disappear any time soon.

If any pan-democratic Legco members were to bolt and go over to the dark side, supporting the Partystate's fake universal suffrage proposal, that could deal a fatal blow to the pro-democracy movement; indeed, the Partystate originally considered passage of fake universal suffrage as crucial in undermining the pro-democracy movement once and for all. But short of that, it looks to be around for a long time to come. If there's anything, though, that working within a movement teaches, it is how inherently fragile such a movement can be. So we shouldn't take its staying power for granted.

Diversity of tactics

Arguably, one of the strengths of the movement is that since the end of the occuapations, a plethora of groups has significantly diversified tactics. And while its highly decentralized nature can make it often appear a mess from the point of view of organization and coherent mobilization, it certainly isn't lacking in new initiatives from a large variety of sources.

Still, amidst all that diversity, one area that has proven crucial in other contexts and has hardly figured in HK is mass boycotts and strikes. There was the one-week student boycott of classes, and once the police teargassed the people, Hong Kong Federation of Students called for an indefinite boycott, but it doesn't appear that was ever really followed through on. Likewise, the Professional Teachers Union, HK's largest pro-democracy union, called a strike in the wake of the teargasing, but it appears there was little to no uptake from teachers, and that call faded into oblivion as well. Many have argued that such boycotts and strikes would at any rate not be very effective in Hong Kong. Whatever the case, the lack of large-scale collective action on the part of workers or consumers can be considered a limitation of the movement up to now, especially when the need to escalate arises. You saw this during the occupations. When HKFS declared it would escalate, the best it could think of to do was to surround the Chief Executive's office. What really needed to happen was for a new wave of people to join the movement and act outside of the occupation zones.

Co-option of opposing elites

Back in October, at the height of the occupations, when Chenoweth was interviewed, virtually no progress had been made in this area, and the same can be said today. In that sense, on the surface at least, the Partystate has been remarkably effective in shoring up its support. In HK, the forces supporting and protecting the Partystate include:

- the tycoons and more generally, the business community, including the major chambers of commerce;
- large segments of the media;
- the HK government and police;
- and the many Partystate front organizations, including political parties, unions and so-called patriotic associations

That's a formidable list. None has shown the least inclination to budge. Some quietly resent the pressure put on them to support the Partystate and would just as soon stay out of politics altogether, but when push comes to shove, they still see their interests as aligned with those in power.

That's just within HK. A salient feature of the HK situation is that, structurally, it is really a classical colonial model—the real power rests far away, in Beijing. The mainland economic elites haven't so much as blinked at what's going on in HK; it doesn't even play into their calculations. The Partystate has such a stranglehold on the media that the people on the mainland receive little to no accurate information about the HK political situation, and the result of that has been striking ignorance and antagonism ("spoiled little HKers—we give them everything and look how ungrateful they are") when, really, our interests are closely aligned. Within the Partystate itself, Xi Jinping is waging such a ferocious battle over control (under the guise of an anti-corruption campaign) that nobody is about to risk crossing him over such a relatively paltry matter as HK. At other times one might have detected a greater range of opinion within the Partystate, but now they're all in a race to appear more hardline than thou. As for the People's Suppression Army, it would be hard to find an issue to which it's less sympathetic than HK freedom.

So, as far as co-option of any of the forces supporting the Partystate, the HK pro-democracy movement has struck out completely. I agree with you, Mr Sackur, we have failed. Indeed, we've hardly even tried, so futile have such efforts appeared.

What's worse, meanwhile, as we consider co-option of forces supporting the Partystate, the Partystate ramps up its divide-and-rule tactics and redoubles its efforts to mainlandize HK society. Indeed, one could argue that it's far more likely the Partystate will split the pro-democracy movement than the opposite.

The global context

Rarely is it the case, though, that elites suddenly "see the light" and start to support pro-democracy movements. More often than not, they make a calculated decision that it is more in their interest to remove support from the regime. What that means is that if they do so, that might help to shift the balance of power, but the question is whether that shift will be decisive and enduring. In the case of Egypt, for example, the military withdrew its support from Mubarak, causing him to fall, but then waited in the wings to return to power, and three years after the fall of Mubarak, rather than democracy, there is effectively military dictatorship in Egypt that is even harsher than Mubarak. So co-option of the elites is also playing with fire.

The Egyptian example is instructive also because it shows just how illusory short-term gains can sometimes be. Coupled with the examples of the Indian freedom struggle and the struggle for racial equality in the US, the lesson learnt is that freedom struggles are almost always long-term processes. Even decisive victories are not final victories. The struggle goes on and on.

Indeed, the long-term results of "victories" in freedom struggles are a mixed bag, to say the least. Transitions to democracy are arduous.

Most of the former republics of the Soviet Union are not doing too well. The exceptions are the Baltic states, Estonia, Latvia and Lithuania. Ukraine could be coming around, though it's too soon to say.

The USSR's former satellite states are faring somewhat better, especially Poland, East Germany and the Czech Republic. But then there are Bulgaria and Romania, which have never fully managed the transition, Hungary which is backsliding, and Slovakia, which can often seem neither here nor there.

In South America, Argentina, Brazil, Chile and Uruguay have all made impressive transitions to democracy, Paraguay and Peru somewhat less so. But overall, for a region that used to be overwhelmingly dictatorial, it's made remarkable progress. Central America, on the other hand, continues to struggle with fragile, easily co-opted state institutions.

In East Asia, Taiwan and South Korea have made impressive transitions.

Elsewhere in Asia, there are signs for optimism in Indonesia. The eighties People Power revolution of the Philippines is in some ways unfinished. Post-Marcos Philippines has been plagued by corruption and the retrenchment of economic elites. That might be changing, but it's still up in the air.

In South Africa, there is much disillusionment with the African National Congress, which has become increasingly corrupt, coupled with the gross income inequality and the exceedingly large number of people still living in poverty. Elsewhere in Africa, you have to really look hard to find any uplifting stories of successful democratic transition.

And of all the countries affected by the Arab Spring, Tunisia appears to be the only one to have turned a corner and made decisive progress toward democracy.

In this global context, HK isn't necessarily doing that bad at all. But equally, it's got a long way to go. We can't count on anything bringing about the decisive victory of the HK pro-democracy movement any time soon. The question is the extent to which it can persevere and strengthen itself in the face of that awareness.

Perhaps one of the most important things to keep in mind is that the HK pro-democracy movement is part of a worldwide movement for democracy. While governments for the most part sit on the sidelines, remaining silent if not downright hostile, all over the world people continue to fight for political freedom. We are part of a much larger struggle. Our freedom struggle is bound up with those of Taiwan, Tibet and the Uighurs as well as of people on the mainland. It is related to those of the people of Southeast and South Asia. We should inform ourselves of other freedom struggles. We should learn from them much more than we do. We should work in solidarity with them. While we decry the fact that few governments around the world have supported our struggle, we should be heartened by the fact that many people do. Our existence is important: We stand for a vision of a fair, democratic society, a society far different from the one that now exists. We are a mote in the dictator's eye. The Partystate stands for oppression; for rule by fiat, not by law; for everything we detest. The real question is: in the long run, which vision will win? This is a question of relevance to the whole world, not just HK.

I'll leave you with a few of Erica Chenoweth's aphoristic tweets from the height of the occupations in October last year:

> Mvmts that win adopt long-term thinking. They put strategy before tactics. They know when to stand their ground & when to retreat & regroup.
>
> NV mvmts don't win b/c they are "morally superior." They win by outlasting or outmaneuvering the opponent.
>
> NV movements that win (1) plan for a years-long struggle; (2) use NV tactics besides just demonstrations (e.g. strikes)
>
> Although NV mvmts face great odds, difficult circumstances do not always predetermine whether they succeed or fail.

Also check out Jay Ulfelder's "How the Umbrella Revolution Could Win" , an application of Kurt Schock's *Unarmed Insurrections* to HK.

A brief encounter with the Hong Kong police

May 1, 2015

. . . which leads me to wonder:

To what extent have the HK police been corrupted by their use as guard dogs of an illegitimate regime?

1

On Saturday, April 25 at around 5 pm, I was walking down the street toward Tai Po Market MTR station. About one-hundred meters from the station, I heard what sounded like the clatter of boots on the pavement approaching from behind. Before I turned, a police officer appeared at my side. She was accompanied by four male colleagues. She asked me for my ID.

"Why?" I replied.

"Under the HK Immigration Ordinance," she said.

"What about it?" I asked.

"We have the right to request your ID under the HK Immigration Ordinance."

"Do you suspect me of a crime, or do you think I have been acting suspiciously?"

"No, we just want to see your ID. "

"Do you suspect me of having broken the Immigration Ordinance or of being in HK illegally?"

"No, but we have the right to ask for your ID."

"Why did you approach me just now?"

"To ask you for your ID."

"Where did you approach me from?"

(Quizzical looks)

"Have you been following me?"

(No answer)

The laws regarding police powers to demand to see an identification document are somewhat unclear. Immigration Ordinance section 17c is pretty unambiguous. According to it, the police have the power, without having to give a reason, to demand that any person produce "proof of his identity" (exactly of what that may legally consist is somewhat open to interpretation). According to Police Force Ordinance section 54, police have the power, in the case of a person "who acts in a suspicious manner", "to stop the person for the purpose of demanding that he produce proof of his identity for inspection by the police officer." Because of the relative ambiguity of the Police Force Ordinance, police seem to prefer invoking the authority of the Immigration Ordinance when stopping people and demanding proof of identity.

The HK government had just launched its "2017: Make It Happen!" campaign to drum up support for its fake universal suffrage proposal, which was presented to the Legislative Council on Wednesday, April 22. Top government ministers, including the three formally responsible for the proposal, the Chief Secretary, the Secretary for Justice and the Secretary for Mainland and Constitutional Affairs, had been riding around the city that afternoon in an open-top bus.

The bus had passed nearby Tai Po Market about a half hour before. I had been there at the time. So had both pro-government and pro-democracy demonstrators, and I had reason to suspect that the police were asking me for identification for political reasons; that is to say, they believed me to hold political views or to have engaged in political acts they considered suspicious, perhaps even conducive to criminal activity.

This was only the second time in my life, including many years of attending demonstrations, that the police had asked me for ID. The first time was during a demonstration for Tibetan freedom and human rights on Tibetan Uprising Day, March 10, 2011. It is striking that both times were in relation to political protest even though on neither occasion did the police say they had reason to believe I had committed a crime.

As I spoke with the five police officers, they called colleagues. Quickly three others arrived. (Hundreds of police officers were at Tai Po Market and several dozen more in the vicinity of the MTR station.) I was now surrounded by eight officers altogether. A crowd of about 20 curious onlookers gathered. Two people began to video us with their mobile phones.

One of the three newly arrived officers was in plainclothes. (I never did ask him for proof of being a police officer, though afterwards I thought I should have.) He told me that I had been at Kennedy Town and Lok Fu, two other places the "2017: Make It Happen!" open-top bus had passed earlier that day. And, he added, I had "been on t.v."

His words lead me to believe that I had not simply been randomly stopped by the five officers who initially approached me, or even that they had followed me from Tai Po Market and stopped me under suspicion of being a pro-democracy activist, but that, instead, the five had been ordered to do so by superiors who had been monitoring me over the course of the day

"Do you think I have committed a crime?" I asked the plainclothes officer. "Is it a crime to be in those locations or to be on t.v?"

"No," he said, "but it is a matter of public order."

"I don't understand: Do you suspect me of having disrupted public order?"

"No," he said, "but we have the right to see your ID."

"But what does that have to do with whether or not I was in Kennedy Town or Lok Fu or on t.v?"

People outside of a restaurant on the other side of the narrow street on which we stood were shouting at the two onlookers videoing our discussion who shouted back. Five people came over from the restaurant side and began shoving the two videographers. Two of the police officers went over to them.

A young person I recognized as a pro-democracy activist happened by and began to video the incident. He asked me to speak to the camera and tell what was happening and then asked the officers what was going on.

Then a citizen journalist I recognized and had seen earlier that day in Kennedy Town and Tai Po happened by and began to observe.

The police demand to see my ID was quickly becoming a spectacle.

2

A lot had already happened that day.

While at Kennedy Town, I had stood on a corner opposite the corner where a large number of pro-government and pro-democracy demonstrators were gathered, squeezed into a small area. From my vantage point, I could look down the street in the direction from which the "2017: Make It Happen!" bus was scheduled to come. The demonstrators would not be able to see the bus until it turned the corner and was almost already past them. When I saw it, I crossed the street and yelled to the demonstrators, "The bus is coming!"

Three police officers grabbed me and pulled me to the sidewalk. The bus turned the corner, and I stepped out into the street to catch a glimpse of it, since, on the sidewalk, my view was obscured by the other demonstrators. One policeman tackled me, another held me down, and a third towered over me. A fourth came quickly, and the four of them took one limb each and carried me to the side of the road while I asked, "What are you doing?"

"Stay on the sidewalk," they told me, and then ran back to where the bus had just passed.

A scuffle broke out between pro-government and pro-democracy demonstrators. When the bus had turned the corner, the pro-democracy demonstrators had pushed toward the street, and the police gathered to block them shoved them backward with an enormous heave. They clattered into the pro-government demonstrators who began attacking them. One heavy-set young man in white pummeled a scrawny young man in white about the head. Two plainclothes policemen I recognized emerged from the crowd. One of them looked stunned. He had gotten caught up in the scuffle, and his colleague was trying to attend to him. I shouted at them that a demonstrator was being attacked, but the one officer lead his dazed colleague off in the opposite direction. It was very difficult to draw police attention to the assault, as the police appeared to think that their only mission was to guard the bus. Now that the bus had passed, the police did intervene, dozens shoving their way into the thick of the crowd, but they clearly had little idea of what was going on, or really didn't care, as they took away the scrawny young man who had been pummeled while the heavy-set man who'd attacked him disappeared into the crowd. I tried to follow him, but he got away. Then I told the police they were dragging away the wrong person, but not a single police officer listened to me. They did not appear to be interested in taking witness statements. Instead, they told me not to follow them.

From Kennedy Town, I went to Lok Fu. I arrived, according to the first person there I asked, a pro-democracy demonstrator, about three minutes after the "2017: Make It Happen!" bus had passed. I dashed back to the MTR and took it up to Tai Po Market. It is interesting that the plainclothes police officer I spoke to near Tai Po Market MTR mentioned that I had been at Lok Fu, since

I'd been there a matter of only a few minutes, emerging from the MTR station and then going right back into it. The fact that the police officer said I had been seen there suggests they were tailing me or monitoring me fairly closely.

At Tai Po Market, there were very few pro-democracy protesters, perhaps a couple dozen altogether. They were outnumbered by the pro-government demonstrators who had set up a stage. In fact, there were so few pro-democracy protesters, I wondered whether the "2017: Make It Happen!" bus had already passed.

While I stood on the wide pavement out front of the market trying to get my bearings, a police officer approached and asked what I was doing.

"I am standing here," I said.

"Be sure not to block others," he said.

"I don't think I am," I said. "Do you?"

He didn't reply.

I saw a scrum of reporters encircling Joshua Wong. Then I turned in the other direction and saw the "2017: Make It Happen!" bus coming swiftly down the street. I wondered whether I was really seeing it because it seemed as if no one else had yet noticed. I shouted, "I want real universal suffrage!" at the bus.

This caught Joshua's attention, and he broke through the media scrum and ran toward the curb. He was almost immediately knocked down by a police officer,[1] though he was doing nothing in the least bit threatening (unless simply moving in the direction of the bus could be construed as threatening).

I started to jog parallel to the bus as it made its way down the street and continued shouting, "I want real universal suffrage!" I was almost immediately blocked by several police officers.

"What are you doing?" I asked.

"Don't step out into the street," one officer snarled at me.

"I'm not. I'm on the pavement," I said.

"You're close to the street," he said. He wasn't interested in fine distinctions.

The officers were simply trying to prevent me from following the bus, although presumably I had a perfect right to do so as long as I remained on the pavement. As soon as the bus turned the corner down at the end of the street, the police backed away and allowed me to proceed.

I continued on down toward the end of the street. I wanted to reach the corner and see if the bus had already disappeared out of site. I passed the pro-government stage. Several people there swore and spat at me.

I stopped and stared at them, then turned to the large group of police officers standing nearby. "Look at what they're doing," I said. The police officers neither moved nor replied. Their faces were entirely impassive, in strong contrast to the one snarling at me moments before.

One plainclothes officer continued to follow me down to the end of the street.

"You will be in trouble if you don't stop," he threatened.

"Why are you following me?" I asked.

When we reached the end of the street, he turned around and headed back to where he'd come from.

From the corner, the bus was nowhere in sight.

By that point, whatever the "objective facts", I definitely felt my freedoms of movement, assembly and association had been unjustifiably infringed. Between the police and the pro-government demonstrators, the atmosphere in Tai Po was menacing.

It was then that I headed back to the Tai Po Market MTR station, taking a different route so as to avoid the pro-government crowd and police I'd just passed, and was stopped by the police officers who demanded my ID.

Our discussion went in circles. They threatened to arrest me and take me to the police station to identify me. I stepped aside and made a phone call to ask for advice. I also hoped the call might signal to the police officers that I was a "somebody" and that treating me as they were could have repercussions. I was advised by my interlocutor to offer to show the police my ID if they agreed not to take down my details.

When I got off the phone, the plainclothes officer who said I'd been seen at Kennedy Town, Lok Fu and "on t.v." had disappeared, but two more uniformed officers had arrived. The total was now nine.

"If I show you my ID, will you record my details?"

"Yes," they said.

"Why do you need to do that if my ID is in order?"

"It is standard procedure," they said, "for the records."

We were at an impasse. Some of the officers looked embarrassed; they just wanted to move on. Two looked very angry at me for giving them trouble. I would not want to encounter them in a "dark corner". If they began to arrest me, I wasn't sure what I'd do. I believe the police are politically profiling people and probably compiling a list of "politically suspect individuals", including those who have never been arrested or convicted of a crime. I did not want to show them my details because I did not trust them.

3

The next day, Sunday, I went on the Remember June 4 26-kilometer run. This event is held every year in the lead-up to the candlelight vigil on June 4. At most, several dozen people turn out for it. We start at Chinese University and run through Hong Kong, finishing at the Central Government Liaison Office where we make a declaration and lay white chrysanthemums. We are just about the most harmless, non-threatening group of mostly middle-aged people you can imagine, and in the ten years of the run, we have never caused the police any trouble at all.

In past years, there was very little police presence along the route. Typically, it increased only at the University of Hong Kong. Around the Liaison Office, there were always a lot of police. Indeed, year after year, the police would find little ways of making our lives difficult (no, you can't bring that Goddess of Democracy statue through; there isn't enough space, etc, and long negotiations would ensue), but then, police behavior in front of the Liaison Office is a category unto itself.

This year, for the first time in my seven years doing the run, there was a continuous police presence along most of the route from CUHK down through New Territories and Kowloon to Hong Kong Island, HKU and the Liaison Office. All of the police were very courteous and some quite solicitous, stopping traffic for us. This, I thought, is what HK police are good at, directing traffic; it is what they should stick to. But I also found it strange that there were so many along the way. Many of them took photos of us. I felt under surveillance.

What did they think? That we were going to suddenly occupy a street? That we could be part of some plot to re-occupy the city? Probably not, but I suspect the police are under orders to do whatever they can to prevent any kind of re-occupation from occurring. Prevention is the order of the day. And that means not only more police in MTR stations and university campuses (which I have also noticed) but also stepped-up monitoring of any group affiliated with the pro-democracy movement.

In HK, there is insufficient oversight of police. Complaints must be made directly to the Complaints Against Police Office, which is within the Police

Force. It, in turn, is monitored by a toothless and quite inactive Independent Police Complaints Council, a government-appointed body, according to a labyrinthine process. There has been no action taken by the HK government or any other official entity to hold the police accountable for police actions during the 79 days of occupations, and no independent investigation of police either. (Pro-government members dominate the Functional Constituency part of the Legislative Council—the part not elected according to principles of universal suffrage—and voted down pan-democratic attempts to pass a motion establishing an independent investigation.) Considering this situation, the risks of abuse of power and infringements of political and civil liberties are present, to say the least, and, for anyone who has been out on the street, quite palpable.

Police were present at both CUHK, the start of the run, and City U, a stop on the route. Also at both were people I took to be mainland intelligence agents. I'd seen the sorts in the past: either thick, stocky and pot-bellied or abnormally skinny, both types in sunglasses and ill-fitting suits or polo shirts. Though I was running and had better things to do, I was so provoked by the ones at City U taking photos of us that I stopped and took a photo of them.

The intelligence guys were standing near the police. I thought to myself, While mainland intelligence personnel spy on HK citizens—nothing new about this, except it's become more blatant—, rather than investigating them since it is illegal for mainland agents to operate in HK, the police exhibit suspicion of HK people due to their political expression. This is not a pretty picture.

At the finish line, the Liaison Office, there was definite police overkill, even more so than in the past: upwards of two-hundred police officers versus under fifty of us. You wouldn't want us to hop the fence and occupy the compound there, would you?!

4

So have the police changed, or am I just making a lot out of nothing? If the police have changed, how much?

Having gone to many pro-democracy demonstrations over the years, I've seen the police do a lot of annoying things, and there's much I could take them to task for.

What immediately come to mind are arrests for things like whistling too loudly in the vicinity of police officers (amazingly, that guy was actually convicted); "assault" for opening a bottle of champagne to celebrate Liu Xiaobo's Nobel Peace Prize at the Liaison Office, some of it allegedly spraying a security guard standing nearby; prominent pro-democracy figures arrested simply for appearing on Citizens' Radio, a station the government has refused to license (when Szeto Wah died, he still had a charge for that hanging over him); and various other arrests that appear more like harassment (or judicial persecution, as it has been called) than law enforcement.

During Li Keqiang's visit to HK in 2011, police appeared to cooperate with mainland security to deprive or infringe civil liberties on numerous occasions. In 2010, the police infamously "kidnapped" not one but two Goddess of Democracy replica statues in the lead-up to the June 4 candlelight vigil and arrested some two dozen people related to Hong Kong Alliance who tried to prevent them from doing so. A couple of legal cases related to those arrests are still on-going five years later.

In that sense, the situation today is not entirely new, though its scale and severity are. Pro-democracy demonstrators have never felt the police are "on our side" or even entirely neutral, but in the last five years especially, they often appear to be against us. Is it an exaggeration to say that political opposition is being increasingly criminalized?

For a stark point of contrast, remember the July 1 march in 2003 when a half million people turned out to protest against impending draconian Article 23 "security" legislation intended to make HK laws dovetail with the mainland's. Considering the enormous crowd, the police presence on that occasion was light. The police regarded their role as that of facilitation, no more, no less. There were no arrests, and the event went off peacefully. In how many other cities around the world could half a million people gather without any destruction to property or other crime? In this respect, it's important to remember that HK people are largely self-policing and nonviolent. The fact that crime rates in HK are relatively low is perhaps more down to the law-abiding character of the population than to the police (though it should be noted that the fact that the HK police are not economically corrupt is a big plus).

Compare the 2003 march to the one on July 1, 2014. Last year was the first time ever that march organizers were arrested for a July 1 march—five of them altogether. Year after year, organizers and police had disagreed about various details of the march, but the police had never before taken the step of arresting them. (As in the case of the vast majority of arrests made by police in connection with the Umbrella Revolution, no prosecution has yet ensued.[2])

Some have compared HK police to police elsewhere and argued we have little to complain about. But most of these comparisons, for instance to police in US cities, are more misleading than instructive. While the Umbrella Revolution has been going on in HK, there have been several notorious cases of unarmed black men (and a child) being killed by police in the US. Some say, Look, hey, here in HK, a little tear gas, a little pepper spray—what's that compared to the fact that police elsewhere, and in a democratic country no less, are killing their own citizens?

But in comparing different situations, it's important to take their different contexts into account. In this case, the US has a "double history" of violence: First, slavery and racial discrimination that, while not as bad as before, continues up to this day; second, gun laws that allow a large number of citizens to carry lethal weapons. The two are a lethal brew, for racist tendencies amongst US police are compounded by their expectation that in any given situation, they could be shot at. The chances of them pre- or over-reacting are great.

By contrast, HK police have it relatively easy. HK is a relatively nonviolent society (at least physically speaking; the structural violence is great, HK being one of the most unequal societies in the world and number one on two out of two *Economist* crony capitalism indices).

A better comparison would be to Nordic countries which, like HK, are small in population, racially homogenous, affluent and have a tradition of relatively nonviolent behavior of both police and citizenry.

In light of that comparison, the behavior of HK police can be seen in relief as well as the fact that its backdrop is the political injustice suffered by the HK people. That is to say, the police routinely infringe civil liberties and abuse their power in order to protect those in power, unlike in the Nordic countries which are amongst the most democratic in the world.

Amongst its many inanities on HK, the UK government judged the police's response to the occupations to be generally proportionate.[3] To the extent that there is any truth to that view, it has to be highly qualified: Yes, after the initial indiscriminate pepper-spraying and tear-gassing which triggered the occupations, they did practice relative restraint, but this was because they had no other option unless they wanted to use even greater force, which was judged politically unviable. They had lost. Not only had they failed to prevent people from occupying the streets (indeed, ironically, it was their act, the teargasing, more than anything else that provoked people to do so), but the general population was incensed at their behavior and at the government's irresponsible order to the police to attack its own citizens (an order it has not even dared to admit it gave). Once they had taken the risk of attacking their own citizens and failed so miserably even in the narrow military sense of defeating them (ie, clearing the streets), all they could do was adopt a defensive stance and wait out the occupations, which is what they did. When the occupied sites were eventually cleared, the occupiers put up no resistance. (The first time the police tried to clear Mong Kok by stealth, it was reoccupied. The second time, after the clearance of Argyle Street, there was resistance in nearby side streets, but by this time, the police felt more confident they could put it down without political repercussions, and this is also where a great deal of police brutality occurred, for example, with police aiming batons at the head level of demonstrators hiding behind umbrellas.)

Even then, to consider their use of force "largely proportionate" is to ignore a large body of evidence to the contrary. Not only were there the indiscriminate tear-gassing and gratuitous use of pepper spray on a number of occasions, individual cases of police brutality during the occupations were widespread, with an especially large number associated with the clearance of Lung Wo Road; the clearance of Mong Kok, especially in the aftermath of the clearance of Argyle Street; and several infamous beatings of individuals, the best known being that of Ken Tsang, but also others for which the officers responsible have not been held accountable, for example, Osman Cheng's beating in Mong Kok.

Police win few points from anyone for the fact that the officers who beat Ken Tsang have not yet been brought to trial. From comments by the Police Commissioner himself defending his officers' right not to cooperate in a criminal investigation in which they themselves are implicated (the Police Commissioner has never defended the rights of other arrestees or suspects not to cooperate), one is left with the suspicion that the police handed a weak or faulty or incomplete report to the Department of Justice in order to make it harder to prosecute the officers. In the meantime, demonstrators have been tried on charges of assaulting officers and obstructing officers and bailiffs.[4]

Few if any of these cases are as clear-cut as Ken Tsang's. Many of them are very flimsy indeed, and on more than one occasion, the judge has criticized the prosecution and testifying officers for their poor, and in some cases, misleading or inaccurate evidence. There was certainly not a single case of demonstrators outright beating an officer. The double standard mars the police's integrity and public trust in it.

In addition to this, at times during the occupations and also since, especially during the anti-parallel trade demonstrations but also during Gao Wu in Mong Kok, it has appeared that the police and counter-demonstrators had a sort of relationship or tacit agreement or that, at the very least, police were more focused on "policing" demonstrators than people attacking them.

In the week leading up to the HK government tabling its fake universal suffrage proposals in Legco, the police arrested two Scholarism students, Ivan Lam and Wilson Li, and the deputy secretary general of the League of Social Democrats, Napo Wong, in connection to incidents that took place way back in, respectively, November 2013 and March 2014. Strange timing, that, and many said it seemed as if the police were trying to intimidate people against coming out to the streets to protest against the fake universal suffrage proposals.

There is also the worryingly large number of reports of HK people being prevented from entering the mainland. It appears there is a kind of blacklist, and it is unclear whether or not HK authorities, perhaps including the police, have cooperated with mainland authorities in compiling it.

But at base, more than these discrete incidents, the political corruption of the HK police by making them serve the ends of an unelected government which is little more than the representative of the largest dictatorship in the world has to do with the decision to tear gas demonstrators on September 28, 2014 for hours on end, far past the point that the teargasing could reasonably have been said to have any law enforcement function, if indeed it ever could have.

In taking that decision, the HK government was essentially turning the police into a militia to protect it and treating the pro-democracy demonstrators as the enemy. This constituted the breaking of a basic social contract that had existed for decades. Remember, it was the first use of tear gas against HK citizens, the first concerted attack on HK citizens since the late 1960s. Back then, at any rate, the police had the justification that their adversaries, Cultural Revolution-inspired leftists, were violent, planting bombs and throwing Molotov cocktails.

Not until both the HK government and the police formally and unequivocally acknowledge their actions, fully account for them, hold individuals responsible for making the decisions to take them, and apologize to the HK people can the HK police really regain their integrity and hope to reform.

The police attack on demonstrators had more to do with regime intimidation than law enforcement. This continues to be the operative paradigm, and at root, this is the problem.

5

You could argue that the police are simply responding as best they can to a new reality, namely, HK people's greater willingness to engage in acts of civil disobedience and their decreasing willingness to abide by the terms of the Public Order Ordinance, which has been criticized both locally[5] and internationally for being open to abuse as a tool to infringe freedom of assembly and association. Yes, sometimes there have been excesses, this line of reasoning goes, but what are the police to do in dealing with an increasingly restive population?

After the Kennedy Town fracas on Saturday, a journalist who is generally sympathetic with the pro-democracy movement said, "I feel sympathy for the police." She meant that the police are put in a difficult position.

I agree, but I also think the question isn't so much whether or not one feels sympathy with police. On a certain level, I feel sympathy with all human beings—life is difficult, after all! The question is what function the police are serving, and whether or not they should be serving that function.

And here, while the behavior of individual police officers is certainly important to address, and individual officers should be held responsible for abuses of power, the problem is more systematic and has to do, fundamentally, with the relationship between the government, the police and the people of HK.

Are the police adhering strictly to the role of law enforcement? Or have they overstepped their bounds, largely due to government orders and the disposition of top officers, in particular the Police Commissioner, and increasingly begun to play the political role of keeping political opposition to the regime in check? To what extent has law enforcement bled into harassment, intimidation, surveillance, and infringement of civil liberties?

Or to put it another way, when the Partystate and the HK government refuse to abide by the Basic Law and international law, when they deny the HK people the basic human right of genuine universal suffrage, when, in effect, it is they who have broken the law, when it is their criminal act that is the "original sin" at the root of the issue at hand, what role should the police play? Arguably, the police should have been arresting the people on that "2017: Make It Happen!" bus responsible for the fake universal suffrage plan and not the people demonstrating against it.

When was the last time the police asked Carrie Lam for proof of identity? When was the last time they asked Raymond Tam what he was doing standing on the pavement? Have they ever ignored Rimsky Yuen when he tried to give them information related to a crime? These are the people who have broken the Basic Law, who have broken international law. If there were any international enforceability in this area, they would be indicted for depriving 7.2 million people of a basic political right. How much are the HK police corrupted when they are continually in the position of defending a government that has committed a crime against the HK people from the HK people who are trying to hold them legally accountable to the Basic Law and international law? It is really an up-is-down, down-is-up situation, which is why it is hard to listen to HK government propagandistic phrases like "the illegal Occupy Movement" with any patience; it should quite literally be "the illegal HK government".

The media should have a pressing interest in asking and pursuing these questions, but you'd be hard pressed to find much in the media about them, apart from news about the most notorious cases, such as the beating of Ken Tsang by seven police officers. But those are easy to write off as "excesses" committed by a few "bad apples" when the problem, as I say, is more systematic. To approach this systematic problem, you need analytical and investigative journalism, of which there is very little in HK, and even less of high quality. And international journalists simply don't have the time or inclination to cover it; HK isn't a high enough priority to their editors on the other side of the world. And so, arguably one of the larger stories of the Umbrella Revolution, whether the police force has been turned into a tool to protect the political power of the regime, goes unexamined in local and international public discourse.

The police who accosted me in the street were not "bad apples", at least not in their handling of me. They were just "doing their job". Yet the job they were doing really shouldn't be their job. They were ordered to do it, and they did it, and in doing it, they were corrupted, not dramatically, not in the sense that they beat me or arrested me and framed me or harmed me physically, but in the sort of subtle way that becomes significant only when you recognize it as part of a pattern.

In a way, all of what I have written here was going through my head when the police requested my ID and goes through my head in any encounter with the police. I am not alone—it is thus for a great many in the pro-democracy movement, and if you spend any time talking with them, you will come away with a great many stories like this one.

The issue of political pressure on institutions—and of their compromising and corruption and degradation—in HK is urgent and has to do not only with police but also the media, education and universities, the law and the judiciary.

One reason the Department of Justice seems reluctant to prosecute pro-democracy demonstrators is it fears the judiciary is not yet sufficiently compromised that the government can expect easy wins that can be parleyed into propaganda (you see: we told you those demonstrators were "illegal"!). The HK government consistently employs the description, "the illegal Occupy Movement," but it has yet to test this assertion of "illegality" in court: Not a single occupier has been tried for unlawful assembly, though the great majority of arrests were for that crime. Some in government and the police must understand that there is a difference between the world of force, which they inhabit, and the world of law as represented by the judiciary and legal community. Unlike the judiciary, the universities, some schools and a few hold-outs in the media, the police, on the other hand, have proven sufficiently pliable. Admittedly, they were the most vulnerable to such corruption to begin with.

The police and the Department of Justice should either make full efforts to prosecute those they arrest, in particular on the charge of unlawful assembly but also in connection with demonstrations, or the police should acknowledge its errors in making those arrests and stop the abuse of their powers of arrest. Otherwise, they are simply using arrests to control people they have no intention of actually prosecuting and who have, until proven otherwise, committed no crime. Their acts are not illegal until proven so in a court of law.

6

Just when it looked as if the police would be carting me down to the police station, the female officer who had been the first to approach me took me aside and said, "Perhaps if you answer a few questions about Hong Kong, we can be assured that you are not an illegal immigrant."

From the point of view of methodology, her suggestion was absurd, but I discerned she was trying to find a face-saving way of ending the encounter.

"OK," I said.

"How long have you been in Hong Kong?"

I answered the question.

"Where do you live?"

I said I did not want to answer the question.

"What district do you live in?"

I told her.

She asked one more question about my marital status (?!) and then said I could go. Good on her for putting an end to the farce.

As I walked away, I glanced at my watch. The whole encounter had lasted 25 minutes.

The citizen journalist who had been observing accompanied me to the station. He said, "I recognize two of those officers."

"From where?" I asked.

"I videoed them at the Yuen Long anti-parallel trade demonstration in March. I saw a blue ribbon attacking a demonstrator there. I chased him and he ran away. He was joined by these two officers. They went into an alley. I told the officers I'd seen the man attack another man. They didn't listen to me. They gave the attacker an iced tea and then said goodbye to him."

He showed me the video. Sure enough, it was definitely the same two officers.

In that small group of officers who stopped me lies a parable. Common sense had eventually prevailed upon the female police officer, and this, too, is a characteristic of many HK police, albeit perhaps dwindling overall. Two of the other officers had at least on one previous occasion "gone over to the dark side". At stake is the soul of the force, which in turn will have much influence on the fate of HK. Which way will it go?

26 years on, we still live in the shadow of June 4, 1989

May 29, 2015

The legacies of '89 are multiple and wide-ranging, affecting China, its imperial peripheries, and the wider world.

1

If you were in Hong Kong last September, you saw how powerful the legacy of June 4 still is.

On the night of September 28, 2014, a rumor circulated that the HK police would escalate their use of violence from tear gas to live ammunition, most probably rubber bullets, but who knew?

"Scary green men" were seen prowling the streets of Admiralty, where the police had first attacked the people with an hours-long barrage of tear gas canisters. The scary green men were HK police, but we'd never seen their kind before. They looked more like soldiers in their green uniforms, gas masks and boots. They carried rifles, which they pointed in all directions.

In the face of the rumor the police would escalate use of violence, Hong Kong Federation of Students and Occupy Central, two of the groups who suddenly found themselves leaders of a sort after tens of thousands of people had spontaneously turned out on the streets earlier that day, called on people to go home.

When I first heard the call, I couldn't believe it. I thought, "You've got to be kidding. Here are all these people out on the streets, and you want them to go home!" I tried to contact HKFS and OC to tell them they were overreacting, but I wasn't able to reach them. Once they had made the appeal, they weren't communicating.

Luckily, the people didn't listen to them, and rather than going home, they not only occupied Admiralty but also Causeway Bay and Mong Kok, initiating occupations that would last longer (seventy-nine days, from September 28 to December 15) than the demonstrations in Tiananmen Square in 1989 (fifty days, from April 15 to June 4).

The situation was confusing that night. HKFS and OC decided it was best to err on the side of caution. They feared the police would open fire, causing massive injuries, even deaths, and they felt responsible; they wanted people to be safe.

Of course, lurking in the back of their minds, hovering over them like a long shadow cast across twenty-five years, was the Tiananmen massacre. They wanted to avoid a second Tiananmen.

Earlier that summer of 2014, in the lead-up to what would become the entirely unplanned occupations, there were regular rumors of People's Suppression Army (after June 4, I cannot stomach using the name they call themselves, the very opposite of what they have shown themselves to be; calling soldiers who kill their own people the "People's Liberation Army" is a grotesque abuse of language and truth, a desecration of the memory of their victims) troop movements in Hong Kong and night sightings of PSA vehicles. One of many questions swirling in the air for weeks was, Would the PSA intervene to defend the HK government?

As it turned out, the HK police did not escalate—those scary green men with rifles disappeared from the streets that night never to return throughout the remaining seventy-nine days of occupation, as if they had been just some mirage, and PSA troops stayed in their barracks. But the rumors showed the extent to which June 4 still permeates the HK psyche, submerged, repressed much of the time but brought to the surface by events such as last year's.

And it's not just a matter of psychology: For all of the Communist Party's attempts to erase June 4 from history, the historical period in which we live is still the June 4 era.

2

China is a schizophrenic place. On the one hand, it is one of the fastest changing societies in the world. Whole cityscapes are transformed in a matter of years. The economy has grown massively since 1989. The society and culture of today would be largely unrecognizable to someone time-travelling from '89. Just the way people looked and dressed in photos from the '89 demonstrations shows the temporal distance.

And yet, politically, China is frozen in time; politically, the date today is the same as it has been for twenty-six years: June 4, 1989.

That isn't to say that there haven't been political changes or developments since 1989 but that the general mode of governance is in the same paradigm as that of 26 years ago; there has been no substantial political reform or change of any kind. We still live under the "dictatorship of the proletariat".

The very low level of the Communist Party's tolerance for open public political discussion is a good litmus test of change. Sometimes I wake up and look around and think I must be dreaming: Pu Zhiqiang, Gao Yu, Chen Yunfei, Liu Xiaobo, others are all in prison. They were all participants in the events of April to June 1989. They were young then. And now, twenty-six years later, they're in prison, all on trumped up if not downright ridiculous charges, this in a country that purports to be moving toward rule of law. Pu and Gao were arrested last year around the time of the twenty-fifth anniversary of the '89 demonstrations, Pu after attending a private meeting about events of '89, Gao on her way to one. This is a clear sign of being frozen in time: 26 years on, the Communist Party still feels threatened by the most moderate of opinions, the most moderate of efforts to move society in a more rights-respecting, less corrupt direction.

As Chinese students studying abroad put it recently in their wonderful open letter on Tiananmen (a must-read for all on this 26th anniversary): *"A classmate of this writer believes that the events from twenty-six years ago are too far back, today's China is getting better and better, and he lives a very happy life. As I walked on the Avenue of Eternal Peace two years ago, I saw no trace of blood or bullets but skyscrapers and the bustling of people and cars. We live in prosperity, but what kind of prosperity it is—our imagination is constantly challenged by the astonishing scale of high and low ranking officials, the marriage of power and money that the students opposed twenty-six years ago has become the prevalent model of the state economy. Xi Jinping's regime waves the banner of anti-corruption, but ordinary people are thrown in jail as trouble makers for holding signs asking officials to disclose their assets. The clans of Deng Xiaoping and Li Peng, whose hands were stained with the blood of students, have become filthy rich. We are shocked to discover that we are governed by officials whose family members live abroad. In other words, we are ruled by a bunch of foreigners, and China is merely the goose that lays golden eggs for them.*

"Twenty-six years ago, students wanted freedom of the press; and twenty-six years later, all media are still controlled by the Party's Propaganda Department,

and journalists and lawyers are being put in jail for invented crimes. Gao Yu's crime was leaking state secrets, or the ruling party's latest ideological guidelines. Some of my friends are of the opinion that those who draw the Party's ire do so because they are famous and conspicuous. We, on the other hand, are mere ordinary people who don't care about politics. But are ordinary people safe from harm? Think about Xia Junfeng (夏俊峰), Xu Chunhe (徐纯合), and the daughter of Tang Hui (唐慧). No one is safe in a dictatorial system."[1]

While the political situation has hardly changed, views on the chances of the Communist Party continuing to rule have. The conventional wisdom used to be, This cannot last, an economy and society so rapidly changing, a political system so stuck in the past. But in recent years, much international coverage and punditry has focused on the Communist Party's ability to adapt, its management of the economy, its fine-tuning of the mechanisms of control, propaganda, censorship. This has lead to very different questions: Is the Communist Party's brand of neo-authoritarianism sustainable? Does it even offer a new model, especially to developing countries, that competes with democracy?

After Tiananmen, the Communist Party made a coerced and implicit pact with the Chinese people: No political reform, no political freedom, but we will allow you greater economic freedom than you have ever had under our regime. You allow us to stay in power and we allow you to get rich.

In order for this deal to work, China had to have sustained and rapid economic growth. This was a matter that was outside the control of the Communist Party for it entailed integration into the global trading system: China had to sell a lot to the rest of the world. It would have been difficult if not impossible for the Communist Party to continue to rule without the neo-liberal globalization that flourished in the nineties; the coincidence was a godsend to the Party.

It's not an exaggeration to say that the number one aiders and abetters of dictatorship in China after Tiananmen have been Western governments' trade policies, Western corporations and Western consumers. That was not their intention—their intentions, respectively, were to improve their economies and/or do the bidding of their corporations (governments), make a lot of money (corporations), and buy a lot of cheap stuff (consumers)—but that was their effect.

That history leads to another important sense in which we are still living in the June 4 era, and not just here in China, in Hong Kong, but globally: we experience a deep confusion about the relationship between capitalism and democracy, or perhaps a deep ambivalence about which we prefer.

3

In the early nineties, democracy was seen to be in the ascendancy worldwide. The Soviet empire had just collapsed. The number of countries that were, at least on paper, democracies was increasing rapidly. OK, China was an anomaly, but it was only a matter of time, right?

The nineties was also the time of the ascendancy of the "Washington consensus", neo-liberal economics, and globalization. The World Trade Organization and free-trade agreements deliberately segregated issues of environmental protection and labor rights from trade issues, prioritizing the latter. They pushed free trade; they didn't push protection of labor and the environment.

There was a lazy and self-serving argument on the part of Western government leaders and their business and finance lobbies that democracy and neoliberal capitalism went hand in hand. This lead to policies of "engagement" with China; basically, do business with them and they'll eventually become democratic. Unsurprisingly, these Western elites were far more interested in business than democracy.

And the Communist Party hit the jackpot: China, with its lack of labor rights, relatively well-educated, healthy and disciplined workforce (the Communist Party did get a few things right in contrast with its democratic counterpart in India), long coast with many ports, improving infrastructure and huge economies of scale, was well placed to take advantage of neo-liberal globalization. Post-Tiananmen, China went from being politically isolated to the center of the global economy in a matter of incredibly few years.

Western capitalist countries threw the Communists a lifeline, and not only did the Communists survive, but the Communist Party is the biggest, most powerful, wealthiest dictatorship in the world, with almost unlimited resources, as well as the number one owner of US Treasury securities (neck and neck with Japan these days, leaving the rest of the competition in the dust).

When push came to shove, seemingly almost by default, as if they hadn't even really considered the matter carefully, Western countries were more interested in capitalism than democracy. This wasn't really a hard sell to Western electorates: as long as they benefitted as consumers, they were easily satisfied, forget the fact that the plethora of cheap goods were made by workers who hadn't the rights Western workers had even as Western countries hemmorrhaged good blue collar jobs.

Then, while it was getting rich from selling the West cheap stuff, the Communist Party dangled a "market of one billion people" in front of salivating multinational corporations. They and their governments became little more than supplicants at the throne of the dragon emperor: We want in, we want in, we'll do anything to get in. The genius of the Communist Party has been, for the most part, not to let them in while at the same time continuing to hold the promise before them. Having to a large extent saturated Western markets and reached their "growth potential", these corporations are desperate for new markets.

PEN American Center recently released an excellent report, *Censorship and Conscience: Foreign Authors and the Challenge of Chinese Censorship*[2], to coincide with Book Expo America's annual conference at which a delegation of over 500 publishing industry bigwigs from China lead by Communist Party officials was Guest of Honor. Why? Because the US book industry sees China as the future, and the road to China leads through the Communist Party. One Barnes and Noble's bookstore in New York where the conference took place was seen (by Xinhua[3]) to have an extensive display by the Chinese delegation in its shop window with Xi Jinping's little red book (well, it's actually beige) taking pride of place. World, how low can you go!?

Last year, the Norwegian government joined the growing list of governments to scurry as far as it could from the Dalai Lama. In 1989, the very year of Tiananmen, the Dalai Lama won the Nobel Peace Prize. Twenty-five years later, upon invitation, he returned to Norway to commemorate the occasion, but not a single Norwegian government official would meet him. The Norwegian government argued it had to repair the damage to its relationship with China caused by the Nobel Committee having awarded the Peace Prize to Liu Xiaobo in 2010 (the damage was actually inflicted by the Communist Party in response to the award). Denmark, which later also hid from the Dalai Lama, couldn't have the same excuse.[4] These are amongst the most democratic countries in the world, and yet they find themselves genuflecting to the will of the world's biggest dictatorship. World, how low can you go?!

The brazen cynicism and cowardice of the governments of democratic countries have been deeply disheartening. Whether they know it or not, they live in the shadow of June 4, their actions and decisions trapped in the dialectic of events that day set in motion. The original logic of "engagement" has been turned on its head: From, "We have the economic power to influence their political change", to, "They have the economic power to influence us to display copies of Xi Jinping's book in our shopwindows and avoid meeting a Tibetan monk." Small prices to pay, of course, for rich (hoped-for) economic rewards. How many small prices to pay before they become one big price?

After the 1990s, the Communist Party got lucky in another way. 9/11 lead to a US fixation on fighting Islamist terrorism. The world, it could be said, took its eye off the ball. In the long term, neo-authoritarianism of the sort seen in China and Russia today is a greater threat to democracy, freedom and rights than Islamist political groups. And yet no Western power has seriously focused on that threat. After Russia's invasion of Ukraine, Chinese Communist dictatorship falls even further down Western powers' list of imminent threats (with the partial exception of the Party's stronger assertion of territorial claims in the South China Sea).

And then the financial crisis hit in 2007, largely caused by business and finance interests predominating in the formulation of Western government policies over the previous fifteen years—again, capitalism triumphing over democracy—especially in the US, the UK and a few other countries.

Apart from economic difficulties, large democratic deficits within Western countries went unaddressed, in the US caused by the huge influence of money in politics and greatly increasing income inequality, in the European Union by the great power of the Commission and the European Central Bank and their distance from and lack of accountability to ordinary citizens as well as the imbalance of power among member states.

In contrast to the nineties democracy boom, over the past decade, indices such as Freedom House's Freedom of the World report and the Economist Intelligence Unit's Democracy Index state unequivocally that democracy is "in decline", "in retreat". And we wonder how it came to this.

Around the world, it's still June 4. June 4 stands for the world's unfinished business. We got to the edge of global democracy and weren't able to turn the corner. Due to consumer capitalism and globalization gaining the upper hand over democracy. Due to lack of vision and commitment to democracy on the part of Western countries and many in the supposedly newly emerging democracies (ie, Russia).

Does China offer a viable model of governance to developing countries? That the question is even asked (and that the authoritarian development model is supported largely by Western aid in countries like Ethiopia) shows how much the world's changed.

Maybe, instead, we should ask, What would the world look like today if the Chinese empire, like the Soviet empire, had turned that democratic corner in '89? Or if the West had considered it more important to turn that global democratic corner than to turn China into the world's workshop? Much of Western punditry, driven by realist thinking in the foreign policy establishment and business and finance thinking in influential publications like *The Economist* and *Financial Times*, will guffaw at such naïve thinking: China is richer, the world is richer, history is inexorable and there's no sense hypothesizing about it. But history is made of decisions. Where we are now is the result of decisions made: the decision to murder people in cold blood on June 4, 1989; the decisions that resulted in neo-liberal globalization; the decisions to "engage" the Communist Party on largely an economic basis (and largely excluding politics). Is there really no way to make the world both richer and more democratic? Is our political imagination really so impoverished as to deal in little more than "the way things are"?

4

Another legacy of June 4 is the Communist Party's continuing adamant refusal to recognize the will of the people. How else to interpret the massacre? This might seem obvious, but the refusal to so much as listen (never a great skill of the Party) has essentially caused the Communist Party to lose the peripheries of its empire. Of course, it hasn't lost them in the formal sense, but the only way it can keep them is through threat and military occupation, for it's so thoroughly lost "hearts and minds."

Hong Kong's not the only periphery that must deal with the long shadow of June 4. Under the current governance paradigm, the situations of Hong Kong, Taiwan, Tibet and East Turkestan cannot be resolved except by force (which is a "negative peace", a fake resolution).

To Tibet and East Turkestan the Communist Party tried to apply the post-Tiananmen lesson learned in its heartland: Give people economic growth and prosperity and they won't care about politics or rights. But the situations in those places today are in many ways more fraught than they ever have been, with constant strife over the past half-decade and more.

After Taiwan saw how intent the Communist Party was on denying Hong Kong the right to genuine universal suffrage, the chance of any rapprochement between it and the mainland is gone for a good long time if not forever. Taiwan most definitely does not want to become Hong Kong. In Taiwan too, the Communist Party's strategy was to undermine Taiwan politically with its economic influence, and the response has been political, the Sunflower Movement. China's treatment of Hong Kong and the Guomindang pushing closer economic cooperation with the mainland look to be two key factors that will likely bring the Democratic Progressive Party to power in the next elections, a party the Communists have always despised as separatist.

The Communist Party appears constantly taken aback that in Hong Kong, Taiwan, Tibet, and East Turkestan, politics trump economics and people care about other things than money. Quite simply, it's really made a mess of things in all of these places, even in the narrow terms of its own objective of attaining firm and complete control. It refuses to listen, or even acknowledge an interlocutor and believes the only approach is to take a hardline. Its response to eruptions of discontent in Tibet and East Turkestan has been brutal, basically a combination of military occupation, police state and isolating those areas as much from the rest of the world as possible. With Hong Kong and Taiwan, where it can't just impose its will by brute force, it simply doesn't know what to do; it's at a loss.

Could it be that one enduring lesson of June 4 is more than idealistic cliché; namely, that the people want the power, and until they get it, political problems cannot be solved through mere force and refusal to so much as engage the other side? The Tiananmen Massacre meant the Communist Party did not have to listen to anyone, and its refusal to even acknowledge issues raised by political adversaries as legitimate must constitute a serious governance limitation of some sort, even in terms of the calculations of realpolitik.

5

One last way in which we are still living in the shadow of June 4:

A keystone of the Communist Party's approach to '89 is to remove it from history. Accurate accounts are not allowed to appear in published books, school textbooks, the media or on the internet. It's simply whitewashed.

Enforcement of historical amnesia is a longstanding policy of the Communist Party's rule: the Cultural Revolution, the Great Famine, the Great Leap Forwards and anti-rightist campaign, the genocides of landlords and Tibetans—you name it, it's off limits.

Of course, many countries have difficulties facing their histories honestly. Japan, the US and Turkey are three that immediately come to mind. Germany is one of the few that does so remarkably well. But the Communist Party is in a class of its own when it comes to the resources it dedicates to enforcing its version of history.

In China, a frequent experience I have is disorientation of a sort verging on vertigo. This is partly caused by the fact that my perception of the country differs so enormously from that of its rulers. It also has to do with what I mentioned at the start of this essay: the schizophrenia of being, on the one hand, one of the fastest-changing societies in the world and, on the other, frozen in time. But it's also because so many people have such a deep misunderstanding or ignorance of their own country's history, are so deeply influenced by the official version propagated by the Party. It has often seemed to me that there is something dangerous in this situation: a society whose attention is so often directed to the horrific atrocities committed by Japan but not to those committed by its Communist rulers which in order of magnitude (number of lives lost) and current impact on society dwarf those committed by any other oppressor.

In this sense, the Party's approach to June 4 is a touchstone indicating the extent to which it will go to perpetuate lies, the extent to which it perceives truth as its enemy.

6

If you say the '89 demonstrations and massacre are discrete events that occurred in Beijing and other Chinese cities, then perhaps they look less relevant today.

But if you look at the ways the regime, the people, and the rest of the world responded to those events, their contemporary significance is great: We are still in the June 4 era.

Arguably, the greatest legacy of June 4 is that we have all contributed to creating a monster: the most powerful dictatorship and one of the largest armies in the world; domestically, a huge "stability maintenance budget" (the Communist Party perceives its own people as the greatest threat to its power) coupled with extensive mechanisms of propaganda and censorship, systematic torture, 95 percent conviction rates, independent trade unions forbidden; internationally, territorial disputes with many of its neighbors (in particular, in the South China Sea with Japan, the Philippines, Vietnam and the borders of occupied Tibet with India).

This is not a pretty picture. This is not where we should be in 2015.

June 4 is not just about justice and rights and freedom, not just about democracy and accountable government, not just about facing history honestly, but also about peace, about how we keep the peace, about the difference between negative and positive peace, and about the future, the sort of society we wish to see and the chances of bringing that about.

In China, in Hong Kong, in Tibet and East Turkestan and Taiwan and the world, how much longer must we continue to live in June 4's shadow?

It's time to make a concerted effort to disassemble the monster we have played a part in creating. Not only that, it's time we clearly realize that decisions made over the past twenty-six years in China and the rest of the world have lead to democracy hanging in the balance worldwide. Do we really value democracy, or do we not? And if we do, how do we apply that value, how do we foster, promote, defend, encourage, support democracy around the world?

In the spirit of June 4, and applying its lessons, constructive responses would include:

As a matter of priority and urgency, consequentially fighting dictatorship and the denial of the people's right to choose their own government wherever they occur, recognizing that this is not only a moral and legal imperative but in the long-term self-interest of the vast majority of people and countries

... and concomitantly, consistently fostering and supporting democracy, including democratic institutions and cultures in China and elsewhere, recognizing that democracy is not only a basic right but also the best way of ensuring political equality and justice as well as positive peace

Subordinating capitalism to democracy, ensuring that the economic growth capitalism seems to be quite good at producing is channeled toward the benefit of all of society, and addressing income inequality as a matter of justice and a threat to national and global security

Fighting the imposition and/or promotion of historical amnesia wherever it may occur, including fighting against censorship and propaganda, key tools of the dictator in enforcing historical amnesia

Expanding our global consciousness so that it embraces all who fight for democracy, human rights and freedom around the world, in order that we may always work in solidarity with them as we learn lessons from them about defending democracy at home

Only if we do these things as part of our responsibility as global citizens can we say that we have honored the memory of the demonstrators of 1989, especially those who were killed by the dictatorship and its army.

It's become abundantly clear that governments won't do this unless they are pushed to do so by their citizens. And perhaps that's the way it should be: democracy is nothing if it is not a people's movement.

I realize this will sound pie-in-the-sky to many. Idealism is not fashionable these days. (Cynicism, arguably, is another powerful legacy of June 4, in China and elsewhere: make money and shut up.) But in Hong Kong, China and elsewhere, we must have a vision of that better society we wish to see. We must fix our eyes on that prize while at the same time seeing where we're at, strategizing with savvy how to get from here to there. Of course, the struggle to get there will entail failure again and again and again. But there will also be victories along the way, and perhaps, occasionally, the big victory that sets the course of history in another direction, that helps us to emerge from the June 4 era, from the long shadow events of that day twenty-six years ago have cast.

Thanks to the people of China in 1989, and people in many other countries around the world time and time again, for reminding us of that.

A tribute to all of the people of the HK pro-democracy movement (because it's not often these days that someone stares down the dictator)

June 19, 2015

On the occasion of the defeat of fake universal suffrage in the Legislative Council on June 18, 2015

1

I'll admit: When I turned up at the Civil Human Rights Front-organized march at Victoria Park last Sunday, June 14 and looked around, I thought, "Where is everybody?!" There were so many fewer marchers (ultimate count: 3,500) than CHRF had said it expected (50,000) that it almost seemed as if someone was playing a trick on us. Well, I thought, it's so hot; maybe people are too lazy and will just gather around the Legislative Council building, the march's terminus and site of the planned encampment in the coming days, instead. But when we got there after a long hot walk, that was not the case either. What's up? Have HK people really faltered at this last step?

Then it struck me: HK people are SO tired. HK people are so so tired. HK people are so sick and fed up with the political charade of "constitutional development" that the Communist Party and the HK government have been conducting in their city over the last twenty months almost as if the people were not there, even though HK people have time and again made it abundantly clear that WE ARE HERE, WE DO EXIST, THIS PLACE IS OURS AND YOU CAN'T DO WITH IT WHAT YOU WISH.

Even in the faces of those who turned up last Sunday, I could see it: They are so tired. And it wasn't just that the temperature was a good 35 degrees and the heat radiated off the pavement. It was a spiritual tiredness, deep in their bones. They had fought so long, so hard. And not only that: Their struggle was a defensive action: to prevent the worst from happening as opposed to working toward achieving the best.

It was not only that they were tired. HK people, and especially young people, had ceased to believe in the efficacy of these marches from Victoria Park to the Liaison Office or to HK government headquarters. You go out, you spend your day in the heat, and what good does it do? We've done this for years, and where has it gotten us? If the CCP and HK government won't listen to 79 days of occupation, then what good is a march going to do? The days of the march may be numbered.

And it was not only that they were tired and had ceased to believe in the efficacy of marches. They were by that point quite confident that the 28 Legco members who'd vowed to vote against the HK government proposals to introduce fake universal suffrage in the "selection" (it's not for nothing that the HK government is addicted to the "s" in front of "election") of the Chief Executive in 2017, thus defeating the proposals, would indeed do so. In that sense, the motivation to come out and "support" or "threaten" them, depending on how you looked at it, did not seem so urgent. In a strange sense, the low turnout exhibited a faith in those members of the Legislative Council who'd said they would vote the proposals down.

Still, I thought, given all that, they still should have been there. I could just imagine the media having a field day: They said 50,000 would be here, and there are 3,500. The vast majority of the media, largely because of their lack of understanding of the pro-democracy movement (or, in HK, because of self-censorship and/or a pro-CCP editorial stance) had time and again counted the pro-democracy movement out: It had failed to achieve anything concrete from 79 days of occupation, it had fractured, it had "descended" into localism, it was ultimately powerless to exert its will upon the HK government and the CCP.

There were two things that those media narratives failed to comprehend:

1) After 17 years of postponement, once the CCP decided to shove fake suffrage down the throat of HK, its introduction became a cornerstone in the CCP end game to exert nearly complete control over HK long

before the 50 years of "one country, two systems" and the Basic Law were due to end in 2047, and it really really wanted it.

2) After the publication of the White Paper in June 2014 and the August 31, 2014 hardline decision of the National People's Congress Standing Committee that virtually stripped away the last vestiges of HK autonomy, at least as far as electoral arrangements were concerned, the basic stance of the HK pro-democracy movement was defensive. The occupations originally happened by accident: They were at first a spontaneous reaction against the decision of the HK government to use the HK police as a private militia to protect itself by attacking its own citizens. They were a big NO: NO, WE WON'T BE INTIMIDATED BY YOU! NO, THIS IS OUR CITY; NOT YOURS. Even once they'd settled in to stay for the long haul of 79 days, they were still a big NO: HANDS OFF OUR CITY, CCP! NO, WE WON'T ACCEPT FAKE SUFFRAGE! Yes, we want genuine universal suffrage, and yes, that has been the main slogan of the of the pro-democracy movement, but we all knew that given the August 31 decision, genuine universal suffrage was the longest of long shots, at least in the short term. Therefore, the objective of this phase of the pro-democracy movement has been to defeat fake suffrage and the CCP imposition of its will on the HK political system.

If you don't acknowledge that the CCP really really wanted fake suffrage and the HK people were set on denying them that, then you will have great difficulty understanding the dynamics of the political situation in HK.

So, standing there in front of Legco with my 3,499 counterparts last Sunday, I was disappointed and I feared the media would have a field day. Then I thought, Wait a minute—give them a break, give the HK people a break. Nowhere else in the world that I can think of have so many turned out over the past year to demand democracy, nowhere else have such large numbers come out to so many pro-democracy events. The number surely runs in the millions. And I did a quick tally in my head:

- June 4, 2014 candlelight vigil: 180,000
- June 22 to 29, 2014 referendum on genuine universal suffrage: 800,000
- July 1, 2014 march: 530,000
- September 28 to December 15 occupations: 500,000
- June 4, 2015 vigil & other commemorations: 138,000

That's 2,118,000 participants total. And the estimate of participants in the occupations is on the low end. Other estimates, extrapolated from surveys, are in the area of 1.2 million, which would put the total number of participants at 2,818,000. And that's just the massive events. There were plenty of others with numbers in the tens of thousands, thousands, hundreds, dozens. So a fairly conservative estimate would place the number of participants in pro-democracy events in HK over the past year at 2.2 million and a moderate estimate would be 2.9 million. That's astounding: 30 to 40 percent of the HK population of 7.188 million, 44 to 58 percent of the 5 million or so HK people eligible to vote, 62 to 82 percent of the 3.5 million people registered to vote in HK. Of course, there are overlaps. For example, I participated in every one of those events, so you're counting me multiple times. A good core of that number is people who came out time and time again. But even taking that into account, it's a lot. It's also worth remembering that HK has a low unemployment rate of about 3 percent along with amongst the longest working hours in the world: It's not as if HK people are sitting around with nothing to do but protest; just the opposite: they made a concerted effort to take time out from their often overly busy lives to stand up for their rights.

Looked at that way, looking at the 3,499 people arrayed in front of me at Legco, I thought, What else do you expect a people to do? How else can they go about expressing their will, their clear demand for real democracy, real autonomy, their demand that HK people choose their own government, their own legislative representatives, that HK people have full political participation and a real say in running their city?

And thinking of the millions who had come out over the past year to demand their basic right and that we were on the brink of succeeding in denying the CCP its desire to infringe that right in a way that would be legally decisive and final (with the implementation of "universal suffrage", the CCP would be under no legal obligation to change the political system further, and HK would essentially be at its mercy, never a good position to be in with a dictator), my eyes were almost filled with tears. I felt love and respect for those 3,499 gathered around me and the millions of others who had raised their voice and spoken out over the past year. They had shown tenacity, perseverance, courage, integrity, principle, morality, creativity, discipline, determination, dedication, commitment to nonviolence, diversity, joy, audacity, humility, community-mindedness and collaboration, anarchy (in the best sense—the ability to live and work constructively together without government), the ability to endure suffering and face the truth head-on, great care and responsibility for their society and future generations and a vision for that society based on equality, freedom and real democracy. And at least in that moment I thought, Yes, perhaps there is still some hope yet for HK. It is not a thought I always have.

2

When I speak of my love and respect for the pro-democracy movement in HK, I must emphasize that I mean everybody in the pro-democracy movement. Everyone has played a role. While we may often appear disorganized and divided, our diversity is also a strength. The diversity produces new ideas, new actions, new initiatives. The movement does not hang its hat on a single peg; it does not become stagnant and stale. It has the ability to re-energize, re-generate. There's always something new coming at the HK government and the CCP—they never know quite which way to turn. They attempt to isolate, suppress, harass, intimidate, imprison, demonize this mole, and another mole pops up.

There are the pro-democracy political parties, which are amongst the oldest elements in the movement, dating back to the 1980s. They have often been criticized over the past year, for being the old guard, for having failed to achieve much, for having ceased to develop, expand, grow the movement, for being stale and just doing the same thing over and over again, for having been co-opted by the establishment, for having lost their way. Much of the criticism has more than a grain of truth to it. And yet, these people have stayed the course. In the moments when the chances for real democracy in HK appeared most remote, they persevered, often, it seemed, without a great number of people supporting them. They kept the flame alive. They have been constant. And of course, in a very real sense, the defeat of fake suffrage depended on them. People (myself included) feared some might bend or break under the pressure. But they didn't. And when push came to shove, every one of the 28 pro-democracy Legislative Council members voted their conscience, voted as they had vowed to do, and defeated fake suffrage. Not only that, but in the eleven hours of speeches in Legco leading up to the vote, in their 15-minute speeches, one after one they spoke truth to power, telling the dictator to go stuff it. It is not often in formal politics these days that you see politicians standing up and saying it like it is, so freely, so eloquently, speaking both from their heart and from their head. People say words don't matter; only action. But words do matter, and not only their vote but their words were inspirational on the day they defeated fake democracy, June 18, 2015.

Much of the credit for promoting the concept of civil disobedience as a means of confronting the denial of a basic right must go to Occupy Central with Love and Peace. The three co-founders shared, in age, in outlook, in temperament (especially the inclination towards moderation) much with the pro-democracy political parties. After the amazing success of its referendum from June 22 to 29, 2014, when 800,000 voted decisively for genuine universal suffrage, OCLP was criticized for its limitations, and indeed, its limitations were significant, especially in terms of strategy, leadership, mobilization and growing the movement. But it put principled, nonviolent civil disobedience on the map in HK. The actual way in which the occupations eventually occurred was something that virtually no one could foresee, and when they did occur, OCLP was essentially along for the ride, no longer in the driver's seat, but without OCLP, it's hard to imagine that the HK people would have been intellectually and psychologically prepared not only for civil disobedience in a one-time-only, one-off sense (as on July 1, 2014 when 511 people were arrested for a sit-in in Central, a kind of precursor to the occupations) but for the grueling months of occupation. The OCLP co-founders left the occupations weeks before they concluded, but by that point, they had already passed on their baton to others, having done indispensible service to the movement.

Then there are the young people, the students, the magnificent young people and students. They are the age group most staunchly opposed to the CCP trampling on HK, the ones who appear to best understand what's really going on here, and most willing to do something about it. With the onslaught of CCP-directed mainlandization which will continue apace regardless of the defeat of fake suffrage in Legco yesterday, people under 30 are perhaps HK's best hope for the future. If they stay the way they are now and maintain their opposition to their rights being trampled and the future of their city being taken away from them, then there's a chance. Of course, it was the young people who triggered the occupations with their class boycott of September 22 to 26, leading to a small number of them occupying Civic Square on the evening of September 26, people coming out in their thousands to support them the next day, the 27th, the police responding with pepper spray and tear gas on the 28th, and the people responding to that with occupations. And with the occupations, their leading groups, Scholarism and the Hong Kong Federation of Students, came to the fore. Previous to that, they'd been forced to take a backseat to the OCLP triumvirate and pro-democracy political parties, but now they were in the lead. That was a very difficult position to be in, to be leaders of essentially leaderless occupations, but they pulled it off with magnificent energy, verve and maturity. Even in regard to the tactical mistakes they might have made, it's hard to hold them solely accountable: they had to contend with the weaknesses of the movement, for example, its inability and/or unwillingness to escalate to the level of general strikes and boycotts outside of the zones of occupation. It's also the young people who are perhaps the most disenchanted with traditional ways of doing things in the pro-democracy movement—the low number of young people at last Sunday's march was notable. Whatever means they decide to adopt instead, whatever positions they decide to take will to a great extent determine the direction of the movement in the future.

Then there are the so-called "radical" groups. First of all, I hate the way the term "radical" is used in HK and elsewhere— to dismiss, to denigrate, to marginalize, to suggest that a group is beyond the pale, not serious. "Radical" comes from the Latin "radix", which means "root". So "radical" etymologically means "getting to the root". If you take "radical" to mean someone or something who gets to the root of things, then I consider it a term of approbation, and it's in this sense I use it. Some of the groups, such as Civic Passion, pre-existed the occupations. Others, such as HK Indigenous, emerged from the occupations, as a reaction against the perceived failings of the occupations, and to more strongly assert and defend an HK identity as distinct from and in opposition to the mainland, especially the mainland under the dictatorship of the CCP. Apart from their direct actions after the occupations, in particular, the anti-parallel trade demonstrations in the New Territories and their support of hawkers in Kowloon during Chinese New Year, these radical groups have been very influential, again especially amongst young people, in putting this assertion of Hong Kong identity on the map. What they say is, Yes, genuine universal suffrage in formal politics is important, but in addition to CCP attempts to bring the political system under its full control, one of the greatest threats to HK is mainlandization, which occurs in a variety of ways and is the CCP's surreptitious way of subordinating HK. It remains to be seen how effective these groups will be in combating them, but they have at least succeeded in putting the issue firmly within the sights of the general populace and media, and in this sense have done a great service to HK and acted indirectly as a support to the struggle for genuine universal suffrage, even as some "moderate" pan-democrats have sought to distance themselves from their perceived "radicalism". To draw a semi-lame analogy, they are Malcolm X (and the eventual Black Power Movement) to OCLP's Martin Luther King, Jr., also in the sense of taking direct actions that are more confrontational. The CCP has to see that if they continue to refuse to address the legitimate democratic demands of HK people, they will face not acquiescence but greater opposition and disillusionment with their rule over HK amongst a growing number of people. In numbers, these "radical" groups are small, but in influence large, with perhaps one in six to one in five HK people identifying with them. The referenda on HK university campuses to disaffiliate individual university student unions from Hong Kong Federation of Students and the decisions by the HKU student union and HKFS not to take part in the June 4 candlelight vigil this year are largely a result of this influence. Many see it as pernicious, and indeed, if it basically turns more "moderate" allies into enemies or becomes nihilistic it could prove to be so, but a lot of this is the fall-out from the occupations and represents a transformation of the movement which may be painful but necessary. At any rate, the contribution they have made to a stronger assertion of a separate HK identity and stronger opposition to mainlandization is salutary.

Besides these, there are many other groups who have contributed to the pro-democracy struggle. Indeed, since the occupations, they have proliferated. Professional groups, youth groups, cultural groups, rights groups, groups to contest upcoming District Council elections. I know the movement fairly well, but I still come across groups I haven't encountered before. For example, at the march last Sunday, I met Cooks for Universal Suffrage (their banner said, CY Leung should be fried like a squid—a Cantonese idiom meaning he should be fired), Radiographers for Universal Suffrage. And on and on and on it goes. The society is in ferment. The roots of the desire for genuine democracy, genuine autonomy are spreading and deepening.

Then, last but first are the people of HK. Without ordinary HK people, the occupations would never have occurred. They are the ones who came out to support the students surrounded by police in Civic Square on September 26 and 27. They are the ones who stayed on and demanded their rights once the students were removed and arrested. They are the ones who burst into the street when their numbers became too many to be contained on the sidewalks. They are the ones who stood up to gratuitous police attacks of pepper spray and tear gas. They are the ones who spread out and occupied different parts of the city. They are the ones who remained for seventy-nine days. They are the ones who have turned out to events and activities in their thousands again and again and again over the years and in the past year in particular. At the height of the occupations in October, *Ming Pao* conducted a survey of occupiers which showed that only 26 percent of them were students. Most of the occupiers were ordinary people, ordinary working people. It was truly a grassroots citizens movement.

3

Out of these millions of people, there are too many stories to tell, and many have been told well elsewhere. To me, at the moment, four come to mind in particular, all from the assembly outside of the Legislative Council on Wednesday evening, after the first day of speeches and before the momentous defeat of fake universal suffrage the next day.

On that evening, we were not many—again, not nearly as many as I thought there might be, perhaps 3,000 to 4,000 and most of those went home early, before 10 pm. But there was a special feeling that evening, a feeling that something was coming to an end, a stage in the struggle for democracy. On the one hand, we felt gratified because we were about to accomplish something for which we'd fought hard for over a year, the defeat of fake suffrage. On the other hand, there was melancholy about the end of this stage, and relief, and uncertainty about the future. There was again, as many times before in the last year, that feeling of being part of history, of being part of something larger than ourselves.

One of the people I met Wednesday evening was a fifty-something taxi driver. He'd been with the movement since the beginning of the occupations. An image of him from September 28 became infamous for gratuitous police violence: he was pepper-sprayed directly in the face by a police officer though he stood a good distance from the barrier separating demonstrators from police and was making no aggressive action toward the police. Once the police started tear-gassing the people, he stood amongst the several hundred young people most directly defying the police. After the end of the occupations, once his taxi-driving shifts were finished, he would come to Tim Mei Village, the small occupation that continued at Legco long after the main one was cleared, park his taxi there, and sleep in it at night. He would often ferry occupiers to places they had to go, or bring take-out dinners to them. That Wednesday, he said: "We are at the kindergarten stage in the struggle for democracy. We still have a long long way to go."

Another person I met that Wednesday was a middle-aged member of the Progressive Teachers Alliance, one of the groups to emerge from the occupations. The Professional Teachers Union is the largest pro-democracy union in HK, but it's been pretty lame in the past year. After the police tear-gassing, the PTU called for an indefinite strike, but there wasn't much response, and since then, we never heard from them. Some teachers became frustrated with the sluggishness of the PTU and set up the Progressive Teachers Alliance. I asked her what she thought about opinion polls that consistently put support for the HK government's fake universal suffrage proposals at 40 to 50 percent. How can that be? I wondered. Do you think they're accurate? "Well," she said, "most HK people deep in their hearts want democracy, want freedom, don't want HK to become more like the mainland, don't want more CCP influence over HK. Polls over the last decades have consistently shown that 60 to 70 percent of HK people want democracy. That is clear. But then there's greed, ignorance, political apathy. You have to remember that political awareness and involvement in politics are relatively new phenomena in HK. Then there's the relentless government propaganda, from both HK and Beijing. There are people who just want a quiet life, don't want any trouble, and think the best way to keep out of trouble is to just go along with what Beijing says as long as it lets them lead their day-to-day lives. Then there are the people who have the illusion that they can just stay out of politics. They don't realize that politics affects them whether they like it or not. Then there is the minority of people at the top and those on the bottom who think their interests are best served by allying themselves with Beijing. The people on the bottom are deluded; the people on the top may be short-sighted; their alliance with Beijing is one of convenience, not of ideology or love. So when you take all these factors into account, maybe it's easier to put those polls into perspective."

The official program of the assembly ended around nine that evening. Very quickly, the stage was taken down, the floodlights turned off and disassembled, the sound system carted away. In the darkness left in their wake, one of the "mobile democracy classrooms" made famous during the occupations sprung up, with about twenty-five people taking part in a discussion that mostly revolved around looking past the vote of the next day to what the future held and how to carry on the struggle. Off to the side of it, two people, a man and a woman, had set a big battered metal pot. From it, they ladled a sugary lemony very cold drink into small cups that they went about offering to the discussants and passers-by. The drink was very refreshing on that hot night when even long past daylight you could feel the heat radiating off the pavement. They told me they had often done this during the occupations; it was their small way to contribute. The earnest act of gratuitous kindness was a characteristic I have often come across in pro-democracy activists, and is why I've said time and again that the pro-democracy movement shows the very best side of HK.

Then there was the most startling, surprising encounter of the night. It occurred as I was leaving. Way back in September, before the occupations began, I was leaving the student class boycott, whose activities for most of the week were centered around Tamar Park, where they had a big main stage. Near the harbor, I passed a young man off by himself strumming guitar. He looked up at me, and I stopped to talk. I asked him what he was singing.

He said, "I'm composing a song for when we get democracy."

"When will that be?" I asked.

"I don't know," he said, "maybe a long time," and smiled.

"Can I listen?" I asked.

"Sure," he said, and I sat there listening while staring out across the water over to the Kowloon side. The music sounded very soft, wispy. I don't remember his words, but I remember thinking they sounded earnest, idealistic. I'd since thought of that guitarist occasionally, but never saw him again.

Until Wednesday evening. I was coming across Tamar Park, where that evening the pro-CCP contingent was headquartered. But they'd departed punctually at 9— rumor had it they'd gone to tour buses at Central ferry pier 8 to collect their money for the day and get a ride home. They'd left all of their things behind, including chairs and tents. A few pro-democracy young people had moved in, to talk and enjoy the view; amongst them, my guitarist. He was playing his guitar and joyfully making a huge racket. Rather than soft, earnest music, this was punk, hardcore. And the words weren't idealistic but in-your-face:

CCP, you can stick it up your ass
CCP, you can stick it up your ass
CCP, you can stick it up your ass
HK is mine, mine, mine
HK is not yours, it's mine
HK is mine

His friends were laughing and helping him to improvise:

CCP, you can stick it up your ass
UK, you can stick it up your ass
EU you can stick it up your ass
Whole goddamn world you can stick it up your ass
HK is mine is mine is mine
HK is not yours, it's mine
HK is mine

How's that for an alternative national anthem?

After the song ended, I applauded and asked if he remembered me.

"Yes," he said. "It's been a long time."

"So long. Do you remember the song you were composing? You said it was for when we get democracy."

"Yes," he said.

"What ever became of that?"

"Well, we haven't gotten democracy yet, but at least we're about to stop the fake kind. I think I still have a while to finish that song."

In such a short time, we've come so far, so much has changed. And yet so much remains the same.

4

Across the broad spectrum of the pro-democracy movement, one of the few things we all agree on is that we don't know what the future holds. I ask people that question all the time. More often than not, the response is a shrug: Who knows?

We've fought so hard to gain so little. Indeed, at most, with the defeat of fake suffrage, we've prevented the worst, and only for the time being, in a most provisional way.

We live in limbo under a creeping shadow and will continue to do so into the foreseeable future. There are 32 years to go before the end of the 50-year "one country, two systems" period, but the CCP is trying to end the game long before then.

Joshua Wong has set the tone in saying the defeat of fake suffrage is not really a victory and not cause for celebration. (He's right, but, c'mon, Joshua, we have to at least congratulate ourselves a bit after all that resistance.)

He goes on to say that we need to be thinking about what happens after 2047. Again, I concur. It is essential to have a long-term perspective, to think in terms of what our ultimate goals are, and to devise a long-term strategy accordingly. We can't just keep dealing with matters as they arise. While we are indeed in an era of resistance, we have to also think about how to aim for what we really want. That's certainly what the CCP's been doing all along, and so much of our work up to now has concentrated on reacting against the CCP or calling for ultimate demands to be met, such as genuine universal suffrage, without having a clear long-term strategy for advancing that cause.

And what do we want? Well, of course, different people in the pro-democracy movement want different things, including some who say their ultimate aim is independence, but it's safe to say that there is general consensus on the desire for real democracy and real autonomy. In addition to that, there's agreement on the aims of greater economic and social justice.

It is also very difficult to strategize in the long term with such a shifting array of characters. The people in the Legislative Council who blocked fake suffrage are the old guard, and they will be moving on before long. The people outside Legco demonstrating are the ones who represent the future.

Outside of Legco, people, young people, were holding debates on revising the Basic Law or drawing up a whole new constitution. It's important to stress that this is the extent to which the CCP's refusal to honor its legal obligation to HK or address the demands of the people of HK in any serious way has essentially torn up the implicit social contract between the CCP and HK. People are now saying 1) the CCP simply didn't honor the Basic Law, so why should we? 2) Anyway, it's proven deficient in protecting the interests, rights and autonomy of HK. 3) And on top of that, we never had any say in it anyway. So either you amend the articles that are sticking points in fulfilling the rights of the HK people and guarding HK's autonomy, or we go back to the drawing board and we draw up a constitution that is the people's constitution and we put it to a referendum.

Indeed, one of the basic issues of debate within the pro-democracy movement at the moment is whether to work within the current system or reject it. Those who say we should work within the system say the problem isn't the Basic Law per se as the CCP's attitude. We won't get a better deal than the Basic Law, at least in the short term, and in many ways, it has worked effectively to protect the interests of the HK people most of the time up to now. The response to that is that the recent debacle has shown clearly the limitations of the Basic Law. Up to now, HK people have patiently abided by the Basic Law, though they had no say in drawing it up and have never given any formal approval of it. They did so in the expectation that one day, their demands for rights promised in the Basic Law would be met, but they have not been, and with the social contract represented in the Basic Law broken, it's time to start all over. Anyway, the whole system imposed by the Basic Law is rigged, and the CCP has shown no inclination to begin un-rigging it any time soon, by allowing universal suffrage for Chief Executive and the Legislative Council. So we should start on that process ourselves, not in the expectation that the CCP will suddenly see the light before long but with the understanding that we must first articulate our goals and then work toward them over a longer period of time lasting probably decades.

Much of how the pro-democracy movement develops from this point on will revolve around how this debate plays itself out.

It's worth noting that most of the political parties represented in Legco—with the exception of People Power, the independent Wong Yuk-man, and possibly the League of Social Democrats (a total of five of the 27 pan-democratic legislative councillors)—have affirmed allegiance to the Basic Law even as they voted down fake suffrage. They basically say the Basic Law is o.k. but the interpretations of the provisions related to universal suffrage by the CCP and the HK government are incorrect. (A very good example of this is the excellent speech against fake suffrage[1] given by Civic Party member and representative of the law functional constituency, Dennis Kwok).

Meanwhile, outside of formal politics, it appears more and more opinions are drifting toward less acceptance of the Basic Law as a sufficient basis for the governance of HK. Joshua Wong of Scholarism raised eyebrows when he spoke in favor of re-examining the Basic Law and the need for amendments of those parts of it which the CCP and HK government have interpreted in such a way as to deny HK people the basic right to be elected. This appeared to be a departure from the position held by Scholarism up to then. If indeed it is, that means that most of the leading pro-democracy groups which don't participate in formal politics and contest elections are taking a far more skeptical attitude toward the Basic Law. Even the relatively mainstream Civil Human Rights Front is jumping on the "amend the Basic Law" bandwagon, making that demand one of two key themes of the upcoming July 1 march[2] (the other being restarting the electoral reform process after the defeat of fake suffrage).

Upcoming District Council elections in November and Legislative Council elections in 2016 will likely sharpen the point of these differences. Do you take part and strive to do as well as possible, or do you say, That's a rigged system and I refuse to legitimize it by taking part in it?

There have been many small pro-democracy groups that have arisen to contest the District Council elections. Up to now, they don't seem to be gaining much traction, though perhaps it's too soon to say. Because the pro-CCP parties are so much better funded than the pan-democratic parties, they have fared much better at District Council elections in recent years. They have a permanent presence in many parts of the city and are hard to unseat without a very well-coordinated, well-organized mobilization effort that the pro-democracy movement hasn't been able to pull off up to now. Anyway, the argument goes, District Councils are not where the battle should be fought; they don't do much anyway. Will the pro-democracy movement participate wholeheartedly in the District Council elections; will it not? How well will it do? The fact that there are reportedly 391,277 young people between the ages of 18 and 30 not registered as voters[3] with a registration deadline of 2 July does not bode well.

Then, of course, the Legislative Council elections of 2016 will be as rigged as ever, since the CCP refused to entertain demands to abolish functional constituencies in 2016, saying first fake suffrage for Chief Executive in 2017 had to be passed before reform of Legco elections in 2020 could be entertained. So, again, do you participate in a rigged system or not? There's probably a stronger argument for doing so. Pan-democratic parties have not done spectacularly well in recent Legco elections, but 2016 represents a real opportunity for them to substantially improve, capitalizing on their success in defeating fake suffrage.

If they can't do better in 2016, then it's doubtful they'll ever be able to increase their representation significantly in subsequent elections.

But they'll have to be much better prepared and, in particular, put up much more appealing candidates than they have recently. The thing is, many of the more charismatic figures in the pro-democracy movement have shown little inclination to enter into formal politics. Even those who believe it's still possible to work within the system think they can accomplish more personally outside of Legco than inside it.

The pan-dems currently have only 18 of 35 seats in the geographical constituencies (those elected in accordance with the principles of genuine universal suffrage). And with the resignation of Ronny Tong, that number drops to 17, under half. That's hardly an impressive record, and the pan-dems' underwhelming performance in recent Legco elections is one reason so many pro-democracy activists have started looking elsewhere for initiative, energy, new ideas and leadership and turning their backs on the formal political process. In that sense, 2016 is really a make-or-break election. All of the pro-democracy movement, regardless of attitude toward formal politics, needs to firmly support the pan-dems' campaigns, but if they don't manage to substantially improve on their current record, then exactly how the pro-democracy movement participates in the formal political system needs to be re-evaluated. By the same token, the pan-democratic political parties need to be much more willing to listen to their pro-democracy allies than they have been up to now.

The pan-dems hold 9 of 35 seats in the largely rigged functional constituencies. The pro-democracy movement should continue to call for the abolition of all functional constituency seats, but in the meantime, it should hotly contest all where it stands a chance. That means also identifying the currently pro-CCP functional constituency seats that are vulnerable. Because of the Democratic Party's bone-headed compromise with the CCP on "reform" of Legco elections starting in 2012, functional constituencies are arguably even more deeply entrenched, and we're stuck with these five weird "super seats", according to which five District Councillors are elected to five seats in Legco. It's a terrible set-up, but also one of the main reasons—whatever else you may think of the pro-democracy movement putting its energies into District Council elections—the pan-democratic camp needs a savvy and well-coordinated strategy to contest DC elections.

It's important to remember just how little power Legco has in our so-called "executive-led" system. Legco members can't even initiate new legislation (unless it costs nothing). That means the best Legco can do is thwart the efforts of the Chief Executive, a role which it has often played well, but which falls short of actually "doing anything". Indeed, one reason the support of pan-democratic parties remains rather limited is that some people look at them and say, What have they done? Of course, the system is designed in such a way that there's little they can. That goes for the pro-CCP parties as well, but the latter have a better track record of taking people to snake feasts and the like, which perhaps makes it look as if they "do something", at least in the eyes of some.

At any rate, there's little that can be accomplished in Legco in terms of fighting for democracy beyond the rearguard actions such as blocking fake suffrage that we have just seen. For precisely this reason, it's tactically important to do as well as possible in Legco: If the pro-CCP side attains a two-thirds majority and can thus pass constitutional amendments, HK is as good as dead, at least as far as hopes for a more democratic, fairer society go.

Outside of the system, there is discussion of setting up a whole shadow or parallel political system. This could include drawing up a new constitution, holding a parallel election for Chief Executive under rules of genuine universal suffrage in 2017, forming a shadow/parallel government, and so on. There are many interesting possibilities here.

Apart from politics, there are many social, cultural and economic issues to be addressed. The anti-parallel trade demonstrations set a good template for that, but keep in mind that parallel trading, as annoying as it is in many places in Hong Kong, as much as it negatively affects the quality of life, is but the tip of the iceberg when it comes to mainlandization. Could an overall plan be drawn up by groups across the pro-democracy spectrum to combat mainlandization in its myriad manifestations?

One of the most positive aspects of the occupations was that it sowed the seeds for many cultural initiatives. Developing a culture that is independent and promotes self-confidence and strengthens HK identity as separate from that of a mainland under CCP dictatorship is to be encouraged.

In general, there are two particular opportunities for the pro-democracy movement: 1) strengthen a sense of HK identity and 2) point out the connection between lack of democracy and crony capitalism, on the one hand, and the fact that HK is the most unequal developed society in the world in terms of income distribution.[4]

Probably one of the effective bulwarks against mainlandization is the development of an HK identity as distinct from that of the mainland. It is already clear that most young people, especially, think of themselves as first and foremost HK people and identify very little if at all with the CCP-dictated mainland. Many recent controversies, in particular the decisions by the Hong Kong Federation of Students and the Hong Kong University Student Union to not participate in the June 4 candlelight vigil, are about this. And this, in return, is a reaction against efforts by the CCP and the HK government to inculcate a stronger sense of "national identity" in secondary students and universities. To the extent that HK people think of themselves as HK people first, that sense of identity can be a strong basis of resistance.

Traditional elements of the HK pro-democracy movement, in particular the formal political parties, have been weak at communicating the connection between lack of democracy and income inequality. They've sought to improve recently, but they still have to get much better at it. This is a key opportunity to strip away support for pro-CCP parties, especially in the many low-income areas of HK where the latter have a strong presence.

But this means going to those areas, having a consistent presence in those areas, and communicating effectively to low-income people how the pro-CCP parties and the HK government are actually and effectively opposed to economic and social justice and are largely involved in preserving the vested interests of the elites. The HK government and pro-CCP parties give the pro-democracy movement plenty of easily available ammunition, such as the argument of CY Leung against genuine universal suffrage on the ground that it would give poor people equal voting rights.

Generally speaking, pro-democracy parties and groups have a fairly strong record in supporting measures that would lead to greater social and economic justice, such as laws on minimum wage, maximum work hours and mandatory overtime pay and the right to collective bargaining, but they need to improve and promote these more strongly, making them a cornerstone of their programs, and developing a fully coherent and comprehensive agenda (that would, among other things, involve a sane housing strategy that would contrast sharply with the HK government's).

If the pro-democracy movement can collaborate on a program of promotion of 1) HK identity and autonomy, 2) social and economic justice, and 3) genuine universal suffrage, and constantly stress the ways in which these issues are inter-related, then I am quite confident they will continue to be a force to be reckoned with in the foreseeable future.

In terms of techniques, after low turnouts for marches on February 1 and June 14, the line goes that many people in the pro-democracy movement don't believe in marches anymore. That's fine. But then, what do you believe in? What is more effective? That question remains to be answered. Ideas for general civil disobedience campaigns such as refusal to pay taxes or rent on public housing apartments have not met widespread acceptance up to now. Likewise, there have been few to no labor actions related to the pro-democracy movement, though many have organized professional groups supporting universal suffrage. Ideas for economic boycotts have not really been realized up to now either. That's not to say there aren't ways to go about these things; just that not much work has been done on them up to now and there's not a general cultural climate of acceptance or experience of such techniques. This proved to be a significant limitation on the effectiveness of the occupations when the question of escalation arose.

We return to the fact that perhaps the number one signal failing of the pro-democracy movement in the past year is that it didn't get any of the regime's allies—tycoons, the business community in general, the largely pro-establishment or acquiescent media, the police—to defect. Are there any strategies of eventually getting them to calculate that their interests will in the long-term be more aligned with the pro-democracy movement than with the regime? This is a key question that is hardly being discussed at the moment, precisely because virtually everyone finds it hard to envision any of those entities defecting or, at the very least, withdrawing their active support of the regime.

Still, where opportunities arise, the pro-democracy movement should work to develop effective channels of communication with these elements. It's important to remember that, deep down, few of them are fervent supporters of the CCP; it's a marriage of convenience.

Many tycoons have resented getting roped into the CCP's anti-democracy propaganda campaign and being made to publicly declare their loyalty. Morale within the police force is low due to its high disapproval rating among HK people. It's hard to imagine any of them suddenly changing sides and declaring their fervent belief in democracy, but it's not as hard to imagine them cutting their business exposure in China (especially if the Chinese economy and business opportunities continue to slow down) and gradually moving some of their business out of HK to less uncertain markets, as people like Li Ka-shing have already been doing. In their place will perhaps gradually arise a business class that is not as beholden to the political powers that be (and the favors they can bestow or withhold) for its profits.

There are many decent police officers who are disgruntled at being co-opted as the guard dogs of the regime. They are aware that the public approval rating of HK police is at an all-time low. Among other things, they see it in people's eyes on the streets every day. HK remains one of the safest, most orderly and most law-abiding societies in the world, first and foremost because it is self-policing, because HK people are highly disciplined and law-abiding. The most lawless elements in HK society, such as the triads and other forms of organized crime, are without exception more closely allied with the regime. As with the business class, the police are hardly going to suddenly switch sides and begin to disobey political orders, and the leaders of the HK police will most likely continue to have the least scruples when it comes to developing ever-closer relations with mainland counterparts, but more and more HK police see that various forms of smuggling and trafficking are far more damaging to law and order than the pro-democracy movement, regardless of CCP and HK government propaganda to the contrary. The aim should be to split the HK police rank and file from the HK police leaders, so that the latter, in order to maintain good relations with the former, will have to track closer to them in practice and away from using the police to conduct surveillance and monitoring and generally persecuting the pro-democracy movement, which is a trend at the moment. Right now, the police leaders think the way forward is to develop "crack units" for online surveillance, covert monitoring, and street policing, but a potential weakness of this strategy is that it will create a rift within the ranks between the absolute loyalists and the vast majority who are really just interested in traditional policing. Isolating and combating the units that engage in what the police consider "preventative" policing (ie, keeping an eye on and pursuing even potentially "criminal" elements) should be a priority of the pro-democracy movement.

For the most part, trying to change the editorial line of the establishment media is a lost cause, but it's important to remember that what will hit them hardest is loss of revenue. Viewership of free t.v. and readership of print news continues to hemorrhage, especially among young people. Indeed, to a large extent, a parallel system of information gathering and dissemination, of opinion formation is already growing up around social media and online media upstarts such as InMedia, SocRec, Stand News, Passion Times, and HK Free Press. This trend will most likely continue, given that it is young people driving it. It is striking the extent to which the editorial position of *South China Morning Post,* for example, is almost diametrically opposed to the views of its readership when it comes to democracy. SCMP supported fake universal suffrage, but a (thoroughly unscientific but suggestive) online poll conducted of its readership found that nearly 80 percent were happy that fake suffrage was defeated. For both business and ideological reasons, it can be said the pro-CCP and/or self-censoring media don't have time on their side, and their main purpose will continue to be to "divide" society, to shore up support amongst the 20 to 30 percent of the population that can be relied on to support CCP policies, however passively, a percentage of society which, due to its age, could be slowly dying out.

My advice is, try everything that you have the capacity for, everything that stands a chance of working and even a few things that don't. The future really is wide open. We need to try new things. It's hard to know what will work and what won't. It's a problem that we don't know where we're going, but it's also an opportunity. The open-hearted and adventurous spirit of the pro-democracy movement over the past year must be retained and cultivated. We must continually search for ways to give young people a real stake, a real voice and real power in pro-democracy institutions, something we haven't been good at up to now. Groups that are youth groups, such as Scholarism, need more support. Scholarism has operated almost in isolation when it comes to outreach to secondary school students. It needs to continue to operate according to its own agenda but help in matters such liaising with progressive teachers and school administrators, contacts, networking, and material help such as support in printing leaflets and lending venues for events would all go some way in helping to develop one of the more promising organizations.

Indeed, one of the main things the pro-democracy movement should be considering at this point is setting up an overall coordinating body as a platform for identifying common opportunities and needs and ways in which we can help each other. It should not "centralize" or be a decision-making body, but it should bring the various elements of the movement into better communication with one another.

We are tired. We need a break. But there is much work to do. And the clock is ticking. The CCP will redouble efforts to rapidly mainlandize with a vengeance after the humiliation of the defeat of fake suffrage. The people of the HK pro-democracy movement have been magnificent up to now, but that doesn't mean we will continue to be so in the future. As ever, it all depends on us.

Commentary on Joshua Wong's essay on the next phase of the HK democracy movement

August 15, 2015

In addition to the article by Joshua Wong mentioned below, Wong and Jeffrey Ngo wrote several more articles about self-determination in 2016, and even got into an indirect debate on the issue with the head of the PRC Foreign Ministry office in Hong Kong. All of their articles can be found through the link in the endnote. [1]

Joshua Wong's August 2 essay in *Ming Pao*, "The next phase of the democracy movement: A referendum on constitutional reform and sustainable democratic self-governance"[2] is the most substantial vision yet presented by a prominent democracy movement leader in HK on the future. In fact, since the Partystate and HK government's fake universal suffrage proposal was defeated in the Legislative Council in June, democracy movement leaders have been conspicuously quiet about the way forward. This is understandable: everyone is exhausted, needs a break and time to think. Still, it has to be said, the HK democracy movement hasn't exactly been blessed by outstanding strategic thinkers down through the years, and you wonder what it says about the movement that one of its best thinkers hasn't yet turned 20.

Indeed, one of the strongest points of Wong's essay is that the pan-democrats have largely been strategizing by default, on autopilot for some years now. They've been co-opted by participation in a rigged system, and it might be even saying a bit much to characterize what they've been doing as "strategizing" since they have been highly reactive, responding to situations and issues as they arise. Wong calls their strategy "fight for every inch" and criticizes it. Among other things, one of the problems with it is that you can be so tightly focused on that inch you're fighting for that you forget to look up and ask yourself, But why am

I fighting over this, where will it get me? We should thank Wong simply for demanding that we look up and think long term. One should hope that his essay (and others like it, for example those he mentions) will lead to a wide-ranging, inclusive debate.

The essay represents a development in Wong's thinking. Already at the time of the demonstrations in June outside of Legco against the fake universal suffrage proposal, Wong was expressing some of the ideas now fully articulated in the essay. It is also quite courageous and forward-looking. He's willing to dispense with old notions that he considers outmoded or failed, even if they're his own. Regarding the recent past, he says we should be clear about two things: 1) We failed to persuade the Partystate to fulfill its promise and legal obligation of introducing genuine universal suffrage to HK, and 2) we should have absolutely no illusions that under the hardline framework laid down by the National People's Congress Standing Committee on August 31 last year—which the Partystate says is indefinitely binding—it ever will. In fact, Wong pretty much concludes we shouldn't even bother fighting for universal suffrage on those grounds; at any rate, it shouldn't be our main focus. In this sense, the essay clearly demarcates: One era has ended, and another must begin. But what is the new era? And what should our focus be?

It should be on what Wong calls "the second question of the future" of HK, namely, what will happen after 2047, the end of the "one country, two systems" period. In contrast, Wong says we have just concluded once and for all the period of the "first question of the future", whether or not there can be such a thing as real democracy in HK under Chinese sovereignty. The National People's Congress Standing Committee decision of August 31, 2014 said an emphatic no to that.

In this new period of HK history, as Wong characterizes it, the long-term goals of the democracy movement, and the goals for HK beyond 2047, should be what Wong calls self-governance or self-determination.

After the debacle of fake reform and the refusal of the Partystate and HK government to heed the voice of the people, Wong sees an impasse and what he calls a predicament for the democracy movement. In thinking his way out of this impasse, it is clear that Wong has been significantly influenced by proponents of localism, with his emphasis on self-governance or self-determination. He seems be saying, I don't think the localists stand much of a chance of appealing to the mainstream because they're perceived as too extreme, but I more or less agree with them, and the question is how to take their basic stance, develop it and make it palatable to ordinary HK people. In this, of course, Wong is distancing himself even further from traditional pan-democrats who, as said, have been largely silent since the defeat of fake suffrage, thus appearing to have no road map of their own. They risk appearing to be a spent force (at least in terms of ideas; they will probably continue to elect a significant number of representatives in the formal political system). Wong differs from some localists in that he doesn't call for independence or even say exactly what the relationship between the Partystate-ruled mainland and HK should be; he appears to think that is for the people of HK to determine. But he thinks that something must be done to encourage HK people to take their fate into their own hands and see themselves as being able to act autonomously from the Partystate. And that something is referendums, and, at a later time, deliberations on constitutional amendments or even a new constitution.

Before commenting on Wong's ideas about referendums, I should mention that it's striking that there is virtually no mention of the Partystate in Wong's essay and no discussion of what the relationship between HK and the Partystate should be. Wong merely states that the fake reform process has shown that it's an illusion to believe that you can ever negotiate in good faith with the Partystate. It seems that, in concluding that, Wong has pretty much written the Partystate off. This is a very interesting stance. At first, I found it peculiar, but then I thought, Yes, why not act as if Beijing had nothing to do with it, as if Beijing's refusal to grant real suffrage to HK renders it irrelevant to the question of deciding HK's future. It had a chance to play a role in determining that, and it missed the boat. Now, Wong seems to say, this is between HK people; it's for HK people to sort out; and we shouldn't just resign ourselves to the idea that our fate lies entirely in the Partystate's hands, let alone waste our time bothering to appeal to it; we must grasp that fate in our own hands. We must act as if that is simply the way that it is until that is the way that it is. We will achieve self-determination with or without you; now, most likely, without you. Of course, Beijing does matter — it's still the gorilla that stands between HK and its aspirations —, but in its refusal to be a partner in HK achieving suffrage, it has rendered itself a bystander. Wong seems to be encouraging HK people to "act as if" — act as if you live in a democratic society in order to realize a democratic society. And his strong advocacy of referendums resembles concepts of the "parallel society": If the government is unelected, lacks legitimacy and stands in the way of the people's aspirations, then construct a parallel society, to reject the illegitimate government, to give people the confidence to take their fate into their own hands and help them to learn to act democratically, to prepare for the day when the people will be their own rulers.

Wong's idea for referendums may be part of the way to go about that. It is very interesting and clearly worth debating. But there is also some fuzziness regarding exactly how he sees them working. In particular, it's unclear what he sees as the relationship between unofficial, autonomous referendums conducted by the people and not recognized by the government, like Occupy Central's referendum on universal suffrage in June 2014, and official referendums held by the government. He seems to think we should start out holding unofficial referendums. This coupled with other pressures will eventually lead to the introduction of legislation legalizing referendums, leading in turn to officially conducted referendums which will eventually encompass constitutional issues such as amendments to the Basic Law, perhaps eventually even replacement of the Basic Law with a constitution more appropriate to HK (and more democratic than the current Basic Law).

Wong is often interested in how realistic a proposal is—he is quite a pragmatic thinker. On pragmatic grounds, he criticizes simply keeping on pushing for universal suffrage as long as the Partystate persists in declaring the 8/31 decision as binding once and for all. But applying that same pragmatic criterion to referendums, it's hard to imagine how we might ever get to the point where the Partystate would allow the HK government to pass legislation to legalize referendums. Of course, referendums could still be held unofficially and could still be an important gauge of public opinion and an important way of encouraging public engagement, but it seems to me that the risk is that, after a while, people will lose enthusiasm when they see that their vote has no effect.

Referendums can be an excellent way to reach out to people who for whatever reason haven't been participating and get them involved, if there are ways of capturing the interest it takes to cast a vote and translate that into more active, consistent and substantive political action, though the democracy movement has not been terribly good at that up to now. 800,000 people voted in Occupy Central's June 2014 referendum, numbers-wise probably the largest participation in any political event outside of official elections. But that may have had a lot to do with the timing, coming right after the Partystate's publication of the White Paper on HK and in the lead-up to the NPCSC decision: It was seen as a crucial historic moment. Previous to that, the 2010 by-elections triggered by the resignation of five pan-democrats from Legco, the so-called five-district referendum, had a turnout of 17 percent. It was considered a failure. Of course, that too is down to specific circumstances, in particular, the pro-Partystate camp's refusal to participate. Wong's idea of tapping into strong public interest in particular issues such as TV licensing and the Northeast New Territories development projects is good but there's also the possibility that after a while, unofficial referendums come to be seen as hum-drum and, yes, ineffectual. There are few societies that use referendums as actively and frequently as Wong is proposing HK should do. Switzerland is one of the few. It would be great if we could be Switzerland; it's just very hard to see that happening.

The same goes for constitutional amendments, a constitutional assembly. Perhaps we should use unofficial referendums and other events outside of the official political system to arrive at a consensus within the democracy movement about which articles of the Basic Law need amending and how, or, alternatively, what a constitution that really suits HK would look like. Among other things, this would increase wider public awareness of the flaws in the Basic Law and shift the political discourse, a message to the Partystate that since it refuses to grant the political rights enshrined in the Basic Law, the people of HK are moving beyond it. It would also, eventually, provide a more concrete and specified vision of what we'd like to see. In this sense, the issues of a referendum law and an officially recognized constitutional assembly can be bracketed off: if we ever get there, great, but if not, the unofficial referendums and other activities on constitutional matters can be useful nevertheless in articulating a united and coherent vision of the future.

Wong's ultimate objectives of self-determination and self-governance are worthy. It's just that perhaps he pins too much hope on referendums as the means of getting there. Perhaps referendums can be one of many ways to work towards those long-term objectives. Perhaps we need to ask, What other actions can be taken to encourage HK people to take their fate into their own hands and to work toward self-determination, self-governance? And then construct a strategy, a roadmap based on our answers to that. Wong's fear here, probably, would be that we get bogged down again in the "fight every inch" strategy which is largely reactive, fighting against the worst rather than aiming for the best. After all, it is often the case that it's easier to get people to say a big no to an imminent danger (Article 23, fake suffrage, etc) and to get people to focus on the short term than to participate in a long-term project towards a positive end, especially when the outcome is far from certain and determining it seems beyond our power. With that in mind, we should aim to be pro-active, asking ourselves what furthers the aims of self-determination and self-governance and aiming to tap into the huge reservoir of frustration of those who participated in the Umbrella Movement and are looking around to see what we can do now. So much depends, as ever, on how many people—both those who have been involved up to now and those who have not—we manage to convince to be politically active in the struggle—which as Wong emphasizes, will play out in the long term, over the decades to come. Having staying power over the long-term also requires the development of organizations and institutions which outlive individuals, and this is one of many areas that needs greater focus.

Hong Kong one year after the start of the Umbrella Movement: Injustice and complete lack of accountability

September 25, 2016

For just the gist, read the italicized bit below. For details, information and logic upon which tthe italicized statement is based, read the rest. For background and substantiation of assertions, see a list after the end of this essay.

A society whose political leader is not chosen freely by its citizens is an unjust society.

A society whose police and public officials are not accountable to its citizens but to its unelected political leader is an unjust society.

Hong Kong is an unjust society, run by an unelected leader supported by police and public officials who are accountable to him, not to its citizens.

The demand for justice and accountability will not disappear.

One year after the start of the HK occupations on September 28, 2014, HK is a society suffering the injustice of the continued denial of the basic right of its citizens to genuine universal suffrage under both the HK Basic Law and HK's international legal obligations as party to the International Covenant on Civil and Political Rights (ICCPR).

In addition, there has been complete lack of accountability of the HK government and police in regard to their actions during the 79 days of the occupations. The government and police refuse to submit to effective oversight and investigation by an independent agency whose authority they recognize.

The results of the denial of the basic right to genuine universal suffrage and the lack of accountability are that, effectively,

1) the HK government is illegitimate and illegal according to international law,

2) distrust of the HK police force is at an all-time high, and

3) the HK government and police have eroded rule of law in HK.

Regarding governance, HK is in a chronic crisis which the HK government and Chinese Partystate refuse to recognize.

Regarding law enforcement, it is very difficult for the HK government and police to act as credible authorities for law enforcement and protectors of the law when they refuse to be held accountable for instances in which they have acted outside of the law.

Both the HK government and police will continue to suffer erosion of public trust and their authority will be ever less recognized and respected as long as these matters remain unaddressed.

The way out is clear:

- *As a matter of urgency, the HK government and Partystate must implement genuine universal suffrage for elections of the Chief Executive and Legislative Council in line with their legal obligations under HK and international law. (It must be stressed that this is the legal obligation of the HK government and Partystate and they cannot blame anyone else for their failure to do so.)*
- *In cooperation with civil society, the HK government must appoint an independent commission with the power to conduct an investigation into HK government and police actions during the occupations and must act on the recommendations of the commission*
- *Individuals within the HK government and police who have committed criminal acts must be criminally prosecuted*
- *The HK government must immediately cease prosecuting citizens for peaceful expression in relation to activities conducted during the occupations*

But one year after the beginning of the occupations, none of this has occurred and there is no sign that the HK government has any intention to take any of those actions.

The discrepancy between the HK government and police refusal to be held accountable, on the one hand, and, on the other, their efforts to prosecute demonstrators is striking.

The occupations lasted 79 days. They were remarkably disciplined and almost entirely peaceful and nonviolent. Nevertheless, nearly one thousand people were arrested. Upwards of 100 have been prosecuted. Several dozen have been convicted of crimes. In the 79 days of occupation, there is clear video evidence of one case of assaulting an officer and one case of property damage. One demonstrator was convicted of assaulting a police officer and sentenced to three months in prison. Four people have been convicted of criminal damage, three of whom have been sentenced to three months in prison each. It is worth noting that this incidence of criminality at occupation sites is actually significantly lower than the ordinary urban crime rate.

Meanwhile, the HK government has initiated no investigation of government and police actions, and not a single police officer has been held accountable, whether administratively or criminally, in spite of abundant video and photographic documentation of disproportionate use of force, including tear gas attacks, indiscriminate use of pepper spray, systematic aiming of batons at demonstrators' heads in Mong Kok, multiple beatings of fleeing demonstrators with batons from behind during the clearance of Lung Wo Road, the infamous case of the eight officers beating an arrested and cuffed demonstrator, various cases of individual police officers gratuitously attacking demonstrators with pepper spray and batons, a repeated pattern of police failure to protect demonstrators from violent attacks by thugs in Mong Kok that lead to suspicions that police were actually colluding with the thugs, and dozens of cases of police attacking and arresting journalists and preventing journalists from doing their work.

A society whose authorities refuse to be held accountable is not only an unjust society but one on its way to tyranny. Hong Kong usually appears a prosperous, efficient, well-run, disciplined, law-abiding, stable and peaceful society. But it is also a society in perpetual political crisis, a crisis which the Partystate and the HK government appear unwilling or unable to resolve in an equitable and just manner. The actions of the Partystate, the HK government and police in the past year are unjust and detrimental to HK. Their refusal to be held accountable does not bode well for HK's future. HK people will not simply forget the denial of their basic right to genuine universal suffrage and the unaccountable actions of the HK government and police during the occupations.

Recently the new HK police commissioner warned HK people against any "misbehavior" related to the first anniversary of the start of the occupations. Venturing to speak on behalf of HK people, though he is not their representative, he said HK people don't want another Occupy. Well, I thought, if they don't, then maybe you shouldn't attack citizens with teargas.

His statement, while rather innocuous, was in keeping with the general obliviousness of the HK government and top police officers. It showed just how little they have learned from the past year and, therefore, just how necessary an independent investigation of HK government and police conduct related to the occupations is.

Just after the last of the three occupied sites, Causeway Bay, was cleared by police on December 15, then police commissioner Andy Tsang announced the police would conduct a three-month investigation into the "principal instigators" of the occupations. There was never any subsequent announcement about the completion of that investigation, and it is unclear what ever became of it. But, again, I thought to myself, well, look no further than the mirror! The police were apparently interested only in conducting criminal investigations of demonstrators but not in conducting investigations into their own conduct, not even when it appeared criminal, as in the infamous beating of the demonstrator, Ken Tsang. (One year on, while the seven police officers involved were arrested and suspended from duty, no decision has been made as to whether or not to prosecute them.)

There is quite wide consensus amongst most everyone but the HK government and police that the main precipitator of the occupations was the eight-hours-long police tear gas attack on HK citizens of September 28, 2014. To mark the first anniversary of the occupations, a rally will be held, at the center of which is a moment of silence beginning at 5:58 pm on September 28, 2014. The time marks the moment the tear gas attack commenced, thus indicating that for most people, the tear gas attack is synchronous with the beginning of the occupations.

Amazingly, to this day, almost nothing is publicly known about the tear gas attacks. Who ordered them? Was it someone within the police force? If so, who? Was it someone in the HK government? If so, who? Was it someone from the Partystate? If so, who, and how? This is a basic question that must be answered in order to merely begin the process of accountability. Days after the tear gas attacks, an interview appeared in *SCMP* with an anonymous police superintendent (in a police station, and with the permission of his superiors) who claimed that he was the immediate supervisor of the officers who fired the tear gas at 5:58 pm and that he had ordered the attack without consulting his superiors. As the one and only explanation of the attack, this is far from sufficient and hardly credible. Even assuming his assertion was true, that would reflect poorly on the police, allowing a police officer to take such a momentous decision without consultation with superiors. It seems more likely the top police officers, the HK government and the Partystate were hiding behind that one relatively low-ranking officer. And the officer certainly couldn't have ordered the sustained attacks which went on for eight hours until 2 am.

Even on basic points of supposed "fact", the details of the tear gas attack are unclear. At one point, the police announced that there were "87 rounds" of tear gas. Since then, it's become almost common knowledge that 87 canisters of tear gas were fired. All over the city you can find the silkscreen print of 87 on umbrellas and t-shirts to commemorate the attack. But we really don't know whether that's true, or whether 87 rounds means 87 tear gas canisters or something else. None of that has been independently corroborated or properly investigated, nor has the police ever given any detailed account of the attack.

The only HK government and police justification for the tear gas attack was that it was needed in order to get demonstrators to move back from police cordons. But taken at face value, this explanation makes almost no sense. To begin with, if the police were worried about demonstrators pushing up against their cordons, why would tear gas, fired into the indeterminate distance, be the best means of getting those only centimeters away from the police to move back? Presumably the idea was that if those behind the people in the front lines were dispersed with tear gas, then perhaps those in the front lines would move back too, but that has never been explained, and it still seems rather far-fetched. On top of that, the tear gas attacks went on for hours, long after the justification of using tear gas to force demonstrators to move back from police cordons could be credibly made, for by that point, there was no situation in which demonstrators were too close to police cordons. So even assuming the police's justification makes sense for the beginning of the attack, it makes no sense for the rest of it. Indeed, past a certain point, it appeared that the police were shooting tear gas randomly because they didn't know what else to do.

Apart from that, assuming the police intended the tear gas attack as a crowd control measure, the police have never explained why its measure failed so miserably as to essentially trigger the very last thing it presumably wanted to see, the occupations. Putting aside issues of rights and legality for a moment, what kind of bad policing is that?!

Indeed, from a strictly policing perspective, the police made a series of bizarre and poor decisions that lead up to that catastrophic one, including the following: 1) they took more than twelve hours to clear from Civic Square the 61 students who were occupying it, 2) while they waited, they used pepper spray indiscriminately on those outside of Civic Square who the police claimed were assembled illegally, thus provoking more people to come out in support of their fellow citizens under attack, and 3) they prevented access to Tim Mei Avenue where the newly arrived demonstrators wished to go, thus creating an impossible crowd control situation on Harcourt Road that lead to demonstrators stepping out into the road, since they had nowhere else to go, so crowded had the sidewalks lining the road become. Then they fired the tear gas. If you didn't know better, you'd almost think the police deliberately created the occupations through their blunders. And yet, no investigation. As far as we know, there was not even an internal investigation from a strictly policing point of view. In March, such an investigation was announced, but no further word was heard of it.

In the absence of a transparent independent public investigation determining to the contrary, there exists strong suspicion that the police were ordered to attack citizens with tear gas by their political superiors in the HK government and/or Partystate. If so, then rather than being a law enforcement decision, the tear gas attack was a political decision. The people of HK deserve to know whether or not this was the case. If it was, the implications are grave, for it essentially means that the HK government turned the police from a law enforcement agency into its own private militia to defend its interests. Indeed, ever since, amongst many HK people, the police has been perceived as a guard dog of the regime. If the police force truly wishes to clear its name, the best way to do so would be to establish exactly how the decision was taken, unless, indeed, it was a political decision and they wish to keep that hidden.

There are four basic principles for judging police use of force, according to the United Nations Basic Principles on the Use of Force and Firearms by Law Enforcement Officials and outlined in the new Amnesty guidelines for implementation of those principles. They are legality, necessity, proportionality, and accountability. In other words: Is the force used for a lawful law enforcement purpose (as opposed to, for example, defending the political interests of the regime)? What necessitates force being used at all and what determines how much force should be used? Is there a balance between the benefits of the use and the possible consequences and harm caused by its use? These principles should be used as the criteria to judge the HK police tear gas attacks and other cases of police use of force during the occupations.

As regards the legality of the tear gas attacks, only a day after they occurred, HKU law professor Simon Young examined them against the backdrop of HK law and concluded, "Thus it seems the Hong Kong Police Force have more than a clear case to answer to justify their use of force on the protesters." The HK police still have not answered that case or explained how they legally justified their use of force.

It seems quite clear to me and to many an HK person that the tear gas attacks were neither necessary nor proportionate. As concerns necessity, they achieved the exact opposite purpose they presumably intended. As concerns proportionality, HK demonstrators were peaceful. There was not a single act of violence or destruction of property, impressive considering the situation and large number of people. Police claimed demonstrators were threatening police cordons. But video evidence does not suggest this, and they were certainly not doing so through either threat or use of violence. At innumerable demonstrations down through the years, demonstrators stood close to police cordons without police deeming it necessary to attack them with tear gas for doing so. Prior to the attack, police had raised their infamous flags declaring the assembly "unlawful", but they never gave demonstrators an opportunity to assemble elsewhere besides the road, for example, in nearby Tamar Park, which at the time the attacks commenced was mostly empty.

Indeed, the police tear gas attack needs to be set in the wider context of possible infringements of freedom of assembly that had occurred for days leading up to the attack. The student class boycott, scheduled for September 23 to 26 in Tamar Park, was kicked out of the park on its last day, the 26th on the grounds that, as the Leisure and Cultural Services Department put it, groups could reserve park facilities for up to three days maximum, a rule that up to then no one had ever heard of (officially sanctioned events run for upwards of a week or more on a regular basis in Victoria Park), and that another group had requested use of the park on the 26th. No one was surprised to learn it was a pro-Partystate group. That group was granted permission to use the park on the 26th, not even to hold an event but to make preparations for October 1 celebrations, though that date was five days away. As it turned out, the group hardly used the park at all that day, just delivering its equipment but not really getting going until the weekend, the following day. While there were perhaps one or two dozen members of the pro-Beijing group in the park setting up, the students had no recourse but to crowd onto the sidewalks along Tim Mei Avenue on the last day of the class boycott when there was an even larger number of students than on previous days since it was the only day of the secondary student class boycott and many secondary students joined. It was pathetic to see how squeezed in they were, sitting on the sidewalk in neat rows in their school uniforms. They were participating in a full day of lectures, debates and discussions while nothing was occurring in the park from which they'd been evicted. It was that evening that the students "reclaimed" Civic Square—reclaimed because they were going into a place that had been free for the public to use only two months before, when the government made the abrupt decision (taken without so much as pro-forma public consultation) to seal off the public space from the public and erected a high fence around it. Then, when supporters of the students gathered on the sidewalks outside the square along Tim Mei Avenue, where the students had formerly been allowed to gather for the last day of the boycott, the police declared their assembly "unlawful" and used pepper spray indiscriminately against them, though, again, they were entirely peaceful and nonviolent. And finally, when more people arrived to support them, numbering in the thousands, police did not allow them to enter Tim Mei Avenue nor did police make any effort to accommodate them or suggest an alternative space (such as Tamar Park). All told, the HK government and police had denied demonstrators use of Civic Square, Tamar Park, and the sidewalks of Tim Mei Avenue and had barred people from entering Tim Mei Avenue. So where were they supposed to go then? The street, obviously. This pattern must surely constitute unreasonable restrictions on the freedom of assembly, especially given the fact that, to emphasize, the demonstrators were entirely peaceful and nonviolent.

The crowd clearly had a right to assembly peacefully and it was the responsibility of the police to facilitate their exercising that right in an orderly manner, not to prevent them from doing so, though the latter appeared to be the police's intent. Indeed, the police, at least in terms of the orders given from above, appeared to treat the demonstrators as their adversary, if not downright enemy. The perception of demonstrators as the enemy appears to be an attitude that began to be inculcated in at least some members of the police force some years back, roughly corresponding with the former police chief Andy Tsang's tenure, and a thorough independent investigation would look into this matter of police culture: Were there practices, statements or orders that encouraged police to regard demonstrators as an opponent or adversary? Were any orders given that were based on this perception? The July 1 pro-democracy march of 500,000 people was a case in point: For the first time ever, five march organizers were arrested, one for idling the engine of the lead vehicle of the march! Once again, the huge march was peaceful and nonviolent—the organizers should have been praised for holding such an orderly march, but instead they were arrested. Police actions appeared exceedingly petty, to say the least, and seemed to reveal an animosity toward demonstrators on the part of top police officers.

In this sense, the tear gas attacks were the culmination of a series of decisions made by the HK government and police that resulted in infringements on freedom of assembly around government headquarters. In a sense, with the occupations, they got what they were asking for. From this angle, the police use of tear gas was a desperate attempt to correct previous blunders it had made. It could hardly be considered proportionate.

As regards the fourth principle, accountability, there has been none. Up to now at least, the HK government and police have clearly failed where that principle is considered, not having made a single effort to investigate matters related to accountability.

Indeed, what the past year has made clear is the complete inadequacy of the sole mechanism (short of criminal prosecution) that exists for accountability regarding police behavior. That is the Independent Police Complaints Council, which monitors the Complaints Against Police Office, an office within the police force. Complaints against police must first be made to the police (CAPO), which then decides which complaints are "reportable" and sends them on to the IPCC. Of the hundreds of complaints against police related to the occupations, CAPO ruled 172 "reportable" and forwarded 150 to the IPCC. The IPCC has reported it is actively investigating 16.

Up to now, the IPCC has amazingly considered only one complaint actionable, the infamous case of Police Superintendent Franklin Chu gratuitously beating a demonstrator with his baton in Mong Kok. It was a pretty clear cut case, well-documented with irrefutable video evidence. Indeed, the IPCC, facing intense political pressure, ruled that Chu had assaulted the demonstrator. The police disagreed. The IPCC has no power to impose its decision upon the police or in any other way hold the police to account in cases of disagreement. In other words, all the police have to do is disagree and nothing happens. In cases where the two disagree, the Chief Executive is the only one with the power to make a decision. Don't expect one from him any time soon. The Franklin Chu case was the first time in years that the IPCC had attempted to hold the police accountable, and it failed. As an accountability mechanism, it is little more than a charade.

Apart from this mechanism, there are only criminal procedures. The seven police officers who were filmed beating Ken Tsang after having arrested and handcuffed him were arrested and suspended from duty. But nearly a year after that occurrence and months after the police apparently finished its investigation and sent its report to the Department of Justice, there has been no word as to whether or not the latter intends to prosecute. So far, a dead-end there too.

In short, even in the most clear cut and obvious individual cases of illegitimate if not criminal use of force, there has up to now been no accountability.

This is not to even consider cases of what appeared to be systematic illegitimate use of force of the kind that leads one to suspect that frontline officers were given orders to act in such a way, cases such as officers aiming baton blows at demonstrators' heads in Mong Kok, or officers beating fleeing demonstrators from behind while clearing Lung Wo Road, or the many cases of indiscriminate use of pepper spray.

But going back to the tear gas attacks for a moment longer:

Some might think, What's the big deal? After all, no one was killed or even seriously injured. Police do much worse many other places in the world. But for HK, in the HK context, it was a cataclysmic, paradigm-shifting, historical event. A year on, it may be easy to forget just how profoundly shocking those attacks were to virtually the whole HK population. After all, it was the first time since the leftist riots of 1967, which involved a considerable degree of violence and terrorist bombings on the part of the demonstrators, that the HK police had attacked its own people with tear gas. In the days immediately after the tear gas attack, people across the political spectrum (with the notable exception of the stalwart pro-Partystaters) expressed their indignation, consternation, outrage.

In one of the strongest statements it's ever made, the Hong Kong Bar Association said it was "deeply disturbed by, and deplores and condemns, the excessive and disproportionate use of force" by police. It went on: "There can be scope for disagreement on the underlying political debate or demands leading to the demonstration. Some demonstrators may have committed criminal offences... However, none of the above matters justify the use of excessive or disproportionate force by police against unarmed civilians as a matter of law and common decency."

Peter Mathieson, the president and vice-chancellor of HKU, in an email to students, staff and alumni, said HKU "profoundly regrets the escalation of events in recent days. We condemn violence of any kind by any party. We cannot understand the use of tear gas yesterday: the police and the government are accountable for that decision."

Twenty-three pan-democratic Legco members issued a joint statement calling for an emergency meeting to debate a motion to impeach CY Leung. The statement said, "We urge the administration to stop suppressing the people violently, it should talk to the people; it should also re-open Civic Square and resume the people's reasonable right to use the area."

Legco member Wong Yuk-man said, "Not a stone or a glass bottle has been thrown over the past week, but police decided to resort to tear gas. All people did was raise their hands."

Former Chief Secretary Anson Chan said: "This is a sad day for Hong Kong. Pictures of our Police Force firing pepper spray and tear gas into the faces of unarmed protestors will shame our government in front of the whole world."

In all, pupils and teachers from at least 31 secondary schools went on strike to protest the police attack on civilians. Lee Shing-ho, a co-organizer of the strike at CNEC Lee I Yao Memorial Secondary School, said, "The senior students took the initiative to leave their classrooms. This is not a strike led by the teachers. We want to protest the police's violent behavior." Liu Cheuk-laam, from SFTA Lee Shau Kee College said, "We're in a totally different situation now after the tear gas. All students should protest." The Professional Teachers Union, the largest union in HK and one with a long pro-democracy history, called on teachers to go on strike. PTU president Fung Wai-wah said, "We're talking about what's right and wrong. . . It's important to let students discuss and express their feelings. Teachers cannot escape from this."

Don Chan Hing-lung, chairman of the Swire Beverages Employees General Union, said 200 delivery workers at the Swire Coca-Cola were on strike to support the civil disobedience movement. "We don't care if we lose money. We are here for the future. If we don't come, there won't be one."

A spokesperson for Swire Coca-Cola was amazingly understanding, stating, "delivery staff members of Swire Coca-Cola HK who are members of a union have been on strike today and staged a sit-in outside the Siu Lek Yuen plant. . . . The Company understands that it is an action in response to union calls for strike in support of the Occupy Central protests. The strike was initiated by the related staff of their own volition and the company has expressed understanding about the action."

Spencer Wong, chief executive of advertising company McCann Worldgroup Hong Kong, said in a message to his staff, "It's up to you whether you come to work or not. The company will not punish anyone who supports something more important than work."

About 1,000 social workers and social work students gathered at Polytechnic University to protest police violence and show their support for the movement. Social worker Simon Lai said, "I could not believe that the police used tear gas against student protesters. . . The students were not armed. There were tens of thousands of them yesterday and the tear gas could have led to a stampede."

It was one of those brief moments in history when virtually an entire population was unified in condemnation.

The HK government decided the best thing to do was to just wait it out. It stuck tightly to script: appropriate force, appropriate force, only occasionally slipping up: Chief Secretary Carrie Lam once referred to the police attacks as "appropriate violence" but her press office immediately corrected the slip.

The government apparently thought it could just ignore the problem until it went away. But when you don't deal with a serious problem, it festers, mutates, becomes worse, metamorphoses. In this case, it has resulted in a serious lack of confidence in the police force as an impartial law enforcement agency. The latest HKUPOP survey in June on the popularity of the Hong Kong disciplinary forces and the PLA Hong Kong Garrison showed police popularity at its lowest since 1997, when the survey began, even lower than in December 2014, when the occupations concluded. The HK government and police have clearly not understood that police actions during the occupations have seriously undermined public confidence, and as recent statements suggest, intend to continue to bury their heads in the sand.

Yet, except when they were at their worst, I often found myself sympathizing with the police (at least the frontline officers, at least the ones who didn't violently attack protesters; their superiors are another matter) for they were put in the difficult position of defending an unlawful government intent on continuing to deny its citizens the basic legal and human right of genuine universal suffrage. A police force is meant to serve and be accountable to the citizens, but in this case, it served an unlawful government defending itself against the citizens.

In response to the occupations, the HK government quickly devised a propaganda template, according to which the occupations were always referred to as the "illegal Occupy movement", parroting none other than Xi Jinping himself (and in so doing, showing exactly whom it served). It was hard to see how a whole movement—especially a peaceful, nonviolent movement—could simply be characterized as illegal in one big brush-stroke, especially when its illegality had not been tested in a court of law. In what sense illegal? More or less illegal than denying a people their right to choose their own government through free and fair elections, their right to run for and be elected to office, even when universal suffrage was stipulated in the mini-constitution of the territory, even when the mini-constitution explicitly stated that as party to the International Covenant on Civil and Political Rights, HK was obliged under international law to uphold and implement the rights contained therein, including free and fair elections and the right to vote, run for office and be elected according to the internationally recognized principles of universal suffrage? More or less illegal than that?

While it is perhaps easy to fixate on the police, since they are one of the most tangible faces of injustice and lack of accountability, it is important to remember that they are only a secondary problem, a problem caused by the underlying problem of the denial of the basic right to genuine universal suffrage by the HK government and Partystate.

That is the basic injustice that pervades HK politics and society, a fundamental problem that the Partystate and HK government can't just simply wish away. It will fester and mutate as long as they continue to deny justice to the city.

When the government insists that others follow the law while it itself breaks both HK and international law, when the government itself is technically "illegal" (since it is not elected by universal suffrage as required by both HK and international law), it perverts the whole meaning of law, threatening to undermine rule of law by placing itself above it. That is why recent Partystate statements to the effect of the Chief Executive being "transcendent" and there being no true separation of powers in HK have caused alarm: It becomes apparent that the objective of the Partystate and HK government is that the HK government eventually attain a position similar to that of the Partystate on the mainland; namely, of being above the law and therefore of being, in effect, "the law," all the while being, quite literally, an outlaw.

We are accustomed to being so confident of the foundations of the rule of law in HK that people tend to laugh off warnings about the Partystate and

HK government seeking to move in the direction of placing the unelected Chief Executive and government above the law, but given recent trends, and the pattern of statements and logic on the matter emanating both from the Partystate and the HK government, we should be on guard. Their respect for the law is less than exemplary, to put it mildly. It is typical Partystate practice to break the law, to act above the law, and then to say that actions were taken "in accordance with the law". It is rule by fiat, not of law, and signs of it can be seen in HK as well, especially in regard to the HK government's defiance of the law regarding universal suffrage and its refusal to hold itself accountable for actions taken and decisions made during the occupations.

The refusal of the Partystate and HK government to follow the law also highlights a major problem with international law. It is clear they are breaking international law, but there are no enforcement mechanisms when it comes to human rights, especially in this part of the world, (In Europe, for instance, there is the European Court of Human Rights where citizens can bring cases against their governments), and not even any effective sanctioning mechanisms. In October 2014, the UN Human Rights Committee, a panel of 18 experts that monitors implementation of the ICCPR, called on China to implement universal suffrage in HK and stressed that meant not only the right to vote but the right to run and be elected to office. It expressed concern that China intended to effectively pre-screen candidates based on their political opinion and stated this would constitute an "unreasonable restriction". The problem is, there has been no follow-up on its conclusions. The UN Human Rights Council has failed to act. The Council is made up of states elected to the council by other states. That is to say, it is not a independent judiciary organ or group of experts but a political organization, and it acts as such. States are more interested in advancing their interests than in safeguarding and promoting human rights, which includes sanctioning states that break international human rights law. Though the Partystate and HK government are defying international law, there are no international mechanisms to compel them to follow it. This problem is exacerbated by the fact that no other country has individually been willing to call China out on the matter and say in no uncertain terms that it is not abiding by its obligations under international law.

A third and final matter in regard to injustice and lack of accountability:

There has been insufficient monitoring of the actions of the police and Department of Justice in regard to arrests and prosecutions related to the occupations. While media have reported on individual cases, no independent NGOs or, specifically, human rights organizations have consistently tracked the patterns that have arisen.

To my knowledge, my own documentation is the only that exists and can be viewed publicly that has attempted to do that, but my work is insufficient for a number of reasons: it is based solely on monitoring of media reports and the few reports by organizations that have emerged, all of which are incomplete, and I can hardly give my full attention to it, which means, for instance, that my overview of legal cases hasn't been updated in two months, though many related occurrences have taken place.

What has emerged from the overview is the following: Upwards of a thousand were arrested in relation to the occupations (1,500 if you include the over 500 arrested last July 1, which I do). The vast majority of those have not been charged or prosecuted. A little under 100 have been prosecuted on a variety of charges including assaulting police, obstructing police, obstructing bailiffs, contempt of court, resisting arrest, behaving in a disorderly manner in a public place, failing to produce ID when demanded by police, criminal damage of property, inciting unlawful assembly, unlawful assembly, and obstructing traffic. Of those, about 30 have been convicted of crimes. That means a tiny percentage—about three percent—of those arrested have been convicted of a crime.

This begs the question of why so many were arrested in the first place: were the arrests preventative? In other words, did the police really suspect those arrested of having committed crimes or were they arresting them simply to "get them out of the way" or to retaliate? If the police did suspect those arrested of having committed crimes, why did they not follow through, press charges and send a report to the Department of Justice so that that latter could prosecute? Was there insufficient evidence? If so, what does that say about the police record in making arrests? If there was sufficient evidence in a large number of cases of those arrested, why weren't more prosecuted?

And how did the police and DoJ select the one-hundred or so cases they have decided to prosecute? The whole process has an arbitrary, inconsistent, incoherent quality to it, especially considering that the former police chief announced a three-month investigation into the "instigators". That suggested police and DoJ would weigh relative severity of crimes and responsibility for occupations in deciding whom to prosecute. Some prosecutions were for fairly high-profile and well documented incidents, such as of people smashing Legco windows (four were convicted of criminal damage and unlawful assembly, the latter charge rather mysterious—why them and virtually none of the hundreds of others arrested on that charge?). But many prosecutions seemed very random, many for what appear to be the most minor of crimes, for example, those prosecuted for obstructing police in Lung Wo Road—they were sitting on the pavement, no different from thousands of others in the occupied areas.

And while several elderly or seemingly eccentric blue-ribbons have been prosecuted for fairly mild attacks on demonstrators (such as poking a demonstrator's throat with an aggressive finger) or threats to attack them (such as one threatening to light himself and nearby demonstrators on fire with paint thinner), not a single thug has been prosecuted for what appeared to be systematic and perhaps triad-orchestrated attacks on demonstrators in Mong Kok. Indeed, to public knowledge, there has been no police investigation of any kind into those attacks, which appeared to be coordinated. Because of many cases of police treating the thuggish attackers leniently by leading them away from the scene and releasing them (as if their first priority were to protect the attackers from demonstrators), police are suspected by many of having colluded with the thugs.

Many of the cases that have actually gone to trial have been of exceedingly poor quality. The conviction rate has been far below the average conviction rate for all criminal trials (something like 25 percent for the occupations versus 50 percent overall). Given that the police and DoJ had upwards of one-thousand cases to choose from, that police were constantly recording the demonstrations with special video teams, and that abundant video and photographic documentation of the demonstrations exists in the media and social media, it seems that the police and DoJ should have been able to make good decisions as to which cases stood a strong chance of resulting in convictions. Instead, on numerous occasions, video evidence has shown that police testimony was inaccurate, and on numerous occasions, magistrates have criticized the police and DoJ for presenting false, misleading and unreliable evidence.

Of course, the most convincing reason for the low number of prosecutions as a percentage of arrests, low number of convictions as a percentage of prosecutions, and low quality of many cases brought to court is that hardly any crime occurred in relation to the occupations. Considering the very large number of people involved—in the hundreds of thousands—it is really quite remarkable how little criminality there was. Of course, that's not surprising at all, considering HK pro-democracy demonstrators are largely self-policing and have over the years assembled again and again in the hundreds of thousands without any crime at all.

But the police and DoJ were probably under pressure from the HK government to produce a semblance of "illegality" and this may be one reason why they've brought such poor cases to court. Once the Partystate and HK government settled on the propaganda term "illegal Occupy movement", perhaps they felt they needed to back that up with convictions. But 30-some convictions out of the hundreds of thousands who participated does not an "illegal" movement make; quite the contrary: It puts paid to the HK government's characterization of the "Occupy movement" as "illegal".

The only conceivable charge with which the DoJ could credibly nail demonstrators is unlawful assembly, but up to now, there have only been five prosecutions and convictions for unlawful assembly (and in all five cases, defendants were charged with another crime which was essentially the primary one). Why have the police and DoJ decided not to prosecute unlawful assembly? Is it because they don't want to face legal challenges to the Public Order Ordinance, which has been repeatedly criticized as written in such a way as to lend itself to unreasonable infringement of freedom of assembly?

And why, up to now, have the police and DoJ not prosecuted any of the "instigators", which the previous police chief singled out for investigation?

Partial answers to these questions may come soon since the police have recently charged three student leaders with unlawful assembly and inciting unlawful assembly in relation to the occupation of Civic Square on the evening of September 26, 2014, preparing the way for their almost certain prosecution. These would be the first "instigators" to be prosecuted, and for a crime, no less, which they arguably did commit. (Arguable because they entered what had been and really should have still been a public space.) It also appears that at least two student leaders will face contempt of court charges related to the police clearance of Mong Kok. These charges are ludicrous—I'm amazed that the police and DoJ intend to pursue them, and it would be outrageous if an HK court actually convicted them. The student leaders were drug by police out of a crowd on Nathan Road and wrestled to the ground. In no sense were they "in contempt of court" unless the DoJ can successfully argue that simply being present at the scene constituted contempt, and if the court accepts that argument, then so much for freedom of assembly.

In short, an overview of the record of arrests and prosecutions related to the occupations shows that justice has not been delivered by the police and DoJ. In fact, a separate investigation should be made into the questions presented here, in order to get to the bottom of why the police and DoJ approaches to prosecution have been so scattershot, arbitrary, inconsistent and incoherent.

The upside is that the HK judiciary has so far stood up pretty well to attempts by the HK government to prosecute people essentially for their political beliefs and expression. It is highly probable that one ulterior motive of the HK government has been to prod the courts to see if there are any weaknesses that could allow it to compromise the independence of the judiciary. Some magistrates have made some questionable decisions, in particular convicting based on insufficient evidence or relying solely on police testimony. But they have also forced the DoJ to drop a good many cases as frivolous.

Thus, we find that one year after the beginning of the occupations:

The Partystate and HK government continue to deny the basic right of genuine universal suffrage to the people of HK, and the HK government therefore continues to be illegal under both HK and international law, resulting in a situation of basic injustice and a chronic governance crisis;

The HK government and police have refused to be held accountable for their decisions and actions related to the occupations and have undertaken no accountability initiatives, resulting in public lack of confidence and trust in the HK government and police and the prospect of the HK police being increasingly used as tool of the government rather than being accountable to the people and the law;

Actions taken by police and the Department of Justice in regard to arrests and prosecutions of demonstrators have been systematically arbitrary, inconsistent, incoherent and flawed, calling into question their competence and integrity.

A society whose political leader is not chosen freely by its citizens is an unjust society.

A society whose police and public officials are not accountable to its citizens but to its unelected political leader is an unjust society.

Hong Kong is an unjust society, run by an unelected leader supported by police and public officials who are accountable to him, not to its citizens.

The demand for justice and accountability will not disappear.

My account of the 6 to 7 November demonstrations against the impending interpretation of the Basic Law by the National People's Congress Standing Committee

November 7, 2016

A brief explanation of what demonstrators were protesting against

The National People's Congress Standing Committee is about to issue an interpretation of the Basic Law, reportedly Article 104, which has to do with swearing oaths upon taking office. The interpretation will almost certainly seek to exclude two members from Legco, Baggio Leung and Yau Wai-ching of the new political group Youngspiration, which arose after the 2014 occupations. They won seats in the September 2016 Legco election. On the oath-taking day, October 12, most Legco members were sworn in without controversy, but the secretary general of Legco declared five oaths invalid, including those taken by Leung and Yau. Leung and Yau showed banners that said "Hong Kong is not China" and they also made changes to the written oath when they spoke it.

A huge propaganda campaign against them ensued, lead by the Partystate, the HK government and pro-Partystate political parties and the Partystate's United Front in HK. The newly elected Legco president, a pro-Partystater himself, invalidated a sixth oath, but said that the two, Leung and Yau, as well as the three others whose oaths had not been accepted the first time around and the one that he himself invalidated could all take their oaths again.

But the next week when Legco met on October 19, after two of the five retakers took their oaths and before Yau and Leung did, the pro-Partystate faction called for a quorum count and then walked out, thus ensuring there was not a quorum to hold the meeting.

The day before that meeting was adjourned, October 18, the HK government applied to the HK High Court for a judicial review, citing the Legco president and Yau and Leung as defendants, and claiming that the two should not be allowed to retake their oaths and their seats should be vacated. It was unprecedented for the HK government to essentially sue Legco as well as to attempt to disqualify elected Legco members. The High Court judge did not grant an immediate injunction against them retaking their oaths, but he did agree to hear the case on November 3.

The Legco president then changed his mind and said the two could not retake their oaths until the court ruled on the judicial review. The following week, on October 26, it was the pro-democracy camp that prevented Legco from meeting by walking out in protest at the Legco president's reversal.

And the week after that, Yau and Leung entered the Legco chamber demanding to retake their oaths, though the president had forbidden them to do so. The Legco president moved the meeting to another room, but when Yau and Leung attempted to enter there, he adjourned the meeting for the third time in three weeks due to safety concerns. That was November 2.

The next day, November 3, the High Court heard the judicial review. It was argued on narrow legal grounds with the two sides debating whether the oath-taking was a constitutional matter for the courts to decide (the government's position) or a matter of separation of powers and immunity of Legco members (the Legco president's and Yau and Leung's positions). The judge did not rule at the end of the hearing but said he would do so soon.

In the meantime, there were already rumblings that the NPCSC was going to interpret the Basic Law even before the court judgment. This would be only the fourth time overall since the handover in 1997 that the NPCSC would do so, and the first time to pre-empt an on-going court case.

Virtually everyone in HK who is for democracy is outraged by the expected intervention, which is regarded as an infringement on HK's autonomy as well as on the independence of the HK judiciary, and thus, damaging to rule of law in HK, which in turn is regarded as one of the few things keeping HK from becoming much like the mainland.

Thus, the protests.

The pro-democracy movement believes this is yet another instance of the Partystate attempting to gain greater control over HK. For the first time ever, Legco members face the prospect of losing their seats for words spoken and actions taken within the space of a couple of minutes. Yau and Leung were democratically elected. The Partystate and HK government attempt to expel them is a clear infringement on the already highly constrained democratic rights of the HK people. Among other things, it fails to take into account the rights of voters to have those they have elected represent them.

You have the extraordinary situation of an unelected HK government and an unelected Partystate trying to bar two elected members of Legco from taking their seats. If there were ever any situation to prove—if proof were needed—that Partystate intentions in the infamous hardline August 31, 2014 ruling of the NPCSC denying genuine universal suffrage were not to move in the direction of greater democracy in HK, this is it.

The Partystate says it is a matter of national security, but Yau and Leung have not been charged with any crime, and it appears the Partystate and HK government are just making up the rules as they go along in order to suit themselves.

The NPCSC is literally above the law: Any interpretation it makes of the Basic Law automatically becomes the law of HK. There is no avenue to contest it judicially and no way the NPCSC can be held legally accountable.

The march and subsequent Liaison Office protest

The day started around 3 in the afternoon at Luard Road in Wan Chai. Civil Human Rights Front had called a march against the National People's Congress Standing Committee interpreting the HK Basic Law. The route was from there to the Court of Final Appeal in Central.

Many groups gathered in Southorn Playground before the march began. The only localist group I noticed there was Youngspiration, whose two Legco representatives, Yau Wai-ching and Baggio Leung, are at the heart of the current controversy.

Otherwise, the make-up of the march was old-style pro-democracy, with most of the pan-democratic parties present, including Democratic Party and Civic Party. The march wasn't one of the "mega-marches" of hundreds of thousands we have seen through the years in HK, but it was substantial. *SCMP* eventually estimated 13,000, and *SCMP* usually errs on the low side. I would guess somewhere around 15,000. Of the dozens of people I spoke to, I didn't meet a single one who was pro-independence. Quite a few (mostly older) people were critical of Yau Wai-ching and Baggio Leung's oath-taking, and several went out of their way to emphasize that they didn't support them but they were even more strongly opposed to the interference of the Communist Party in HK affairs and that was why they'd come.

I was near the front of the march throughout and didn't see what went on behind. The march was fairly uneventful, winding down Queen's Road, until it got to the intersection of Queen's Road Central and Ice House Street. At that point, the march was to turn right into Ice House Street to proceed to the Court of Final Appeal, its destination, about a block away. Demosistō, which had been at the front of the march, immediately split into two groups, with one group peeling off to continue up Queen's Road Central and the other following the scheduled march into Ice House Street. Of its leaders, Nathan Law and Agnes Chow went up Queen's Road Central, and I lost Joshua Wong in the crowd and assumed he continued to the Court of Final Appeal, though he later showed up at the Liaison Office. League of Social Democrats wasn't far behind Demosistō, and they too continued up Queen's Road Central. Not far behind them was the Labour Party and the Hong Kong Confederation of Trade Unions, which joined the Queen's Road contingent. They made up the nucleus of the group intending to go to the Liaison Office, but there were hundreds of unaffiliated others as well, eventually maybe somewhere between one-thousand and two-thousand over all.

This is not an unusual practice of demonstrators in recent years, to break away from the "official" demonstration near the end and go to the Liaison Office. Demosistō (and its precursor Scholarism) and LSD are especially practiced in this art. And the police have almost a ritual approach. Early in the march, they bring out their yellow banner and declare the march an unlawful gathering. The demonstrators proceed to ignore the police warning, and the police eventually accommodate the march, at least until the Liaison Office, and then what the police decide to do depends on the situation. That's what happened this time as well. This time, though, the number of protesters was significantly larger than usual.

The police declared the march an "unlawful assembly" under the HK Public Order Ordinance. International authorities on human rights law including the

United Nations Human Rights Committee and Human Rights Watch have repeatedly for years criticized POO as being written in such a vague way so as to leave itself unduly open to police interpretation, and this, in turn, they argue, could lead to unreasonable restrictions being placed on freedom of assembly. In recent years, especially since the 2014 occupations, various pro-democracy groups have increasingly ignored the terms of the POO, which stipulate that if you intend to organize an assembly in which you expect more than 30 people to participate, you must notify the police and receive a notice of no objection from them in order to go ahead. The official justification for this is that police need to make arrangements for traffic and public order. The rebuttal to that is that people should have to do no more than notify the police, not await a notice of no objection—essentially permission—from them, and there should be allowances for spontaneous gatherings as well. In other words, spontaneous gatherings shouldn't be immediately "outlawed", which appears to have become an HK police habit. The UNHRC is the body legally empowered to monitor compliance with the International Covenant on Civil and Political Rights, to which HK is party. Even though it has repeatedly expressed concerns about POO, the HK government has made no effort to amend it to address the UNHRC's concerns. This raises the question of how lawful POO is in light of international law, and it's one reason the Department of Justice has until recently been relatively reluctant to prosecute demonstrators arrested on unlawful assembly charges.

The march that split off from the "official" march and headed toward the Liaison Office did not apply for a notice of no objection. March leaders warned participants of this, saying they might get arrested. As it turned out, none did. Not en route to the Liaison Office at least. The arrests came later.

I was surprised that HK police didn't appear entirely prepared for the "unauthorized" procession, given the high tension in the city surrounding the impending NPCSC interpretation of the Basic Law. Ever since the 2014 occupations, if anything HK police have had a tendency to come overprepared, to put it mildly, for possible "disruptions to public order". Still, the police accommodated the march all the way to the Liaison Office.

And then another part of the ritual began: Police routinely block marches, even authorized ones, right before they get to the Liaison Office on Connaught Road. Then they decide what to do. If the march is small and authorized, they often open a corridor, a bit like a gauntlet, and allow demonstrators to pass by the Liaison Office in single file. If it is not, they often refuse to allow demonstrators to pass. For years, various groups have complained that the area around the front of the Liaison Office has been designed so as to constrain the right to protest there. Raised flower beds have been erected, and police are always on guard duty there. When a demonstration comes, police set up barriers that make demonstrators feel like cattle going through a chute.

It's safe to say that there are few places in HK as sensitive when it comes to demonstrations as the Liaison Office and the police are under strict orders to ensure nothing undo happens. The police have often been overzealous about arresting people there. When Liu Xiaobo won the Nobel Peace Prize in 2010, a demonstrator was arrested for "assaulting" a security guard when spray from a bottle of champagne she opened inadvertently hit the guard. She was not prosecuted.

This time around, there was virtually no chance the police would let the demonstrators pass. On top of being "unauthorized", the march was simply too large to take the risk. Most of the time when police refuse to allow demonstrators to pass, I think it's unreasonable, but this time, they might have been wise. Usually when the police block demonstrators, they eventually leave. This time, they didn't. They stayed put and stood firm. There is a large penned area to the east of the Liaison Office on Connaught Road that is set up to accommodate demonstrators. This area was filled and demonstrators were backed onto the stairs and pedestrian bridge at the corner of Connaught and Western Streets, and spilled down around the corner onto the Western Street sidewalk.

At a certain point in the evening, some demonstrators who were penned in attempted to step out into Connaught Road. Police reacted swiftly and aggressively, unleashing massive amounts of pepperspray that hit not only some of the people stepping out into the road but also a great many others simply standing in the penned area nearby, including journalists. Many reported that their skin stung for hours afterwards. Some reported their phones ceasing to work after being hit. Avery Ng, one of the leaders of LSD, was arrested at this point, and one other person was arrested. As far as I know, these were the only two arrests of the night, remarkable given what was to come.

Not long after that, some demonstrators went to Des Voeux Road abutting the Liaison Office on the back side and occupied the road there. These demonstrators had not participated in the "official" march earlier in the day. Quite a few wore masks and protective gear. They appeared to be more affiliated with localist elements and had come directly to the Liaison Office upon hearing others were gathered there.

Eventually, more and more demonstrators on Connaught Road, attracted by the commotion on Des Voeux Road and sick of being penned in, made their way into Western Street and Des Voeux Road, and the "occupation", if that's what it should be called, began. Western Street and Des Voeux Road were effectively closed to traffic from this point on. A major tram line runs on Des Voeux Road, and eventually more than a dozen tram cars were blocked and parked back nearly two blocks to the east on the road.

At this point, I estimated there were somewhere between 3,000 and 4,000 demonstrators, and this was probably the peak in terms of numbers. Quickly a stand-off commenced on Des Voeux Road between police and demonstrators, with several meters between them. Demonstrators had their umbrellas ready. Police tried to disperse them with pepperspray, but to no avail. At the same time, once most of the Connaught Road demonstrators had gone into Western Street and Des Voeux Road, police pushed up into Western Street and set up barriers there. So there were at this point police cordons on Western Street and Des Voeux Road, but still there were not terribly many police visible; in the hundreds yes, but I would have expected more. It appeared that what these police intended to do was keep the situation stable until reinforcements could arrive. Quickly, a kind of stalemate ensued.

Nathan Law of Demosistō spoke to the crowd. He seemed ambivalent about remaining, asking what could be gained by occupying the road. Many voiced their displeasure with his speech. I was a bit puzzled too.

It made one wonder what Demosistō thought it was doing in the first place going down to the Liaison Office. Either it had some secret plan that was thwarted by the police not allowing demonstrators to proceed past the office, or it just thought it would go there and then leave.

And so the occupation continued. There weren't really any leaders, and few people spoke on loudhailers to the crowd. Nathan said he wasn't against people staying or more people coming but emphasized that safety came first and if police attacked with tear gas, people should leave. Hardly a rousing endorsement of proceedings.

Behind this reluctance on his part and others to take the lead and emphatically call for more people to come out was a tension amongst the demonstrators. To put it simply, it was between the localist sorts who tend to speak more in terms of an "HK nation" if not independence and those like Demosistō who advocate self-determination. No localist groups (such as HK Indigenous or Civic Passion) were "officially" there by name, except perhaps Youngspiration. At the same time, no traditional pan-democratic parties, except perhaps Labour Party, were there either, and the vast majority of those gathered were young people.

Once this scene had been set, not that many more people arrived to add to the ranks of the demonstrators. When I asked demonstrators about this, I got two answers. The first was that it was Sunday evening and people had to work the next day. The second, mostly from the self-determinationists, was that people were afraid of being "used" by localists, or of being drawn into a situation in which demonstrators used violence.

This reflects the ambivalence of many pro-democracy types I met on the march who, on the one hand, are critical of how Yau Wai-ching and Baggio Leung took their oaths and don't support HK independence, but, on the other, are appalled by the Communist Party's intervention. At any rate, this probably explains the fact that the crowd did not get significantly larger from this point on. Indeed, one of the more frequent slogans shouted at the demonstration was "HK independence!" Though it was only a certain portion of the demonstrators shouting this, I could imagine there were a good many pro-democracy people who wouldn't want to be present at a demonstration where that was one of the main shouts. There have been many conspiracy theories about for a good long time to the effect that the Partystate and HK government are deliberately stoking the independence flame in order to justify a heavier crackdown, and many in the pro-democracy movement are leery of being manipulated.

By this point, both at a press conference and at the demonstration, police were alleging that people were taking bricks from the pavement and warning against doing so. Perhaps they intended to stress that this was their bottom line, and to warn that if there was any brick-throwing, there would be a hard crackdown. But they may have also wished to smear the demonstrators as "violent" and portray the situation as on the verge of "riot", evoking what happened in Mong Kok during Chinese New Year on 8 and 9 February.

Perhaps some people did take bricks from the pavement, but if so, I didn't see it. I surveyed the whole area several times over several hours and didn't see a single demonstrator with a brick. So if the brick people existed, they were a tiny minority. Police also mentioned demonstrators potentially using bamboo poles as offensive weapons. Again, I didn't see any bamboo poles, and if some had them, again, they had to have been a tiny minority. The vast majority of demonstrators were entirely nonviolent and were exhorted repeatedly by other demonstrators to remain so.

I did see some of the localist types throwing plastic water bottles at police when the latter charged. I repeatedly asked them not to. Because I didn't think a principled argument for nonviolence would go over that well with them, I told them that if they were caught, the police and Department of Justice would do their utmost to prosecute them for assaulting officers and try to get them jail time; otherwise, there was little the police could charge them with that would stick in a court of law. Plastic bottle throwing continued into the night, though. I personally am against it because I believe in resolute nonviolence, but it is also stupidly ineffectual and gives the police license to take actions they otherwise are not justified in taking as well as an opportunity to brand demonstrators as "violent".

A little bottle throwing happened when police formed a cordon at the top of Western Street, above the police station, and came partway down the street. This was a little after 10 pm. One purpose of this new cordon appeared to be partly to allow more police to enter police station headquarters through a gate on Western Street. The other intention was to enclose the demonstrators on three sides. Since police left Des Voeux Road to the east unblocked, from this point on the police tactic became clear: to eventually force demonstrators down Des Voeux Road to the east. But still, at that point, there were not many police visible and they hadn't the numbers yet to conduct the operation.

So everyone just stood around, waiting for something. For what exactly? For the police to take action. I was struck that the demonstrators didn't really seem to have any ideas or plans for where to go from there. Now that they were in the road, what should they do? And this was the purpose of the police, to neutralize. The police appeared to take their sweet time getting ready to clear, in the hope that the demonstrators might trickle away of their own accord. Only a few did, but at the same time, the crowd was not growing at that point.

By this point, virtually all police were wearing riot helmets with clear plastic visors pulled down over the faces. The police on the frontlines held two-meter-high clear plastic shields. They had an array of devices to shoot pepperspray. They brought in dogs. Some had tear gas rifles. Some people speculated that some of these rifles were to shoot bean bags of pepperspray. And it appeared there were also some rifles that might have contained rubber bullets or even live ammunition. (I am no weapons expert and base this observation on the fact that the barrels of rifles were narrow, unlike the barrels of the tear gas rifles, which are fat. I was later told the narrow-barreled rifles were paint guns for marking demonstrators. To my knowledge, they've never been used before by HK police.)

Shortly after midnight, Nathan Law and Baggio Leung both called on demonstrators to move towards Central, given that their position was not "advantageous". Even before making that call, both had expressed some ambivalence about the gathering, Baggio more in the sense that he worried there were just too many police there, Nathan because he wondered about the efficacy of the street occupation.

Around 12:30 am, police began to move in, pushing from three directions. At this point, in the lead were the so-called "raptors", a unit of blue-uniformed officers from the counterrorism and airport special unit who had a reputation for being especially aggressive. They had been used to clear Mong Kok on November 26 and Lung Wo Road on December 1 during the 2014 occupations. And they used a similar technique this time, pushing rapidly from three directions and forcing demonstrators down Des Voeux Road to the east. Demonstrators did not resist. I was a little surprised that demonstrators didn't make alternative plans to occupy streets elsewhere. Not long after, most of the main groups at the protest, namely Demosistō, the Labour Party and Baggio Leung and Yau Wai-ching called on people to go home, and this appeared to take most of the spirit of struggle out of the demonstration, if it wasn't already dissipating of its own accord. Police continued to push demonstrators down Des Voeux Road over the course of more than two hours, eventually going as far as Bonham Strand West. By that point, it was nearly 3 am, and there were only small pockets of demonstrators remaining.

While police were resolute, it appeared they were trying their best not to resort to actually clubbing demonstrators with batons, as they had done frequently in the past, and also to avoid arrests. As noted above, the two people arrested in the first police pepperspray attack earlier in the evening were the only two arrests I heard of the whole night. The police's main objectives appeared to be to keep people away from the Liaison Office and clear the streets.

On the Hong Kong government charging nine pro-democracy leaders with "inciting public nuisance" for the Umbrella Movement

March 28, 2017

Two and half years after the fact, the government is essentially asserting that these nine are primarily responsible for starting the Umbrella Movement. Ironically, though, the police themselves were the "principal instigators".

On 27 March 2017, nine HK pro-democracy leaders were arrested and charged with various counts of "inciting public nuisance". They are the first of some 1,000 people arrested in connection with the Umbrella Movement to face this charge.

The Umbrella Movement Nine are Benny Tai, Chan Kin-man and Chu Yiu-ming, the three co-founders of Occupy Central with Love and Peace; Tanya Chan, a prominent politician in the Civic Party who won a seat in the 2016 Legislative Council elections; Shiu Ka-chun, currently the Legco Social Welfare functional constituency representative; Raphael Wong, vice-chair of the League of Social Democrats; Lee Wing-tat, a politician in the Democratic Party; and Eason Chung and Tommy Cheung, who at the time of the 2014 demonstrations were leaders in the Hong Kong Federation of Students.

In charging the nine with the crime of incitement to public nuisance, the Hong Kong government is effectively arguing that they were the ones primarily responsible for sparking the Umbrella Movement. This harks back to an announcement made by then-Police Commissioner Andy Tsang on 15 December 2014, the day of the police clearance of the last of the three occupation sites in Causeway Bay. He said the police would conduct an investigation into the "principal instigators" of the occupations, and he hoped the investigation would be completed within three months.

From January to March 2015, 43 pro-democracy leaders were called to police headquarters for "arrest appointments". They were interviewed and then released. Many at the time expected that charges would soon follow. But none did. Until now.

When Tsang made the announcement, I wondered how he could do so with a straight face, since the obvious "principal instigator" of the occupations was the police themselves. From 5:58 pm of 28 September to approximately 2 am of 29 September, they attacked nonviolent demonstrators with 87 rounds of teargas. In doing so, they outraged Hong Kong people who came out in ever greater numbers to stand up to the police attack and show solidarity with the demonstrators under assault. If the police had not engaged in those futile eight hours of attacks, it is doubtful that the occupations would have ever taken place; at any rate, they would not have started as they did.

For the fact of the matter is, *nobody* planned the occupations, *nobody* planned the Umbrella Movement, and no single individual or group is responsible for "inciting" the Umbrella Movement. It occurred as a spontaneous direct response to the police teargas attacks, and, in the second instance, to the hardline National People's Congress Standing Committee decision of 31 August which effectively ruled out genuine universal suffrage while purporting to allow it.

The Hong Kong government's prosecution of the nine once again raises the issue of government and police accountability. Immediately after the teargas attacks, many people in Hong Kong, including pro-democracy Legco members, called for a formal independent investigation of the roles of the Hong Kong government and police in deciding on the eight-hour-long teargas attacks. In Hong Kong, there is a specific Commissions of Inquiry statute that allows the Chief Executive to appoint an independent commission to carry out an inquiry into a specific issue of great public interest. Recent commissions appointed under the current Chief Executive Leung Chun-ying include one looking into the Lamma ferry disaster and another into excess lead found in drinking water. But the Hong Kong government, pro-Communist Party Legco members and the police stonewalled all attempts to carry out an independent investigation of any kind. To this day, no Hong Kong government official or police leader has been held accountable for the decision to attack nonviolent demonstrators for eight hours on 28 and 29 September.

The only explanation the police ever gave was that it was to stop demonstrators from charging police cordons. The claim is doubly misleading: police cordons were not being charged by the crowds and even if that justification might appear credible in regard to the first few teargas shots fired around 6 pm of the 28th, it entirely fails to explain why the attacks continued for eight hours.

No Hong Kong government official or police leader has ever taken responsibility for making the decision to attack nonviolent demonstrators with teargas or explained the decision-making behind the actions. In one newspaper interview with an anonymous police superintendent held at police headquarters, the superintendent claimed that he alone took the decision. Again, this strains credibility, given the facts that it was the first time since 1967 Hong Kong police had attacked their own people with teargas and the attacks went on for eight hours. A single police superintendent surely couldn't have been solely responsible for all that with no direction whatsoever from his superiors.

And here we are, two and a half years later, still with no genuine universal suffrage, with yet another tiresome charade of a Chief Executive selection process having been completed (when the real decision is made by the Communist Party), and the Hong Kong government is trying to pin the blame for the Umbrella Movement on these nine. It's really quite perverse. They were simply amongst hundreds of thousands fighting for the basic human right of all people, including Hong Kong people, to genuine universal suffrage, a right denied by the Hong Kong government under the Communist Party for nearly twenty years now. So the Communist Party and Hong Kong government abuse the rights of the Hong Kong people (and break both international and the Hong Kong Basic Law in doing so) and then punish people for demanding their rights. Dictatorship in a nutshell.

The funny thing is, none of the nine charged really played any particularly large role in "inciting" people to public nuisance. The Hong Kong government may have some evidence which it believes will allow it to nail the nine legally, but they were really not the main forces behind the occupations.

It's important to note that in charging the six non-OCLP leaders with incitement, the police said that it was in connection with actions they took from 27 to 28 September 2014. So what they were doing in that two-day period right up to the start of the teargas attacks and occupations will be crucial in deciding whether or not they are guilty as charged in a court of law.

OCLP is bit different since the police said the charges relate to a period from 27 March 2013, when OCLP was founded, to when OCLP leaders turned themselves in to police in early December 2014. The OCLP Three are being charged with "conspiracy to incite public nuisance", which presumably means the government is trying to convict them for promoting the concept of civil disobedience for a period of more than a year before the occupations. Throughout that period, though, the OCLP leaders (one of whom is a law professor) were careful to avoid directly "inciting", and to the extent they can be said to have incited to any specific act of civil disobedience at all, it was not the Umbrella Movement but something else which was pre-empted by it and never occurred.

The OCLP Three actually did not want to join in the demonstrations when they began with the occupation of Civic Square on the evening of 26 September. On the morning of 27 September, Benny Tai and Chan Kin-man showed up to support the people occupying the square, but despite calls to join, they were resistant to declaring Occupy Central open, much to the frustration of some in the crowd who actually heckled them. In fact, they had been planning a small-scale "wedding banquet" for the upcoming 1 October holiday in Central, and one very much had the impression that they didn't want what was happening before their eyes to pre-empt their plan. As the crowds grew over the course of the 27th, they changed their mind, and in the middle of the night from 27 to 28 September, Benny Tai announced Occupy Central was open. But by then, they were joining forces with a demonstration that had already been underway in one form or another for more than twenty-four hours. Never once did they call for long-term occupations of the sort that eventually ensued.

As for Tommy Cheung and Eason Chung, it is presumably in their capacity as leaders of HKFS that they are being charged. The top leaders of HKFS, Alex Chow and Lester Shum, had been arrested on the morning of Saturday 27 September for occupying Civic Square. The police kept Chow and Shum in prison for the entire weekend, supposedly because they were investigating but really to prevent them from getting out and re-assuming their leadership roles. In fact, it was only when fellow arrestee Joshua Wong's lawyer forced the police to release him with a writ of habeas corpus from the High Court and Chow and Shum's lawyers threatened the same that the police let them go Sunday night, after the police teargas attacks had started. (Chow and Wong were eventually convicted of unlawful assembly in July 2016 and given, respectively, a suspended sentence and community service. The government regards the sentences as too lenient and is appealing.)

That meant that during that crucial weekend, the top leadership of HKFS was behind bars. Cheung and Chung undoubtedly played an important role in assuming the reins of HKFS in their absence, and among other things, they helped MC on the HKFS stage next to Civic Square while the weekend demonstrations were happening, but they have never been perceived as "inciting" crowds to take any particular action.

In fact, the amazing thing is, on the evening of 28 September, after the police teargas attacks began, both HKFS and OCLP called on demonstrators to *leave* and *go home*. They did this primarily out of concern for their safety since over the course of the evening there were rumors that the police would escalate to use of rubber bullets and even live ammunition. (Yes, the shadow of the June 4 Tiananmen massacre definitely loomed.) I remember this very clearly because I couldn't believe my ears when I first heard it: You've got all these people on the streets, and you're telling them to go home?! So the ironic thing is, at that moment at least, rather than "inciting public nuisance", OCLP and HKFS were telling people to leave.

And here again is proof that it was really the people who made the movement: The demonstrators ignored the calls of OCLP and HKFS and remained on the streets, even while the police continued to attack them.

As for Tanya Chan and Shiu Ka-chun, I remember them well, but primarily for their roles in acting as MCs at the HKFS stage over the course of the weekend, again filling in for the student leaders in prison. I don't remember much of what Shiu said, but I remember very clearly my impression that Chan, rather than inciting, had a moderating influence. She certainly had no plan to "incite public nuisance". If anything, she was just trying to manage the crowd. She kept telling people to calm down and not do anything rash.

I have to say I don't even remember seeing Lee Wing-tat at all that weekend. He may have been there, but I am highly skeptical that he played any major role in "inciting public nuisance". Raphael Wong was always in the mix, always around, but again, I fail to recall a single instance in which it appeared that he was making any particular effort to "incite public nuisance." For all I know, maybe the police have some evidence on him relating to one of the other occupation sites besides Admiralty.

To put it simply, the police have the wrong people. Who are the right people, then? Yes, the police. And the people themselves, the Hong Kong people, who in the face of hours of police teargas attacks refused to leave the streets. No one told them to stand up to the police; they did so on their own. And they did so to say, We've had enough! This is our city! We refuse to allow you to intimidate and brutalize us! We demand our basic human right of universal suffrage!

Essentially, in prosecuting the Umbrella Movement Nine, the Hong Kong government is using them as proxies for the people, for it cannot send all the people to jail. In prosecuting them, it is prosecuting the Hong Kong people. It is the government against the people.

The tragic thing is that the situation had gotten to the point where the people felt they had no other option than to camp out in the streets of their own city for 79 days to get genuine universal suffrage. And they still haven't gotten it. It is Hong Kong's festering sore, and will continue to be. Hong Kong is a city in perpetual political crisis. Rather than addressing that crisis, the authorities are trying to imprison people who were demanding that it be addressed in a way consonant with Hong Kong's obligations under international law.

When the new Chief Executive, Carrie Lam, was selected on 26 March, she said she wanted to "unite" the city. Who is she kidding? If there is a lack of unity, the reason for it is the lack of justice. There will be no "unity" without justice. And she stated clearly in the run-up to the selection that she had no intention to work on political reform.

The willful blindness of the Communist Party and the Hong Kong authorities to the real issues of the city and their insistence on taking a hardline (disqualifying Legco candidates, attempting to disqualify elected pro-democracy Legco members, and handing down a special NPCSC Basic Law interpretation to do so, thus further undermining "one country, two systems" and rule of law) is a political dead end that has left this city more pessimistic than I have ever seen it.

One final note: The Department of Justice's explanation of why it has taken two and half years to bring charges against the Umbrella Movement Nine is ludicrous. It said it had to consider "the material submitted by the Police in respect of another group of 287 arrested persons (including about 335 investigation reports, 300 witness statements, 130 hours of video recordings and 80 items of non-video exhibits) and the relevant legal issues"; in effect, it had so much work. But that is an excuse. It is the responsibility of the DoJ to prosecute in a timely manner, among other things because doing so is important to protecting the rights of the accused. Two and a half years is not timely and not necessary given the nature of the charges brought against the nine. On the very same day that the nine were charged, a Hong Kong police officer named Franklin Chu was also charged with assault for hitting people with a baton in Mong Kok during the occupations. His actions were captured on video and broadcast the very same day, 26 November 2014. And yet it has taken the DoJ 853 days to bring charges against him. It has as yet made no statement attempting to explain that delay.

I hope the pro-democracy movement will use the opportunity of the prosecution of the Umbrella Movement Nine to focus on the need to continue pressing for justice, for self-determination and democracy. One probable reason for the timing of the arrests was that the Hong Kong government hopes they will have a deterrent effect. After Carrie Lam was selected as the new CE, Demosistō stated that it would hold a "civil disobedience protest" on 1 July, when Lam will be formally appointed CE, most likely by Xi Jinping on a visit to Hong Kong to "celebrate" the 20th anniversary of HK's "return to the motherland". It will be interesting to see what exactly happens on that occasion. But believe me, in saying that, I'm not "inciting".

The Hong Kong government's all-out attack on Demosistō and League of Social Democrats

August 18, 2017

How do you destroy your political adversary in a society that supposedly has rule of law and protects civil rights (some at least, to some degree)? The HK government's post-Umbrella Movement attack on Demosistō and LSD is a case study.

The HK government is cracking down on the pro-democracy movement in general and has been for some time. Since the Umbrella Movement of 2014, it has brought 39 legal cases against 26 pro-democracy leaders, successfully applied for High Court judicial reviews which banned from office six elected pro-democracy Legislative Council members and effectively cancelled the votes of over 180,000 voters, and prosecuted dozens of others pro-democracy activists. In this week alone, it has successfully appealed the original sentences of 16 pro-democracy activists, including Umbrella Movement leaders Joshua Wong, Nathan Law, Alex Chow and Raphael Wong, with the High Court sentencing them to between six and thirteen months in prison for the nonviolent protest-related crime of unlawful assembly.

But within the pro-democracy movement, Demosistō and League of Social Democrats have been hit particularly hard. Of those 39 legal cases brought against pro-democracy leaders, six are against Demosistō and 10 against LSD:

Joshua Wong, Secretary General of Demosistō, has faced three prosecutions. In addition to Joshua's unlawful assembly conviction for occupying Civic Square on 26 September 2014, for which he was yesterday sentenced to seven months in prison, on 6 July, he acknowledged contempt of court in relation to the clearance of the Mong Kok occupation on 26 November 2014. In that case, he's on trial together with 20 others, half of whom have refused to acknowledge contempt, and the judge has said he will consider sentencing once the trial concludes, probably within the next month. Joshua could very well receive additional time in prison. Joshua has previously been acquitted of obstructing police for a June 2014 protest against the White Paper at the Chinese government Liaison Office.

Nathan Law, chair of Demosistō, has faced two criminal prosecutions and a judicial review. The prosecutions are for the same cases as Joshua's above. He was acquitted of obstructing police at the White Paper protest, sentenced to eight months in prison for inciting unlawful assembly in relation to the Civic Square occupation, and ejected from Legco by the High Court for using an inflection in his pronunciation of the People's Republic of China during the Legco swearing-in ceremony which the judge, following a Basic Law interpretation by the National People's Congress Standing Committee, found to be lacking in "solemnity". As many have pointed out, the prison sentences also mean that Nathan and Joshua will be disqualified from running for elected office for the next five years.

In addition to Joshua and Nathan, two other core members of Demosistō, **Derek Lam** and **Ivan Lam**, also face prosecutions. Both Derek and Ivan are to go on trial together with seven others on 23 August for a 6 November 2016 protest against the NPCSC Basic Law interpretation that eventually lead to Nathan's ejection from Legco, Derek for inciting disorderly conduct and Ivan for unlawful assembly. Ivan was this week sentenced to 13 months in prison for unlawful assembly for a protest in June 2014 in Civic Square against an HK government northeast New Territories development project. That protest lead to the government closing Civic Square to the public. Joshua, Nathan and Alex Chow have just been sentenced to prison for re-occupying Civic Square in September that year.

Raphael Wong, vice-chair of LSD, has faced four prosecutions. Together with Ivan and 11 others, he was sentenced this week to thirteen months in prison for unlawful assembly. He was acquitted of obstructing police for the same June 2014 White Paper protest as Joshua and Nathan. And he's currently on trial in the same case as Joshua for contempt of court for the 26 November 2014 Mong Kok occupation clearance. Unlike Joshua, he's refused to acknowledge contempt. The verdict will most likely be within a matter of weeks. Raphael is also one of the Umbrella Movement 9 who will go on trial on 19 September, essentially for instigating the movement. He faces two counts of inciting public nuisance.

Long Hair (Leung Kwok-hung), former chair of LSD, has faced two criminal prosecutions and one judicial review. He was acquitted of misconduct in public office on 31 July over his alleged failure to declare a HK$250,000 donation from Jimmy Lai. His trial for contempt of Legco related to a November 2016 incident in which he grabbed some papers belonging to a government minister will begin soon. Like Nathan, he was disqualified from Legco by the High Court on 14 July over his swearing-in.

Avery Ng, chair of LSD, faces three prosecutions. He is currently on trial for assaulting a police officer with a thrown sandwich at a September 2016 protest against Chief Executive CY Leung on Legco election day. He will face trial for disclosing the identity of a person under investigation by the Independent Commission Against Corruption. And like Derek and Ivan, he goes on trial on 23 August in relation to the protest against the NPCSC Basic Law interpretation; in his case, the charge consists of two counts of disorderly conduct.

Dickson Chau Ka-faat, LSD deputy secretary general, will be on trial in the same case, on charges of obstructing and assaulting police.

As you can see, quite a few of these cases involve collaboration between Demosistō and LSD. The two were the leaders of the Black Bauhinia protest on 28 June against the treatment of Liu Xiaobo and the 20th anniversary of the handover of HK from the UK to China. Altogether, 26 were arrested at that protest, including Nathan Law, Joshua Wong, Agnes Chow, Long Hair, Avery Ng, Raphael Wong and several other members of Demosistō and LSD. So far, no charges have been brought, but they very well may be.

It's not only through the courts that the HK government has gone on the attack, presumably with the intention of destroying the organizations. Demosistō was founded in early 2016. At that time, it applied to the Companies Registry, a governmental agency, for legal recognition. In HK, there's no law about political parties, so parties typically register as companies in order to become legally recognized entities. It usually takes a matter of days for an application to be approved. Indeed, HK is renowned as one of the easiest places in the world to start a business. But nearly a year and a half later, Demosistō still has received no response to its application. In practice, this means it cannot open a bank account in its name, which in turn makes it more difficult to solicit donations. Unless you hand-deliver your donation, the only way you can get it to the party is to send a cheque to Joshua Wong's P.O. Box in Wan Chai, this for one of the most internet-savvy parties in HK.

Why is the HK government going so hard after these groups? Arguably because they're the ones who embarrass the government the most. LSD is one of the most progressive and assertive pro-democracy parties. Demosistō is arguably an even greater threat as it is in the forefront of the HK self-determination movement that is an outgrowth of the Umbrella Movement. It also represents the more assertive political role of young people in HK since the Umbrella Movement. The HK government is acting ever more like the Communist Party: It wants to cut off the head of the chicken to scare the monkeys. As far as the Communist Party and the HK government were concerned, the striking victories of many of the newly formed political groups in the September 2016 Legco elections, many of whom were leaders in the Umbrella Movement, was the last straw. The regime could not stand to have such a strident political opposition inside of the formal political structure, even though it is already rigged to ensure dominance by Communist Party allies. Ever since then, the regime's efforts to eject the newly elected from Legco and eviscerate their parties have been stepped up.

In appealing the sentences of the 16 convicted of unlawful assembly, the government was trying, as the Secretary for Justice Rimsky Yuen put it, to get the High Court to "lay down guidelines for sentencing for these kind [sic] of crimes". In other words, to send the message that you will be punished much more severely than in the past for taking part in what's either at the time of the act or retrospectively designated by the police an unlawful assembly. That is potentially chilling to the right of freedom of assembly. The crime of unlawful assembly falls under the already problematic Public Order Ordinance. For years, both the UN Human Rights Committee and Human Rights Watch have said POO needs to be revised to meet international standards, to avoid being used to unreasonably restrict the right to freedom of assembly or grant arbitrary powers to police. But rather than fix POO, the HK government is sending a warning that the government is getting tough on behavior at public gatherings, with all the attendant risks that brings of unreasonable restrictions on the right to freedom of assembly.

Now, when the HK government invokes "rule of law", I'm sickened: Coming from their mouths, it sounds the same as from the mouths of Communist Party officials (ie, rule by law). How can these people who have refused to comply with the Basic Law and international law by denying the basic human right of universal suffrage to the people of HK invoke the rule of law to oppress the very people fighting for that right? It's perverse.

Overall, behind the persecution of Demosistō and LSD is the government's vision, inspired if not directed by the Communist Party, of a "managed" society: Everyone should behave just as the government wishes and all shall be fine. Tellingly, the government has brought relatively few prosecutions against traditional pan-democrats, even though they represent a much higher percentage of those arrested during the Umbrella Movement, presumably because, overall, they are seen to be generally "well behaved". Indeed, their demands remain about the same as they were before the Umbrella Movement, genuine universal suffrage as promised in the Basic Law, whereas most of the groups that have come up since the Umbrella Movement, such as Demosistō, have given up on that possibility as long as the Communists are in power and instead are seeking self-determination or, in some cases, independence.

Apart from the human rights abuses perpetrated by the HK government on Demosistō, LSD and others in the pro-democracy movement, what damage have the attacks caused? After all, HK is already undemocratic. It suffers a perpetual governance crisis due to the illegitimacy (and from the perspective of international law, illegality) of the unelected government, coupled with the fact that it has shown itself consistently to be primarily an administrative organ of the Communist Party rather than a representative of the HK people. So how could what it's doing now make things worse? Well, in order to go after political opponents, it is compromising the police force, the judiciary and the Legislative Council. All are institutions important to a well-functioning, fair and democratic society. Of course, it presumably wishes to compromise these entities, or doesn't care, or considers such compromised institutions more "loyal" and "patriotic", echoing the 2014 White Paper statement that the judiciary is an administrative organ whose functionaries must be "patriotic". It certainly represents yet another significant step backwards in the political development of HK, a slide toward greater authoritarianism.

What we the people of HK owe Demosistō and LSD is precisely what Joshua Wong said before he went to prison: We have to stay strong, and we have to carry on. The Communist Party and HK government's attacks on the pro-democracy movement are meant, among other things, to affect the general atmosphere in HK, and they certainly have. I spend a lot of time arguing with people over their pessimism. It's not that there isn't reason to be pessimistic; the problem comes when the pessimism leads to defeatism, resignation, fatalism, apathy, giving up. That's just what the Communist Party wants. If HK people follow the lead of Demosistō and LSD, we will win in the long run. The Communist Party's policy on HK is unsustainable because in order to control it, it must destroy it. As long as HK people continue to resist, democracy and self-determination will prevail. In this sense, as always, the freedom struggle is as much a struggle within ourselves as with our adversary.

Advocating independence for Hong Kong is neither illegal nor against the Basic Law

September 19, 2017

In attempting to ban all discussion, let alone advocacy, of independence on campuses across the city, the Hong Kong government, university authorities, and Communist Party allies are waging a campaign of intimidation that runs counter to the letter and spirit of international and HK law.

Recently, HK government officials, university heads and Communist Party allies have declared in chorus (indeed, it seems suspiciously orchestrated) that advocating independence for Hong Kong is illegal and against the Basic Law. Most legal experts, who tend to be pro-democracy, say that it is not illegal, though they seem less certain of whether it violates the Basic Law. Indeed, in a recent interview, University of Hong Kong law professor and co-founder of Occupy Central, Benny Tai was quoted as saying it does.[1] Even the most recent statement by 12 university student unions, who have bravely lead the defense of the right to freedom of expression over the HK independence posters and banners on campuses, only defends the right to "discuss" independence without mentioning whether or not that extends to the right to advocate it.[2]

In this charged environment, it may be useful to clarify that advocacy of independence for HK is neither illegal nor against the Basic Law. (Here, "illegal" means a criminal offense; "against the Basic Law" means unconstitutional.)

Let's start with the issue of illegality since that is more straight-forward. No one has ever been charged with a crime, let alone prosecuted or convicted, related to advocating independence. There is no statute in the Crimes Ordinance which specifically forbids independence advocacy. Basic Law Article 39 states, "The rights and freedoms enjoyed by Hong Kong residents shall not be restricted unless as prescribed by law." In other words, if you say some kind of speech is illegal, you have to point to a law that forbids it; otherwise, it's not only permitted but protected.

Most of those who say independence advocacy is illegal don't bother to cite any law, but those who have, such as two former Bar Association chairs, Ronny Tong[3] and Winnie Tam[4], say that it may violate the statue on seditious intent (Chapter 200, section 9 of the Crimes Ordinance). Since the handover, no one has ever been prosecuted for this crime. It is a problematically vague old colonial relic. It defines seditious intention as an intention to "bring into hatred or contempt or to excite disaffection" against the Queen or HK government or to "raise discontent or disaffection" amongst HK people against same. But firstly, this is an exceedingly low threshold: In general use, seditious speech means that which incites rebellion against a state. Secondly, it is within my right to criticize the government, even with the intent of bringing it "into hatred or contempt or excite disaffection". Indeed, it could be argued the Party and HK government do that better than anyone else, though probably without that intention. And lastly, the banners do no such thing: they advocate a particular political status for HK. The whole issue of HK's political status is unsettled and is surely to arise come the end of the "one country, two systems" period in 2047. Rather than being unlawful to discuss HK's political status, it is responsible to do so and certainly not "seditious" whether intentionally or not.

In 1997, just before the handover, the Legislative Council was for a very brief time controlled by democrats. (At the stroke of midnight, July 1, 1997, the Communist Party kicked them out and installed its own entirely unelected Legco.) That pre-handover Legco contemplated abolishing the seditious intent statute entirely and then decided to keep it, fearing that the Communist Party might use lack of anything of the sort to justify rushing introduction of Article 23 legislation on treason, secession, sedition, subversion and the like. Instead of abolishing it, Legco inserted restrictions intended to prevent it from being misused. As it happened, the Party did rush Article 23 legislation anyway, in 2003, and was roundly defeated by the people of HK who came out to the streets half a million strong to say no. As a result, there are no laws forbidding advocacy of any forms of political status for HK, whether its present form or any other. While the government has rumbled and thundered about independence advocacy's illegality, it's so far taken no action. If it does, it will be a watershed moment for HK, yet another attack on a basic right that will test the independence of the judiciary.

Turning to whether independence advocacy "is against" or "violates" the Basic Law: Really what people who say things like this mean is that it contradicts the Basic Law, which, to be clear, is no crime. They usually refer to Article 1: "The Hong Kong Special Administrative Region is an inalienable part of the People's Republic of China." On the surface, that sounds quite unequivocal, but within constitutional documents such as the Basic Law, there are often tensions between different clauses. Constitutional issues are open to interpretation — that's why many countries have constitutional courts.

Basic Law Article 39 says HK is party to both the International Covenant on Civil and Political Rights and the International Covenant on Economic, Social, and Cultural Rights. The very first right — Article 1 in fact — guaranteed in both the ICCPR and ICESCR (indeed, it's the only right to appear in both) is the right of self-determination, which includes the right of peoples to determine their political status: "All peoples have the right of self-determination. By virtue of that right they freely determine their political status and freely pursue their economic, social and cultural development."

How to resolve the tension between Article 1, which asserts that the HKSAR is an inalienable part of the PRC, and Article 39, which obliges HK to comply with the ICESCR and the ICCPR, including their guarantee of the right of self-determination?

When Article 1 asserts the HKSAR is an inalienable part of the PRC, we should ask, Says who? Who made the Basic Law? It certainly wasn't HK people. In fact, HK people had no formal or representative participation in its articulation. The whole process was controlled by the Communist Party. And HK people had no opportunity to formally approve the Basic Law, for example by a referendum; it was imposed upon them. Indeed, in their entire modern history, under both British colonial and now Communist Party rule, HK people have never been granted the right of self-determination, which includes the right to determine their political status. If HK people had formally agreed to being handed over by the UK to the PRC, had participated in the articulation of the Basic Law, and had voted in free and fair referendums to be transferred to PRC sovereignty and to approve the Basic Law, one might say, HK people, you have made your bed and now you must sleep in it. But that is not the case. HK people have never made their bed; it's always been made by someone else. And no state has the right to determine a people's political status on their behalf, especially by incorporating them into said state without their formal approval.

From the point of view of international law, therefore, in the case of HK, the right of self-determination trumps state claims to sovereignty. Even international law experts who argue for a very restrictive interpretation of the right of self-determination allow that when rights have been denied and there is no other recourse to gain them, the right of self-determination is invoked.[5] Surely, even according to the strictest interpretation, the Communist Party's denial of genuine universal suffrage on 31 August 2014 triggered this right. Indeed, we could say that a dictatorship not only denying a people their right of self-determination but then declaring their territory an inalienable part of the state ruled by the dictatorship and then on top of that, refusing to fulfill the legal obligation to grant them full and genuine universal suffrage, is the very definition of tyranny.

Thus, HK people are perfectly within their rights, as articulated in both the Basic Law and international law, to advocate independence and to determine their political status.

If I were to make this case before the HK High Court, would the judges rule in my favor? Probably not: They tend to be conservative, hewing closely and selectively to precedent, and pay little heed to HK's obligations under international treaties to which HK is party. On top of that, the right of self-determination has never been specifically "implemented through laws of the HKSAR", as Article 39 requires HK to do. And even if the judges did rule in my favor, ultimately HK is not ruled by law but by an entity called the National People's Congress Standing Committee, which is not an independent judicial organ but essentially an arm of the Communist Party. So HK is ruled not by law but by the Communist Party. And the chances of *it* ever ruling in my favor... well, that happens to be one of the reasons many think HK will never get justice (or genuine universal suffrage) under this regime and that some other solution, such as independence, must be found to guarantee HK people's full democratic and political rights.

Assessing the Umbrella Movement three years on

September 25, 2017

Hong Kong's Umbrella Movement accomplished much more than conventional wisdom gives it credit for but had serious limitations that the pro-democracy movement still has not addressed.

Not long after the end of the occupations in December 2014, I started to hear participants say things like, "We accomplished nothing." Most though not all of these voices belonged to young people. I was a bit taken aback because during the occupations, most occupiers had quite realistic expectations. No one thought the Communist Party was suddenly going to see the light and hand genuine universal suffrage to HK on a platter. Why, then, this downbeat, categorical assessment afterwards?

After so many had fought so long and hard, camping out on the streets for 79 days, being teargassed, peppersprayed, beaten and arrested by police, the bitterness was understandable: It's one thing to know something in your head, another to feel it deep in your heart. In the aftermath of the Umbrella Movement, it was dawning on many HK people, especially young people, just how deeply unjust their society was. They were coming to terms with the "nature of the beast", the Communist Party, their implacable adversary which had spent over sixty years jealously guarding its monopoly on power on the mainland, annihilating any challenge to it. Existing as they did a step removed from the full force of that power, a good many HK people hadn't fully understood the Communist Party. But they did now. Or it was dawning on them with awful clarity. Accompanying this growing awareness of injustice and of the ruthlessness of the oppressor was a deep sense of powerlessness. Much of the disillusionment turned inward: people were disappointed with themselves and with the leaders of the occupations.

But while emotionally understandable and partially accurate, the assessment that the Umbrella Movement accomplished nothing disregards a wide array of positive outcomes, both intended and not. While some can be classified as objectives met others are perhaps more like side effects. A fuller understanding of what the movement was about, what it did and did not accomplish, is, among other things, useful in strategizing for the future.

In one sense, "We accomplished nothing" is right: The Communist Party made no concrete concessions nor even exhibited a willingness to engage, let alone negotiate. The Umbrella Movement did not lead to genuine universal suffrage. On the surface, it did not force the Party to budge an inch.

The Umbrella Movement's lack of accomplishment of any concrete immediate positive objective was not dissimilar to the cases of many other recent nonviolent popular movements and uprisings going back to the huge global demonstrations against the invasion of Iraq in 2003 and up through the Occupy movement and the Arab Spring. These movements are all different from one another, but a clear pattern is emerging: It's become harder for nonviolent political movements to accomplish concrete positive objectives in the short term.

But there is a difference between acknowledging the fact that the key positive objective of genuine suffrage hasn't been accomplished and saying that nothing has been.

Before outlining the movement's main accomplishments and failings, it's important to consider a few important contexts.

The Umbrella Movement was the largest manifestation of resistance to Communist Party rule since the 1989 demonstrations across China. While those demonstrations were violently crushed, the Umbrella Movement fought the Communist Party to a draw: Neither was able to achieve its primary aim (for the movement, genuine suffrage; for the Party, fake).

Once the Communist Party came out with its decision of 31 August 2014 that virtually ruled out genuine universal suffrage, it committed itself irrevocably to taking a hard line on HK. From that point on, it could not show the least bit of "weakness". This hardline stance is a Communist specialty, and more so than ever under Xi Jinping. It is similar to Party policy on Taiwan, Tibet and Xinjiang, which in turn is based on an awareness that the Communist empire is contested at its peripheries. Indeed, from the Tibetan uprising of 2008 to unrest in Xinjiang to the Sunflower Movement of Taiwan and the HK Umbrella Movement of 2014, we see a clear pattern of resistance to Party rule (in the case of the Sunflower Movement, Party influence).

In all of these places, it hasn't gotten the loyalty and obedience it wants. And whenever people rise up, its reflex is repression: it's backed itself into a corner with its hardline policies. Of course, the underlying reason for this is that it rules by force and without the formal consent of any of its people. So if you think the Umbrella Movement failed, just look at the messes the Party's made for itself all over its empire. From 31 August 2014 onward, then, it was fairly certain what the Party response would be to any mass resistance in HK. Indeed, resort to use of the military was more likely than substantial concessions.

Also important to remember is that the occupations began spontaneously as a form of resistance rather than as an expression of a positive demand. They were first and foremost a big NO to the eight-hour-long police teargas attack on HK citizens on 28 September and to the fake suffrage stipulated in the 31 August ruling. Of course, demonstrators desired genuine suffrage; that was their primary positive objective. But they also wished to block the worst, fake suffrage, from happening, and in this, they succeeded: The Umbrella Movement torpedoed any chance of an HK government proposal based on the 31 August ruling ever passing in the Legislative Council. And sure enough, the Communist Party's fake suffrage was defeated on 18 June 2015.

If "We accomplished nothing" is true, the same can be said for the Communist Party. Fake suffrage was an important part of the Party's plan to bring HK under its full control far before 2047. With fake suffrage, the Party would have achieved a complete and final stranglehold over the formal political system. Since it called what it was proposing "universal suffrage", it would have also been relieved of the legal obligation enshrined in the Basic Law to introduce it. It would have been under no further legal obligation to allow any subsequent political development in HK whatsoever. Fake suffrage was checkmate. For this reason, defeating fake suffrage, while a long way from achieving the realization of genuine suffrage, was a crucial accomplishment. It also fulfilled the original objective of the demonstrators, to say no.

In this sense, judging by the criterion of the spontaneous motivation to come out to the streets on 28 September, the Umbrella Movement accomplished its primary objective. Indeed, whenever HK people have had the power to do so—Article 23 "security" legislation in 2003, the national education curriculum in 2012, the fake suffrage of 2015—, they have consistently thwarted the Communist Party's efforts to exert greater control over HK.

The Umbrella Movement can be considered to have "failed", to have "accomplished nothing" only if it is regarded as the climax of a campaign, rather than part of a much longer history of political struggle which began long before the movement and will continue far into the future. In that broader context, the accomplishments of the Umbrella Movement were various and profound:

It drew much greater attention, both in HK and internationally, to the Communist Party's stepped-up efforts at mainlandization (political control coupled with infrastructural, economic and cultural integration of HK with the mainland) and brought the political situation in HK to the attention of the rest of the world in a way that no other event had ever done before, establishing HK as contested political territory.

It brought HK to a new stage in the struggle for democracy and self-determination, initiating an era of long-term resistance, cultivating a deep and healthy distrust of the Communist Party that pervades greater swathes of HK society than ever before, and, with that, increased vigilance.

It did more than any other event to promote a politically conscious and active citizenship, and this especially amongst a huge majority of young people—upwards of 80 to 90 percent—who are in favor of democracy and genuine autonomy. This resistance is a factor that the Party will have to contend with for years and perhaps even generations to come; indeed, it could outlast the Party itself. It is not going too far to say that the fate of HK rests on what this generation of young people decides to do.

It raised the political awareness of HK people generally, and especially that of many previously apolitical people. They realized how emotionally attached to HK they are. They strongly identify with it and want to defend it. It got people talking politics and thinking about the future of the city. It made more people aware of HK's many deficits, of the failings of the HK government, and the relationship between the city's drawbacks and the fact that it lacks democracy. And it motivated a larger number of people than ever to stand up for themselves and for HK.

It made HK less submissive, less controllable. As Jacques Semelin said in reference to civil resistance to Hitler in occupied Europe, "When a society feels less and less submissive, it becomes more and more uncontrollable. Then even if the occupier keeps its power, it loses its authority." That's HK today.

The Umbrella Movement delegitimized Communist Party rule in HK and made people see more clearly than ever before what the Party was doing to HK. What government can fail to respond to such a huge number of its citizens in such great open rebellion that they take over large parts of the city for months and retain even vestigial legitimacy? Because of the unfulfilled promise of universal suffrage, HK was already in perpetual political crisis before the Umbrella Movement, but the movement made the contradictions and injustices of Party rule even more acute. And the only way the Party knew how to respond, doing nothing to reform and instead tightening the screws, has discredited it further. This model of governance—an essentially unelected government whose first priority is to implement the agenda of the Communist Party in a city of citizens aware of and demanding their rights—is unsustainable, however stable it may sometimes appear on the surface.

Related to the above, the movement specifically doomed Chief Executive Leung Chun-ying and his administration to illegitimacy and ineffectuality. One of the very first and most concrete demands the movement made was that Leung resign to take responsibility for failed political reform and the police teargas attacks. I recall clearly at the time many long-time China watchers scoffed at the idea that the movement could force the Party to dump Leung. Oh, I said to them, it may not come now, but it will come, it will come. Remember Tung Chee-hwa? He was actually the first CE whose reign was terminated due to a people's movement, the half-million-person march in 2003 against the Party-directed Article 23 "security" legislation. He resigned for "medical reasons" in 2005. In 2016, Leung decided not to run for a second term for "family reasons". He had rendered himself so unpopular by doing the Party's dirty work that the Party dumped him. Both Tung and Leung had their reigns shattered by people's movements against Party attempts to impose its will. The only CE to complete his two allotted terms so far is Donald Tsang, and he was subsequently convicted of corruption and sentenced to prison for crimes committed while in office. There's no greater indictment of the HK governance model than the fact that even in a system where the CE is appointed rather than elected, he still cannot complete two terms.

The Umbrella Movement was an ultimatum to the Communist Party: Either you give us what you promised, or all bets are off; the implicit social contract of the last seventeen years, according to which we grudgingly went along with your rule in exchange for you fulfilling your promise of allowing real autonomy and granting genuine suffrage, is torn up and we start from scratch. We will no longer wait around for you to deliver, we will take our fate into our hands. There is a growing awareness that it is the Basic Law itself that is problematic (or the Party's interpretation of it, which amounts to the same thing), and fewer people will abide by it as the basis of a just political solution for HK. Indeed, the suffrage struggle lead to today's calls for self-determination and independence.

The Umbrella Movement brought into relief two clearly contrasting sets of values, those of HK and the pro-democracy movement, on the one hand, and the Communist Party's authoritarian political culture, on the other. It provided a vision of just what a better place HK could be — fairer, more egalitarian, more communitarian, more vibrant, caring, generous and creative, happier, and of course, more democratic. This vision stands in stark contrast to what the Party wants it to be — authoritarian, rigidly hierarchical, inegalitarian, docile, passive, prostrate, obedient, plodding, cutthroat capitalistic and exploitative, resigned and pessimistic. For the Party, the model HK citizen is the dull and unswervingly loyal HK government political appointee: He can't think for himself, but he's good at executing orders. The Umbrella Movement vision is a template for a different sort of society not governed by the dictates of authoritarian turbo-capitalism with political and economic power concentrated in the hands of a tiny minority. The movement's art, creativity, anarchic collaboration, egalitarianism, communalism, emphasis on values other than the economic, idealism, generosity of spirit and action, dedication, commitment to the common good, to ideals higher than oneself, one's pocketbook, one's family, opened HK people's eyes to one another, to a common HK identity both already existing and still emerging, and to the possibilities of a truly self-governed, democratic HK. This heartened people and gave them confidence in themselves, their comrades, their allies, the better angels of HK's nature. People who participated in and were inspired by the occupations continue to resist and to fight for justice in ways big and small, as a movement, in groups and as individuals in many areas of society. They carry the flame of the movement deep in their hearts.

The Umbrella Movement dealt a blow to the international reputation of the Communist Party, as it became clear that it had no intention to fulfill its legal obligations. While the Party exercises greater economic and military influence globally than ever before, its "soft power", its ability to inspire any kind of affinity based on the attraction of its system as a political model and of its society as a cultural model is close to zero.

The Umbrella Movement smashed any hope the Communist Party may have had that Taiwan would ever willingly reconcile with the mainland as it is now ruled. The last thing Taiwanese want is to become like HK.

The Umbrella Movement accomplished all of the above nonviolently and with courage and dignity in the face of violent attacks by the police and thugs. It preserved the moral upper hand. It showed that nonviolent resistance is, among other things, the most sustainable option, working as a platform for future action, even if it doesn't necessarily immediately lead to the fulfillment of the most desired objectives.

That list of accomplishments and successes is far from everything but it is certainly more than nothing.

But then what were the movement's failures and limitations? What were the main reasons it was not able to accomplish its primary positive objective of genuine suffrage?

Simply put, it didn't have enough power to force the Communist Party to grant it.

Why didn't it have enough power? There are three main reasons: It didn't have enough people, it hadn't the capacity to "escalate outward" effectively, and it failed to convince supporters of the Party to withdraw their support or defect to the other side.

Estimates for participation in the occupations themselves range from 836,000 to 1,300,000. That's between 13 and 20 percent of the 6,401,600 HK people over the age of 15. In addition to that, there were the nearly 800,000 who voted in the Occupy Central with Love and Peace referendum on universal suffrage of 22 to 29 June 2014 and the 510,000 who marched on 1 July that year. In all, in events ranging from the 22–29 June 2014 OCLP referendum to the defeat of fake suffrage in June 2015, an estimated 2,156,000 to 2,620,000 people participated—an astounding 33 to 40 percent of the over-15 population. Even if one assumes that many people participated in all events, the referendum, the march and the occupations, that is still an extraordinary participation rate. Scholar of nonviolent resistance Erica Chenoweth says that most any movement with a participation rate of 3.5 percent is likely to succeed. The Umbrella Movement far exceeded that. But still, that was not enough. Too many HK people, for whatever reason, decided not to get involved at a historically crucial moment. This was indeed a weakness, but not really one for which the movement itself could be blamed; it was a general problem of HK people.

One could also argue that indeed enough people participated but those huge numbers could eventually be contained because of the movement's biggest internal weakness, its inability to "escalate outward" when the moment demanded. It couldn't expand the movement beyond street occupations. Past a certain point, it was insufficient to just have people in the streets or even to use those people to, for example, surround government buildings. The problem was that, going into the movement, which, again, began spontaneously, the pro-democracy movement and civil society generally were organizationally too weak and without the requisite culture to accomplish outward escalation. That would have meant, for example, labor union strikes, rent strikes of public housing tenants (who make up about half of all HK people), and economic boycotts of entities supporting the Communist Party. Imagine, for instance, if teachers, bus drivers and MTR train drivers went on strike. Both the Confederation of Trade Unions and the Professional Teachers Union called strikes in response to the police teargas attacks of 28 September, but little came of them. Traditionally, the pro-democracy movement had been weak at organizing, and it showed in the Umbrella Movement, when it needed to be able to call on a base of already-organized people to mobilize in different areas of society. As a result of the movement's inability to escalate outward, the Communist Party was reassured after the first week or so that it could be contained, and thus it and the HK government adopted the strategy of simply waiting it out.

The movement's other big weakness was an inability to get supporters of the regime to either defect or withdraw their support. Most nonviolent resistance movements that succeed are able to persuade the security apparatuses protecting the regime or the business elements that see themselves as benefitting from it to calculate that they'd be better off no longer supporting it. Loyalist defections are identified by nonviolent resistance scholars as amongst the most decisive turning points. But no one amongst the HK tycoons and business establishment, the pro-Party media, HK government political appointees or civil service or the HK police, let alone the Communist Party's army or mainland Chinese citizens changed sides or even withdrew support. Again, this had the effect of reassuring the Communist Party that it could wait the movement out since it wasn't eroding support amongst its allies.

There were other weaknesses—in leadership, strategy, communication, coordination and decision-making—but these were not of decisive significance, nor was the fact that the movement received no significant moral or rhetorical support from foreign governments.

Weighing all of the above, the conclusion is that there was little else the Umbrella Movement might have accomplished, considering the circumstances, and that what it did accomplish was of great significance. It was a watershed of HK history. Its legacy will be felt for years to come. Indeed, we are living in the post-Umbrella Movement era: Virtually every significant political development in HK since then has its origins in the movement or reactions against it.

Unfortunately, the assessment that "we accomplished nothing" has lead to wrong lessons being learnt. In the aftermath of the movement, there were recriminations and disunity amongst various factions within the HK pro-democracy movement which should have, over the past three years, been collaborating and cultivating a sense of common purpose. The underlying weakness of an insufficiently organized civil society generally and pro-democracy movement in particular has not been addressed. Much of the deep pessimism that can easily be found amongst activists and others in HK these days might also be tempered by greater confidence in our own power. Pessimism risks becoming fatalism or defeatism or resignation, which is exactly what the Communist Party wants. When it comes to power, the Party sees everything as a zero-sum game: its goal is the absolute annihilation or submission of the enemy. Don't do the Party's work for it.

The real lessons to be learned from the Umbrella Movement are the necessity for unity and solidarity amongst all those in HK who want democracy and self-determination and the importance of addressing the pro-democracy movement's underlying weaknesses in strategy, organization and mobilization. For HK, there is always hope as long as people continue to resist, especially if they do so in unity and solidarity and with a clear goal and plan to achieve it.

Three years on, the fallout from the Umbrella Movement determines the politics of Hong Kong today

October 3, 2017

Virtually every major aspect of the political situation in HK today has its origins in the Umbrella Movement, with an illegitimate and outmoded political system in perpetual crisis and a pro-democracy movement searching for the way forward.

The rise of localism; a nascent self-determination movement; candidates disqualified on political grounds from running for Legislative Council seats; Umbrella Movement leaders and grassroots activists getting elected to Legco… and then six of them getting disqualified for the way they took their oaths (but in reality for their political views); the elaborate charade of the Chief Executive "election" that installed the deputy of the deeply unpopular predecessor; prosecutions of 26 pro-democracy leaders and hundreds of ordinary activists and the jailing of 16 of them….

This does not look like a stable, just, well-functioning or legitimate political system based on the will of the people.

HK has been in slow-burn political crisis for many years, but in the aftermath of the Umbrella Movement, the dysfunctionality, injustice and illegality of its formal political system have become more acute and lead to alarming developments, including greater persecution.

The Party

From the above characterization, one might conclude that the 2014 struggle for genuine universal suffrage "did no good", but the current situation is to be expected when those responsible for it, the Communist Party and HK government, refuse to even acknowledge very basic structural problems of governance, let alone address them. The system is cracking while the rulers pretend everything's o.k. Controlled by the largest dictatorship in the world, this system purports to have aspects of liberal democracy such as rule of law and protections of some political and civil rights, while the leader, the Chief Executive, is appointed by the Party to do its bidding amongst a populace ever more resistant to Party imposition. The question is whether it will reach a point at which it can no longer bear the burden of its deep contradictions.

It doesn't exactly suit the Communist Party to have HK in such a mess, for it reflects poorly on its rule, but the Party far prefers the status quo to any of the alternatives, in particular, to genuine suffrage and autonomy. It hopes to slowly but surely tighten its grip on virtually every area of society, but in doing so, it may strangle the city entirely, the Party's hold a potential death grip. Its main lesson from the Umbrella Movement was that it had to make the hard line even harder. It has stepped up efforts to control and mainlandize in the hope of eventually forcing surrender and obedience.

The pro-democracy movement

While the Party's boxed itself in by its own hardline position, the pro-democracy movement, in all its fractious diversity, is, as ever, trying to get its act together and figuring out which objectives and strategies to adopt.

On 20 August, a march was held to show solidarity with 16 activists who had been sentenced the previous week to six to 13 months in prison for the non-violent protest-related crime of unlawful assembly. Amongst them were Joshua Wong, Alex Chow and Nathan Law, imprisoned for seven, six and eight months respectively for their roles in the occupation of Civic Square on 26 September 2014, which triggered the street occupations that became known to the world as the Umbrella Movement. The march turnout was unexpectedly high—in excess of 100,000 people, I estimated[1]—, and generally agreed to be the biggest demonstration since the Umbrella Movement. Apart from the high turnout, most striking was the diversity of the participants. Of course, there were the die-hard pro-democracy marchers who have seemed to be the only ones consistently showing up at demonstrations for much of the nearly three-year period since the Umbrella Movement. But in addition to them were groups that had been shunning demonstrations as ineffectual, in particular, localists such as Hong

Kong Indigenous and many students and young people. The reason was clear: All of the 16 imprisoned activists were young, many were students, and many were associated with the more radical wing of the pro-democracy movement. (By "radical" here, I mean more willing to engage in direct action and make political demands which go beyond the traditional pan-democratic demand for genuine universal suffrage in compliance with the Basic Law.)

Edward Leung, the Hong Kong Indigenous leader, said after the march, "Even though, in the past, we have different strategies [and] different ideologies during the whole struggle, at this moment we think stand[ing] in solidarity is the most important thing today, so that the government will know that we are not really afraid. Even though we are facing huge political oppression."[2]

To which I say: Great, you're right, but what took you (and just about everyone else in the pro-democracy movement) so long?! Hopefully this is the beginning of a new phase of solidarity, unity and cooperation. Time will tell. If there was any lesson that should have been learned from the Umbrella Movement, it was the necessity of unity, of common purpose, of better coordination and cooperation between groups within the pro-democracy movement (understood in its widest sense to encompass also localist and pro-independence groups). That doesn't mean that everyone needs to have the exact same agenda, just that everyone needs to recognize we're allies, on the same side, with a common adversary, and it strengthens us all to work together.

In December 2014, towards the end of the Umbrella Movement, leaders such as Benny Tai (now on trial) and Alex Chow (now in prison) proposed that a coalition or coordinating body be set up afterwards. But that is not what occurred. Instead, ensuing developments could be characterized as "fragmentation", if you choose to put a negative spin on it, or "ferment, innovation and initiative", if you prefer the positive.

Things moved so quickly it was hard to keep up. There was the virtual disintegration of Hong Kong Federation of Students through a disaffiliation referendum campaign, resulting in five student unions leaving HKFS, including the largest and most influential, the University of Hong Kong's. There was the rise of localism and the high-profile anti-parallel trade protests. There was the founding of new political parties like Demosistō, Youngspiration and Democracy Groundwork. There were the Chinese New Year 2016 clashes in Mong Kok between police and protesters, many of whom came from localist backgrounds. There was the remarkable success of new, young candidates in the 2016 Legislative Council elections, including Chu Hoi-dick (who got more votes than any other Legco candidate ever), Nathan Law, Lau Siu-lai, Baggio Leung, Yau Wai-ching, Cheng Chung-tai and others.

All of this happened almost as if through a process of spontaneous combustion. No one controlled it, and sometimes there seemed little rhyme or reason to it. Out of these action-packed three years since the Umbrella Movement, what has emerged in terms of ideologies, objectives and strategies? Is the whole wide spectrum of the pro-democracy movement really any closer to the kind of mutual solidarity and cooperation which Edward Leung advocated on 20 August?

Looking back to look forward

In the aftermath of the Umbrella Movement, two key questions faced young people especially: 1) where to go in terms of ideology and objective and 2) whether or not to seek to participate in the rigged formal political system.

For many, the Communist Party's refusal to allow genuine universal suffrage, in spite of the huge pro-suffrage campaign, was a clear signal that it will never grant real suffrage. That refusal effectively tore up the implied contract of the last twenty years between Party and HK people, according to which HK people would grudgingly recognize the Party's sovereignty over HK in return for the Party grudgingly allowing HK people to elect their own Chief Executive and representatives in the Legislative Council (currently only half of the 70 are elected according to principles of universal suffrage). Now that the Party has not only showed that it will not honor its pledge but is also further tightening the screws on HK, what to do?

The main ideological responses to this dilemma have been to call for either self-determination or independence, both of which eschew as futile the decades-long demand that the Party comply with the Basic Law and international law and enact genuine suffrage. Indeed, these positions regard the whole Basic Law skeptically as an impediment to their aims rather than the guarantor of their rights (the premise heretofore). Now that the Party has reneged on its promise, all bets are off, and HK must go its own way.

The self-determinationists, such as Demosistō and Chu Hoi-dick, stress that HK people have never in their history had the right to decide their political status, even though this is a basic human right, the only one that appears—as

Article 1 no less—in both seminal international human rights treaties, the International Covenant on Civil and Political Rights and the International Covenant on Economic, Social and Cultural Rights. (HK is party to both covenants and Basic Law Article 39 obliges it to uphold all rights in both.) Self-determination encompasses all possible options, from full assimilation with the People's Republic of China to perpetuation of the "one country, two systems" policy to full independence. Whatever the case, the argument goes, it should be up to the HK people to decide.

Those advocating independence say self-determination is just pussy-footing around; HK would be far better off independent, and it's important to stand strong for a clear, unambiguous goal.

The localists

Since the Umbrella Movement, localism has undoubtedly been the most influential political force, not so much in terms of the impact of specific localist groups as in terms of the appeal of its ethos of defending HK and asserting a distinct HK identity. There has been great enthusiasm for this newfound "HK nationalism" across wide swathes of society, including many who wouldn't identify themselves as localists.

In June 2015, at the protests outside of the Legislative Council just before the defeat of the HK government's fake suffrage proposal, Joshua Wong was already starting to articulate his ideas about self-determination. These were clearly influenced by localism. Even more traditional pan-democratic parties such as Civic Party[3] and ADPL[4] published manifestoes with localism-tinged statements. The localists were obviously on to something, both in terms of identifying a major issue, the mainlandization of HK, and tapping into the desires and resentments of HK people, especially young people.

But localist groups have largely failed to articulate a positive vision or an overall strategy for combatting mainlandization. Some localists have advocated independence, but beyond saying they think HK should be independent, they've done little to flesh out that idea, let alone sketch out a road map leading to that goal. The manifestations of mainlandization in HK are numerous, and the Party has stepped up its efforts to control and integrate HK with the mainland. A serious comprehensive localist strategy would identify these and devise ways of opposing them.

Instead, the localists have largely confined themselves to street protests. While the anti-parallel trade protests of spring 2015 resonated because many in HK found parallel trading and the related presence of tens of millions of mainland tourists per year annoying, in the bigger scheme of things, parallel trading doesn't even rank close to the top of the list of threats posed by mainlandization.

Localism was the main influence on the campaigns for university student unions to disaffiliate themselves from HKFS. These achieved their immediate goal of the disaffiliation of five student unions, but they destroyed a perhaps flawed but influential organization without replacing it with anything else.

Indeed, much of the localists' political work has had a nihilistic edge to it, and also a tendency toward what Liu Xiaobo would call "enemy thinking", an at-times xenophobic tinge and a propensity to attack its natural allies. This has lead to little to no cooperation with others in the pro-democracy movement (indeed, some localists even go so far as to disavow belonging to that movement). Localist anger at their elders in the resistance is understandable, but acting it out has not been politically astute.

On top of all that, their role in the Mong Kok clashes with police during Chinese New Year 2016 has put them on the defensive. Through prosecutions, the Hong Kong government is attempting to decimate them, and they've all but gone underground. In fact, the 20 August march was the first time in ages I'd seen groups like Hong Kong Indigenous, replete with banners, out in public.

Localist groups have been strategically naïve, taking the substantial momentum they had and driving it down a dead-end street. There are still many in HK, especially young people, with a generally localist outlook, but localism as a political force appears stalled and even threatened, much of the damage being essentially self-inflicted.

While calls for HK independence have attracted a lot of media attention and Party opprobrium, there isn't really a pro-independence movement. A lot of sentiment in the city leans in that direction, and these days even a good many middle-of-the-road people dream of independence, but that's different from it emerging as a political force. So far, the HK National Party is the only one to advocate independence as part of its platform. While many in the media have characterized Baggio Leung and Yau Wai-ching as "pro-independence" and they have made statements encouraging such characterization, their party, Youngspiration, has not officially advocated independence. In fact, its original position was much closer to that of Demosistō: It too called for a referendum to determine HK's political status.

It remains to be seen whether any actual political movement will grow out of the groundswell of grassroots enthusiasm for independence. The recent appearance of HK independence banners and posters at six universities in the first week of the school year indicated both that the aspiration is alive and, because almost all were put up anonymously, the trepidation independence advocates feel about stepping out of the shadows given the intimidation by the Party and HK government.

The crucial question regarding both self-determination and independence is, how to get there? Their advocates are often criticized for being "unrealistic". But after the fake suffrage fiasco of 2014–2015, can it really be said that continuing to demand genuine universal suffrage is any more realistic than, say, self-determination or independence? The dilemma of the HK people is that we have no "realistic" recourse to gain our basic human rights, whether the right to universal suffrage or the right of self-determination.

The head-on collision: when localists and self-determinationists tried to enter the system

After the Umbrella Movement, apart from the question of which ideological position to adopt in response to the Party's refusal to grant genuine suffrage, there was the question of whether or not to attempt to enter the formal political system. To do so would risk conferring legitimacy on a system that both independence advocates and self-determinationists regard as illegitimate, while not doing so would lock them out of a platform for propagating their ideas. Eventually, virtually all decided to run for Legco.

The result has been like watching a head-on collision. First, the Electoral Affairs Commission, a governmental agency, disqualified some candidates on political grounds, due to suspicions that they did not truly, deep in their hearts, accept the Basic Law, especially Article 1 which asserts that the Hong Kong Special Administration Region is an inalienable part of the People's Republic of China. In spite of this, the new candidates who were allowed to run did remarkably well.

The Party and HK government couldn't abide their success and tried to kick out as many out as possible. They have succeeded so far in ejecting six,

Baggio Leung, Yau Wai-ching, Leung Kwok-hung, Lau Siu-lai, Nathan Law and Edward Yiu. This has sent the message that there is no room for the political views of a great many HK people inside a political system that is rigged to begin with, further constricting the political space in HK. (The six received 185,727 votes, over 8 percent of the 2,202,283 total votes cast.)[5]

In flushing them out, the Party and HK government have put their finger on an inherent tension: Can you have so many representatives operating within a system which they do not regard as illegitimate? Up to now, pan-democrats have sat in Legco even though they do not accept the lack of universal suffrage, but they never questioned the political status of HKSAR as "an inalienable part of the PRC". Now the Party was faced with the prospect of a growing number of representatives who regarded the Basic Law and "one country, two systems" as failed and in need of substantial reform if not replacement.

Democratic political systems that work are based on wide consensus that the system is legitimate. When a substantial portion of the population does not consent to the political system, there is a political crisis. Such is the situation in HK at the moment. Rather than acknowledging and addressing the problems, the Party and HK government's response to this crisis has been to further restrict participation, going beyond the tried and true rigged system—which guarantees that the CE and a majority in Legco are Party loyalists—to devising new methods (EAC disqualifications, Basic Law "interpretation", disqualifications of elected Legco members, and criminal prosecutions which render threatening potential candidates ineligible to run) to simply exclude those who symbolize the lack of consent. These actions accomplish little more than to further discredit the system.

The pan-democrats

The traditional pan-democrats, meanwhile, have largely buried their heads in the sand. Their response to the Party's denial of universal suffrage has been to continue to demand universal suffrage. They can sometimes seem to be caught in a time warp: Hello? Didn't the Party already rule that out?

Their decision to support establishmentarian par excellence John Tsang in this year's Chief Executive selection threw into question whether they had learned much at all from the Umbrella Movement. The pan-democrats had several hundred votes, more than ever before, in the closed-circle process involving about 1,200 electors, but there were no pro-democracy candidates. Though reluctant, Long Hair declared his candidacy, as he believed there needed to be a protest candidate. The pan-democrats didn't back him since he stood no chance of getting elected. Instead, styling themselves kingmakers, they went for John Tsang, the Finance Secretary in the despised Leung Chun-ying administration. Not only was Tsang about as firmly establishment as you can get, his financial policies had for years been to the detriment of the great majority of HK people, contributing to the greatest income inequality in the world amongst developed economies. It was as if the pan-democrats didn't understand that the CE selection is rigged, the result predetermined by the Communist Party. Their support for an establishment candidate with no track record of advocating genuine suffrage leant legitimacy to what, from the perspective of international law, is an illegal process (for it constitutes the appointment of the head of the government by means other than universal suffrage). After all these years, how could they be so naive? Their actions cast serious doubt on their acumen as political strategists as well as on how clearly they are able to see the nature of their adversary after all these years. The pan-democrats have some good young politicians and a solid vote bank, representing moderate voters, so they have a recipe for survival, and their ability to work within the system to express displeasure with the government and frustrate its efforts to enact unjust policies is valuable, but it's hard to see how they can possibly take the lead in finding a way forward. They operate ever more as traditional political parties in a system that is acutely distorted.

Making the most of the era of resistance

The above characterizations of localists, self-determinationists and pan-democrats might lead some to conclude that the pro-democracy movement is directionless and diffuse. There's some truth to that, but it's also developing and not necessarily that far from consolidation.

Many within the movement have lamented a lack of leadership, and in particular of charismatic leadership, but one shouldn't wish for a savior. The strength of the movement is that it's based on the people. Remember: It wasn't because OCLP or HKFS gave the command that the Umbrella Movement took off—the people followed their own conscience. Basically what those looking for strong leadership mean is they want a unifying figure, a Mandela. But we are capable of achieving that unity ourselves. There are lots of good leaders out there, pretty much across the pro-democracy spectrum. Joshua Wong, Nathan

Law, Long Hair, Fernando Cheung, Adrian Yeung, Ted Hui, Lau Siu-lai, Chu Hoi-dick are the ones who immediately come to mind, but there are plenty of others.

Leadership isn't really the main problem of the pro-democracy movement. The key weaknesses are lack of unity and insufficient strategizing and organizing, and these have been present for years, preceding the Umbrella Movement. Independent civil society is still weak. Pro-democracy political parties are pathetically small. For that reason, when the Umbrella Movement needed to "escalate outwards", for example through labor stoppages and rent and consumer boycotts, it hadn't the culture or organizational foundation upon which to do so. The pro-democracy movement needn't and shouldn't be Leninist (like the Party), but it needs to be less laissez-faire and more pro-active in comprehensively and strategically diagnosing and addressing its deficits.

What is needed at the moment is a kind of council bringing the whole pro-democracy spectrum together. It would foster unity and solidarity as well as coordination, communication, and strategic thinking and planning. Maybe, after the 20 August demonstration, the movement is finally ready for what Benny Tai and Alex Chow proposed way back in December 2014. Call it the Resistance Coalition. The need for resistance, after all, is something all groups can agree on, whether localist or self-determinationist or pan-democrat, whatever their other differences.

Apart from resistance, which is essentially defensive, the movement also needs to work toward a positive goal. Here, the umbrella term can be self-determination. Thus, a Resistance and Self-Determination Coalition. Even a good many pan-democrats espouse what they call "internal self-determination", which pretty much means simply what was promised to HK by the Party to begin with, namely, a "high degree of autonomy", so it shouldn't be all that hard to unite under that term.

As with all coalitions, it would mean everyone compromising in some area. Pan-democrats and localists would have to swallow their dislike of one another. Pan-democrats would also have to stand up to the Party propaganda that would brand them crypto-independence advocates for even associating with localists. The localists, in turn, would have to agree to not advocate violence and also downplay any independence aspirations they may have.

We are in the era of resistance, and this truth must be embraced. Much of the disillusionment in the aftermath of the Umbrella Movement was due to a desire for quick fixes or magical solutions. We must rid ourselves of that illusion and see long-term resistance as the effective strategy that it is. Indeed, the fact that widespread resistance exists is in itself an accomplishment as well as a foundation upon which to build the future. It's often said that it's very hard to mobilize people around most any long-term objective; people will much more readily come out in reaction to something in particular, like the jailing of the 16 political prisoners in August. But resistance is a culture. It needs to be cultivated, and rather than grim, it can and should be very joyful.

The Resistance and Self-determination Coalition would, in one sense, function much as the working group that already exists amongst pan-democrats in Legco but be broader and embrace groups both in and outside of Legco. It would work at articulating and coordinating both defensive strategies and tactics—how to prevent the worst from happening, how to resist—and positive ones—how to move toward fulfilling the movement's goals and objectives, how to attain self-determination.

Apart from providing leadership to the movement, it must also work to strengthen the presence of the resistance at the grassroots level, through local committees in neighborhoods and public housing estates, so that it has a presence everywhere in the city. In short, the movement has to organize.

There is a difference between mobilizing and organizing. The pro-democracy movement is pretty good at mobilizing, getting people out on the streets. But it's poor at organizing. That's where the focus needs to be. A more organized movement would also make it easier to mobilize when necessary.

Most in the pro-democracy movement are still wedded to a mobilization model. In this sense, very little's changed since the Umbrella Movement. According to that model, you have a small cohort of activists who are basically doing it full-time, surrounded by a small core of supporters who can be counted on to mobilize whenever needed. Between them and the masses, there is a large gap. This leaves the full-time activists and their supporters isolated and the masses passive and uninvolved, except on the few occasions, like the Umbrella Movement, when they're motivated to join in.

The gap between the full-time activists and their supporters, on the one hand, and the masses on the other needs to be bridged in a long-lasting way, not just a one-off. The pro-democracy movement has to have a presence in every community in the city, every neighborhood, every public housing estate, and that presence has to be people who live in those places. Those are the sorts of leaders the movement really needs. If you go to a public housing estate, where half of HK lives, the first thing you see is the DAB office of the local district councilor. It's as if the pro-democracy movement has conceded that whole territory to the adversary. Cultivating a strong, widespread, enduring network is a basic principle of organizing that the movement hasn't even started to come to terms with. This period when people don't see any immediate breakthroughs or advances on the horizon and seem to be waiting for "the next big thing" is the perfect opportunity to do that sort of constructive, long-term work.

The political situation in HK is at an impasse, perhaps even a breaking point, but then again, it has been for years, and while it has become even more acute since the Umbrella Movement, the current situation can continue indefinitely. The Party sees this as working to its advantage: While shoring up the status quo, it is increasing its control. But the more it imposes control, the more it alienates, and every act of oppression is an opportunity the pro-democracy movement can take advantage of.

After the imprisonment of the 16 — all excellent, good-hearted, idealistic young people —, it's become widely apparent to HK people that the Party and HK government are ready and willing to eat our kids. The opportunities for resistance that awareness provides are numerous. Part of the formula of the Umbrella Movement, remember, was people coming out to protect and stand in solidarity with the students.

As long as people continue to resist in significant numbers, the Party, no matter how much it might putatively control, simply can't have its way in HK. It's up to HK people to support and join the political groups leading the resistance. It's up to those groups to improve their abilities to collaborate, strategize and organize. If localists, traditional pan-democrats and self-determinationists can find ways to cooperate and support one another, their power will increase exponentially.

That's easier said than done, and it's important to recall that some of these groups are under such fierce attack by the Party and HK government that their very existence is threatened. A Taiwanese academic recently asked me how I foresaw links between the HK pro-democracy movement and the progressive political forces of Taiwan developing in the next five years. Well, I said, that depends first and foremost on whether or not some of the HK groups even exist in five years. Nothing should be taken for granted. The Party would like to emerge from this period having obliterated any group that does not abide by the terms of its rule. Then again, the HK resistance and self-determination movement could very well outlast the Party itself. That's how precarious and volatile the situation is. HK could go in many different directions, and while the Party will do its best to control every element it can, the direction HK goes will largely depend on the actions of the HK people.

Mainlandization: An overview of Communist Party attempts to control and assimilate Hong Kong

October 15, 2017

Mainlandization preceded the Umbrella Movement. Since then, the Party has stepped up and expanded it.

The primary dynamic of the current political situation in HK is a contest between Party-driven mainlandization on the one hand and democracy and self-determination movements on the other. The current article examines mainlandization. A following article will look at self-determination.

Make no mistake about it: Communist Party-driven mainlandization is the biggest existential threat facing Hong Kong.

"Mainlandization" means attempts by the Communist Party and its allies to exert greater control over HK politically, economically, socially and culturally, with the objective of assimilating it and integrating it into the mainland as much as possible before the end of the 50-year "one country, two systems" period in 2047.

Before the Umbrella Movement of 2014, the Party already had a plan to achieve that. Indeed, the fake suffrage it attempted to implement in 2014 and 2015, against which the Umbrella Movement was a reaction, was a key part of that plan. The Party has not taken HK people's defeat of fake suffrage lightly. Its main response has been to speed up mainlandization and expand it into areas where it had previously made few inroads. It appears to believe that if the changes come fast and furious, shock-and-awe style, HK will simply be overwhelmed and "hostile elements" will not have the strength to withstand them all. Its strategy is to transform every aspect of governance and society while preserving the veneer of allowing HK institutions to continue to exist as before.

Below is an overview of various aspects of mainlandization, divided according to sector of society. The sectors are

- Government, civil service, Legislative Council and police
- Cross-border abductions
- Mega-infrastructure projects
- Demographics and tourism
- Business and the economy
- Civil society (the United Front)
- Media and the book industry
- Education
- The judiciary and rule of law

The overview ends with education and the judiciary because these are the areas which, prior to the Umbrella Movement, had been the most resilient in withstanding mainlandization, and for that very reason, they are ones into which the Party and HK government have invested major effort in the post-Umbrella period.

This overview is not exhaustive; much more could be said about each area as well as about other areas not covered here. It is primarily intended to map just how pervasive the mainlandization of HK is and to show a pattern of imposition: Perhaps if one looks at one or two manifestations of mainlandization, one may not see the aspect of imposition, but take the manifestations as a whole, and it's hard to ignore.

If, after reading, you feel Armageddon's upon us, the overview has achieved its intended effect. But none of the ways the Party is trying to make HK more like the mainland are irreversible. Many of the Party and HK government's attempts to mainlandize are encountering strong resistance. Meanwhile, democracy and self-determination movements continue to develop. Weighing the balance between mainlandization and democratization, the conclusion is HK is up for grabs. But the threat of mainlandization needs to be seen for what it is and strategically and systematically countered.

Government, civil service, Legislative Council and police

The Communist Party's failure to implement fake suffrage was monumental. It would have given it a permanent stranglehold over the formal political system with no legal obligation to implement any further changes. But even without fake suffrage, its control over the HK government is nevertheless greater than ever.

The Chief Executive and her political appointees act as little more than proxies of the Party, especially when it comes to issues which the Party sees as core interests. It is hard to recall a case in which the HK government differed with the Party, even when it appeared the interests of the HK people and the Party were at odds. Recent examples of the lockstep routine include co-location for the express rail link, the Party's Basic Law interpretation over oath-taking, a new mainland law criminalizing insult of the national anthem which the Party intends to insert into an annex of the Basic Law to give it legal effect in HK, and Party agents' abductions of Lee Bo and Xiao Jianhua in HK and their spiriting across the border. On all these matters and others, the HK government simply adopts the Party line. A memorable nadir was the 2016 annual policy address by former Chief Executive Leung Chun-ying in which he mentioned the Party's "One Belt One Road" initiative 48 times,[1] a project in which HK people have next to zero interest. He sounded like a ventriloquist's dummy in an unintentionally comic performance, illustrating perfectly the relationship between the Party and HK government.

A relatively non-corrupt, efficient and unpoliticized civil service has been one of HK's saving graces, but since the Umbrella Movement, the government has increasingly used various agencies and departments to further the Party's agenda, largely through denial of services and facilities to perceived enemies. The Leisure and Cultural Services Department banned the pro-independence HK National Party and the localist Youngspiration from the Victoria Park New Year's Market on ludicrous "public safety" grounds[2] and refused to publish a line in the bio of a theater director from Taiwan that said she had gone to Taipei National University of the Arts.[3] The Companies Registry continues to refuse to register the pro-democracy self-determinationist political party Demosistō more than a year after it applied, without giving any reason for the delay. It also rejected the application of the National Party. Before the 2016 Legislative Council elections, as the nomination period was about to open, the Electoral Affairs Commission suddenly demanded that prospective candidates sign a new additional form pledging fealty to the Basic Law, in particular Article 1, which asserts that the Hong Kong Special Administrative Region is an inalienable part of the People's Republic of China. The EAC's returning officers then proceeded to disqualify half a dozen potential candidates on political grounds having to do with their unsubstantiated and uncontestable suspicions that the applicants would not uphold Article 1.

The Legislative Council was already a rigged institution, but it is descending to even lower depths. With only half of its 70 seats filled through free and fair elections according to principles of universal suffrage and the fact that it is hardly a legislative body in that members cannot introduce any legislation which costs government money, it was hardly a paragon of democracy to begin with. But now it is apparently to be scrubbed of any elected representatives with political views deemed unacceptable by the Party. Of course, there are the infamous cases of the six pro-democracy Legco members, elected with 183,236 votes total, who were disqualified after the National People's Congress Standing Committee interpretation of the Basic Law on oath-taking in November 2016. In addition, the HK government has brought six criminal cases against five elected pro-democracy Legco members for statements made and actions taken as part of their work in Legco: Cheng Chung-tai was convicted of desecrating the PRC and HKSAR flags; Long Hair was acquitted of misconduct in public office and is awaiting trial for contempt of Legco; Kenneth Leung is being personally sued by former CE Leung Chun-ying for defamation; and Baggio Leung and Yau Wai-ching await trial for unlawful assembly outside a Legco chamber. This pattern represents a new trend: previously, the HK government left Legco's matters to Legco to sort out, whether oath-taking or disciplinary issues. Its interventions are unprecedented attacks on the little democracy HK has, and indeed on the concept of representative government and the will of the people.

The police force has more links than ever with its mainland counterparts, and both top officers and ordinary officers go to the mainland in greater numbers and more frequently than ever. Since the Umbrella Movement, the police force has become more insulated than ever from accountability, and there is still exceedingly deep distrust of the force on the part of a great many HK citizens. (A recent conversation: Me: "When it comes down to it, police officers are just ordinary people, like most everyone else." Interlocutor: "Maybe, but when they're ordered to shoot you, they'll shoot. So whose side are they on?") Upwards of a third of its 28,705 officers were used to guard both Zhang Dejiang and Xi Jinping during their respective 2016 and 2017 visits to HK. This number far exceeded that needed to address legitimate security concerns. Their primary purpose was to protect the Party leaders from encountering protest by HK people or any other "embarrassing" situations. Both during the Umbrella Movement and since, in lieu of viable solutions to political problems, they have been used as the guard dogs of the regime. And they have been impotent in pursuing potential crimes in which Party agents are implicated (see below).

Cross-border abductions

This is an entirely new category of mainlandization that has arisen since the Umbrella Movement. Prior to the abduction of Lee Bo in December 2015, few people thought the Party would be so brazen as to kidnap people off the streets of HK and transport them to the mainland. Indeed, even though it involved no more than a single individual, no other event has so damaged people's confidence in "one country, two systems" and protections of civil rights as Lee Bo's kidnapping.

And then it happened again, this time to the mainland tycoon Xiao Jianhua staying at the luxury Four Seasons hotel in January 2017. This abduction didn't excite nearly as much alarm, perhaps because it was seen as an internal Party matter, Xiao being a politically well-connected businessman. But it should have, especially coming so soon after Lee Bo's abduction. Until then, some might have argued Lee Bo was a one-off, perhaps even a "mistake", but after Xiao Jianhua, it's clear that when the Party feels the need, it will not allow something as inconsequential as the law to prevent it from abducting people in HK.

Just as alarming as the actions of Party agents in HK has been the utter incapacity (or perhaps lack of will) of the HK government and police to do anything about them. In neither Lee Bo's nor Xiao Jianhua's case did the police so much as even determine that a crime had been committed, nor did they get to the bottom of what exactly had occurred. So HK people are left with the prospect that the government and police either can or will not protect them even within HK, let alone elsewhere (HK permanent resident Gui Minhai, the bookseller kidnapped by the Party in Thailand, has been held incommunicado in detention without trial for over a year). Of course, it all depends on who's doing the kidnapping: By contrast, when the Bossini clothing heiress was kidnapped in HK in early 2015, HK police worked closely with mainland police to apprehend the suspects, and by the middle of 2016, nine kidnappers had been tried in Shenzhen and one in HK.

Mega-infrastructure projects

These include the HK-Macau-Zhuhai bridge, the rail link to connect HK to the mainland express rail system, and related to that, the plan to "co-locate" mainland immigration authorities at the express rail terminus in HK. To this can be added the annex to the Palace Museum in Beijing, an entire museum in its own right to be built at the West Kowloon Cultural District, where the express rail link terminates. All of these projects were initiated by the Party and implemented by the HK government with minimal participation or approval by HK people. They are enormously expensive, unnecessary, and largely unwanted. Their main purpose is political.

The transport links are meant to integrate HK more closely with the mainland. The vision is of a Pearl River Delta mega-city with Shenzhen and Zhuhai. The Party's name for the plan is the "Greater Bay Area". Ultimately, HK is to be rendered virtually indistinguishable. The expenses of the HK portion of the projects are borne for the most part by the HK government, mostly through tax and land sales revenues (the bridge partly through loans and the museum capital expenses entirely through donation from the HK Jockey Club).

The express rail link was originally estimated to cost HK$39.5 billion. Then the cost rose to $65 billion, and now, most recently, to $84.42 billion, more than double the initial estimate. Seven years after the HK government got initial approval for funding from a Legco dominated by Party allies, it finally announced its agreement with the Party for a co-location arrangement, according to which mainland immigration authorities will be allowed to operate in HK, in direct contravention of Basic Law Article 18. Prior to this agreement, it did not consult the people of HK and says it won't now either, apart from moving a non-binding Legco motion. Thus, the project has become the Party's Trojan horse, introducing mainland law enforcement into HK.

The cost of the main section of the HK-Macau-Zhuhai bridge is unknown, though announced to have gone over the initial estimate of HK$17.74 billion, with HK contributing $7.62 billion. In addition to that, HK will spend $48.5 billion on the HK section of the bridge infrastructure.

So, just on those two projects, a minimum of HK$140.54 billion from HK government coffers for primarily Party priorities whose purpose is to link HK closer to the mainland.

The Palace Museum annex in HK is the result of a secret agreement between the HK government and the Party. The content of the discussions between the Party and the HK government regarding co-location was also secret, but at least the HK public was informed they were going on. In the case of the museum, no one knew about it until it was announced. Astonishingly, not even the board of the West Kowloon Cultural District Authority, itself a government agency, was informed of the agreement until after it had been made, let alone given any say in the matter. The site where the Palace Museum annex will be built was originally intended as a major performance venue. That idea was scrapped after the government said it had not been able to procure funding. But it had no problem funding the HK Palace Museum: Part of the secret agreement was that HK$3.5 billion in capital would be provided by the HK Jockey Club. Since it is a non-governmental entity, the HK government does not have to seek approval for funding from Legco, and there is therefore even less public oversight of the project than of the other two major infrastructure projects. It is unclear who will administer the museum, but it will presumably involve mainland government agencies given that the collection it houses will continue to belong to the Palace Museum in Beijing. Apart from the entirely opaque decision-making process, many object to the concept of Chinese-ness foisted upon HK by the Palace Museum annex at a time when fewer HK people than ever identify themselves as Chinese, 21 percent overall and only 3 percent of young people.[4] What, after all, does the Palace Museum have to do with HK? It is as if the Party were planting its assertion that HK is Chinese right in the middle of the city, on the site of the HK government's largest ever cultural initiative. The West Kowloon Cultural District was originally intended to put HK on the global map culturally. The Palace Museum annex subverts that outward-facing intention, instead emphasizing a particular vision of Chinese culture.

Demographics

According to HK government statistics, from 2003 to 2014, 828,000 mainlanders settled in HK, about 11 percent of the overall population, 63,000 new arrivals every year.[5] Mainland immigration is by far the biggest contributor to population growth in a city with one of the lowest birth rates in the world. The vast majority of these mainland immigrants arrive through the One-Way Permit Scheme, which has the intended purpose of family reunification, but the Party, not the HK government, has control over who comes; indeed, final approval is given by the Ministry of Public Security. The process has no transparency, and little is known about how it is determined who exactly comes.

HK is an immigrant city par excellence. Virtually everyone came here from somewhere else (mostly China) within the last century. But many feel that the post-handover immigrants are different and represent an attempt by the Party to change the demographic composition of HK to one more favorable to Party rule. Prior to the 1997 handover, the brunt of mainland immigration to HK occurred before the 1970s. Only after the handover was an official policy to facilitate immigration in large numbers from the mainland implemented. In the past, many immigrants fled the mainland due to political turmoil or famine, and therefore tended to have at the very least an ambivalent attitude towards the Party, but post-handover immigrants appear to be apolitical or inclined to support the Party, not necessarily actively but because the mainland's is the only political culture they've ever known. Political docility probably comes top of the list of the Party's desired attributes in its subjects. It is unclear the extent to which the Party has recruited recent mainland immigrants to participate in United Front organizations (see below). Indeed, little is known of them in general.

In addition to immigrants, over 40 million mainland tourists visit HK every year, more than five times the size of HK's population, enough to have a decided impact on the cityscape. This number has risen from 4 million per year in 2003, due not least of all to HK government efforts to reorient the economy towards mainland tourism. This has driven up retail property prices, turning central shopping areas into meccas for global luxury brands and displacing many smaller locally owned businesses. Because of the tourists and the immigrants, Putonghua is heard with increasing frequency on the streets of many central areas and in neighborhoods and public housing estates where recent immigrants are clustered.

Business and the economy

Since the handover, HK's business elites have had a cozy relationship with the Party, which regards them as a major ally. After it ruled out genuine suffrage in HK in 2014, it expected trouble, and so it summoned 70 tycoons, lead by Tung

Chee-hwa, the HKSAR's first Chief Executive and a tycoon himself, to Beijing[6] to remind them of the importance of loyalty.[7] The Umbrella Movement erupted a week later. The tycoons stood by the regime throughout. Both the HK General Chamber of Commerce and the Chinese Chamber of Commerce are allied with the Party and have supported Party political initiatives[8] and spoken out against pro-democracy initiatives,[9] all in the name of business advocacy of course.

These days, however, the sands are quickly shifting beneath the tycoons' feet. The Party is shunting them aside in favor of mainland companies, many Party-owned or with close links to the Party.[10] According to a *Reuters* report, "Chinese companies are consuming ever bigger chunks of the city's key sectors including real estate, finance, power, construction and the stock market."[11] "Seven developers—controlled by Hong Kong's richest men—used to win 45 per cent of all residential land sites sold in the city as recently as in 2012. That ratio halved to 22 per cent by [2016].... Mainland Chinese developers won about one plot out of every three on sale through government tender in 2016."[12] Mainland banks account for 40 percent of retail bank branches in HK, and mainland companies for over 60 percent of market capitalization on the Hang Seng Index, compared to 20 percent in 1997. In 1997, all top 10 companies on the Hang Seng were HK companies; now 6 of 10 are mainland companies, and 4 of those Party-owned. Last year, 92 percent of all initial public offerings were from the mainland.[13] Especially after the 2008 global financial crisis, when the Party injected large amounts of liquidity into the mainland economy to offset the downturn, money sloshing over the border has been one of the main causes of an increase in property prices that's put the goal of owning a home far out of the reach of most people and made HK the least affordable housing market in the world.

That HK's economy has become increasingly dependent on, linked to and colonized by the mainland's is not entirely due to the gravitational pull of the latter due to its sheer size. It has been driven by government policy on both sides of the border. The economy is the area of mainlandization where the Party faces the least resistance, and this is to due to the fact that most businesspeople either support or don't dare object to it while HK government officials refuse to use the mechanisms at their disposal to regulate it.

HK could promote a more diverse economy, by both supporting local initiatives and facing outward toward East and Southeast Asia and beyond, positioning itself not as "a China growth derivative"[14] as one market analyst put it but as a regional hub. A developed, post-industrial economy, HK is well-placed to be a regional leader in environmentally friendly urban design. As a city with an English-language heritage and solid universities, it could also be a regional education hub.

Civil Society (the United Front)

The term United Front (統一戰線) refers to the various organizations in HK aligned with the Party and used by it to further its interests. This includes loyalist political parties, the Federation of Trade Unions, the Heung Yee Kuk of New Territories rural committees, and so-called "patriotic" associations often named after the places in China from which their founders originally came. These groups have an especially strong presence in lower-income and working-class parts of HK, for example, the public housing estates. The Party is attempting to extend its tentacles all the time: Derek Lam of Demosistō recently reported, "Of Hong Kong's six major religions, five are already firmly under the control of the Chinese Communist Party."[15]

The Democratic Alliance for the Betterment and Progress of Hong Kong is the largest political party in HK. Since HK has no law on political parties (they are registered as companies in the Companies Registry) or on their funding, they are required to divulge only their income, not their funding sources. This allows parties to receive funding in complete secrecy. To get a sense of both sources and size of funding, one can only look at the tip of the iceberg: At the DAB's annual fundraising auction in 2014, it raised HK$68.38 million, with some of it coming from HK tycoons purchasing auctioned calligraphy and paintings made by Party officials working in HK[16]—a perfect illustration of how the combination of tycoons, Party officials and United Front organizations works. This was in contrast to $2.8 million and $2.35 million raised, respectively, by the pan-democratic Democratic and Civic Parties at their auctions. The DAB's total income for 2008 to 2014 was HK$460 million.[17] This money is largely used to maintain a permanent presence in as many parts of the city as possible, especially lower-income areas, which in turn function as its vote banks.

As much as anything else, the United Front is meant to promote a Party-friendly environment. Many UF groups are known for their low-cost banquets and excursions for the elderly in parts of the city where there are few other affordable entertainment options. The FTU is known for its adult education classes. People who avail themselves of these opportunities tend to be disproportionately older and relatively uncritical of the Party.

UF members and supporters are also mobilized when needed. For example, on the last day of the week-long student strike in September 2014 which eventually lead to the Umbrella Movement, the Leisure and Cultural Services Department, a government agency, denied the main venue in Tamar Park where the strike took place to Hong Kong Federation of Students, though it had already been there for three days, and gave it to the Federation of HK Guangxi Community Organizations, an archetypal UF group, to celebrate October 1, though that was still five days away.[18] The United Front is also the primary pool for rent-a-crowd mobilizations when the Party thinks showing a street presence will be of some benefit in projecting an image of a "divided" city. There have been numerous cases of pro-Party "demonstrators" being paid stipends and provided with meals and transportation to attend events. A classic example occurred in the lead-up to the Umbrella Movement, when in August 2014, several thousand were mobilized to march against the pro-democracy movement's threat of civil disobedience. Out of that arose the infamous interview in which one marcher, when asked why she was there, simply answered, in shaky Cantonese, "Shopping."[19]

The United Front's biggest challenge is recruiting the next generation. Its membership skews elderly, and most HK young people despise the Party. Recent mainland immigrants (see above) may be its most promising replenishment pool. Its efforts at appealing to the young often take bizarre and maladroit forms such as the Hong Kong Army Cadets Association, of which the wife of former CE Leung Chun-ying is "commander-in-chief".[20]

As Christine Loh put it in her 2010 book, *Underground Front*, HK is the only place in the world where the ruling party is underground. That continues to be the case—it's everywhere and nowhere all at once. It wants to be the air you breathe.

Media and book industry

The HK media is widely regarded by both journalists themselves and the public to practice substantial self-censorship.[21] Freedom of the press is seen as increasingly threatened.[22] It is unusual to come across criticism of the Party's top leaders in the mainstream press, or for that matter, even of the Party.

The Party owns outright its low-circulation mouthpieces, *Wen Wei Po* and *Ta Kung Pao*. There is a number of other news outlets considered pro-Party, either due to their ownership or their editorial stance or both. There are two reputable neutral daily newspapers, *Ming Pao* and low-circulation *Hong Kong Economic Journal*. One of *Ming Pao*'s editors, Kevin Lau was nearly hacked to death in a cleaver attack while walking on the street in 2014. Another was fired in 2016, supposedly for business reasons, to the outrage of the *Ming Pao* Staff Association and much of the public. *Apple Daily* is the only explicitly pro-democracy daily. During the fight for genuine suffrage in 2014, it suffered cyberattacks on its website, its distribution center was picketed by Party supporters, its newspapers were destroyed at pick-up points, and its owner, Jimmy Lai, had his electronic communications hacked, his house firebombed, and was physically attacked by Party supporters at the Admiralty occupation. The biggest English-language daily, *South China Morning Post*, was bought in 2016 by Alibaba, which has close ties to the Party. It announced it purchased *SCMP* to, among other reasons, provide a better image of China to the world. Even before that, its editor in chief, Wang Xiangwei, was a mainlander and a representative to the Chinese People's Political Consultative Conference. Its owner at the time, pro-Party tycoon Robert Kuok Hock Nien, consulted the Liaison Office before appointing Wang.

While television has always been the least diverse medium, with the fewest outlets, new digital t.v. ventures briefly gave some hope of more variety. One of these was ViuTV which had a show titled "Travels with Rivals". It had invited Billy Fung, the former head of the HKU Student Union and an advocate of HK independence, and Wang Dan, the 1989 student leader in Beijing, to appear together on a trip to Japan. But after the pair debated HK independence at the Foreign Correspondents Club of Japan,[23] ViuTV suddenly cancelled the show.[24]

Apparently, word had come down from above that no substantive discussion of HK independence, especially by its advocates, could be allowed on television. The largest free television station in HK, TVB, has long been criticized as having an editorial board that hews far too close to the Party line. Indeed, its nickname within the pro-democracy movement is CCTVB, combining the name of the Party broadcaster, CCTV, with TVB. It is owned by mainland media mogul Li Ruigang through a nearly impenetrable web of business relationships and company structures apparently in breach of HK government regulations restricting ownership of HK broadcasters by non-HK entities.[25]

The only other pro-democracy journalism can be found in online-only media outlets. These are the main sources of news for many HK people, especially young people.

The Party's Liaison Office is HK's biggest owner of book distributors and retailers. It has an 80 percent market share and owns 51 bookstores.[26] It appears to have deliberately camouflaged its ownership: It owns Guangdong New Culture Development, which in turn owns New Culture Development HK, which in turn owns Sino United Publishing Group, which in turn owns Commercial Press, Joint Publishing, and Chunghwa, three major bookstore chains.[27] Several reports have documented the chains' censorship of books on "sensitive" political topics, such as the Umbrella Movement, which are not presented from the Party's point of view. Like Li Ruigang's ownership of TVB, this ownership structure is apparently in violation of HK law, in this instance Basic Law Article 22.

Education

Post-Umbrella, the Party and HK government have put significant effort into exerting greater control over universities. Their lesson from the Umbrella Movement was that, since students played a central role, more attention had to be given toward better "educating" them. Universities have been relatively free spaces in HK society, and up to the Umbrella Movement, the Party had made few substantial inroads there. Post-Umbrella, universities have become key battlegrounds.

In his first annual policy address after the Umbrella Movement, in January 2015, Chief Executive Leung Chun-ying criticized the HKU Student Union magazine, *Undergrad*, for publications on self-determination, self-reliance and HK people deciding their own fate. The attack was tantamount to a veiled declaration of war on pro-democracy forces on university campuses.

Upon the request of the government's Education Bureau, the HKU governing council, dominated by government appointees, made repeated attempts to punish Benny Tai and the HKU Public Opinion Programme for conducting the OCLP referendum in June 2014 in which nearly 800,000 people voted for real universal suffrage, this in spite of the fact that the HKU administration under vice-chancellor Peter Mathieson had already cleared Tai of any wrongdoing. Benny's been singled out for attack in Party-owned newspapers and, most recently, by pro-Party Legco member and Lingnan University governing council member Junius Ho, who in a rally dedicated to driving Benny from the university also said independence advocates should be killed.

The Party and HK government have pressured public university governing councils to play a more pro-government role. The Chief Executive is nominal chancellor of all public universities. By tradition, this role has largely been ceremonial. Leung Chun-ying used it to drive his political agenda, for example by appointing Arthur Li as head of the HKU council over the objections of large numbers of students, faculty and alumni. Li compared students who participated in the Umbrella Movement to Cultural Revolution Red Guards. The head of HKU, Peter Mathieson, resigned prematurely, supposedly because of the attraction of an academic post elsewhere, but one couldn't help but think the constant political interference from above must have been stifling. His own governing council, which appointed him, blocked his preferred candidate for pro-vice-chancellor, Johannes Chan, who was head of the HKU law faculty and also happened to be Benny's boss and himself a proponent of democracy. Thus, during Mathieson's whole tenure, he was never allowed to put his own leadership team in place.

Resistance to the political interference has been strong, with calls to end the CE's position as chancellor of all public universities and for diversification of university councils. This has headed off greater incursions, at least for the time being. But as has been seen in the recent controversy surrounding the appearance of HK independence banners on campuses in the first week of the school year, the pressure has chilled university administrations into falling into lockstep with the Party line and students know they will likely be punished for making political statements to which the Party takes exception (in particular, for advocating independence—tellingly, the banners appeared anonymously). Much circumstantial evidence suggests that professors consider the "sensitivity" of an issue when deciding whether or not to pursue research, organize conferences and teach it. The Party's effort to control universities is a long-term project. The ultimate aim is to get universities to practice more extensive self-censorship similar to the media.

The Party's efforts to mainlandize secondary and primary schools are long-standing. In 2012, a large campaign by a coalition of civil society groups forced the HK government to all but scrap its about-to-be-implemented Moral and National Education subject, the impetus for which was a statement by then Party General Secretary Hu Jintao that HK had to foster "a strong sense of national identity" amongst young people. The subject was regarded as brainwashing by the pro-democracy movement, for which the government's climb-down was a significant victory, but the government has said that it still intends to introduce elements of national education into the school system through a variety of avenues, and there are frequent protests against introduction of new materials, such as those meant to promote the Party line on the Basic Law or, most recently, a booklet intended to promote Chinese identity.

Language is a political battleground in Hong Kong. Cantonese is widely considered central to Hong Kong identity. There is persistent controversy surrounding the HK government's long-standing policy, going back to 2003, of promoting the teaching of Chinese in Putonghua, even though there is no scientific research that shows HK children learn Chinese better in Putonghua than in Cantonese, the native language of 90 percent of them. While the decision is ultimately left up to individual schools, HK government efforts to promote teaching Chinese in Putonghua had by 2015 resulted in 72 percent of government-funded primaries and 37 percent of government-funded secondary schools teaching Chinese in Putonghua. Some, especially secondaries, have recently switched back to Cantonese after becoming disillusioned with the results of teaching Chinese in Putonghua. But given government backing, the pressure to teach Chinese in Putonghua is bound to continue.

Judiciary and rule of law

Along with education, the judiciary and rule of law were seen, prior to the Umbrella Movement, as the other area of HK society which had largely buffered itself from mainlandization. But since the Umbrella Movement, the judiciary's come under heavy pressure and there are signs that it is changing in ways that only Party loyalists can see as positive.

While most of HK responded with varying degrees of shock and indignation to the White Paper on HK issued by the Party in June 2014 (it provoked a backlash days before OCLP's scheduled referendum on genuine universal suffrage), the legal community in particular was up in arms since the White Paper characterized the HK judiciary as an "administrative" body that had to cooperate with other parts of the HK government and be "patriotic". Lawyers, who were not given to street protest (indeed, this was only their second since the handover), demonstrated by holding a silent march dressed in black suits from HK's High Court to its Court of Final Appeal. To the legal community, the independence of the judiciary and the rule of law were sacrosanct.

Since, then, the Party has pushed HK to fulfill to its vision of the judiciary articulated in the White Paper. The HK government originally planned to use prosecutions of the more than 1,000 arrested during the Umbrella Movement to test judicial independence, but the majority of its cases were so weak, it never got far with that plan, prosecuting upwards of 250 people and getting around 85 convictions. The Party and HK government labelled the whole movement "illegal", but they couldn't prove that in the courts.

Then along came their godsend, the Chinese New Year 2016 clashes in Mong Kok between police and protesters. If there's anything the generally conservative judiciary abhors, it's violence by non-state actors. The HK government's been aggressively prosecuting Mong Kok defendants and getting a much higher percentage of convictions than usual as well as long prison sentences of three years each for "rioting". This seems to have shifted the priorities of at least some in the judiciary away from paying due regard to civil rights and toward "deterrence", a word that's crept into many decisions as if implanted there.

With newfound confidence, the HK government appealed the community service sentences of 15 activists (and suspended sentence of one) in two separate cases, one related to the Umbrella Movement, one preceding it, and got prison sentences for all 16, ranging in duration from six to thirteen months. This, even though the crime committed by all 16 was the nonviolent unlawful assembly, and most sentences for this crime in recent years have ranged from fines to three weeks to three months in prison. Both High Court judgments made reference to "violence", though the crimes of which the 16 were convicted did not involve violence. Parts of the judges' rulings sounded politically biased, referring to "unhealthy trends in society" (civil disobedience and what they saw as disrespect for the law) and again invoking "deterrence" to justify the much harsher-than-usual sentences. It was hard to avoid the conclusion that HK now had its first full-fledged political prisoners, serving prison sentences not based on the nature of their crime but on the lead judge's views on the "health" of society. It was as if these defendants were being held responsible not for unlawful assembly but for the "unhealthy trends in society". None of the judges mentioned the "unhealthy trend" of HK still being denied universal suffrage in contravention of both international and HK law.

Probably the single most damaging act against the independence of the judiciary has been the NPCSC's interpretation of the Basic Law, handed down in November 2016 in the midst of an on-going court case brought by the HK government against Legco members Baggio Leung and Yau Wai-ching over their Legco oath-taking. The interpretation was retroactive since it supposedly only clarified what was stated in 1997, in clear contravention of a basic judicial principle that new laws should not be applied retroactively. It all but compelled the High Court judge to decide in favor of the HK government and disqualify the two from Legco. For the second time in less than three years, the law community marched against the interference. But the HK government wasn't done there. Flush with its success, it applied to the High Court to disqualify four more elected members of Legco, and the High Court gave them the boot as well.

An unelected government, with the indispensible help of a dictatorship's ruling, was using the High Court to kick democratically elected representatives out of office.

Whatever else may be said about the High Court's disqualification of six elected Legco members, it is clear that it has not protected the rights or interests of voters, and therefore has failed to protect the few, highly circumscribed democratic rights HK people enjoy, deciding that a dictatorship's edict has far greater legal weight. Indeed, one of the most troubling aspects of rule of law in HK has been the inability to hold those who most egregiously refuse to follow the law accountable. In continuing to deny universal suffrage in line with international law and standards to the people of HK, the Party and HK government are in breach of the Basic Law, yet there is virtually no legal recourse to justice in regard to this breach which deprives an entire population of a basic human right. There is the great irony that those protesting the denial of that right have been convicted and imprisoned while those who continue to deny that right are above the law. What does that say about the state of rule of law in HK?

Conclusion

The overall effect of the many manifestations of mainlandization outlined here is a crisis of public confidence in the "one country, two systems" policy and the supposed guarantee to HK of a "high degree of autonomy" in all matters except those related to defense and foreign affairs. There is widespread public distrust of the HK government, the police, the Party, and, increasingly, of other institutions such as the judiciary and university administrations.

Some might argue that closer ties between a country, such as the PRC, and its newly incorporated territory, such as HK, are both inevitable and normal. But the pattern mapped out here shows not closer cooperation but imposition. And the whole point of "one country, two systems" and a "high degree of autonomy" was that such imposition should not occur.

A substantial number of HK people have concluded not only that "one country, two systems" isn't working properly but that it really no longer exists and the Basic Law has failed HK. One increasingly hears phrases like "one country, one-point-five systems" which will eventually lead to one country, one system. More HK people feel compelled to look for other solutions, whether self-determination or full independence, as the only means of preserving what they thought had been promised to them and protecting and achieving their basic rights.

Hong Kong's right of self-determination: The only way left?

October 23, 2017

The primary dynamic of the current political situation in HK is a contest between Communist Party-driven mainlandization on the one hand and democracy and self-determination movements on the other. A previous article looked at mainlandization. This article examines self-determination.

What is the right of self-determination and how does it apply to Hong Kong? After the Communist Party's denial of genuine universal suffrage, and in light of its continual efforts to infringe and restrict other rights, is a push for self-determination the only viable option for HK people?

Catalonia, Iraqi Kurdistan, Puerto Rico, Scotland, Kosovo, East Timor, South Sudan, Montenegro: In the last fifteen years, a strikingly high number of peoples have either held independence referenda or declared independence. In doing so, all invoked their inherent right of self-determination. That list excludes the dozens of new countries formed as a result of the demise of the Soviet Union in the nineties—republics of the USSR, republics of Yugoslavia, Slovakia—and other referenda that took place in that decade—for instance, in 1995, 93 percent of registered voters took part in a Quebec referendum on independence, voting narrowly (50.58 percent to 49.42 percent) to remain part of Canada.

Some on that list are amongst the poorest on the planet. Some were brutally oppressed. Some are relatively prosperous with fairly well protected rights. Some undertook self-determination processes that were recognized and supported by the countries from which they considered separating; others did so against the will of those countries. Some became independent. Some did not. They are European, Asian, African and Caribbean. We tend to think of the world map as more or less fixed, but in fact, it has undergone significant changes in the last three decades and is continually evolving.

What lessons do the cases of peoples who have considered independence hold for Hong Kong people who have never in their modern history been granted the right of self-determination? On what legal and moral grounds is the right of self-determination based?

The background

The very first article of both of the world's two foundational, legally-binding human rights covenants, the International Covenant on Civil and Political Rights and the International Covenant on Economic, Social and Cultural Rights, reads as follows:

Article 1

1. All peoples have the right of self-determination. By virtue of that right they freely determine their political status and freely pursue their economic, social and cultural development.

2. All peoples may, for their own ends, freely dispose of their natural wealth and resources without prejudice to any obligations arising out of international economic co-operation, based upon the principle of mutual benefit, and international law. In no case may a people be deprived of its own means of subsistence.

3. The States Parties to the present Covenant, including those having responsibility for the administration of Non-Self-Governing and Trust Territories, shall promote the realization of the right of self-determination, and shall respect that right, in conformity with the provisions of the Charter of the United Nations.

Self-determination is the only right to appear in both treaties, with the exact same wording. Why?

As with most fundamental and constitutional documents that are supposed to have a whiff of the eternal about them, the ICCPR and ICESCR are flecked with historical contingency. They came into existence in 1966, as dozens of peoples around the world were achieving independence from colonial domination.

There's no mention of the right of self-determination in the Universal Declaration of Human Rights, the non-legally-binding document of 1948 from which the ICCPR and ICESCR derive. Self-determination is mentioned in the

United Nations Charter of 1945, though not explicitly as a right. It was newly independent states that pushed for the Covenants, 18 years after the UDHR, and also ensured that the right of self-determination came first in each. The logic was that the only way to ensure that peoples had all other rights was if they had the right to determine their own political status; having done so, the thinking went, they would be in control of their destiny and thereby more able to ensure the other rights, dependent as they are on political freedom.

As far as the UN, an organization made up of states, was concerned, this was the high-water mark for self-determination. Never since have states, for obvious reasons of self-interest, been so keen on this right. They have generally gone out of their way to emphasize state sovereignty over self-determination. In the most recent cases, the Catalans and the Iraqi Kurds, you have to look hard to find a state that supports their right of self-determination. Still, numerous peoples over the last half-century have asserted their right, some much more successfully than others, and they continue to do so.

Hong Kong people and the right of self-determination

That HK people have this right is indisputable—all "peoples" do.

Even from a strictly legalistic perspective, Basic Law Article 39 states that HK is party to both the ICCPR and ICESCR, which, as we've seen, guarantee the right. In 1975, the UK inserted a reservation into the ICCPR regarding HK and the right of self-determination. Given that HK's political status has changed since then, with the handover from the UK to the PRC in 1997, there is some dispute as to whether or not the UK's reservations on HK still pertain. The UK also made a reservation regarding HK and the right to universal suffrage, but the UN Human Rights Committee, which monitors states parties to the ICCPR, has said it no longer applies since the Basic Law explicitly recognizes the right and promises to realize it. China, unsurprisingly, doesn't agree and has argued that all reservations on HK that it inherited from the UK continue to apply. HK is also party to the ICESCR, becoming so in 1997 since the PRC is a party (the PRC is not party to the ICCPR), and there is no reservation regarding HK and the right of self-determination under that covenant.

The main issue at stake is, are HK people a "people"? The right of self-determination, unlike, say, the right to freedom of expression, is a group right, not an individual right. While it's usually pretty easy to determine what an individual person is (short answer: every human being), it's not always as easy to define a "people". To complicate matters, there is no international consensus on the legal definition of a "people".

Still, generally speaking, the standard criteria are quite clear: a group of people who share a common heritage, history, culture, language, a clearly defined and usually geographically contiguous territory, and often but not always a separate jurisdiction, and, by virtue thereof, have an identity distinct from their neighbors'. On all these counts, HK people do indeed constitute a "people" and thereby qualify to partake of the right of self-determination. Even if you say HK people are Chinese, they are also distinct from other people considered Chinese based on most of the above criteria.

The thing is, while definitely a "people", HK people have never once in their modern history, from the time of the British takeover in 1842, been allowed to exercise this right: Their political status has always been determined by others. First they were a UK colony. Then they were handed over to the Communist Party like a present (indeed, the Party chose its own birthday, 1 July, for the handover date). HK's "mini-constitution", the Basic Law, was articulated and implemented by the Communist Party with virtually no participation by the people of HK, certainly not in any formal, representative sense. Nor did the Sino-British Joint Declaration or Basic Law ever go through any kind of formal approval process, such as a referendum, whereby the people of HK had an opportunity to either accept or reject those documents determining its current political status. The HK people never formally agreed to be part of the PRC any more than they agreed to be a UK colony.

Self-determination versus state sovereignty

Nobody would probably even be discussing self-determination if the Communist Party had just respected HK's supposedly "high degree of autonomy". But it hasn't, and that's the crux of the matter. Its denial of genuine suffrage in 2014 and 2015 was the last straw. What made it all the worse, and all the more ominous, was that in asserting that it was allowing "universal suffrage", it disingenuously pretended to grant the very thing it withheld. Either the Party was not acting in good faith or its understanding of universal suffrage was so divergent from international law and standards as to fail to constitute it. On top of that, the Party says its 31 August 2014 decision denying genuine suffrage stands for all time and will not be amended. In other words, HK is indefinitely stuck with the denial of this basic human right. The chances of the Party ever allowing the suffrage which the Basic Law legally obliges it to grant are exceedingly low, so low that one can say the Party has reneged on its implicit contract with HK, according to which HK people would tacitly recognize PRC sovereignty in exchange for real autonomy and the right to form their own government. And if that is the case, it surely justifies the demand for self-determination, for it has been shown that the basic rights of HK people will not be respected or realized under HK's current political status as a Special Administrative Region of the PRC.

It has been frequently pointed out that there's no internationally recognized right to secession. But not only is that right implied and embodied by the right of self-determination, but the fact that HK was first a colony of a state on the other side of the world long after most other colonies ceased to exist and then a Special Administrative Region of the world's largest dictatorship, improves HK people's argument for the right of self-determination, whether that entails secession or another option. In other words, HK people's political status is contested, and the fact that the current governing power refuses to grant it promised rights improves its case.

Even conservative scholars of international law who argue that the right of self-determination must be highly circumscribed and that state sovereignty and territorial integrity are paramount allow that "a general right to secede [exists] if and only if [the people] has suffered certain injustices, for which secession is the appropriate remedy of last resort."[1] This is known as Remedial Right Only Theory. What constitutes "certain injustices"? Iraq's genocide against the Kurds is undoubtedly a "certain injustice", even though Iraq's no longer ruled by the genocidal dictator. What about the Party's denial of universal suffrage to HK? After all, it involves no direct physical violence or atrocity. Yet it constitutes the indefinite denial of a basic human right promised to HK. And as for "of last resort": Over 20 years now, HK people have tried just about everything to get the Party to honor its promise, and finally, rather than doing so, it redefined the term "universal suffrage", twisting it beyond recognition, in order to continue denying it. That's what the Umbrella Movement was about. It said, We've had enough, what else can we do? And that didn't work. So now what? We've reached the last resort.

Wherever balance is struck between state sovereignty and territorial integrity on the one hand and the right of self-determination on the other, sovereignty cannot trump the right of self-determination in undemocratic states

(China, HK) and places where the people have never had an opportunity to freely determine their political status (HK). Dictators' assertions of sovereignty are tantamount to tyranny. The whole logic underpinning international human rights law, whether as regards the right to universal suffrage or the right of self-determination, is that it is the people, not unelected leaders or dictatorial regimes or even states, who are sovereign.

When the Communist Party argues that Basic Law Article 1 states unequivocally that HKSAR is an "inalienable" part of the PRC, one must ask, Says who? HK people themselves have certainly never consented to this designation; it was imposed upon them. There is strong irony in the fact that the Party wields that adjective over HK, for HK people have "inalienable" (a term present in the preambles of both the ICCPR and ICESCR) human rights not only inherent to them by virtue of being human beings but also via Basic Law Article 39, including the right of self-determination, which they have always been denied.

The recent history of the self-determination movement in Hong Kong

The right of self-determination first entered mainstream political discourse within the HK pro-democracy movement shortly after the end of the Umbrella Movement in December 2014 and even before the Party's fake suffrage was finally defeated in the Legislative Council on 18 June 2015. I clearly remember Joshua Wong discussing self-determination at a panel discussion at the protest camp outside of Legco in the days leading up to the vote on the fake suffrage proposal. It was indicative of the mood in the pro-democracy movement that many were already moving beyond the suffrage debate since it was clear that under the Communist Party, genuine suffrage would never be granted to HK. The question was, well, then, what next?

Joshua proposed self-determination as the next step of the pro-democracy movement in his first essay on the topic in August 2015.[2] The political party which he eventually co-founded in April 2016, Demosistō, has made self-determination one of the cornerstones of its mission.[3]

Proponents of HK self-determination have gone out of their way to state that while they don't rule out independence as one of the possible outcomes, they don't support it either. Their point is that even more basic than determining what HK's political status should be is that it should be HK people themselves who determine it. Apart from full independence, other options are full assimilation into the PRC and some form of autonomy, presumably similar to the "high degree of autonomy" HK's supposed to enjoy now.

However, the fact that the Communist Party has never allowed genuine autonomy in the PRC and that the regions in the PRC designated as autonomous (Tibet and Xinjiang, for example) are ironically the most tightly controlled by the central government, should give autonomy proponents pause for thought. Quebec, Greenland and Åland are often held up as successful examples of "internal self-determination", but it should be noted that all three are within states (Canada, Denmark and Finland respectively) which are stable liberal democracies with solid protections for minority rights (ie, a far cry from the PRC). There are no successful examples of internal self-determination under dictatorships.

At one point, HK people might have been content with the "high degree of autonomy" they were promised, but now that that has been significantly eroded and is perceived by many to be quickly disappearing, it is indeed less likely HK people would settle for this, if for no other reason than that it appears unsustainable under Party dictatorship. Thus, it's understandable why the Party, not for propaganda reasons alone, conflates self-determination and independence: It seems to recognize that, in the eyes of many HK people, it has lost the moral right to rule HK.

The rise of self-determination and the Party backlash

For a time, the rise of the idea of self-determination in HK seemed inexorable. Even moderate pan-democrats were catching self-determination fever.

In April 2016, about thirty self-described "young democrats"—moderate politicians, activists and academics—calling themselves ReformHK published a "Resolution on the Future of Hong Kong" which advocated self-determination, invoking international law as outlined above to buttress their argument, and proposed "perpetual self-rule" for the city.[4] They appeared to be hedging somewhat, especially in comparison to Joshua, as they spoke in terms of "internal self-determination". It was hard to know how exactly this was different from what HK people understood the Party was supposed to allow them all along, a "high degree of autonomy" and "HK people ruling HK", except that the group advocated continuing these policies beyond the end of the 50-year "one country, two systems" arrangement in 2047. (The Party has refused to discuss arrangements beyond 2047, and much of the self-determination push has had to do with what happens after then.)

In March and June 2016, two moderate pan-democratic political parties issued manifestos that stressed HK people's right to rule HK. The Association for Democracy and People's Livelihood called for self-determination.[5] Civic Party, while not using the term "self-determination", spoke of defending HK, of autonomy, of ensuring that HK people decide what happens to HK after 2047, noting that they had not had any say in the Joint Declaration or Basic Law.[6] The idea was in the air.

By October 2016, Joshua and Jeffrey Ngo were actually engaging in a media debate with Song Zhe, the Commissioner of the Foreign Ministry of the PRC in HK. The latter's "Self-determination in Hong Kong is a Non-Issue" appeared in *The Wall Street Journal* in mid-October.[7] Of course, Song Zhe would not acknowledge he was debating the two, but between 14 October and 9 November, Joshua and Jeffrey wrote six articles and Song Zhe two which were obvious rebuttals of Joshua and Jeffrey's.[8]

(Joshua and Jeffrey focus on the PRC's successful effort in the early 1970s, shortly after it supplanted the Republic of China as the representative of China at the UN, to have HK removed from the United Nations Special Committee on Decolonization's List of Non-Self-Governing Territories.[9] They say this amounted to stripping HK of its right of self-determination. While this is important history, I don't think it's crucial to the question of the right of self-determination since, according to international law, basic human rights are inalienable—they can never be taken away, and HK people retain their identity as a "people". How, after all, could a people have their status as a people and the right of self-determination taken away by a dictatorial regime at a time when it did not even exert sovereignty over them? At most, the revocation of status makes it more difficult for the UN as a body to recognize HK's right of self-determination, but the chances of the UN doing that anyway were low to non-existent. See the recent case of the UN Special Committee on Decolonization refusing to accept the petition of 1.8 million West Papuans for an example of how this works.[10])

Then the Party got freaked out by how well advocates of self-determination did in the September 2016 Legco elections, entering into the formal political system, and has since gone on the attack, doing whatever it can not only to dislodge them from Legco but also to eviscerate their organizations.

After the purge, Eddie Chu Hoi-dick, the top vote-getter ever in Legco elections, is one of the few outspoken self-determinationists still left in Legco. While he shares with Joshua and Demosistō the same objective of self-determination, the two have quite different ideas on how to get there. Both regard self-determination as a long-term project, with the goal being for HK people to determine HK's political status after 2047.

Joshua, though, envisioned developing a culture of referenda that would eventually lead up to a referendum on HK's post-2047 political status to be held some fifteen years down the road, around 2030. The justification for putting it off that long was to give HK people time to acquaint themselves with the referendum mechanism and debate the political status options so that they could use their vote responsibly and fully avail themselves of the opportunity. The major unanswered question was how in the world did Joshua imagine the Party and HK government would ever recognize such a referendum as legally binding? The hinted answer seemed to be, We'll cross that bridge when we get there.

Eddie Chu, on the other hand, thought working through the existing political system was the answer. Shortly after his victory in September 2016, he envisioned that within four to eight years, the self-determination camp would be the biggest in Legco.[11] Less than a month later, the HK government initiated legal proceedings to dislodge first two elected Legco members and eventually four more. Of these six, four were explicit proponents of self-determination, and the other two were very sympathetic to the cause. So much for the Party and the HK government allowing representatives holding such political beliefs to hold office within the formal political system.

Recently, neither Joshua nor Eddie have said much about self-determination, presumably because they've been rather busy fending off attacks by the Party and HK government. (ReformHK recently published a book focusing on self-determination and setting it in an international context.)[12] Joshua's hardly mentioned self-determination of late, presumably for fear of losing international support at a time when the Party is on the offensive and throwing people in prison, where he himself now sits. At any rate, both of their ideas for advancing the cause of self-determination, through referenda and Legco, face clear obstacles.

This would seem to support critics' views of self-determination and independence advocates. They say the ideas are simply unrealistic. But what's so realistic about continuing to push for real universal suffrage? Are the chances of getting that any greater than they are for self-determination? You could say self-determination is almost the only option remaining for HK people. What other recourse do they have to secure their basic human rights?

The Party clearly perceives self-determination advocacy as a threat. Will it succeed in destroying the advocates? Its current crackdown is so intense and widespread that it affects most everybody in the pro-democracy movement, which has the ironic effect of actually bringing them together. Self-determination was originally inspired by localists. Many moderate pan-democrats have inched their way in that direction, as witnessed by the Civic Party and ADPL manifestoes of 2016. Legco member Claudia Mo left Civic Party to start Hong Kong First. Another Legco member Fernando Cheung of Labour Party "caucuses" with the self-determinationists. Then you've got Demosistō, Democracy Groundwork, Eddie Chu, League of Social Democrats, People Power, Civic Passion, Youngspiration, Hong Kong Indigenous. Just about the only prominent pro-democracy group that hasn't indicated support for one form or another of self-determination is the Democratic Party. Looked at that way, a wide swath of the pro-democracy movement is already self-determinationist. What remains to be seen is whether they will manage to meld the self-determinationist cause, for which there is widespread support, into a political force. Doing so while under Party attack is challenging, to say the least.

Meanwhile, the forces of Party-driven mainlandization cast an ever-longer shadow over HK, where time does not stand still. The clock is ticking. Which side will win in the end?

On its side, the Party has military force, economic might, an ideology that prioritizes maintaining its empire (which it calls "state sovereignty") above almost all else, and the state-centric bias of the international community's preference for the status quo.

HK people have international law, justice and morality on their side — not necessarily a winning combination, but neither should it be underestimated. Oh, yes, and people power. That coupled with determined, unified resistance and a clear game plan focused on achieving a positive common objective would constitute at the very least a force to contend with.

The struggle continues. Underlying the issue of self-determination is the question of who does a people, a land belong to? Does HK belong to the Party, to China, to HK people? The Party-stoked nationalism on the mainland has led many Chinese to see HK as belonging to China, not HK people. The latter need to fight to ensure that, after 175 years, that question will finally be up to the HK people to decide.

Booing the Party anthem means our souls have not been harmonized

November 13, 2017

For 15 straight home football matches dating back to June 2015, fans of the Hong Kong national team have booed the anthem of the Chinese Communist Party. The Party has just promulgated a new anthem law for the mainland and inserted it into Annex III of HK's Basic Law, requiring the HK government to pass local legislation which will in all likelihood include criminalization of "disrespect" of the anthem.

Annex III is the part of the Basic Law having to do with mainland laws to be enforced in HK. Six laws were listed there at the time of the handover in 1997. One was added in 1998 and another in 2005. The anthem law will be the ninth, but it is the first that is meant to stop pre-existing behavior in HK. The HK government has announced it intends to introduce statutory legislation related to the law in the first quarter of next year. Fans booed again at the first match after the law was inserted, a friendly against Bahrain on November 9.[1] The football team plays its next home match on November 14 against Lebanon, an important qualifier for the 2019 Asian Cup.

1. #NotMyAnthem explainer

First, let's get a few things straight. I don't consider what the Communist Party calls the "national anthem" the national anthem. It is the Party anthem. I don't consider what the Party calls the "national flag" the national flag. It is the Party flag. I don't consider what the Party calls the People's Republic of China a people's republic. It is the Party's republic.

All of these, anthem, flag and republic, were decided by the Party without the people's participation. All are symbolic of dictatorship and directly related to Party rule. None existed before the Communist seizure of power in 1949.

One of the primary objectives of Party propaganda is to elide the difference between the Party and the nation, to inculcate in its subjects the idea that the two are virtually synonymous. According to this logic, loyalty to the Party and patriotism — love of country — are one and the same.

In order to resist this insidious message, it is important to insist on the distinction between Party and nation. Whatever I may feel about China, I detest the Party and what it stands for. I don't recognize the Party as the legitimate ruler of China because it is unelected. This is not just a matter of opinion but of international law.

So when I boo the Party anthem, I am not booing China or Chinese people. I am booing dictatorship. I am resisting complicity in dictatorship. I am booing the Party's betrayal of HK, its refusal to allow genuine universal suffrage and autonomy as required by both HK and international law. I am saying no to the Party's vision for HK. I am asserting a separate HK identity. I am standing up for HK.

I dream that one day 1.4 billion Chinese people will wake from the Party's "China dream" and understand that what they have been told was the Chinese flag is really the Party's flag, that what they have been told is the Chinese anthem is really the Party's anthem, that what they have been told is the people's republic is really the Party's republic. On that day, the portrait of the mass murderer responsible for the deaths of tens of millions of Chinese people will be removed from Tiananmen Gate and his likeness will disappear from every banknote. That would be a good day for China and a bad day for the Party. That's my China dream.

2. Just how impervious are HK people to enforced "patriotism"?

It was my daughter's first day of school.

My wife was dreading it. She says the HK education system stole her childhood and killed her creativity and imagination. She doesn't want that to happen to her daughter.

But, I remind my wife, the students of the Umbrella Movement got the very same education as you.

Miracles do happen, she replies.

The principal, who has a reputation as an authoritarian, commenced the beginning-of-year assembly with a flag-raising ceremony.

As trained, the older children raised the flag, accompanied by a tinny recording of "March of the Volunteers".

Next to me, my wife trembled with anger. We're under occupation, she muttered.

Yes, I agreed, it felt like that. It is in these small ways that HK people feel increasingly marginalized within their own city, within their own home.

If it had been another occasion, I would have started singing "Raise Our Umbrellas", the theme song of the Umbrella Movement and hopefully the future national anthem of HK.[2] I would have sung it as loud as I could and drowned out that tinny recording of "March of the Volunteers". But it was my daughter's first day. I didn't want to ruin it for her.

Then I looked around: In that gathering of hundreds of students, teachers, parents and staff, only one single person was singing, a woman who worked in the school office. Some of the older students who had learned but half-forgotten the anthem's lyrics in past years were dutifully mumbling along, their embarrassed heads bowed, facing the ground. All of the teachers and parents were silent. Some probably did not like to sing. Some probably did not know the words. (I estimate that only about 25 percent of HK people can sing the nine-line anthem. There isn't even a Cantonese version, so people are forced to sing an anthem which they are told is their national anthem in a language that is not their own. Contrast this with South Africa's beautiful anthem in Xhosa, Zulu, Sesotho, Afrikaans and English, five of the country's eleven official languages.)[3] Some probably, like us, resented the whole proposition that our children's school year should begin like this, in obeisance to a colonial ruler.

Based on that random sample and multiple other occasions where I noticed people were less than enthusiastic about the anthem, perhaps the Party has not burrowed into our flesh, has not seeped into our bones, is far from winning the proverbial hearts and minds. Twenty years on from the handover, however weak, cowardly, craven, stupid, unthinking and "pragmatic" a good many HK people may be (a good many human beings, for that matter), it will take a whole lot more to make them swallow this Kool-Aid.

3. Only the unloved could outlaw being unloved

The people who boo the Party anthem at football matches are the HK national team's most ardent fans. Without them, the team would have few loyal fans at all. The atmosphere at the matches is wonderful because of them: In the October match against Malaysia, there were only 6,000 spectators in 35,000-seat Hong Kong Stadium, but they got the place rocking.

Believe it or not, the booing of the anthem is good-natured. It's not as if the fans come only to boo. For them, the booing is just part of the routine: You come, you cheer the team, you boo the anthem, you go back to cheering the team. And they're deeply respectful of the opposing team's anthem, remaining utterly silent.

What does it say about the regime that it can't even tolerate a little booing? All dictatorships have one thing in common: No sense of humor. Nor do they have much sense of irony: "March of the Volunteers" evokes righteous, brave young men fervently marching off to join the cause of the defense of the motherland, but "respect" of the song will no longer be voluntary. The anthem's most uplifting phrase is "起來！起來！起來！"—rise up! rise up! rise up!, but then when you do, the Party slaps you down. How reactionary the revolutionaries have become!

China had managed to get by just fine without an anthem law up to now. I have never heard any report of a mainlander "disrespecting" the anthem. Therefore, it appears that for the first time ever, the Party has promulgated an unnecessary law on the mainland specifically to get it enacted in HK, simply to stop behavior it could not tolerate.

HK football has no hooliganism, no problem with violence of any kind at matches. You couldn't ask for better fans. And yet they must by criminalized to save Party face.

The anthem law is of a piece with the modus operandi of the Party: compulsion. It seeks to coerce loyalty to the Party, which it calls "patriotism". It seeks to erase from the public arena any trace of dissent. If you do not love me, I will force you to remain silent and pretend.

The booing is of a piece with the soul: It wants to be free. It knows that love cannot be coerced.

4. China is one of the few countries in the world to criminalize disrespect for the anthem and has the most severe punishment.

China's criminalization of behavior related to the anthem puts it among a small minority of countries in the world. Many countries have national anthem laws, which often include codes of conduct, but few criminalize anthem-related behavior. In many countries there is an expectation that respect be shown toward the anthem, but this is a matter of custom, not law.

Apart from China, at least seven countries criminalize behavior related to the national anthem (maximum punishments in parentheses): Botswana (US$75 fine),[4] Germany (up to 3 years in prison),[5] India (up to 3 years in prison or a fine or both),[6] Malaysia ($24 fine or up to 1 month in prison),[7] Singapore ($734 fine),[8] Turkey (6 months to 2 years in prison),[9] Uzbekistan (25 minimum monthly wages or up to 3 years in prison),[10] and Egypt (up to 1 year in prison and a $1,699 fine).[11] Of these seven countries, only two, Botswana and Germany, are rated "free" (as opposed to "partly free" and "unfree") in the Freedom in the World Report 2017.[12] Only Germany and India have punishments as severe as China's. These types of laws are often referred to as "insult" laws and, from a human rights perspective, are considered highly problematic and potentially unreasonable infringements of the right to freedom of expression.

All except one of the above-mentioned anthem laws prohibiting insult to the anthem are decades old. The newest, Egypt's was implemented in 2014 by the military rulers after they overthrew the elected government in 2013. Strikingly, not even some of the most severe dictatorships in the Middle East have such laws, though many recent incidents involving Islamists refusing to stand for the anthem have upset them.[13]

In addition to China, there have been recent attempts to criminalize behavior related to the anthem in the Philippines[14] and Russia.[15] In November 2016, the Supreme Court of India issued a controversial order that the national anthem must be played in all movie theaters and that those present must stand for it, but the order entails no penalty or punishment for failure to comply and refers to no criminal statutes to enforce the order.[16] What all four countries and Egypt have in common is governments that manipulate nationalistic sentiment to remain in power.

While Japan has no national law criminalizing behavior related to the national anthem, it does allow local jurisdictions to make their own rules.[17] Tokyo and Osaka have passed regulations requiring education authorities to record the names of teachers who do not stand and sing the national anthem in school. As a result, hundreds of teachers have been disciplined. The national anthem is an expression of loyalty to the emperor and considered by many to evoke Japan's militaristic past.

Thailand is well-known for playing the national anthem at 8 am and 6 pm daily, with all expected to stand in silence, but it has no law requiring people to do so. There have been two convictions under the country's lèse-majesté law for not standing while the royal anthem (different from the national anthem) was played in movie theaters. One conviction was eventually overturned and the other resulted in a suspended sentence.

In the United States, standing for and singing the national anthem is customary, but there are no laws criminalizing behavior related to the anthem and previous attempts to enact and enforce related laws have been struck down by the Supreme Court on First Amendment (free speech) grounds.[18] HK Executive Councillor Fanny Law has falsely compared China's new anthem law to the situation in the U.S.: "...Donald Trump has been criticising American football players for kneeling to protest during the playing of the US national anthem."[19] But while he has criticized them, his government is not prosecuting them, nor can it do so, while the new amendment to Chinese Criminal Law Article 299, based on the Chinese anthem law, expressly criminalizes "disrespect" with a penalty of three years' imprisonment.[20]

In 1977, the Sex Pistols shocked many in England when they released "God Save the Queen".[21] The BBC banned the song, but there was and is no UK law criminalizing conduct associated with the national anthem and there was never any question of the Pistols being prosecuted. Johnny Rotten said, "You don't write 'God Save The Queen' because you hate the English race, you write a song like that because you love them; and you're fed up with them being mistreated."[22]

5. There *is* another kind of patriotism

Apart from encouraging people to confuse loyalty to Party and love of nation, another key objective of Communist propaganda and coercion is to make people think that there is no other way, that somehow Party diktat is natural or even reality itself. For that reason, it is a form of resistance to remind ourselves of just how false that is.

I am skeptical of patriotism of all kinds. My loyalty is to humanity. It's human beings we must care for, regardless of their nationality. Human beings have human rights, regardless of where they were born or live. But in general, I am more sympathetic to the patriotism of small, threatened countries, whether Palestine or Tibet or HK. Their nationalism arises as a reaction to attempts by a greater power to swallow them up, and they use it to defend themselves, as did the Irish against England or the Baltics against the Soviet Union, and many others.

If big countries don't possess a high degree of self-critical awareness—and few do, Germany being an exception—their patriotism can easily become jingoistic, aggressive, ugly, hateful, and potentially dangerous, especially if rooted in grievance, the "big country as victim complex". China, for example, has convinced itself that it was a victim of imperialism (this part is true) but the Party will make it great again, while at the same time invading and occupying Tibet in the name of "returning it to the motherland", invading India and Vietnam, claiming most all of the South China Sea as its own, and having outstanding territorial disputes with several of its neighbors. Its toxic promotion of Party-centric "patriotism" is often directed at some "enemy" target like Japan or the Dalai Lama or "ungrateful and spoiled" HK people fighting for their rights.

I lived for several years in Norway, which is as close as human beings have come to a perfect society. Norwegians also happen to be intensely patriotic. I've lived in many countries, and Norwegian patriotism is the only kind I admire. Its key attributes are a belief in fairness, egalitarianism, solidarity ("we're all in this together") and respect for and identification with nature, of which there's plenty. It represents a consensus on basic values arrived at through shared experience and the continual democratic process.

I'm no fan of kings, but I was impressed with a down-to-earth speech defining Norwegians that the Norwegian king gave last year.[23] With compassion and generosity, he stressed diversity and inclusivity. Could one ever imagine a Party leader saying anything like, "Norwegians are girls who love girls, boys who love boys, and girls and boys who love each other. Norwegians believe in God, Allah, everything and nothing"? Could one ever imagine a Chief Executive saying anything inspirational about what it means to be HK people?

Norway has been fully independent for only a little over one hundred years. It endured centuries of colonial domination first under Denmark, then Sweden. When Norwegians got their independence, the first question they asked was, Do we want a monarchy or a republic? Norway is the only country I know of that voted by referendum to have a king.

The main event of Norwegian national day, May 17, is not a military parade but a children's parade to the palace where the royal family waves to them from the balcony. The symbolism is not tokenistic. Most every society has some rhetoric to the effect of children being our future, but Norway's is one of the few to actualize the words through consistent policies. Indeed, it could be said the whole society is designed to promote children's welfare. There is 12 months' paid parental leave, and everywhere you go, whether the bank or a restaurant, you find a play area or family area.

I often compare Norway and HK. Both are prosperous and have relatively small, homogeneous populations. With the HK government's wealth, we too could afford a decent social welfare system, a universal pension system, lengthy parental leave, adequate child and elderly care support for families, solid labor laws and minimal poverty (HK's poverty rate is 19.7 percent and rising,[24] versus 9.3 percent in Norway).[25] The main difference? One place is democratic, the other is not. Political power in HK is concentrated in the hands of a tiny Party-allied minority who are antagonistic to the very concept of the common good, or equate it with their own self-interest.

Norway has no legally designated national anthem. For over a century, "Yes, we love this country" has been the de facto anthem.[26] With lyrics by a famous Romantic nationalist poet of the nineteenth century, its most frequently sung verses focus on Norway's nature. After the 2011 massacre of 77 people, 69 of them at a youth camp, the most widely sung tribute to the country was "My little country".[27] It is shorter, simpler, more down to earth, and composed recently, in 1994. A nice song, though I had to laugh: You can call Norway many things, but it most certainly is not "little"—if you tipped the country upside-down, it would stretch to the bottom of Europe. Of course, the diminutive was a term of endearment, not a reference to size. While other countries have pompous dreams of greatness, it's striking that this new quasi-national anthem by popular acclaim characterizes the big country as little. The modesty is refreshing.

In response to the massacre, Norway's biggest single loss of life to violence since World War II, the Norwegian prime minister said, "We will respond with more democracy, more openness, more humanity but never naivety."[28]

Meanwhile, in HK, a few people boo the Communists' anthem, and they pass a law banning "disrespect".

6. Communist Country versus Umbrella Country

> *"I didn't think I was interested in politics before the revolution. I was interested in finding a way to make myself heard when it felt like the whole world wanted to forget me. Now I know that's what politics is."*
>
> — a mahragranat musician, from *The Egyptians: A Radical History of an Unfinished Revolution* by Jack Shenker

The Egyptian revolution and the Umbrella Movement have many differences, but in one respect they are similar—the eventual retrenchment of the status quo ante, with a vengeance. Shenker characterizes post-revolution Egypt as consisting of what he calls Mubarak Country and Revolution Country. Mubarak Country has political power and controls the security forces and the economy. But Revolution Country is still very much alive and can be found in the many cracks and crevices of society, the rise of mahragranat being an example. These manifestations of Revolution Country among activists, workers, the poor, intellectuals, writers, artists and musicians elude regime attempts to extinguish them. The two have diametrically opposed visions of what Egypt should be. This too sounds like HK.

What is happening in HK now is people are thinking about the sort of society they want, the sort of society that corresponds to how they want HK to be. That cultural efflorescence is almost diametrically opposed to Party rule, which is why the Party does what it can to wipe it out.

When HK fans boo the anthem, it's like the tip of the iceberg of Umbrella Country poking into the public sphere, and Communist Country and Umbrella Country collide. The Party's only way of resolving the difference is by force. It promulgates a mainland law and inserts it into the Basic Law. The rigged HK government and Legislative Council then pass local legislation to criminalize formerly legal behavior.

Virtually every recent Party initiative taken in regard to HK has been to restrict: the 2014 ruling out of genuine universal suffrage; the 2016 interpretation of the Basic Law regarding oath-taking, which was used to kick six elected pro-democracy members out of the Legislative Council; and now, the anthem law.

I wish to live in a society where rights are continually expanded and better protected, not one where they are continually reduced and eroded. That is why I boo. I boo in the hope that one day Umbrella Country will prevail over Communist Country. The booing will soon make me a criminal. But at least this criminal's soul will not be harmonized.

The disqualification of Agnes

January 31, 2018

The Hong Kong government's combination of prosecutions, banning from candidacy, and disqualification from Legco of pro-democracy leaders constitutes a sustained attack on political opposition and creates so many uncertainties and roadblocks as to heavily compromise the only free and fair elections Hong Kong has ever had.

On Saturday, January 27, Agnes Chow Ting was notified by the Returning Officer of the Electoral Affairs Commission of Hong Kong that she would not be allowed to run in the March 11 Hong Kong Island by-election to fill the Legislative Council seat left vacant by the disqualification from Legco of her Demosistō party fellow Nathan Law.

This is a momentous event in Hong Kong history. The reasons for that are complex.

The article below is divided into three parts:

1. Background: How the Communist Party and Hong Kong government have further restricted democratic rights since their refusal to introduce universal suffrage in 2015;
2. The disqualification of Agnes; and
3. The implications of the disqualification.

If you're already familiar with the background, feel free to jump to part 2.

1. Background: How the Communist Party and Hong Kong government have further restricted democratic rights since their refusal to introduce universal suffrage in 2015

On August 31, 2014, the National People's Congress Standing Committee of the People's Republic of China issued a decree on elections in Hong Kong. It said that it would allow "universal suffrage" for the election of the Chief Executive, but its terms were so circumscribed that the Hong Kong pro-democracy movement cried foul: Rather than offering universal suffrage, the 8/31 decree would, if implemented, cement Communist Party control over the election because it stipulated that only "2 or 3 candidates" could run and that they must be "patriotic" (Communist code for loyal to the Party) and chosen by a committee controlled by the Party. The Umbrella Movement, which ran from September 28 to December 15, was a reaction against this decree.

Rather than listening to the United Nations Human Rights Committee, which has the legal responsibility to monitor Hong Kong's compliance with the International Covenant on Civil and Political Rights, to which Hong Kong is party, or to the Umbrella Movement or the wide variety of suggestions by Hong Kong people of ways to comply with international law, the Hong Kong government simply went ahead and made a proposal to the Legislative Council based on the terms of the 8/31 decree. The pro-democracy movement had large enough representation in Legco to veto the proposal. And so, universal suffrage in Hong Kong was dead on arrival.

Since then, not only have the Hong Kong government and Communist Party done nothing to implement genuine universal suffrage or broaden the democratic rights of the Hong Kong people, they have made sustained and extensive efforts to further restrict those rights.

This started with the Legislative Council elections in 2016.

Only 35 of Legco's 70 seats are filled by elections that can be considered free and fair and conducted in accordance with the principles of genuine universal suffrage (ie, complying with ICCPR Article 25). These geographical constituency seats are the only positions in any branch of the Hong Kong government which are thusly filled. That's how small and restricted the area of true democracy in Hong Kong is. And now it's shrinking further, as the government imposes various additional conditions and restrictions on participation.

The other 35 Legco seats are for the so-called functional constituencies representing various professional and other interest groups and sectors of society. There are only about 225,000 electors to 30 of those seats, versus about 5 million eligible voters in the 35 geographical constituencies. The functional constituencies are stacked with Communist Party allies, ensuring their control of Legco. The pro-democracy movement has always won the majority of the seats in the freely and fairly elected 35 geographical constituencies. Allies of the Communist Party have always won a huge majority in the functional constituencies.

The pro-democracy movement has always called on the Communist Party and Hong Kong government to scrap functional constituencies, in accordance with their obligation under the Basic Law to introduce full and genuine universal suffrage. In 2014, the NPCSC handed down a decree that allowed "universal suffrage" in the election of the Chief Executive in 2017 and stipulated that if that was achieved, it was possible to allow "universal suffrage" in Legco elections in 2020. Now, rather than acting to abolish functional constituencies, the declared ultimate objective, the Party and HK government have sought to control both candidacy for and representation of the only 35 freely elected seats, in the geographical constituencies.

In 2016, six applications for Legco candidacy were rejected. The reasons given were political: The applicants were suspected by the Returning Officers of the Electoral Affairs Commission of being advocates of independence for Hong Kong. Never before had applications for candidacy been rejected on political grounds. The Returning Officers justified their decisions by saying they did not believe the applicants could comply with a requirement of office holders in Hong Kong to uphold the Basic Law since Article 1 says Hong Kong is an inalienable part of China.

Previously, the function of the EAC Returning Officers was solely administrative, ensuring forms were filled out fully and correctly, but now, with the disqualifications they were making political and legal judgments which went far beyond the intended scope of their role. Not only were they serving as political arbiters, but there was no recourse: If your application was rejected, there was nothing you could do about it, no one you could appeal to. Suddenly the EAC, previously regarded as non-partisan and neutral, was conducting political screening, exactly what the UNHRC said made the 8/31 decree fall short of Hong Kong's international human rights obligations. Rather than going forwards toward greater democracy, Hong Kong was going backwards.

Two of the disqualified have filed challenges, or so-called election petitions, at the Hong Kong High Court. One, Andy Chan, is the head of the Hong Kong National Party, the first party to explicitly advocate independence. The court heard his case in May 2017 but strangely has yet to issue a decision. The other petitioner is Edward Leung, a former leader of Hong Kong Indigenous, a localist party with pro-independence inclinations. But when Leung filed his application to be a candidate, he eschewed independence. Not only that, he had been allowed to run for Legco in a by-election held only a few months before, in February 2016. Why had he been allowed to run in February but not in September? Nothing had changed. If anything, his political stance, as he articulated it, had moved away from pro-independence. And yet he was disqualified. The High Court, again for reasons that are unclear, has yet to hear his challenge, though it was filed in October 2016. To complicate matters further, and make the process appear even more arbitrary, some applicants who appeared to have in the past at the very least expressed sympathy with the pro-independence cause were allowed to run for Legco.

After the Legislative Council elections were held in September 2016, elected Legco members took their oath of office in October. The Hong Kong government reacted to the ways six pro-democracy representatives took their oaths by attempting to disqualify them, on the basis that they had failed to fulfill the requirement of successfully completing their oath of office.

This, again, was unprecedented. In the past, the oath of office had been used by some elected Legco members to protest. In some cases, the Legco secretary refused to accept their oaths as valid, and the Legco president required them to retake the oaths. This was customarily regarded as an intra-Legco matter, in which the Hong Kong government should not interfere, and Legco had shown itself competent in dealing with past controversies. Indeed, the new Legco president had already acceded to requests from the six Legco members to retake their oaths (though after the government announced it would bring legal cases against Baggio Leung and Yau Wai-ching, he revoked his permission in their cases).

The Hong Kong government brought its case against Leung and Yau to the High Court. While the case was on-going, the National People's Congress Standing Committee, the same entity that had issued the 8/31 decree denying genuine universal suffrage to Hong Kong, issued a new "interpretation" of the Basic Law article pertaining to oath-taking.

It would have been one thing if the Hong Kong government had said, We are warning you. We will no longer tolerate these antics. And from now on, new rules will apply. But instead, the Party and Hong Kong government made up new rules and then applied them retroactively, going against one of the basic principles of common law, that you can't hold someone legally accountable based on a law that did not apply at the time of the commission of the act in question.

The High Court judge subsequently disqualified Leung and Yau. Fresh off that success, the Hong Kong government brought cases against the four other elected pro-democracy Legco members and by mid-2017, managed to get them disqualified as well.

In all, six applicants for candidacy were disqualified, and six elected Legco members were disqualified. While the six applicants for candidacy were all suspected of harboring pro-independence views, the six disqualified Legco members had various political views: Leung and Yau were regarded as having pro-independence sympathies, though their party, Youngspiration, did not explicitly advocate independence. Nathan Law and Lau Siu-lai were in favor of self-determination (more on the meaning of that below). Leung Kwok-hung (Long Hair) was a staunch and outspoken opponent of the Communist Party, but up to then had never expressed pro-independence or self-determinationist views. And Edward Yiu was a mild-mannered professor who was simply pro-democracy. The High Court ruling emphasized they were being disqualified not for their political views but for their failure to successfully take the oath of office, but given the NPCSC's intervention in the midst of the case and the enormous pressure this put on the High Court judge to produce a decision amenable to the Party, it's hard to regard that ruling as anything but politically compromised.

In disqualifying the six Legco members, the High Court ruling disregarded the rights of voters. As a result, a few words uttered while taking the oath of office were made to cancel out tens of thousands of votes. Indeed, 183,236 people had voted for the six. Should not the will of the people and their democratic rights outweigh the judgment that their elected representatives had taken invalid oaths, especially when the representatives were ready and willing to retake the oaths? Would not a more reasonable judgment have been to require them to take their oaths properly? The Hong Kong government's cases against the six were politically absolutist and the judge's ruling legally fundamentalist in its failure to pay due heed to the principle of balancing constitutional rights and responsibilities. The judge was arguably boxed into a corner by the NPCSC interpretation of the Basic Law, probably the single-most egregious example since the 1997 handover of the Communist Party interfering in judicial processes in Hong Kong and the most damaging to the rule of law.

2. The disqualification of Agnes

Why, given the fact that the EAC Returning Officers already rejected six applications for candidacy in 2016, is Agnes' disqualification precedent-setting?

First of all, Agnes was the choice of the pro-democracy movement as a whole. She was running to replace her disqualified fellow member of Demosistō, Nathan Law. In the other two geographical constituencies in which there will be by-elections in March to replace disqualified Legco members, the pro-democracy movement held primaries to choose the candidates, but on Hong Kong Island, it ceded to Demosistō the right to choose Nathan's replacement, and Demosistō chose Agnes. Whereas the six disqualified in 2016 could be seen as representing only themselves or their parties, Agnes represented the pro-democracy movement as a whole, a consensus candidate of the whole spectrum of the movement, from traditional pan-democrat to self-determinationist. In rejecting Agnes, the government is rejecting the candidate of the pro-democracy movement, its main political opponent.

Secondly, the explanation given by the Electoral Affairs Commission is that Agnes was disqualified because of the self-determination stance of her party, Demosistō. This marks the first time that a Hong Kong government entity has taken a concrete action based on the view that advocating self-determination is tantamount to advocating independence. The Communist Party's consistent propaganda line has been to conflate independence and self-determination. Now the Hong Kong government has shown that propaganda is its official position as well.

The Hong Kong government asserts that self-determination is against the Basic Law. Therefore, logically, anyone belonging to a party that advocates self-determination cannot run for Legco because they can't be regarded as upholding the Basic Law, in particular Article 1 on Hong Kong being an inalienable part of China. But as in the case of Edward Leung (allowed to run in February 2016 but not September 2016), the Hong Kong government is moving the goalposts, making up the rules as it goes along.

In September 2016, Nathan Law, also of Demosistō, was allowed to run for Legco without objection by the EAC. Now, Agnes is not. What's changed? Why? What does this have to do with law? It appears to have much more to do with the changing political calculations of the Party and Hong Kong government. Eddie Chu Hoi-dick was elected to Legco in 2016 with the largest number of votes ever for a Legco candidate. He is a prominent advocate of self-determination. The government allowed him to run for office and has not (yet!) attempted to disqualify him. The lack of consistency merely serves to emphasize the arbitrary nature of these decisions.

Not only that, but the Hong Kong government's assertion that self-determination is inconsistent with the Basic Law is simply factually inaccurate. Basic Law Article 39 says, "The provisions of the International Covenant on Civil and Political Rights, the International Covenant on Economic, Social and Cultural Rights, and international labour conventions as applied to Hong Kong shall remain in force and shall be implemented through the laws of the Hong Kong Special Administrative Region. The rights and freedoms enjoyed by Hong Kong residents shall not be restricted unless as prescribed by law." Article 1 of both the ICCPR and the ICESCR says, "All peoples have the right of self-determination. By virtue of that right they freely determine their political status and freely pursue their economic, social and cultural development." There are some details of these articles that require interpretation (for example, what does "as applied to Hong Kong" mean? And what is a "people"?) which I have gone into elsewhere, but basically, not only is it untrue that self-determination is incompatible with the Basic Law, the Basic Law actually protects the Hong Kong people's right of self-determination.

One might argue that there is some tension between Hong Kong being an inalienable part of China (Article 1) and the right of self-determination (Article 39), but then the challenge is to reconcile that tension. It is a sleight of hand to regard one and disregard the other. The Hong Kong government's assertion that advocacy of self-determination is incompatible with the Basic Law is simply a political judgment and its disqualification of Agnes is a political ruling. It is dispensing with law and ruling by decree.

Even if a potential candidate is seen to be challenging or disagreeing with certain aspects of the Basic Law or other laws, it is perfectly within her rights to do so. One purpose of candidates is to propose changes which they believe will improve Hong Kong, and there's nothing that says changes to the Basic Law cannot be proposed, whether by an ordinary citizen, a political candidate, a Legco member, or a government official. To have an iron-clad policy of arbitrarily deciding that certain political views are contrary to the Basic Law, outside of any judicial proceedings or due process, and to disqualify candidates based on that judgment is to deny the very agency to political actors which is at the heart of the philosophy of democracy, that people are elected to change things.

As for what "self-determination" means, that depends on who you ask. At one time or another, quite a few groups in Hong Kong have advocated self-determination, including the traditional pan-democratic Association for Democracy and People's Livelihood[1] and various members of Civic Party, including a sitting Legco member, under ReformHK.[2] Some have used terms such as "internal self-determination", which basically means just having the autonomy Hong Kong people believe they were promised by the Communist Party to run their own government.

Given that different people and groups have advocated self-determination and defined it in different ways, does the disqualification of Agnes on grounds that she belongs to a party advocating self-determination mean that anyone advocating self-determination in any form is to be barred from running for Legco? If so, we're in for a rout. And if not, then where are the boundaries? One suspects that the uncertainties arising from her disqualification are intended to intimidate people against using the dreaded term.

Not long after the Umbrella Movement, Joshua Wong began to advocate a form of self-determination which included the possibility of eventually (he proposed in about 2030) holding a referendum to determine the fate of Hong Kong after 2047, the end of the "one country, two systems" period.[3]

More recently, Demosistō has downplayed that idea and spoken vaguely about self-determination.[4] On its website, it declares, "Demosistō aims to achieve democratic self-determination in Hong Kong. Through direct action, popular referenda, and non-violent means, we push for the city's political and economic autonomy from the oppression of the Communist Party of China (CPC) and capitalist hegemony."[5] Also posted there is a more extensive statement, "Democratic self-determination — Demosisto's roadmap for the self determination of the Hong Kong people".[6]

Not only is Demosistō fully within its rights in advocating self-determination, but the way in which it has done so is exemplary for any responsible citizen. Its concern is for what is to happen to our city after 2047, and this is a matter about which all citizens should be concerned, for no one knows what will happen then.

Demosistō's strongest assertion is that it is Hong Kong people who should determine what happens then. Never in our entire history have we decided our political status or even been so much as involved in determining the basic political parameters of our society. Why should it not be us who decides now?

The Communist Party has not presented its vision for what is to become of Hong Kong after 2047: Will it preserve the supposed "one country, two systems" model at which it is incessantly whittling away? Will it attempt to fully assimilate

Hong Kong into the mainland? It has not made its intentions clear, and this in itself should be cause for worry.

In disqualifying Agnes, the Hong Kong government is clearly siding with (more likely taking orders from) the Communist Party: Hong Kong people are not allowed to determine our own fate; only the Party has that right. This is dictatorship versus popular sovereignty in the starkest terms. The Party is showing itself to be as hostile as ever to the will of the people.

The third reason the disqualification of Agnes is precedent-setting is that the Electoral Affairs Commission has acknowledged it consulted the Hong Kong government in arriving at the decision to disqualify Agnes. While a government agency, the EAC is putatively independent. The reason for this is that it must be regarded as an impartial arbiter in order to legitimately carry out elections. With its previous disqualifications on political grounds and the disqualifcation of Agnes, coupled with its acknowledgment that this was done in consultation with the government, it can no longer be regarded as that impartial arbiter. Rather, it is acting on behalf of the government to conduct political screening. This is enormously damaging to the EAC as an institution and to the only free and fair elections that exist in Hong Kong, those for the 35 Legco geographical constitutency seats.

It is part of a broader pattern: The Party and Hong Kong government are asserting greater political control over institutions, undermining the judiciary, the universities and the EAC, which have up to now been essential in protecting the already insufficient rights and liberties that Hong Kong people do have. It is clear from this pattern that Hong Kong is going backwards, moving ever closer to the mainland model, where the Party exerts full political control over all institutions of government and society.

To give this story an even wickeder ironic twist: the EAC consulted the new Secretary for Justice Teresa Cheng,[6] who, since taking office, has been found to have at least ten illegal structures on multiple properties. So you have the spectacle of a Secretary for Justice who has apparently broken the law with total political impunity giving supposed legal advice to disqualify a political opponent.

And then there's Agnes herself, a highly conscientious, principled, astute young activist with a political wisdom and maturity far beyond her years. She would have been an excellent representative in Legco (perhaps that is exactly what the government was afraid of). She is exactly the sort of person any self-respecting democratic society would want to encourage to become involved in politics. Instead, she is excluded from it. Ultimately, her disqualification is a condemnation of the Hong Kong government for its cowardice and subservience to Communist dictatorship.

The larger issue is that talented, assertive young people have a dwindling stake in their own society. They are either driven to the margins or forced to emigrate. The Party and Hong Kong government's efforts to retain absolute power are destroying Hong Kong. They are attempting to construct a rigidly hierarchical system with unelected and unaccountable leaders and a citizenry whose chief "virtues" are obedience and subservience.

On my way to the Sunday rally to protest the disqualification of Agnes, I passed a street station canvassing support for her opponent, Judy Chan of the pro-Communist New People's Party. I had to laugh: at that moment, Judy Chan was essentially running unopposed. I stopped and told one of her supporters, "Your slogan should be: Vote for Judy, she's the only candidate." How free and fair is that? Yes, the pro-democracy movement has lined up Au Nok-hin as Agnes' replacement, but even if the EAC allows him to run (as of early Tuesday, January 30, one day after the nominations deadline, his candidacy still has not been confirmed), Au will start at a distinct disadvantage, given that both Agnes and Judy Chan have already been campaigning for weeks. It appears that one of the intentions of the Hong Kong government in disqualifying Agnes is to make pro-democracy supporters so disenchanted with the process as to discourage their participation in elections. It's not an exaggeration to say that in the eyes of many, free and fair elections are a thing of the past.

3. The implications of the disqualification

Localists and advocates of independence and self-determination need not apply. In brief, that is the message.

Those groups represent a large proportion of the Hong Kong electorate that is being disenfranchised. Previous surveys have indicated that upwards of 16 percent of Hong Kong people support localism. In the 2016 Legco elections, 173,122 people voted for successful candidates who advocated self-determination (Eddie Chu—84,121, Nathan Law—50,818, Lau Siu-lai—38,183) and 113,136 voted for successful candidates who were considered localists (Cheng Chung-tai—54,496, Baggio Leung—37,997, Yau Wai-ching—20,643). That is a total of 286,258 votes, not including votes for unsuccessful localist and self-determinationist candidates—such a large number of votes as to effectively render Legco elections a joke now that their candidates are excluded. Under such circumstances, how can elections be considered free and fair?

After the Umbrella Movement, many new groups sprung up. They tended to be more strident and demanding than the traditional pan-democratic parties. Their starting point was: The demands of the Umbrella Movement were not met, so what do we do now? One of the first decisions they faced was whether to participate in the formal political system even though they regarded it as illegitimate (because rigged and undemocratic). If they participated, were they not just legitimizing it? Would it not be better to work outside of the system? Virtually all of those groups, from Hong Kong Indigenous to Youngspiration to Demosistō, decided to take part in the formal political system and run for election. They believed it was preferable to work within the system to change it. They have been excluded from that system. Now what?

The Hong Kong government is clearly out to destroy them, not only by excluding them from formal politics but also by prosecuting many of their leaders and regular members. In January alone, there have been 7 trials of 56 pro-democracy leaders and activists. Does the government believe it can stamp out localist, pro-independence and self-determinationist sentiment simply by excluding advocates of these positions from formal politics?

Demosistō will certainly have to reconsider its strategy given that it cannot expect that any of its members will be allowed to run for office again. Anyway, the Hong Kong government's gotten Joshua Wong sentenced to a total of nine months in prison and Nathan Law to eight, rendering them ineligible to run for office for the next five years (unless those sentences are overturned on appeal). So it's employed a variety of means to gut the party.

A whole generation of young people is being dissuaded from participating in the formal political system, becoming ever more hostile toward it if not cynical, regarding it as the preserve of elites who have as their chief aim shoring up the power of the Party and the financial interests that control a large portion of the economy.

And what are the implications for the wider pro-democracy movement? Will the pan-democrats simply express their outrage and then continue with business as usual? Can the pro-democracy movement adopt strategies outside of the political system that are more effective than participation in it?

One might expect the traditional pan-democrats to continue as is. After all, they have not substantially refined their demands since the Umbrella Movement, continuing to simply call for political reform even though it is abundantly clear that for the Party this is entirely off the table for the foreseeable future.

But what about the self-determinationists? They are now all but forced to reconsider their strategy. In 2016, there was an indirect debate between Joshua Wong and Eddie Chu regarding how to pursue self-determination. Joshua thought it was through referenda. Fresh off his huge election victory in September, Eddie thought it was through Legco, and he predicted that within one or two elections, half of Legco would be self-determinationist.[7] The disqualification of Agnes puts paid to that aspiration. So what now?

Perhaps the self-determinationists have put too much faith in Legco as a pathway to anything. Essentially powerless, and now with the entrance to it jealously guarded by Party gatekeepers, Legco's an eternal cul-de-sac intended to keep the pan-democrats going in endless circles. Perhaps it's a blessing in disguise to be excluded. It seems that the success of self-determination will depend on a broad-based mass movement, and this requires reaching out to the people and deep organization, not just mobilization for the occasional elections. Right now, there are many extremely angry and frustrated young people who need to be empowered to take the future of their city into their own hands, and the movement must reach out to them and get them involved.

Meanwhile, the government is trying to do away once and for all with the pro-democracy movement's veto power in Legco, to capture Legco in order to have its way with Hong Kong, which could very well include introducing Article 23 "security" legislation and even a new proposal on fake suffrage.

At what point does something gotta give?

With the disqualification of Agnes, we have entered a new phase in Hong Kong history. The future is very uncertain. All that is clear is that the Communist Party and the Hong Kong government will continue in their efforts to politically control Hong Kong and further restrict Hong Kong people's already highly circumscribed right to political participation. Far less clear is how the people will react.

Why Joshua, Nathan, Alex and the Umbrella Movement would be an excellent choice for the Nobel Peace Prize

February 8, 2018

On January 31, a bi-partisan group of U.S. lawmakers nominated Joshua Wong, Nathan Law, Alex Chow and the Umbrella Movement for the Nobel Peace Prize. They're the first nominees from Hong Kong ever, eight years after Liu Xiaobo became the first Chinese laureate.

It is very heartening that twelve United States lawmakers nominated Joshua Wong, Nathan Law, Alex Chow and the Umbrella Movement for the Nobel Peace Prize.[1]

The nomination comes at a time when the pro-democracy movement is under sustained attack by the Chinese Communist Party and Hong Kong government. Their primary means of attack are criminal prosecutions of pro-democracy leaders and activists and disqualifications from candidacy and elected office. Through these means, they have barred virtually all groups which grew out of the Umbrella Movement from participating in the formal political system and are attempting to destroy the groups they find the most threatening. They intend especially to intimidate young people against getting involved in politics, in the classic Communist ploy of "killing the chicken to scare the monkeys."

All three of the leaders singled out in the nomination have been sentenced to prison (Joshua to nine months in two different cases, Alex to seven, and Nathan to eight) in relation to their role in occupying Civic Square on September 26, 2014, triggering the start of the Umbrella Movement two days later. On February 6, their prison sentences were overturned by the Hong Kong

Court of Final Appeal, nearly two years after the trial began on February 29, 2016. Joshua is now awaiting the appeal hearing of his other, three-month prison sentence. In addition, Nathan was disqualified from the Legislative Council along with five other pro-democracy lawmakers after having won the seats in the only democratic elections Hong Kong had.

It was especially gratifying that the US lawmakers praised the nominees for, among other things, fighting for self-determination in the very same week that the pro-democracy candidate for the Hong Kong Island Legislative Council by-election in March, Agnes Chow, was barred from running on the grounds that she and her party, Demosistō, advocate self-determination. She was seeking to fill the seat left vacant by the disqualification of Nathan. Self-determination is in fact a basic human right. According to the Hong Kong government, it does not comply with the Basic Law even though the international treaties which guarantee it are enshrined in the Basic Law.

But being politically persecuted—prosecuted, disqualified, intimidated, vilified and physically assaulted (assailants have been convicted for attacks on both Joshua and Nathan)—is in itself insufficient grounds for winning the Nobel Peace Prize.

True, the persecuted make up an illustrious list of laureates, including, just in recent decades, Liu Xiaobo, Shirin Ebadi, Kim Dae-jung, Nelson Mandela, Aung San Suu Kyi, Rigoberta Menchú, Desmond Tutu and Lech Walesa, and these, it's safe to say, have been amongst the Norwegian Nobel Committee's best choices. But they won not primarily because they were persecuted but because they were freedom fighters and human rights defenders under oppressive regimes.

Joshua, Nathan and Alex certainly fit that description, and there are plenty of positive reasons the three young men and the Umbrella Movement should join that revered group of laureates. The US lawmakers have already written an eloquent letter to the Norwegian Nobel Committee outlining those reasons, and the statement the three made in response to the nomination also makes their Peace Prize-deserving qualities abundantly clear.[2]

Following on that, there are a few other arguments in their favor, which can be summarized in the following sentence:

They are *young people* **taking the future of their society into their own hands and** *collaboratively leading ordinary citizens* **in the** *long, hard, nonviolent struggle* **for** *democracy* **and self-determination.**

The phrases in italics are discussed below.

Democracy

The number one issue of our times is the global battle between democracy and authoritarianism. The world hangs in the balance: In the coming years and decades, it could easily become more authoritarian or more democratic. Other issues, such as climate change, must also be urgently addressed, but the question of whether the world goes in a more democratic or more authoritarian direction will have great bearing on that and all other urgent global issues.

As the most powerful dictatorship, China is the ringleader of a club of dictators who have a vested interest in ensuring the world goes in a more authoritarian direction. This club includes major countries like Russia, Turkey and Egypt.

Prominent democracies, such as the U.S., India and the Philippines, have leaders with authoritarian tendencies. Brazil and South Africa, major regional powers that have shown great democratic promise, have experienced democratic crises related to corruption. In large swaths of the Middle East and Central Asia, democracy is close to non-existent, and other areas such as Southeast Asia are not much better. Even the most democratic part of the world, Europe, has experienced challenges to democracy in a number of countries, most notably Hungary and Poland.

Both the Economist Intelligence Unit's Democracy Index[3] and the Freedom House Freedom in the World report[4] have tracked the decline of democracy worldwide for upwards of a decade.

Giving the peace prize to Joshua, Nathan, Alex and the Umbrella Movement would be a recognition of the urgency of this issue and send a signal to people around the world of the importance of democracy. Hong Kong, being a "Special Administrative Region" in the world's largest dictatorship, is on the front lines of the battle. Recent visits to Europe and the U.S. gave me the impression that Europeans and Americans don't fully appreciate the threat that China poses to democracy worldwide. A Nobel Peace Prize to the Umbrella Movement would alert them to that.

Youth

Very few young people have won the Nobel Peace Prize. This is understandable: it often takes decades of work to bring about greater peace and justice. But it is important to recognize both the great contributions of young people to peace and their immense potential to bring about a more peaceful and more just world.

Young people were not the only ones who took part in the Umbrella Movement, but they certainly played a leading role. At a crucial moment in Hong Kong's history, they stood up and said, I demand a say in my own society! What's more, since then they've continued to do so, demonstrating admirable persistence, resilience, creativity, determination and courage. They are Hong Kong's future. And while often little more than a well-worn platitude, it is nevertheless true that young people the world over are the future. In order to make the world a better, more peaceful place, it is necessary to tap their energy and ideals. Awarding the Peace Prize to Joshua, Nathan, Alex and the Umbrella Movement would be an inspiration to young people everywhere.

Nonviolent people's movements

Malala Yousafzai is the only recent young Peace Prize laureate. She has admirably harnessed the notoriety gained from the near-fatal attack on her to campaign for education for girls worldwide. But Malala received the award as an individual, sharing the prize with Kailash Satyarthi.

The prize has most often gone to individuals, non-governmental organizations, politicians, and inter-governmental organizations (such as the Intergovernmental Panel on Climate Change and the International Atomic Energy Agency).[5]

The Umbrella Movement came in the wake of the Arab Spring, which the Norwegian Nobel Committee has acknowledged, though with something of a sideways glance. The 2011 prize went to Yemeni activist Tawakkol Karman, together with the Liberians Ellen Johnson Sirleaf and Leymah Gbowee, "for their non-violent struggle for the safety of women and for women's rights to full participation in peace-building work". In 2015, the National Dialogue Quartet won the prize "for its decisive contribution to the building of a pluralistic democracy in Tunisia in the wake of the Jasmine Revolution of 2011". While both awards had to do with people's movements for democracy, one focused more on women's participation and the other on a group that, once the movement had succeeded in toppling the dictator, played a crucial role in bringing about a transition to democracy.

Giving the prize to the Umbrella Movement and its young leaders would be recognition of the importance of ordinary citizens working together to peacefully bring about more just and democratic societies.

The long, hard nonviolent struggle

The Umbrella Movement did not achieve its main positive objective. In this, it is similar to other recent movements like the Arab Spring, the Iranian Green Movement, the Occupy movement, and the worldwide demonstrations against the invasion of Iraq in 2003.

An estimated 1.2 million people participated in the 79-day-long occupations of three hubs of Hong Kong in late 2014. Before that, going back to 2003, hundreds of thousands had demonstrated down through the years for basic rights and universal suffrage. And since then, the struggle continues.

A Peace Prize to the Umbrella Movement would send the message that the peaceful struggle for rights and democracy is long and hard, there are no easy victories, but it is necessary to keep on fighting.

It took Gandhi and the anti-colonial movement of India decades. It took King and the Civil Rights Movement of the U.S. years, and that struggle for full equality is still unfinished. How long will it take us against the biggest dictatorship in the world? How long will it take all the others struggling against authoritarian regimes the world over?

It's up to us, the people, to fight on, but a Peace Prize to the Umbrella Movement would be a beacon of hope to all engaged in the long, hard nonviolent struggle for freedom and the right to make decisions for ourselves and our own societies.

Will the Norwegian Nobel Committee give the Nobel Peace Prize to Joshua, Nathan, Alex and the Umbrella Movement?

This is, of course, impossible to know. There are almost certainly many other worthy nominees.

The conventional wisdom is that it's a long shot. In reaction to Liu Xiaobo receiving the Peace Prize in 2010, the Chinese government punished all of Norway. For six years, there was virtually no contact between the Chinese and Norwegian governments. During that time, the Norwegian government was pressured by its business community to come to terms with China. When the two countries signed an agreement at the end of 2016 to "normalize relations", many saw Norway as capitulating to China, and, in doing so, betraying its own values.[6]

I was in Norway last summer before Liu Xiaobo's death and spoke with many Norwegians about this. They felt somewhat uneasy about what their government had done but few criticized it. They thought it had made a pragmatic decision and got the best deal it could. It didn't necessarily mean, they believed, that Norway would no longer stand up for rights abroad.

I took this general attitude to be the result of the years-long lobbying effort by the Norwegian business community, lead by its fish farmers. Norway believed it needed better relations with China for the sake of trade, in spite of the fact that it is an exceedingly wealthy country, due first and foremost to oil, and it has a well-managed sovereign wealth fund that guarantees its prosperity for generations to come. If any country was in a position to stand up to China, it was Norway. And yet it didn't.

Then Liu Xiaobo died in custody. And the top leaders of the Norwegian government, the ones responsible for the deal with China, said not one word during the excruciating weeks the story of his dying played out in the international media. Even when backed into a corner by the press, Prime Minister Erna Solberg refused to utter Liu's name, as if it were a magical incantation that would spell doom.

Harald Stanghelle, the editor-in-chief of *Aftenposten* (Norway's *New York Times*), wrote an editorial reminding Norwegians of how Norway had stood up for Andrei Sakharov, Nelson Mandela, Aung San Suu Kyi and many more. In backing down to China, Norway was losing its identity as a small nation whose foreign policy was based on democracy and human rights.[7]

Many Norwegians I spoke to agreed, not enough to make a dent in opinion polls (the conservative coalition government was narrowly re-elected in September 2017), but awareness was growing that being "pragmatic" came with moral and political costs that should perhaps be calculated more carefully. Who would bother to take the little country that traded freedom for fish seriously anymore?

In contrast to the silent government, Berit Reiss-Andersen, the chair of the Norwegian Nobel Committee, sent a heartfelt video message to the Liu Xiaobo memorial held in Hong Kong.[8] She also attended the memorial service held in Washington, DC in October. It was clear Liu Xiaobo meant something to her.

Now the Umbrella Movement has been nominated. The threatening rumble from Beijing began the day after that was announced.[9] While confining its criticism to the US lawmakers, China recited the same well-worn propaganda lines it used in the case of Liu Xiaobo, against "foreign interference" and about how the movement was "illegal" and "not peaceful" and the young men nominated were "criminals". The Communist Party's rhetoric wasn't nearly as shrill as it might have been, but that's because this is meant as only the initial warning salvo. The threats are bound to pick up closer to the time in early October when the winner will be announced.

Rarely has the Norwegian Nobel Committee faced such bullying tactics. Will it dare? If the people of Hong Kong can stand up to Beijing, the people of Norway, whom it costs much less, surely can too.

But does it really matter?

It would be a welcome acknowledgement, especially at a time when the pro-democracy movement is under sustained attack.

It wouldn't immediately change anything, and there would in all likelihood be some backlash from the dictatorship. But the Peace Prize would reiterate that the Communist Party has a formidable opponent to contend with. Its demands for basic rights will not simply go away. It will not be destroyed.

It would be a reminder that the rest of the world is watching and give hope and inspiration to young people, persecuted people, and political movements fighting for democracy and other rights around the world.

Awarding the Nobel Peace Prize to Liu Xiaobo had zero effect. Since then, the regime's doubled down on oppression. Even after his death, Xiaobo's wife, Liu Xia, is still extrajudicially held incommunicado from the rest of the world. But that's to be expected from a regime that controls all levers of power.

Hong Kong is different. It has a modicum of freedom and civil liberties. Due to censorship, many Chinese never even knew who Liu Xiaobo was and have only vaguely heard of the 1989 pro-democracy demonstrations, if at all. Everyone in Hong Kong knows of the Umbrella Movement. It has determined almost every aspect of the political moment in which we now live.

Last Thursday evening, I was at the protest against the disqualification of Agnes Chow held outside the Hong Kong government's briefing session for candidates in the upcoming Legislative Council by-elections to fill the seats of four of the six disqualified pro-democracy Legco members.

Agnes, Joshua and Nathan had managed to get inside the session, which was closed to the public, as assistants to Agnes' replacement, Au Nok-hin. I was standing near the back door when suddenly it flew open and before my eyes Agnes was unceremoniously tossed out by a clutch of security guards. At the same moment, Joshua and Nathan were similarly ejected via the front door. It suddenly hit me that the dictators in Beijing are terrified of these brave, articulate, and passionate young people.

A memory followed in the train of that epiphany: In 1989, I was teaching at a university in China when, just four months after the June 4 massacre, the Nobel Peace Prize was awarded to the Dalai Lama. Some of the students at the university had been killed on June 4, others had been imprisoned, still others were on the run, wanted by the authorities. The school year opened with compulsory military training and political education for all students. They were deeply depressed and refused to work. This was back in the days when universities still assigned graduates jobs at work units, and almost all of the students were being punished for their participation in the demonstrations by being sent to the least desirable work units in rural areas.

When the news broke that the Dalai Lama had been awarded the prize, the students were shocked and disappointed. They'd had years of brainwashing by the Communist Party that he was an evil separatist: why would the Norwegian Nobel Committee give the Peace Prize to such a person?

I tried to explain to them as best I could who the Dalai Lama really was and why he deserved the prize, but deep down, I was disappointed too. Even while I recognized that the Dalai Lama would have been an excellent choice in any other year, the students had been hoping that their pro-democracy demonstrations would be awarded the prize, and who could blame them? They had tried to peacefully change China for the better and had been killed, imprisoned and punished in myriad other ways for doing so.

Not long after that, Western democracies mostly resumed "normal relations" with the regime under cover of the cynical euphemism of "engagement", whereby the prerogatives of capital and trade were prioritized over freedom, democracy, and human rights.

It's hard not to feel, looking back, that the Norwegian Nobel Committee missed an opportunity. If the prize had been awarded to the young Chinese who'd stood up for their country, it might have set a somewhat different tone on the world stage and affected the dynamics of what was to come.

Since then, China has failed to democratize. The regime has hardly changed at all. The Committee tried to make amends with the award to Liu Xiaobo, but it was arguably too late: The movement of which he'd been a part had been obliterated decades before, he was in prison, and the Party was already in the process of destroying the fragile beginnings of the independent civil society for which he stood.

Awarding the Nobel Peace Prize to Joshua, Nathan, Alex and the Umbrella Movement would be exceedingly timely, recognizing a movement that is still very much alive and still has a chance of changing Hong Kong for the better, and perhaps even positively affecting the rest of China. Beyond that, it would be a beacon of hope to people everywhere who yearn for freedom, democracy and human rights.

Has independence become the secret dream in many hearts?

April 16, 2018

The Communist Party's propaganda and intimidation are driving the Hong Kong resistance underground, eroding freedom and maybe even helping to germinate the very seed the Party wants to eradicate.

Observations on the Saturday, April 7 rally for Benny Tai and the pro-independence gathering next door

1. "Where their heart lies"

Outside, there are some five dozen of them, the pro-independence advocates, gathered on the pavement between the Legislative Council building and Tim Mei Avenue.

Inside, there are 2,000 to 3,000 at the rally organized by the pro-democracy movement to support Benny Tai, who for nearly two weeks has been under sustained attack by the Communist Party, the Hong Kong government and their allies for having done something he didn't do—advocate independence—, something that even if he had done it, he had a perfect right to do.

People are angry. The chants are loud. Rarely seen in public these days, the Reverend Chu Yiu-ming appears in support of his Occupy Central with Love and Peace co-founder. Now 74, he's aged considerably since the Umbrella Movement three and a half years ago. Long Hair and Lee Cheuk-yan give well-received fiery speeches. The loudest chants of the night are in response to Lee's call to "end one-party dictatorship", a classic pro-democracy slogan down through the years and a gesture in defiance of recent suggestions by Party allies that people who make that call will no longer be allowed to enter Legco due to the latest changes in the Chinese constitution.

The rally is held in the designated Legco protest area on a Saturday evening. (I want to protest against the designated Legco protest area. Something in me recoils at the idea of protesting where the government tells you to.) Legco is dark; there is no one inside; the same for the surrounding government buildings. And all of adjacent Tamar Park is empty too, except for the young lovers, who can hardly hear the noise of the crowd and aren't distracted from their common purpose. I wonder about the point of shouting at an empty building and think of the koan, "If a tree falls in a forest and no one is around to hear it, does it make a sound?"

The crowd is full of pro-democracy stalwarts, familiar faces I've seen for years; its average age makes me feel almost like a youngster. There are probably more young people among the five dozen pro-independence advocates outside than the thousands gathered inside.

I turn to a woman of long acquaintance, someone who was one of the 1,000 arrested in the Umbrella Movement, the 250 prosecuted and the 90-some convicted, in her case of obstructing police for sitting on the pavement just around the corner from where we now stand. She's a middle-aged professional who as recently as last year expected to die of cancer. I ask, "What do you think of them?" gesturing toward the pro-independence group.

"I agree with them," she says.

I am surprised. She's been in the pro-democracy movement for years and even belongs to one of the traditional pro-democracy parties which certainly does not espouse independence.

"They're right," she continued. "It's all we have left. We have nowhere else to go."

There is a pause. A silence hangs between us. I'm waiting for her to tell me more.

"You know Gwangju?" she asks hesitantly.

"You mean Gwangju, Korea?"

"Yes."

And then it is as if she doesn't dare say more, or doesn't know quite how to say it, as if saying it might make it happen and she isn't sure whether she wants that or not.

It takes me a moment to follow her unspoken train of thought. On May 18, 1980, the people of Gwangju rose up against dictatorship. It was not an altogether peaceful uprising. They stole arms from police stations and armories.

Hundreds were massacred by the South Korean military. As a battle, the people lost, but the uprising inspired a movement that went on less than a decade later to set the country irreversibly on the path to democracy.

I'm not shocked by her intimation that it might take outright rebellion and a violent crackdown to catalyze the next stage of the freedom struggle. Since last summer, I've come across more than a few who have spoken of armed uprising. It's easy to dismiss this kind of thinking as crazy, deluded, wishful, irresponsible, but the very fact that such ideas are in the air says something about the political climate in Hong Kong these days. And these people have done their homework: Hers is the first allusion to Gwangju I've come across, but several others have compared Catalonia's nonviolent struggle for independence negatively to Euskadi Ta Askatasuna's violent fight for a Basque country, arguing the latter got more from Spain for the Basques than the former has for the Catalans.

But most of the people I've spoken to who are thinking along these lines are localists or independence advocates. I am so struck by the thoughts of this woman whom I thought I knew well that I decide to pose the same question—what do you make of the independence advocates?—to others who'd come for the main rally inside.

The traditional pan-democratic political parties and many of their supporters have given the pro-independence types a wide berth. They either disagree with them in principle, suspect they've been infiltrated by Communist agents who are driving their agenda, or are afraid of being smeared with the separatist label themselves, which ironically is just what's happening now with the tarring of Benny Tai, of all people, as a separatist. (Prior to the Umbrella Movement, Benny would often joke about how ironic it was that such a staunch moderate as himself ended up leading the most "radical" organization yet in Hong Kong, Occupy Central with Love and Peace, but radical only in the sense that it advocated civil disobedience; it never objected to the Communist Party's assertion that Hong Kong is "an inalienable part of China".) As recently as the annual January 1 pro-democracy march, when a pro-independence group, including some of the same people out tonight, appeared in the marchers' midst, big gaps opened up both before and after it—none of the traditional pro-democracy people wanted to be associated with them, almost as if they were toxic. And at the march on November 6, 2016 against the Party's impending interpretation of the Basic law on oath-taking, which was subsequently used to disqualify six democratically elected Legco representatives, many in the crowd went out of their way to say they were protesting against the Basic Law interpretation but they did not support the actions of Baggio Leung and Yau Wai-ching who during the taking of their Legco oaths of office displayed banners that read, "Hong Kong is not China".

I end up asking nine others. They range in age from their mid-thirties to mid-fifties. All are veterans of the pro-democracy movement, from before the time when even the idea of an independent Hong Kong occurred to most people. All are acquaintances. They feel comfortable talking with me and might say something quite different to strangers, especially given the atmosphere of suspicion and intimidation that pervades Hong Kong these days, in particular on this supposedly "sensitive" issue.

In all, of the ten people I ask, all separately from one another, six express sympathy with the independence advocates demonstrating outside and four are critical.

Of those four, two seem to simply have a visceral reaction against them. I don't get the impression they've thought carefully about the issue. When I ask them if they have anything against Hong Kong being part of China, they don't answer directly but instead say they support democracy in both Hong Kong and China. To me, they represent the traditional pan-democrats whose thinking really hasn't changed much since the Umbrella Movement, who've refused to even engage with the many issues that have arisen since then regarding the strategy, purpose and goals of the pro-democracy movement. The two others disagree with calling for independence on grounds of strategy: Yes, "one country, two systems" is broken beyond repair, but advocating independence plays into the Party's hands, presenting it with a convenient justification for a military crackdown to take full control of Hong Kong long before the end of the "one country, two systems" period in 2047. Notably, none of the four opposes independence on the grounds that they feel Chinese and want to be part of China. It's safe to say that within the pro-democracy movement, you'd be hard pressed to find many who identify with China. The days when the pro-democracy movement was lead by people like the deceased Szeto Wah—who co-founded the first post-1989 pro-democracy party as well as Hong Kong Alliance in Support of Patriotic Democratic Movements in China and the Hong Kong Professional Teachers Union and was himself steeped in Chinese culture, believing deeply in both democracy and being Chinese—are well and truly over.

Of the six who sympathize with the independence advocates, I don't get the sense any are fervently committed to that cause. Rather, their sympathy is related to a lack of faith that the Party will ever abide by the terms of "one, country, two systems", which, among other things, would mean implementing genuine universal suffrage and allowing real autonomy. They simply don't think anything good can come of Party rule over Hong Kong. In fact, the idea makes them despair. So, like the first woman I spoke with, they feel backed into a corner with no way out.

All ten express deep pessimism about the direction Hong Kong is going. One says, "If the Party and Hong Kong government really wanted to stamp out calls for independence, the most effective thing they could do is to ensure affordable housing and decent-paying jobs for young people. The problem now is that people, especially young people, see no future for either themselves or Hong Kong, and they see their personal fate and the political fate of their city as closely related."

A professional woman in her mid-thirties says, "Of course I agree with them. I think most everyone of my generation shares that sentiment—they think Hong Kong would be better off independent. That's where their heart lies."

"Where their heart lies...." The phrase keeps returning to me. As much as anything else, the sympathy with the independence advocates comes out of a feeling of heartache for Hong Kong. It is a heart argument. When you feel you can do nothing else, you still have your heart and what is within your heart, if you haven't relinquished it, if it hasn't been possessed by demons.

These informal interviews, in addition to much else that I've heard and seen since last summer, lead me to wonder about the extent to which resistance to Party control of Hong Kong is being driven underground, especially with the increasing number of individuals and groups excluded from Legco and subjected, like Benny Tai, to witch hunts. More than ever before, authorities are declaring a range of political beliefs "illegal" and unacceptable. As a result of these exclusions and attacks, people are discouraged from expressing their political views—it's always safer not to. But that doesn't mean those views disappear; instead, they remain within the heart and mind, they go underground. And what happens when a substantial part of political life begins to exist out of public view? What are the implications of this resistance of the heart?

These closet independentists make my own self-determinationist position seem like watered-down agnosticism. I advocate self-determination because I insist on it as a basic human right, enshrined in the International Covenant on Civil and Political Rights, the International Covenant on Economic, Social, and Cultural Rights, and, through Basic Law Article 39, in Hong Kong law. I insist on Hong Kong people's right to decide their own political status, a right that in their whole modern history they've never been granted, and I am willing to go along with whatever Hong Kong people decide, as long as they are allowed to do so freely and fairly. But isn't this an intellectual position? What is really in my heart? If Hong Kong people could exercise their right of self-determination and hold a referendum on Hong Kong's political status today, what would I vote for? Isn't the choice almost made for me by process of elimination? Full assimilation into a China ruled by the Communist Party? No way. Maintaining a "one country, two systems" arrangement which the Party already refuses to honor and is steadily eroding? Only for dupes. So...?

Is the Party right after all that self-determination is just a veiled form of independence? If Hong Kong people could really follow their hearts, would they choose independence? Is that why the Party is attempting to nip any talk of independence in the bud now, before it festers? So that Hong Kong never gets to the point of Catalonia or Scotland or Iraqi Kurdistan where millions openly advocate independence? I still think most people would be satisfied with genuine universal suffrage and real autonomy, but they think that's impossible, and where does that leave them to go? It's as if independence is the inevitable conclusion staring us all in the face.

2. The dynamics of political crackdown: Freedoms eroding, the resistance driven underground

But if these six sympathize with the independence advocates, why don't they join them? Two cannot advocate independence publicly because of their jobs. For the others, doing so would represent a decisive step they simply are not ready to make. Some are undecided exactly what they think. It's also a matter of difference: The cultures of the independence advocates and the pro-democracy movement are different. No pro-independence leaders have yet arisen who make it seem like the "respectable" thing to do. They are seen as angry young men.

That taking the leap to advocating independence should be perceived as so decisive, a bit like coming out, a point from which there is no turning back, is also a sign of the extent to which Party propaganda and intimidation has affected the political climate in Hong Kong: Are you ready to make yourself a target? After all, Benny Tai's become a target simply for hypothetically mentioning the idea of independence. By contrast, millions flooded the streets of Catalonia last year to support the independence referendum, and it did not appear that fear of losing their jobs or otherwise suffering retaliation was a deterrent.

Observing the independence advocates, I can't help but observe the police as well: they are filming them the whole time, as I have seen them do on multiple occasions.

Anyone who has attended pro-democracy protests in Hong Kong is familiar with police filming them. It is an abuse of civil liberties that Human Rights Watch[1] and the United Nations Human Rights Committee[2] have repeatedly criticized, though most people in Hong Kong, including pro-democracy activists, don't seem to blink an eye at it. The police say they have a right to film in any public place. But in practice, they tend to film those they suspect of being engaged in unlawful activity. For example, whenever they declare a protest "unlawful", the cameras come out. Even this use of cameras is questionable, especially considering the police have no publicly available guidelines regarding filming of protests, but the independence advocates are certainly committing no crime. Though the police must have hundreds of hours of video footage of them by now, no one has ever been prosecuted in Hong Kong for advocating independence, in spite of the fact that the Hong Kong government has repeatedly said it is "illegal" and "against the Basic Law". (It isn't.[3]) And yet the police continue to film them continuously, without pause, whenever they come out to the street.[4]

Whenever I see police filming protesters, I talk with them about it. Most refuse to engage with me, but on this evening, a polite and earnest officer is willing to entertain my questions. Like colleagues of his I've spoken to before, he begins by invoking the police's right to film in public. I reply that this overlooks the fact that the police are different from ordinary citizens, and police filming of people exercising their right to freedom of expression and assembly can have the effect of intimidating and stigmatizing them. "Can you imagine how it would make you feel if the police followed you around pointing a camera at you, and what it might make others think of you?" He then tells me they're engaged in "crime prevention", to which I respond, "What crime are you preventing, and how?" At that point, the officer says he has given me his explanation. "But wait," I say, "now let me give you mine: What you are doing has little to nothing to do with law enforcement. Your bosses are ordering you to carry out the political agenda of the government, and your filming amounts to intimidation. You should either arrest these people and charge them with a recognizable crime or stop pointing your cameras at them." He pretends he hasn't heard me.

No one knows what the police do with the video footage. Are they conducting facial recognition studies of it? Are they building a database of independence advocates? Are they monitoring them? Are they compiling a dossier for the government? Could they be sharing it with mainland authorities? There is no independent oversight of or accountability for this dubious police work.

In that light, it isn't difficult to see why those harboring pro-independence sympathies might think twice about voicing them. The use of the police to carry out the regime's political tasks is one aspect of the deterioration of HK's political climate. When freedom erodes, it is hard to contain the erosion; it tends to occur in small, sometimes almost indiscernible ways in multiple places in society at the same time.

We are far along that slippery slope, and the goalposts of the permissible keep moving:

In February 2016, the at-the-time Hong Kong Indigenous leader Edward Leung (now in prison while standing trial on "riot" charges) was allowed to run in a Legco by-election. He did well and was expected to win a seat in the general Legco elections of September that year but was disqualified from running. First move of the goalposts.

His ally, Baggio Leung, was elected in his stead. Then Baggio and his Youngspiration party fellow Yau Wai-ching were kicked out of Legco. Second move of the goalposts.

That effectively put an end to pro-independence involvement in formal electoral politics in Hong Kong.

But the Party was not done there. It began to equate independence and self-determination. The two are very different concepts with very different implications for Hong Kong, but the regime essentially makes no distinction.

So, four more elected pro-democracy Legco representatives were kicked out. Two of them, Nathan Law and Lau Siu-lai were self-determinationists, one was a long-time "radical" thorn in the government's side (Long Hair), and one simply happened to occupy a seat that Party allies wanted back (Edward Yiu). Third move of the goalposts.

When Nathan Law's Demosistō party fellow Agnes Chow attempted to run in the March 2018 by-election to fill his vacant seat, she was barred on grounds that her party advocated self-determination, though Nathan had been allowed to run a year and a half before. Fourth move of the goalposts.

From that point on, not only independence advocates but self-determinationists are effectively and arbitrarily barred from holding public office, all of this though courts have never ruled on whether independence or self-determination advocacy is "illegal" or "against the Basic Law" or tantamount to not being able to uphold the Basic Law, a requirement for holding public office.

Now, for the first time, the Party is going after a traditional pan-democrat, Benny Tai, alleging ludicrously that he advocates independence.[5] Fifth move of the goalposts, and a clear warning to other traditional pan-democrats that they had better watch their step.

But why Benny Tai, someone who's never said anything that could remotely be construed as "against the Basic Law"? Precisely for that reason: to scare everyone else who thought they were safe up to now, to make everyone think twice about what they say, how they say it, where they say it, and to whom.

The campaign against Tai is orchestrated. It's the first time I can remember the Hong Kong government ever singling out a particular individual for political criticism,[6] something which is in itself chilling and simply unacceptable. It appears that the fact he gave the speech in Taiwan particularly incensed the Party, sensitive as it is to cooperation between Hong Kong and Taiwanese pro-democracy and independence activists.

Tai's been attacked for ages. After the Umbrella Movement, the governing council of the University of Hong Kong, dominated by Party allies, forced the university to discipline him for alleged improprieties involving donations to OCLP that passed through the university, even though the university administration had conducted its own investigation and found no evidence of wrongdoing. It also rejected vice-chancellor Peter Mathieson's nomination of Johannes Chan, pro-democracy head of the law faculty where Tai works, to pro-vice-chancellor, in apparent retaliation for the fact that Chan defended Tai. Lunatic Party allies like Junius Ho (who said independence advocates should be "killed mercilessly") have tried to get Tai fired. This long-standing campaign goes back to former Chief Executive Leung Chun-ying's astounding attack in his annual policy address of January 2015 on an undergraduate magazine and is meant to cast a pall of self-censorship over university campuses and restrict academic freedom. Now with Mathieson, who had no toleration for political interference, gone, maybe they think they've got another chance to kick Tai out. Apart from restricting academic freedom, The Party is also cleansing public institutions such as Legco and universities of "hostile elements".

Some speculate the attacks on Tai are paving the way for introduction of draconian Article 23 "national security" legislation, but the Party doesn't need to attack Tai to do that. Its constant anti-independence propaganda is sufficient. It's likely, though, the Party is using the attack to test the waters: how much resistance might there be this time around to what many expect to be a more draconian slate of laws than what was tabled, and defeated, in 2003?

The attacks on Tai are also part of a Communist-style campaign to replace truth with proclamation: Henceforth, whatever the Party says is the truth, no evidence needed. This corruption of language and disregard for accuracy are part of the mainlandization of Hong Kong's political climate.

But at its root, this is the Party's fight against any kind of speech which even mentions considering political arrangements for Hong Kong other than the status quo. The Party simply doesn't want Hong Kong people to think about the future of Hong Kong, especially not out loud, in public. It is implacably hostile to popular sovereignty, the idea that Hong Kong people should have any say at all in deciding their political fate. Meanwhile, it refuses to reveal its plan or ideas for what it thinks should happen after the end of the 50-year "one country, two systems" period in 2047, and it wants to head off any discussion of that by Hong Kong people: We shouldn't get any ideas in our heads that we will have any say in a matter that is exclusively for the Party to decide.

The Party is steadily constricting political space, ringfencing a very small circle of "acceptable" opposition groups that will be allowed to participate in formal politics, and excluding an ever wider range of other groups.

I'm often reminded of the Martin Niemöller ditty: First they came for the independence advocates, and I did not speak out, because I was not an independence advocate. Then they came for the self-determinationists, and I did not speak out, because I was not a self-determinationist. Then they came for Benny Tai, and I did not speak out, because I was not a moderate. Who's next?

If you're talking localists, independence advocates, self-determinationists, and anyone whom the Party and Hong Kong government arbitrarily decide to label as such, that's a substantial part of the population, perhaps upwards of 25 percent, which is effectively disenfranchised from participation in the few and highly circumscribed free and fair elections Hong Kong has had. These elections are now so compromised as to pose a dilemma to the pro-democracy movement of just how much to even participate in such an illegitimate process.

One of the main effects of all this—the disqualification of candidates and elected Legco members, the Party attacks on Benny Tai on false premises, the police filming of independence advocates, not to mention the dozens of prosecutions of pro-democracy leaders and activists—is to silence people. They lie low and retreat to the resistance of the heart.

Even the outspoken have had to negotiate this thicket of accusation and denunciation. Self-determinationists, though they advocate a right enshrined in the Basic Law, have been de-emphasizing this key political aspiration in order to continue to participate in the increasingly narrowing formal political sphere. By late 2016, there were burgeoning discussions of self-determination. After his election victory, having received the most votes ever for a Legco candidate, self-determinationist Eddie Chu Hoi-dick said the goal was to eventually make the self-determinationist camp the largest pro-democracy camp in Legco.[7] Now, he is the only self-determinationist remaining in Legco, Nathan Law and Lau Siu-lai having been kicked out, and recently he has downplayed self-determination. The same goes for Demosistō. When Agnes Chow began campaigning to fill Nathan Law's seat in January 2018, she played down the party's call for self-determination. It barely featured in her campaign. Demosistō feared the government might use that as grounds to bar her and also, even if it allowed her to run, would smear her as pro-independence. In the end, of course, Agnes was disqualified anyway, precisely on those grounds.

3. As the Party constricts political space and the resistance submerges, reality becomes harder to discern

These are the dynamics of political crackdown. With the dozens of prosecutions of pro-democracy leaders and activists, with the exclusion from elected office of an ever-expanding range of groups and individuals, with attacks on freedom of speech, resistance is being driven underground, and exactly what is happening becomes harder to discern, even for those involved.

Yes, crackdown frightens people away from political participation. But can you scare people into submission as successfully in a semi-free place like Hong Kong as in an unfree society like the mainland?

What are the risks to the Party in alienating ever more people from its rule? Does it believe that it can eventually isolate and contain its political enemies while the majority of the population will more or less go along with whatever it decides to impose on the city? Is that objective attainable?

Or is the increasingly hidden political life of Hong Kong a sign that the crackdown is merely germinating the seeds of the next uprising, whatever form that might take?

Is the resistance weakening, or lying low while deepening and transforming? What is the worth of a resistance that, at least for the time being, remains largely within the secrecy of the heart?

What happens when you drive a people into a corner, with nowhere else to turn, or, as *People's Daily* puts it in typically bombastic and violent language, apply a "sledge hammer" to them?[8]

The gamble is that they surrender, are obliterated, disappear. But there are other possibilities too.

Are those five dozen independence advocates who appear to be a tiny minority really only the tip of the iceberg?

Turning Hong Kong's Legislative Council into a mini-National People's Congress

May 12, 2018

Through prosecutions, disqualifications and rule changes, the Chinese Communist Party and Hong Kong government are moving toward their vision of a "loyal", "patriotic" Legco meant solely to rubber-stamp their initiatives.

On Saturday, May 5, Democratic Party Legislative Council member Ted Hui was arrested on suspicion of assault, dishonest access to a computer, obstructing a public officer in the execution of her duty, and criminal damage.

What had he done to merit this? Snatch a mobile phone from a Hong Kong government official whom he suspected of monitoring Legco members. He returned the phone and apologized, but the amends were insufficient to head off, first, condemnation by the Hong Kong government and the Communist Party's Hong Kong allies and, now, arrest and possible prosecution.

All of this was pretty predictable. What Hui did was stupid. You don't go around snatching other people's phones, even if you suspect they're spies. His act simply handed the Hong Kong government a golden opportunity to persecute yet another pro-democracy Legco member.

But in all the controversy, the symbolism of the moment and its wider context have been largely overlooked. It appears Hui was correct in suspecting the government official was monitoring Legco members. She seems to have been sent on an errand to herd pro-Communist Legco members into meetings in order to ensure a quorum.

This is part of an initiative undertaken by the government to counteract what it perceives as obstructionism on the part of pro-democracy Legco members who have used Legco rules and procedures to force adjournments and delays of meetings on government initiatives they oppose but ultimately do not have the votes to block.

The first part of the initiative was to pass anti-filibustering rule changes in December 2017.[1] But the government apparently thought that in itself was insufficient; thus, its shepherding project. This would be funny if it weren't so inappropriate and ominous: The pro-Communist Legco members are so inept that they can't themselves figure out how to get the requisite number of bums on seats in meetings.

But the government monitoring is part of a darker trend: its trespassing into areas previously considered the purview of Legco. Rule changes are the least of its arsenal. The more potent weapons are disqualifications and prosecutions of sitting pro-democracy Legco members and blocking potential candidates from running for Legco on political grounds.

The ultimate objective is to defang an already mostly powerless Legco and turn it into a harmless rubber stamp body along the lines of the National People's Congress. According to this vision, Legco should project an image of representative participation in the political process without the messiness of opposition and resistance, let alone any real power. In this sense, it is part of the larger project of the mainlandization of Hong Kong institutions and norms.

How did we get here?

It's important to remember the baseline: According to the Basic Law (Article 68), the Legislative Council is ultimately to be elected entirely according to principles of genuine universal suffrage. That means one person, one vote, all votes counting equally, for all Legco seats.

As it stands, Legco is effectively rigged in favor of Party and Hong Kong government allies.

Thirty-five of its 70 seats represent geographical constituencies. Until the recent disqualifications of elected Legco members and the barring of candidates on political grounds, these were the only elections for high-level political office in Hong Kong which were free and fair and conducted according to principles of universal suffrage.

The other 35 seats represent so-called functional constituencies. Only members of those constituencies, most of which are formed along professional or vocational lines, can vote for those seats. Whereas the overall number of registered voters is about 3.8 million (with a total of somewhere around 4.8 million people eligible to vote), only 236,859 voted in 30 functional constituencies in the 2016 Legco elections: 4 percent of the electorate elected 42 percent of the representatives. Unsurprisingly, most functional constituencies are controlled by entrenched interests allied with the Party and Hong Kong government.

On top of this, it should be remembered that Legco is not really a legislative body in the normal sense of the word. It cannot initiate its own legislation (except in special cases which do not entail any government expenditure), only vet government-initiated legislation. For that reason, I avoid calling Legco members "lawmakers" or "legislators"; these terms are, strictly speaking, misnomers and they convey the impression that Legco isn't much different from legislatures in democratic countries.

Twenty years after the handover, universal suffrage in Legco elections is no closer to being realized. Indeed, from a very undemocratic starting point, we're moving backwards to an even more restricted, less open, less representative political system.

When the Party supposedly decided in 2014 to allow Hong Kong to elect the Chief Executive, it said that once that was achieved in 2017, there would be the possibility of implementing universal suffrage in Legco elections earliest 2020. But, of course, the Party refused to allow the Hong Kong government to put forward a proposal to elect the Chief Executive according to principles of genuine universal suffrage, and its fake suffrage proposal was rejected by pro-democracy Legco members in 2015. This means the implementation of universal suffrage for Legco is also indefinitely stalled.

It's worth stressing that according to international human rights law, it is states that have the responsibility of realizing and protecting human rights, including the right to universal suffrage (Article 25, ICCPR, to which Hong Kong is party). The Chinese and Hong Kong governments are legally obliged to realize universal suffrage. They cannot blame failure to do so on anyone else, nor can they postpone their realization. Whereas the principle of progressive realization (gradually realizing a right) applies to economic and social rights, since some of them require money to realize (like schooling for all children), it does not apply to political and civil rights. Legally speaking, the Chinese and Hong Kong governments have no excuse for the continued delay in implementing universal suffrage for elections of the Chief Executive and Legco. Indeed, until they do, the Hong Kong government and Legco, from the perspective of international law, are illegal.

Rather than implementing genuine universal suffrage without delay, the only actions the Party and Hong Kong government have undertaken in regard to Legco since the defeat of their fake suffrage proposal in 2015 have gone in the opposite direction, further restricting the rights of sitting Legco members, of potential candidates, and of voters.

The turning points here are clear: First, the 2014 Umbrella Movement; then, the rise of localists and independence advocates; then, the police-protester clashes in Mong Kok during Chinese New Year in 2016; and finally, the 2016 Legco elections. The Party looked at these developments and concluded it had to take steps to combat "hostile elements". Hong Kong people were simply getting too uppity. For the Party, the last straw was how well new post-Umbrella candidates did in the 2016 Legco elections. This was something it simply could not abide. And it was around that time that its current policy of political warfare was consolidated.

And now, here we are

Here is a list of candidates representing new pro-democracy parties who were elected to Legco for the first time in 2016, along with their eventual fate:

- Baggio Leung, Youngspiration—disqualified, convicted of unlawful assembly
- Yau Wai-ching, Youngspiration—disqualified, convicted of unlawful assembly
- Nathan Law, Demosistō—disqualified, convicted of unlawful assembly
- Lau Siu-lai, Democracy Groundwork—disqualified
- Cheng Chung-tai, Civic Passion—convicted of desecrating PRC and HKSAR flags
- Eddie Chu Hoi-dick, independent—nothing so far, apart from death threats

See a pattern? The only one of the six who has not been kicked out of Legco and/or prosectued is Eddie Chu. He also happens to be the candidate who won the most votes ever in any Legco election, 84,121. The government has apparently concluded that, for the moment, he's untouchable, and the strategy is to isolate him by removing his allies, rather than attack him directly.

Ted Hui is part of a group of new, young candidates who were elected from Civic Party and Democratic Party, the established and relatively moderate pro-democracy parties, which includes Alvin Yeung, Jeremy Tam and Lam Cheuk-ting. He is the first of this group to be targeted, almost as if the government had just been waiting for the opportunity.

Of course, it's not only the new, young pro-democracy Legco members the government's gone after. If it decides to prosecute Ted Hui for the phone-snatching incident, he will become the 13th pro-democracy Legco member to face, in all, 19 legal proceedings brought by the Hong Kong government against sitting Legco members since the Umbrella Movement. Here is the full list, as it now stands, of 12 Legco members facing 18 cases:

- Baggio Leung (disqualified over oath taking)
- Yau Wai-ching (disqualified over oath-taking)
- Leung Kwok-hung (disqualified over oath-taking)
- Lau Siu-lai (disqualified over oath-taking)
- Nathan Law (disqualified over oath-taking)
- Edward Yiu (disqualified over oath-taking)
- Wong Yuk-man (convicted of assault for throwing glass at CE in Legco)
- Nathan Law (convicted of unlawful assembly related to Umbrella Movement)
- Cheng Chung-tai (convicted of desecrating PRC & HKSAR flags in Legco)
- Baggio Leung (convicted of unlawful assembly in Legco)
- Yau Wai-ching (convicted of unlawful assembly in Legco)
- Albert Chan (acquitted of obstructing police)
- Leung Kwok-hung (acquitted of misconduct in public office)
- Leung Kwok-hung (contempt of Legco prosecution thrown out by judge)
- Leung Kowk-hung (on trial for assault outside Legco in April '17)
- Tanya Chan (on trial for inciting public nuisance at Umbrella Movement)
- Shiu Ka-chun (on trial for inciting public nuisance at Umbrella Movement)
- Kenneth Leung (sued for defamation by former CE CY Leung)

(Note: This list includes three cases of charges being brought against Legco members after they were kicked out of Legco: Baggio Leung and Yau Wai-ching for unlawful assembly and Leung Kwok-hung for assault. All three cases are related to incidents occurring while they were still Legco members. The 15 other cases were brought by the government against sitting Legco members.)

There are currently 25 pro-democracy Legco members. Prior to the six disqualifications, there were 29. (Two of four seats left vacant by the disqualifications were filled by pro-democracy candidates in March by-elections this year.) Of that latter number, 12, or 41 percent, have faced judicial proceedings since the Umbrella Movement in late 2014.

And of those 18 cases, 13 relate to actions taken or words spoken by Legco members while carrying out their duties as elected representatives within Legco (as opposed to, say, taking part in street protests—four of the remaining five relate to that). Prior to the Umbrella Movement, disciplinary matters were considered the purview of Legco, but now the Hong Kong government is using the courts to criminally prosecute pro-democracy Legco members.

Many consider this new practice to constitute unjustifiable intereference by the executive branch in the legislative branch of government (setting aside for a moment the fact that Legco is not really legislative since it can't initiate bills). It certainly runs contrary to the basic principle of democratic culture and governance that those in power should avoid using the machinery of government to carry out their agenda against political enemies.

It also seeks to influence the judiciary to turn in a more authoritarian direction. We can see its success in the series of anti-democratic decisions rendered by the High Court in the disqualification cases and the imprisonment of pro-democracy protesters. Of the 18 cases brought so far by the government against Legco members, there have been six disqualifications, five convictions, two acquittals, and a judge threw out the prosecution of Long Hair for contempt of Legco on grounds that a Legco member cannot be charged with that offense (the government is appealing the ruling). Four cases have not yet gone to trial or are yet to be decided. Altogether, the government has succeeded in 11 of the 15 cases yet decided, a success rate of 73 percent, far higher than the average conviction rate of 40 to 50 percent in recent years.

And it sets precedent. Just to take the example of the six disqualifications over oath-taking: In the past, a tradition had developed of using the oath-taking event as an opportunity for political protest, and the six who were disqualified were acting in that tradition. In the past, the oaths were in some cases accepted in spite of the minor protests or, at most, the oath-taker was made to retake the oath. Even if you say that the tradition of using the oath-taking occasion to protest is one that must end, fair play dictates that you don't change the rules after the fact and then apply them retroactively, which is what happened in that case.

Pro-democracy Legco members have been tried for throwing a glass, attempting to enter a chamber where Legco was meeting, turning mini-flags upside-down, snatching a pile of papers from a desk where a government official was sitting, and saying that the Chief Executive was being investigated by tax authorities abroad. Will Ted Hui be next for snatching a phone? Some of these actions may be improper or unbecoming of elected officials (I, for one, don't approve of throwing a glass, even if you don't hit or even intend to hit someone), but there's a substantial leap between impropriety and crime.

Many of these cases have the aura of a surreal nightmare in which your every peccadillo is magnified and punished disproportionately. Meanwhile, the systematic injustice of which the punishers are guilty—the continuing denial of universal suffrage—remains, entirely unaddressed, indeed, more deeply entrenched than ever. I still can't get over the fact that a judge ruled a few words spoken, a few actions taken in a matter of seconds during oath-taking could cancel out 183,236 votes just like that, an evil spell cast upon the body politic. And there is no way to judicially address the fact that the very formation of the HK government and Legco is, according to both its own mini-constitution and international law, illegal. So much for "rule of law".

There is simply no way a formal political system can be considered functioning and legitimate when such a large number of elected representatives are facing legal proceedings brought by the government.

And I've hardly mentioned the other new tactic employed by the government to further restrict political access: disqualifications from candidacy for Legco. Altogether, in the 2016 Legco elections and the March 2018 by-elections to fill four of the six seats vacated by the oath-taking disqualifications, nine candidates have been barred from running on political grounds, or, to put it more precisely, on the exceedingly vague justification that the candidate cannot be expected to "uphold the Basic Law" due to the candidate's in some cases suspected, in others professed political beliefs. Two of those candidates, Edward Leung in 2016 and Agnes Chow this year, stood a good chance of winning (and their replacements, Baggio Leung and Au Nok-hin respectively, did eventually win).

If you look at the full pattern of prosecutions, disqualifications, and barring potential candidates from running, what emerges is the following picture: The Party and Hong Kong government are moving toward a rubber-stamp NPC model for Legco. Yes, because Hong Kong's system is (still) different from the mainland's, some opposition representatives will be allowed, as long as they "behave themselves". But access will be tightly restricted. All those who are suspected of espousing political views and objectives which the Party finds unacceptable, in particular pro-independence and self-determinationist, will be excluded, regardless of the facts that there is the most tenuous of legal bases for such exclusions and they indeed run counter to basic principles of democratic governance and culture. Those few opposition politicians who will be allowed to enter Legco will be like caged animals in an exhibit to demonstrate the regime's infinite tolerance.

In the face of this deplorable situation, both the United Kingdom[2] and the European Union[3] have recently concluded that, all in all, "one country, two systems" is working pretty well. To which I, and most of the pro-democracy movement,[4] can only say, "?!?!?!?!" True, both expressed concerns over various matters, which in diplomat-speak represents a slight ratcheting up from previous expressions of full complacency, but this makes it all the more lamentable that they show their awareness of much evidence of interference and yet make the conclusions they do. One of the more disheartening aspects of Hong Kong today is that its mainlandization is not clandestine but occurring out in the open, right under the nose of a willfully blind world. Given that nearly half the political opposition's elected representatives are on trial, not to mention a plethora of other problematic situations such as prosecutions of dozens of pro-democracy leaders and activists, the ceding of Hong Kong territory to the mainland at the express rail terminus without any legal basis whatsoever, and the imminent introduction of a law prohibiting insult to the Party anthem, what exactly would it take to conclude that "one country, two systems" isn't working well? Nothing, it seems, short of total collapse or tanks in the streets.

What to do?

But is much of the pro-democracy movement nearly as willfully blind as these foreign governments? Whenever some new trespass occurs, it protests, but at what point does it have to begin seriously considering whether or not it is really justifiable to participate at all in a formal political system which has been so compromised? To put it more directly, have we reached the point where the pro-democracy movement should consider simply boycotting Legco elections?

Some think doing so would be a catastrophic strategic blunder, for it would allow the Party to entirely have its way in Hong Kong, including enacting draconian Article 23 "national security" legislation and fake suffrage. With that prospect in mind, would it not be grossly irresponsible of the pro-democracy movement to boycott Legco? After all, whatever happens, it has to continue using its presence in Legco to fight a rearguard action for as long as it can, heading off the worst from coming to pass. Really, since it is rigged and members can't initiate legislation of their own, all Legco can be used for is defensive purposes, and the movement should avail itself of the body toward that end, whatever else happens. The Party is just waiting for the movement to take such a false step, indeed may even be trying to provoke it to do so.

That is certainly a strong argument. But if the pro-democracy movement were to boycott Legco, it would show up the system as entirely illegitimate and bring it to the point of crisis. Something would have to give. The fear is the Party would simply fill the political vacuum and things would become worse. Are we nearing the point where we have to accept that things may have to become worse before a possibility of improvement arises? Do we have to take bolder political risks? Or is the best we can do to hunker down and fend off the worst from happening for as long as we can, up to the point, perhaps, when there is little left to defend?

Criminalizing the opposition in Hong Kong

May 28, 2018

A review of the major prosecutions of pro-democracy leaders and activists and a discussion of their impact on rule of law

The Chinese Communist Party and the Hong Kong government are using the courts to drive their agenda of criminalizing and marginalizing political opposition as part of their unprecedented crackdown on the pro-democracy movement and the mainlandization of Hong Kong.

This article follows up on a January preview[1] of some of the cases and an article[2] started in April 2017 and regularly updated that monitors the cases against pro-democracy leaders specifically. In both, additional information on the cases can be found. The most up-to-date information on the cases, including from after the publication of this article, can be found in "Regularly updated overview. . . ".[3]

After the Friday, May 11 convictions of Avery Ng in one trial[4] and Baggio Leung, Yau Wai-ching and their three assistants in another,[5] there will most likely be no further verdicts for some time in the remaining trials of Hong Kong pro-democracy activists. Now is a good time to step back and review.

In the period immediately following the 2014 Umbrella Movement, I began to track arrests and prosecutions related to it.[6] From 11 June 2014 to 25 April 2015, 1,505 people were arrested in relation to protests against the attempt by the Chinese Communist Party and Hong Kong government to foist upon Hong Kong fake universal suffrage. Of those, 668 were arrested during the Umbrella Movement from 28 September to 15 December 2014, 724 were arrested before it, and 113 were arrested after it.

By early 2016, it seemed that the Hong Kong government had nearly come to the end of its Umbrella prosecutions. The Secretary for Justice reported to the Legislative Council, "As at January 31 this year [2016], a total of 216 persons have undergone, are undergoing or will undergo judicial proceedings. Amongst them, 182 persons have gone through the judicial process and 116 of them have to bear legal consequences, including 74 who were convicted and 42 who were bound over upon conclusion of court proceedings."[7] Over the course of 2016, four more persons were prosecuted and convicted, bringing the total by early 2017 to at least 220 prosecuted and at least 78 convicted, mostly of minor offenses.

All but five of those 78 convicted were given non-custodial sentences. The longest prison sentence for a demonstrator was 10 months, for assaulting a police officer in Admiralty Centre on 1 December 2014. Following government appeal of original sentences of community service, three people were sentenced to three and a half months in prison each for breaking into the Legislative Council building on 19 November 2014. Ken Tsang, the victim of the infamous "dark corner" police beating broadcast on television, was sentenced to five weeks in prison for assaulting officers and resisting arrest. The total amount of prison time to which demonstrators were sentenced was one year, nine months and three weeks.

Up to that point, the Chinese Communist Party and the Hong Kong government had constantly referred to the "illegal Occupy movement" in their propaganda but were having very limited success proving that illegality in Hong Kong courts. In fact, eight police officers have been sentenced to more prison time for crimes committed while policing the Umbrella Movement than all protesters put together. The seven officers convicted of beating Ken Tsang received two years in prison each, amounting to 14 years total. An eighth officer, Frankly Chu, was sentenced to three months in prison in a separate case. In all, police officers were sentenced to 14 years and three months. All eight are appealing their sentences.

The trial of Joshua Wong, Nathan Law and Alex Chow for occupying Civic Square on 26 September 2014, triggering the start of the Umbrella Movement two days later, was one of only two Umbrella Movement-related trials to begin in 2016. It started in February and concluded in August. It was not the first post-Umbrella prosecution of pro-democracy leaders, but it was the first related to the Umbrella Movement. Still, people didn't seem too worried because, after all, the offense with which they were charged, unlawful assembly, was non-violent and usually punished by a sentence of community service and/or a fine. Indeed, Wong and Law received community service sentences and the judge accommodated Chow's desire to study abroad by giving him a suspended prison sentence.

But then the Hong Kong government appealed the sentences, and it began to appear that something new was afoot, especially as in late 2016, the number of prosecutions of pro-democracy leaders started to increase.

The violence between police and protesters in Mong Kok at Chinese New Year in February 2016 appeared to have emboldened the government to aggressively pursue protest-related prosecutions in the courts using the blanket argument that protests of all kinds, including nonviolent ones, endangered law and order.

But the prosecutions of pro-democracy leaders were not only related to protests. In September 2016, new and young post-Umbrella candidates did impressively well in Legislative Council elections. This development, along with the rise in calls for self-determination and independence, seemed to have alarmed the Party and Hong Kong government, spurring them to take action to snuff out any nascent movements they feared they could not control. They almost immediately initiated disqualification proceedings against six pro-democracy Legco members (five newly elected, one re-elected) and the prosecutions of pro-democracy Legco members and other leaders of political parties and student organizations increased rapidly.

In April 2017, two years and four months after the end of the movement, charges were brought against the Umbrella Movement 9, essentially for "inciting" the 79-day-long occupations. At that time, I began to document[8] a clear pattern of the Hong Kong government targeting leaders of pro-democracy political parties and student organizations for prosecution. Up to now, 28 pro-democracy leaders have faced 43 different legal cases since the Umbrella Movement. Most of the prosecutions have started since late 2016.

In January this year, I previewed[9] a series of upcoming trials and have tracked[10] those trials since. It was not only pro-democracy leaders but also ordinary activists who were being prosecuted, the latter often in batches of a dozen or more at a time. Numbers were ballooning. In January, there were six trials of 43 defendants; in February, six of 27; in March, eight of 46; in

April, five of 27; and in May, three of 21. Since the start of 2018, more than three years after the Umbrella Movement concluded, there have been four trials of 47 defendants related to the Umbrella Movement, sending the overall number of those tried to at least 266 and the number convicted to at least 100.

It's not over yet. There are at least 10 on-going or yet-to-begin trials involving 53 defendants, with big ones scheduled in May (the Mong Kok 15), July (the Liaison Office 9), September (the NENT 13), and November (the Umbrella Movement 9), and there may be new cases to come (for example, Democratic Party Legco member Ted Hui was recently arrested).[11]

What has happened so far and what conclusions can be drawn?

Put simply, Hong Kong has never seen anything like this before, so many people in the pro-democracy movement put on trial over such an extended period of time for such a wide array of crimes. One would have to look to places like Turkey or Venezuela to find comparable instances of prosecutions in courts of law being used as a key weapon in campaigns against political enemies.

In addition to the at least 266 prosecuted in relation to the Umbrella Movement, there have been dozens of others, including at least 27 for protesting, 13 for carrying out their duties as Legislative Council members, and at least 2 for other reasons.

As noted above, the Hong Kong government has brought 43 legal cases against 28 pro-democracy leaders. As of 12 May, 25 cases have concluded, resulting in 16 convictions, six acquittals, one prosecution thrown out by the judge, and six disqualifications from Legco. (Note: The discrepancy has to do with the difference between number of cases and number of counts per case.) Five appeals are on-going, four by defendants, one by the government. There have been three prison sentences. One has been served, and the defendants in the other two cases are on bail pending appeal. Three prison sentences were overturned upon appeal.

Of those 28 pro-democracy leaders, 12 are Legco members, who have faced 18 different cases against them.

- Baggio Leung (disqualified over oath taking)
- Yau Wai-ching (disqualified over oath-taking)
- Leung Kwok-hung (disqualified over oath-taking)

- Lau Siu-lai (disqualified over oath-taking)
- Nathan Law (disqualified over oath-taking)
- Edward Yiu (disqualified over oath-taking)
- Wong Yuk-man (convicted of assault for throwing glass at CE in Legco)
- Nathan Law (convicted of unlawful assembly related to Umbrella Movement)
- Cheng Chung-tai (convicted of desecrating PRC & HKSAR flags in Legco)
- Baggio Leung (convicted of unlawful assembly in Legco)
- Yau Wai-ching (convicted of unlawful assembly in Legco)
- Albert Chan (acquitted of obstructing police)
- Leung Kwok-hung (acquitted of misconduct in public office)
- Leung Kwok-hung (contempt of Legco prosecution thrown out by judge)
- Leung Kowk-hung (on trial for assault outside Legco in April '17)
- Tanya Chan (on trial for inciting public nuisance at Umbrella Movement)
- Shiu Ka-chun (on trial for inciting public nuisance at Umbrella Movement)
- Kenneth Leung (sued for defamation by former CE CY Leung)

(Note: This list includes three cases of charges being brought against Legco members after they were kicked out of Legco: Baggio Leung and Yau Wai-ching for unlawful assembly and Leung Kwok-hung for assault. All three cases are related to incidents that occurred while they were still Legco members. The 15 other cases were brought by the government against sitting Legco members.)

There are currently 25 pro-democracy Legco members. Prior to the disqualification of six, there were 29. Of that latter number of 29, over one-third have faced judicial proceedings. And of those 18 cases, 13 relate to actions taken or words spoken by Legco members while carrying out their duties as elected representatives within Legco (as opposed to, say, taking part in street protests or engaging in entirely unrelated activity).

The list of 28 pro-democracy leaders also includes 10 leaders of student organizations and five leaders of political parties who are not Legco members.

Many of those targeted have been young people. In the "batch trials"—the Mong Kok 20, Mong Kok 15, NENT 13, and Liaison Office 9—the vast majority of defendants are young people. The Umbrella Movement 9, with only two young defendants, is the only batch trial that doesn't fit this pattern. All of these are related to protests.

Two political parties have been especially singled out for targeting: Demosistō and League of Social Democrats have had, respectively, 10 and 11 leaders and core members on trial.

Individuals targeted for multiple prosecutions include Long Hair (4*), Raphael Wong (4), Avery Ng (3), Joshua Wong (3), Nathan Law (3*), Ivan Lam (2), Derek Lam (2), Baggio Leung (2*), and Yau Wai-ching (2*). (The asterisks denote numbers that include a disqualification from Legco, which is not a criminal prosecution.) All of those individuals except the last two belong to Demosistō or LSD.

The government's success rate is checkered but looks to be improving. In the early phase of Umbrella Movement trials up to the end of 2015, its record was poor, with convictions in only 74 of 216 prosecutions, or about 34 percent, significantly under the overall conviction rate of about 50 percent for 2014, which itself has been criticized by law-and-order types as lamentably poor.[12] But since the Civic Square 3 case which started in February 2016, its Umbrella Movement record has improved considerably: 23 convictions out of 24 cases. Its record in other cases has improved as well, with, for example, all 13 of the NENT 13 sentenced to the lengthiest prison terms in living memory for unlawful assembly (their appeal will be heard in September), and 19 successful cases against pro-democracy leaders, resulting in either convictions or disqualifications (versus seven unsuccessful cases).

The prosecutions and the state of the rule of law in Hong Kong

The World Justice Project ranks Hong Kong 16th out of 113 countries in its 2017–2018 Rule of Law Index.[13]

In its 2017 report on Hong Kong, the European Union concluded, "The rule of law prevailed and the judiciary continued to demonstrate its independence and consistent respect for due process."[14]

Are these assessments not unjustifiably sanguine?

In its most recent report, the United Kingdom recognizes the situation but refrains from condemning it or assigning responsibility: "The rule of law and independence of the judiciary is the foundation on which Hong Kong's success and prosperity is [sic] built. This reporting period has seen a large number of cases related to the political system come before Hong Kong's courts, including the disqualification of a further four legislators. The judiciary in Hong Kong remains in high esteem. It will be vital that the Hong Kong SAR Government is seen to use the system of justice fairly in all cases."[15]

The threat to rule of law posed by the Communist Party and Hong Kong government should provoke much greater concern, especially if, in addition to what is presented here, the large number of legal cases brought against political opponents, we take into account the larger picture, including such developments as 1) the National People's Congress Standing Committee's intervention in an on-going legal case, the disqualification proceedings against Baggio Leung and Yau Wai-ching, to retroactively determine an outcome in its favor; 2) the ceding of Hong Kong land at the express rail terminus to mainland authorities with no legal basis whatsoever and in direct contravention of the Basic Law;[16] 3) the Chinese government's unilateral insertion into the Basic Law of a new mainland law criminalizing insult of its anthem; 4) the disqualifications of candidates for Legco on political grounds based on entirely arbitrary rulings by administrative officers,[17] coupled with the exceedingly sluggish response of the High Court in addressing election petitions against the practice,[18] 5) the Hong Kong government's "innovative" employment of never-before-or-rarely-used charges against political opponents, such as the "inciting public nuisance" charges against the Umbrella Movement 9 and the charge of "contempt of Legco" against Long Hair; 6) the introduction by the High Court of harsher sentencing guidelines for nonviolent protesters convicted of unlawful assembly, which may result in an increase in the number of nonviolent protesters going to prison in the future and appears to hold nonviolent protesters accountable for any violence which may occur at protests where they are present even if they are not responsible for the violence, and 7) the continued denial of genuine universal suffrage in contravention of both Hong Kong and international law and with no intention on the part of the Party or Hong Kong government to imminently rectify the matter.

All of these developments (except the last, which is on-going) have occurred within the last year and a half. There has been a steady barrage of bad news about rule of law in Hong Kong. Overall, the Party and Hong Kong government are trying to bend the law in a more authoritarian direction and have had some success in persuading the courts to go along with them. This is toxic not only to the rule of law but also to politics and society's sense of fairness and decency.

In light of this grim picture, what do such observers as those mentioned above mean when they say rule of law remains robust in Hong Kong? To a large extent, as the EU acknowledges, they mean the city remains "good for business": "The rule of law, a transparent regulatory framework, very low levels of corruption and crime, along with an efficient public administration and an independent judiciary, contributed to preserving and fostering the favourable investment climate that lies at the heart of Hong Kong's success."

It is true that in non-political areas, rule of law continues to function well and due process is widely respected. The judiciary remains generally quite independent, notwithstanding the influence on it, especially at the High Court, by the constant pressure of propaganda, the Party's interventions, and non-stop prosecutions.

But an assessment that rule of law in Hong Kong is just fine fails to take seriously the prospects when a government begins to employ the courts toward political ends or, in some cases, acts outside of the law (the continued denial of universal suffrage, the ceding of Hong Kong territory to the mainland) and refuses to be held accountable. Surely, this is a sign of a deterioration in respect for rule of law by those in power, the beginning of its undermining, and a drift toward Communist-style "rule by law", made all the more troubling by the fact that the Hong Kong government, like the Party, constantly invokes "rule of law" to defend its actions.

Indeed, this ritual justification, "acting in accordance with the rule of law", appears to have a hypnotic effect on a great many observers, bamboozling them into complacency or somnolence: Oh, well, if it's done in accordance with rule of law—and Hong Kong does have robust rule of law, lest we forget—then, well, even if we don't like it, that's just the way it is. Likewise, the steady drip-drip-drip of one prosecution after another is intended to fly under the radar. To understand the full breadth of the crackdown on the pro-democracy movement and the mainlandization of Hong Kong, and therefore also the threat to the rule of law, one must comprehend the full picture.

Far from being only "fringe" issues, using the legal system to attack political opponents and the multiple infringements on the "one country, two systems" principle are the canaries in the coalmine, and based on those criteria, alarm bells should be sounding loudly.

The prosecutions are just one part of a wider crackdown on the pro-democracy movement and a strategy to mainlandize politics. Besides what has already been mentioned above — barring candidates for Legco —, other means include denial of applications of pro-democracy groups to register under the Companies Ordinance, thus denying them legal status;[19] denial of use of public space to groups which the government has singled out as political enemies; pressuring universities to rein in professors and students; and unsubstantiated declarations that certain speech is "against the Basic Law" as justification for attacks on perceived enemies (most recently, Benny Tai). In all of these cases, the government has invoked both rule of law and the Basic Law to justify its actions, but a clear pattern emerges of the Hong Kong government employing law as a means to attack its political enemies.

While the Chinese Communist Party and Hong Kong government continue to deny to the people of Hong Kong basic human rights, such as the right of self-determination and the right to genuine universal suffrage, they are further restricting other basic rights such as freedoms of expression and of assembly, the right to run in elections and to hold elected public office, and the right to vote in free and fair elections.

The overall objectives of the Party and Hong Kong government in their on-going crackdown on the pro-democracy movement include 1) keeping it on the defensive, thus weakening its abilities to resist and to advance a positive agenda, 2) damaging or destroying certain groups within the movement which they regard as fundamentally "unpatriotic", "disloyal", "seditious" or "illegal", 3) intimidating ordinary Hong Kong people against participating in any oppositional or resistance politics, and 4) ultimately creating a political environment in Hong Kong that more closely resembles that of the mainland.

A review of the major legal cases against pro-democracy leaders and activists over the past year

The following review is not exhaustive and focuses primarily on cases of the past year or so.

In addition to the cases against pro-democracy leaders and activists discussed in this essay, there have also been major trials of other political opponents, in particular of dozens for their involvement in clashes between police and protesters during Chinese New Year 2016 in Mong Kok.

The DQ 6

- **defendants:** *Baggio Leung, Yau Wai-ching, Leung Kwok-hung / Long Hair, Lau Siu-lai, Nathan Law, Edward Yiu*
- **charges:** *failure to meet oath-taking requirements to assume seats in the Legislative Council (non-criminal case)*
- **outcomes:** *All six were disqualified, Leung and Yau on 15 November 2016, the other four on 14 July 2017. Leung and Yau appealed first to the Court of Appeal and then to the Court of Final Appeal. Both courts rejected their appeals. Of the other four, Nathan Law and Edward Yiu decided not to appeal while Long Hair and Lau have appealed. Long Hair and Lau's appeals have been scheduled for April 2019 but they are appealing this date set so far in the future. By-elections to fill the four other seats were held in March 2018.*

The cases were tried in two batches, Baggio Leung and Yau Wai-ching first, the other four following. They are grouped together here due to their similarity; namely, the government brought cases against the six recently elected pro-democracy Legislative Council members and the High Court disqualified them, leaving their seats in Legco vacant.

The government's case was that, during oath-taking, all had acted in ways that constituted failure to take the oath of office and that they thereby lost the right to fill their seats, even though they were elected.

Meanwhile, the government which brought the case against them remains unelected. The juxtaposition brings into relief a clear instance of the law failing to deliver justice.

The cases of the DQ 6 were precedent-setting in three respects.

First, the government had never previously attempted to use the courts to get elected Legco members disqualified. Previously, any acts committed in Legco had been addressed within Legco. A tradition had developed of pro-democracy Legco members using their oath of office to protest. In several cases, the Legco secretary had declared these oaths void. The Legco members were then given the chance to retake their oaths. In the cases of the DQ 6 as well, the pro-Communist Legco president had ruled the six could retake their oaths, but then changed his mind in the cases of Leung and Yau once the government brought the legal cases against them. These cases thus set the precedent that both the executive and judicial branches can intervene in Legco and overturn decisions made by Legco. In this respect, they are similar to the seven criminal prosecutions brought by the Hong Kong government against pro-democracy Legco members for speech and actions in the course of carrying out their duties as Legco members. Such matters were previously dealt with solely by Legco disciplinary committees.

Second, while the first case, against Leung and Yau, was on-going, the National People's Congress Standing Committee issued an "interpretation" of Basic Law Article 108 regarding oath-taking. The purpose of the interpretation was to compel the High Court to disqualify the six. Furthermore, since it was an "interpretation" rather than an amendment, it was to be applied retroactively. It was one of the few cases of the NPCSC intervening in Hong Kong court proceedings since the 1997 handover, and the very first intervention while a case was on-going. Thus, it is the most egregious example thusfar of Party interference in Hong Kong courts and constitutes a major infringement on the principle of "one country, two systems". In his rulings (it was the same judge in both cases), the High Court judge went out of his way to insist he would have come to the same decision regardless of the NPCSC interpretation, but this is hypothetical, and it is clear that the interpretation brought intense pressure on the High Court, not only in these particular cases but more generally. It is perhaps no surprise that the High Court has ruled more harshly than lower courts in some cases involving pro-democracy protesters (such as imprisoning the Civic Square 3 and the NENT 13, overruling magistrates who'd sentenced the defendants to community service).

Third, the High Court judge entirely disregarded the popular will. Five of the six disqualified Legco members had been elected in so-called geographical constituencies, the only free and fair elections in Hong Kong conducted according to the principles of universal suffrage, while the sixth was elected in the Architectural, Surveying, Planning and Landscape functional constituency. In all, 183,236 people voted for the six. Their votes were effectively cancelled out by the judge's ruling that the ways the six took their oaths of office disqualified them from assuming office, barring even a retake.

The rulings damaged faith in the courts to provide at least a modicum of justice as well as faith in the integrity of elections. In 2014, the Umbrella Movement demanded the right to freely elect Hong Kong's government. Not only did the Party and Hong Kong government reject that demand but since then they have actively attempted to determine the only free and fair elections Hong Kong has, by barring candidates from running on political grounds as well as by disqualifying elected Legco members, in the process so constraining the rights to run for office, to be elected, to hold elected office and to vote as to significantly if not fatally compromise these elections.

In March, four by-elections were held to fill vacant seats. In the run-up to the by-elections, the candidate seeking to replace Nathan Law, his Demosistō party fellow Agnes Chow, was disqualified on the grounds that her party advocated self-determination for Hong Kong, which the Returning Officer of the Electoral Affairs Commission, following legal advice from the Hong Kong government, hardly a disinterested observer, said was not in accordance with the Basic Law; this, in spite of the fact that has never been determined in the courts and Nathan Law was allowed to run for office in the September 2016 Legco elections. The case once again showed the Party and Hong Kong government continually and arbitrarily moving the goalposts, always in an ever-more authoritarian direction.

Two seats have still not been filled because the disqualified Legco members are appealing the High Court ruling, but the High Court has not scheduled their appeal until April 2019, two and a half years after they were disqualified.

The Civic Square 3

- **defendants:** *Joshua Wong, Nathan Law, Alex Chow*
- **charges:** *unlawful assembly (Wong and Chow), inciting unlawful assembly (Wong and Law)*
- **outcome:** *Wong was convicted of unlawful assembly and acquitted of inciting unlawful assembly. Law and Chow were convicted of the charges against them. The magistrate sentenced Wong and Law to, respectively, 80 and 120 hours of community service and, upon his request, Chow to*

a suspended three-week prison term so that he could complete his studies abroad. The government appealed the sentences. The Court of Appeal sentenced Law to eight months in prison, Wong to seven and Chow to six and imposed stricter sentencing guidelines for future cases similar in nature. The Court of Final Appeal overturned the prison sentences but upheld the stricter sentencing guidelines.

The three were arrested in relation to the occupation of Civic Square on 26 September 2014, which lead to the start of the Umbrella Movement two days later. The three were leaders of the movement, with Law and Chow leading Hong Kong Federation of Students and Wong, Scholarism.

Law was prosecuted for calling on people to enter the closed square on the evening of 26 September. Wong was arrested moments after entering the square. Chow's prosecution is peculiar and appears highly selective. He was among a little over 60 demonstrators who occupied the square for the whole night and into the next morning, when they were all removed and arrested by police, but he is the only occupier amongst those 60-plus to have been prosecuted, though his actions were no different from those of the others.

The prosecution began on February 29, 2016. On August 15, 2016, the three were convicted. On August 17, 2017, the Court of Appeal sentenced them to prison. On February 6, 2018, the Court of Final Appeal overturned the prison sentences but ruled that harsh new sentencing guidelines imposed by the Court of Appeal were justified. It said the magistrate who originally handed down the community service / suspended sentences had correctly followed the existing sentencing guidelines, and the new sentencing guidelines imposed by the CA could not be applied retroactively.

While the three were set free and the case was finally concluded nearly three and a half years after the incident in question and two years after the trial began, the ruling was ominous insofar as it endorsed harsher prison sentences in the future for convictions on nonviolent unlawful assembly charges at assemblies where "violence" or "disorder" existed, apparently regardless of whether or not the defendants themselves are violent or disorderly.

Law became the youngest ever candidate elected to Legco in September 2016. He was one of four pro-democracy Legco members disqualified in July 2017. Wong is on bail while appealing his three-month prison sentence for contempt of court in relation to the 26 November 2014 police clearance of the Mong Kok occupation during the Umbrella Movement. Both were previously acquitted of obstructing police at a June 2014 protest.

The Hong Kong government was widely criticized for aggressively pursuing its appeal of the original sentencing. The Court of Appeal was also criticized for changing the sentencing guidelines and applying them retroactively.

Both courts repeatedly referred to the issue of unlawful assembly where some violence may occur and this was a major reason for issuing harsher sentencing guidelines. These repeated allusions ignored the facts that 1) the protesters committed no violence in occupying Civic Square (only one protester was charged with a violent offense and he was acquitted), 2) none of the defendants was implicated in any violence but it appears the judges wished to somehow hold them accountable for violence, and 3) the crime of unlawful assembly is a non-violent crime and by issuing harsher sentencing guidelines, the judges are blurring its boundaries, essentially making those convicted of unlawful assembly potential accountable for something they did not do.

In addition, the defendants are victims of double jeopardy, having fully served their community service sentences (in the cases of Wong and Law) and then having served time in prison until they were bailed while awaiting appeal. Neither the courts nor the Hong Kong government have raised the issue of any kind of compensation for this egregious abuse of rights.

For all of these reasons, this case sets a bad precedent that reflects poorly on judicial institutions in Hong Kong. It could lead to prison sentences for nonviolent offenders where previously those committing such offenses were fined and/or given suspended sentences, and thus has negative implications for the right of freedom of assembly.

The NENT 13

- **defendants:** *Raphael Wong, Willis Ho, Billy Chiu, Chan Pak-san, Chow Koot-yin, David Chu, Yim Man-wah, Ivan Lam, Lau Kwok-leung, Kwok Yiu-cheung, Leung Wing-lai, Leung Hiu-yeung, Wong Kan-yuen*
- **charges:** *all: unlawful assembly and attempted forcible entry; Leung Hiu-yeung: obstructing a police officer*
- **outcome:** *All were acquitted of attempted forcible entry but found guilty of unlawful assembly and originally sentenced to community*

service. Leung Hiu-yeung was found guilty of obstructing a police officer. Upon government appeal of the sentences, the High Court sentenced 12 defendants to 13 months in prison and one to eight months in prison. The Court of Final Appeal has agreed to hear their appeal, but not until 7 September. All are out on bail pending appeal, but some served up to six months in prison before being granted bail.

This was one of the first big post-Umbrella cases. It is only one of two related to an incident that occurred before the Umbrella Movement. (In the other, Joshua Wong, Nathan Law, Raphael Wong and Albert Chan were acquitted of obstructing police officers in relation to a protest outside of the Liaison Office in June 2014.)

In June 2014, protesters demonstrated in Civic Square, outside of the Legislative Council building, against the government's Northeast New Territories development plan. They were acting in solidarity with villagers who would be forcibly displaced if the plan were implemented. They barged into the lobby of Legco and were arrested.

In December 2015, they were all convicted of unlawful assembly but acquitted of attempted forcible entry and sentenced a month later to community service . So far, so normal. Prior to the Umbrella Movement, community service and/or a suspended prison sentence and/or a fine were the standard sentences for those convicted of this nonviolent offense.

But the government successfully appealed the sentences at the Court of Appeal, which sentenced 12 of the demonstrators to 13 months in prison, and one to eight months. The 13-month sentences were by far the harshest ever handed down by a Hong Kong court for the nonviolent offense of unlawful assembly. The Court of Appeal judges said that the magistrate erred in not taking into account the violence at the protest and said the activists did not act in the spirit of civil disobedience. This was a disturbing precedent since the crime for which they were convicted, unlawful assembly, is a non-violent crime. They were acquitted of attempted forcible entry, which arguably suggests a degree of violence. Therefore, it appears they were being sentenced based on actions they themselves were never convicted of having committed.

The 13 were imprisoned two days before the Civic Square 3 (see above) in August 2017, and their cases have two similarities: They were all convicted of unlawful assembly related to Civic Square protests, were all originally given community service/suspended prison sentences, and were convicted by the High Court upon appeal by the Hong Kong government. The cases indicate that the current High Court appears to take a different view of the crime of unlawful assembly from that previously held by the Hong Kong judiciary. The Court of Final Appeal upholding the new sentencing guidelines imposed by the Court of Appeal in the Civic Square 3 may lead to harsher sentences in future.

In response to the 16 imprisonments, 13 in this case and three in the other, many began to speak of a new era of political prisoners in Hong Kong, and at the end of August, 100,000 marched in protest against the prison sentences,[20] the largest protest since the Umbrella Movement.

It is unclear why their appeals at the Court of Final Appeal have been scheduled so far into the future, in September 2018, especially given that the appeals of the Civic Square 3 were heard quite expeditiously, in January 2018. Some have speculated that political decision-making was involved: The Civic Square 3, along with the Umbrella Movement, were nominated for the Nobel Peace Prize, and the government feared if they were in prison, or even on bail awaiting appeal, it might increase their chances of being perceived by the Norwegian Nobel Committee to be persecuted for their political beliefs. One would expect a similar CFA ruling on the NENT 13, given that their case is similar to that of the Civic Square 3, right down to the retroactive imprisonment using new sentencing guidelines which did not exist at the time of the incident nor at the time of the original trial and sentence.

The Mong Kok 20

- **defendants:** *Joshua Wong, Lester Shum, Raphael Wong, Chau Wan-ying, Chu Wai-lun, Chu Pui-yan, Kwok Yeung-yuk, Chiu Chi-sum, Chan Po-ying, Cheung Kai-hong, Kwan Siu-wang, Hung Cheuk-lun, Fung Kai-hei, Choi Tat-shing, Jason Szeto Tse-long, Mak Ying-sheung, Cheung Kai-yin, Ma Po-kwan, Wong Lai-wan, Yeung Ho-wah.*
- **charges:** *contempt of court*
- **outcome:** *All 20 were found liable on 17 January 2018. Nine had plead liable, 11 had plead not liable. Seventeen were fined between HK$10,000 and HK$15,000 and given suspended prison sentences between four and six weeks. One was not fined. Joshua Wong was sentenced*

to 3 months in prison, Raphael Wong to 4 months and 15 days. On 23 March, the Court of Appeal rejected Raphael Wong's appeal and sent him back to prison to serve out his sentence. On 16 April, he was released after having completed his sentence (with an automatic time reduction). Joshua Wong was granted bail pending appeal and is currently awaiting a court date.

On 25 and 26 November 2014, the police cleared the occupation in Mong Kok, one of the three main occupied areas of Hong Kong during the Umbrella Movement. The clearance on the 26th was of the main part, several blocks on Nathan Road. Of the 20 prosecuted in this trial, three movement leaders, Joshua Wong, Raphael Wong and Lester Shum were dragged from the crowd at the start of the clearance. Joshua and Raphael had been using a megaphone to ask bailiffs questions about the clearance. The other 17 simply happened to be there, snatched randomly from the crowd of hundreds.

The High Court judges ruled that simply being present at the clearance constituted contempt of court since bailiffs and police, invoking a court injunction, had instructed people to vacate the area. I along with hundreds of others happened to be present that day. We were not arrested but allowed by police to leave the area under injunction, which they had sealed off. In that light, these prosecutions appear highly arbitrary.[21] In terms of number of defendants, this is the largest single trial related to the Umbrella Movement. It was also the first time anyone in Hong Kong had been tried and imprisoned for contempt of court, not a statutory crime, in relation to street protest.

The Mong Kok 15

- **defendants:** *Chan Wai-fung, Chu Sui-ying, Wong Ka-yee, Kong Kam-to, Chan Ao-tien, Chan Wing-wah, Leung Hon-lam, Siew Yun-long, Man For-on, Lai Yu-sing, Law Wai-yan, Jeffrey Chan, Yung Yiu-sing, Chan Pak-tao*
- **charges:** *contempt of court*
- **outcome:** *Trial proper scheduled to begin on May 15*

This is the second big batch of defendants to be prosecuted in relation to the police clearance of the Mong Kok occupation on November 26, 2014 during the Umbrella Movement. While The Mong Kok 20 included movement leaders, this batch is made up entirely of ordinary people who simply happened to be present at the clearance. The group should really be called the "Mong Kok 17" but for the fact that two, Alvin Cheng and Au Yuk-Kwan, plead guilty and were sentenced on March 30, 2017 to, respectively, three months in prison and a suspended 12-month prison term and HK$10,000 fine. The judge gave Cheng a prison term because he "did not show remorse because he was late for a previous hearing and was 'playing on his phone' during the trial".[22] Seven of the remaining 15 defendants have announced their intention to plead liable: Chan Wai-fung, Chu Sui-ying, Wong Ka-yee, Kong Kam-to, Chan Ao-tien, Chan Wing-wah and Leung Hon-lam. Seven others have said they will plead not liable: Siew Yun-long, Lai Yu-sing, Law Wai-yan, Jeffrey Chan, Yung Yiu-sing, and Chan Pak-tao. An arrest warrant was issued for Man For-on who did not appear at pre-trial review hearings.

"Contempt of court" is not a criminal offense under the Hong Kong Crimes Ordinance. The charging of the 37 defendants in the two above trials was unprecedented. The judge in the trial of the Mong Kok 20 expressed uncertainty as to how to determine sentencing. Given the trials' unprecedented nature, the bar for contempt was set far too low: The judges essentially defined being present as adequate grounds for contempt. Surely, active interference or obstruction in the clearance would have been more appropriate grounds, in which case none of the defendants would have been found guilty. Joshua Wong and Raphael Wong are the only two who the judge regarded as potentially obstructive, though all they did was ask reasonable questions of bailiffs and police about the legal grounds of the clearance. Surely as long as they do not interfere or obstruct, citizens must have the legal right to observe police actions taken in public. The police ended up clearing several blocks of occupied road within an hour and faced no obstruction from citizens.

All of the above cases (the Civic Square 3, the NENT 13, the Mong Kok 20 and the Mong Kok 15) are being tried in the High Court, the Civic Square 3 and NENT 13 upon government appeal. Judging by its record, the High Court appears to have a much less sympathetic view of citizens protesting nonviolently than the magistrates' courts, ruling in favor of the government in all cases except the CFA overturning the Civic Square 3 prison sentences (though it upheld the newly imposed stricter future sentencing guidelines).

The Umbrella Movement 9

- **defendants:** *Chu Yiu-ming, Chan Kin-man, Benny Tai, Lee Wing-tat, Shiu Ka-chun, Tanya Chan, Raphael Wong, Tommy Cheung and Eason Chung*
- **charges:** *conspiracy to create a public nuisance (Chu, Chan Kin-man, Tai); incitement to public nuisance (all nine) ; incitement to incite public nuisance (all except Lee)*
- **outcome:** *Trial proper scheduled to begin November 9*

This case is basically intended to place legal blame on these nine for starting the Umbrella Movement on September 28, 2014, an utterly ridiculous notion to anyone who saw how it actually unfolded. The trial proper is scheduled to begin more than four years after the start of the movement. The government didn't bring charges until April 2017, two and a half years after the start. It has resorted to "inciting public nuisance" charges rarely if ever used in Hong Kong.

Five of the defendants are from Occupy Central with Love and Peace (three) and Hong Kong Federation of Students (two), two of the leading groups of the Umbrella Movement, but strikingly, what both groups have in common is that on the night of 28 September 2014, rather than "incite", they actually called on demonstrators to leave and go home, fearing that the police would escalate from teargas to the use of live ammunition.

Of the other four defendants, three, Lee Wing-tat, Raphael Wong and Shiu Ka-chun, appear to have played exceedingly negligible roles, while Tanya Chan repeatedly beseeched demonstrators to be calm, rational and peaceful and avoid taking impulsive actions which they might later regret—pretty much the opposite of "incitement".

The Umbrella Movement was started by the people, without a leader. It would be hard to find a single demonstrator who could report having participated due to having been "incited" to do so by any of the nine defendants. Ironically, the main "incitement" was the eight-hour-long teargas attack by Hong Kong police on Hong Kong citizens, to which people responded with spontaneous nonviolent outrage, filling the streets. But no member of either the Hong Kong government or police is on trial for that; indeed, no credible account of the decision-making behind it has been offered by police or government, no officially sanctioned investigation into it has ever been conducted, and no one has been held accountable.

In a sense, with this case, the Hong Kong government is indirectly putting the people of Hong Kong on trial for "public nuisance", since we are the "public nuisance" that these nine allegedly incited. Also striking is that of the approximately 1,000 people arrested and 250 prosecuted in relation to the Umbrella Movement, not a single one has been arrested or prosecuted for "public nuisance". So the Hong Kong government is prosecuting these nine for inciting an offense which it has not legally demonstrated was committed in even a single case.

Two of the defendants, Tanya Chan and Shiu Ka-chun, are current Legco members. Those convicted of crimes and sentenced to more than three months in prison are ineligible to run for Legco or serve as Legco members, so Chan's and Shiu's retention of their seats hinges on the outcome of this case. Raphael Wong is currently on bail pending appeal of his 13-month sentence for unlawful assembly in connection with a June 2014 protest at Legco and has served a prison sentence of four months and 15 days in relation to the November 26, 2014 police clearance of the Mong Kok occupation during the Umbrella Movement.

This case is also significant because it represents the first time the government is attempting to "stretch" the law in a court below the High Court, in this case, at District Court. The charges all nine are up on, variations on "public nuisance" are not statutory, meaning they do not exist in the Crimes Ordinance but only in common law. No one in living memory has been charged with "inciting public nuisance". The only apparent reason the government is doing so now is that it comes with heavier maximum sentences than similar charges, such as the familiar "unlawful assembly". Finally, it is significant that in preliminary hearings, the judge in the case denied the defense request to throw out the charge of "inciting to incite to public nuisance" which defense lawyers argued is essentially a duplication of the "inciting to public nuisance" charge. That is a sign that the judge is willing to entertain the government's attempts to "stretch" legal definitions and applications of existing law.

The Liaison Office 9

- **defendants:** *Dickson Chau Ka-faat, Avery Ng, Devon Cheng Pui-lun, Derek Lam, Ivan Lam, Chau Man-wai, Sammy Ip, Lo Tak-cheong*
- **charges:** *Chau Ka-faat: obstructing and assaulting police officer; Ng:*

two counts of inciting unlawful assembly; Cheng: unlawful assembly; Derek Lam: inciting unlawful assembly; Ivan Lam: unlawful assembly; Chau Man-wai: two counts of unlawful assembly; Ip: unlawful assembly, obstructing a police officer; Lo: unlawful assembly
- **outcome:** *Trial proper scheduled to begin July 9; delays caused by prosecution changing charges against two defendants*

These nine are on trial for various offenses related to a protest outside of the Central Government Liaison Office on November 6, 2016 against an impending interpretation of the Basic law on oath-taking by the National People's Congress Standing Committee. The interpretation, which came on November 7, lead to the disqualification of six elected pro-democracy Legco members.

As much as anything else, the nine are being prosecuted due to the location of the protest, the Liaison Office, regarded by the Hong Kong police and government as a highly sensitive area. Police are under strict orders to prevent any kind of disturbance from occurring there, tightly controlling passage in front of the building, supposedly in the name of security but it appears that another objective is to discourage people from protesting there.

On the night in question, the police were up to their old antics, preventing demonstrators from passing in front of the building, but on this occasion, the crowd was so large that it began to spill out into the street. Terrible crowd management by police was exacerbated by its overreaction. It arrested Avery Ng, but the protest escalated, and several thousand protesters filled the surrounding streets, blocking traffic. By the middle of the night, police were able to disperse protesters.

Avery Ng is the only defendant arrested at the protest. The other eight were arrested at their homes two months later.[23] The unlawful assembly charges are particularly peculiar since there were thousands of demonstrators, all presumably "unlawfully assembled"—so why these five, and why did it take months to arrest them?

Two of the defendants are on trial in other cases as well. Ivan Lam was sentenced to 13 months in prison for unlawful assembly at the NENT protest and is out on bail pending appeal. Avery Ng is appealing an assault conviction and was recently convicted of three counts of disclosing the identity of a person under investigation by the Independent Commission Against Corruption.

Most of the defendants are members of Demosistō or League of Social Democrats. One, Devon Cheng, is a former student leader.

The Legco 5

- **defendants:** *Sixtus Baggio Leung Chung-hang, Yau Wai-ching, Yeung Lai-hong, Chung Suet-ying, Cheung Tsz-lung*
- **charges:** *unlawful assembly, with an alternative charge of forcible entry*
- **outcome:** *All five were convicted of unlawful assembly; sentencing at a yet-to-be-determined date*

The charges relate to an incident in the Legislative Council on November 2, 2016. Leung and Yau were newly-elected Legco members at the time. They attempted, with the help of their assistants, to enter a Legco chamber where the rest of Legco was meeting. The President of Legco had barred them from the chamber after having refused to allow them to retake their oaths of office. The President had granted them a retake but then rescinded the offer after the Hong Kong government intervened, announcing it would take the two to court to strip them of their seats. Security guards, on orders of the Legco President, prevented Leung and Yau from entering the chamber where the rest of Legco was meeting.

Five days later, on November 7, in the midst of the government court case against the two over the taking of their oaths, the National People's Congress Standing Committee issued an interpretation of the Hong Kong Basic Law on oath-taking that effectively compelled the High Court to disqualify Leung and Yau from Legco, which it subsequently did. Their seats remained vacant for 14 months and were filled in a by-election on March 11, 2018.

Legco has also demanded of Leung and Yau reimbursement of over HK$933,000 paid out to them while they were Legco members (on the grounds that, according to the High Court ruling, they never were) and is now suing them to recover the money, which they claim was spent on legitimate expenses while they were Legco members.

The Liaison Office 4

- **defendants:** *Albert Chan, Nathan Law, Joshua Wong, Raphael Wong*
- **charges:** *obstructing police*
- **outcome:** *All were acquitted*

The charges are related to an incident outside of the Central Government Liaison Office on June 11, 2014. A small protest was held in which a facsimile of the White Paper on Hong Kong, a document recently released by the Chinese government, was burned. Police attempted to first prevent the burning and then extinguish the flames. The prosecution claimed that the defendants attempted to obstruct the police from doing so.

This was the first high-profile trial of pro-democracy leaders after the Umbrella Movement, though it was in relation to a small protest which preceded the movement by more than three months. The four were arrested 13 months after the incident, and after the Umbrella Movement, provoking suspicion that the prosecution was politically motivated.

Nathan Law, Joshua Wong, and Raphael Wong would all eventually be tried and convicted in other cases, the Civic Square 3 (Nathan and Joshua), the Mong Kok 20 (Joshua and Raphael), and the NENT 13 (Raphael). The Civic Square 3 prison sentences were overturned. Joshua was sentenced to three months in prison in the Mong Kok 20 trial and is on bail awaiting his appeal. Raphael was sentenced to four months and 15 days in prison in that trial and served his sentence after his appeal was rejected. He was sentenced to 13 months in prison in the NENT trial and is on bail awaiting appeal.

The HKU 2

- **defendants:** *Billy Fung Jing-en, Colman Li Fung-kai*
- **charges:** *Fung: disorderly conduct, criminal intimidation, criminal damage, attempted forcible entry; Li: obstructing an ambulanceman*
- **outcome***: Fung plead guilty to criminal damage and attempted forcible entry and was found guilty of disorderly conduct. He was acquitted of criminal intimidation. He was sentenced to 240 hours of community service. Li was found guilty of obstructing an ambulanceman. He was also sentenced to 240 hours of community service. While the government appeared disappointed they did not receive prison sentences, it said it would not appeal the sentencing.*

The charges were brought in relation to a demonstration outside an on-campus meeting of the University of Hong Kong governing council on January 26, 2016. At the time, Fung was the HKU student union president and Li its external vice-president. The hundreds of protesters were demanding that the council reform HKU's governance structures. This came in the wake of several attempts by the Hong Kong government to punish pro-democracy academics and to impose its will upon the university, for example by appointing a deeply unpopular council chair who had leveled scathing criticism against student participants in the Umbrella Movement. For several hours, council members did not leave the meeting room, claiming they were under siege and prevented from doing so by the protesting students. University authorities called police onto campus. Eventually, Fung and Li were the two students charged in relation to the incident. Their convictions are precedent-setting: the first time students have been found guilty of a crime in relation to on-campus political activity.

Cheng Chung-tai

- **charges:** *desecrating the flags of the HKSAR and PRC*
- **outcome:** *convicted on September 29, 2017 and fined HK$5,000; facing censure by a Legco controlled by Communist Party allies*

The charges were brought in relation to an incident which occurred in the Legco chamber on October 16, 2016. Pro-Communist Party Legco members staged a walkout in an attempt to prevent the Legco President from administering the oath of office a second time to recently elected Baggio Leung and Yau Wai-ching, after the two were deemed to have failed to complete their oaths successfully the first time. (The Chinese and Hong Kong governments would eventually intervene and get both disqualified from Legco by the High Court.) The pro-Party Legco members had put mini-flags on their desks to show their "patriotism" as a form of protest against Leung and Yau, who had held banners reading "Hong Kong is not China" while they took their oaths the first time. Cheng turned the flags upside-down, apparently as a kind of prank, which the powers that be did not find amusing in the least. Cheng is the only sitting Legco member to have been convicted.

Long Hair / Leung Kwok-hung

- **charges:** *In three separate trials, 1) misconduct in public office, 2) contempt of the Legislative Council, 3) assault*
- **outcomes:** *1) acquitted of misconduct in public office on July 31, 2017; 2) judge threw out prosecution on charges of contempt of Legco on grounds that a Legco member cannot be prosecuted for this offense; the government is appealing; 3) trial proper yet to begin*

The government has decided to try to get rid of this perennial thorn in its side once and for all. It has, in all, brought four cases against him, the three criminal prosecutions listed above plus his disqualification from Legco. He vies with fellow League of Social Democrats party member Raphael Wong for the title of pro-democracy leader facing the most court cases— four. But of all pro-democracy leaders, Long Hair has also been the most successful so far in defending himself. He lost the disqualification case (which he is the only one of six to appeal) but was acquitted of one charge and had another prosecution thrown out. It was only after that that the government decided to charge him with assault—it appears it will just keep trying until it nails him.

The misconduct in public office charge stemmed from his alleged failure to declare a HK$250,000 donation from Jimmy Lai, the pro-democracy media mogul. A Legco dominated by pro-Communist Party members had already investigated him for the same alleged offense and exonerated him. The underlying issue is that Hong Kong has no law on political parties. Most political parties are registered as companies and are therefore legally required to report revenues but not funding sources. This case hinged on whether Long Hair had accepted the money on behalf of his party, LSD, in which case he did not need to report it, or on his own behalf, in which case, as an elected official, he did. Rather than address the underlying problem of the lack of transparency of political parties, the government decided to try to use a gap in the law to get Long Hair. Meanwhile, we can only speculate where by far the wealthiest party in terms of revenue, the pro-Communist DAB, gets its money from.

On March 5, 2018, a judge ruled that Long Hair could not be prosecuted on contempt of Legco charges since he was a sitting member of Legco and the law did not apply to Legco members but to others who disrupted Legco. The government has announced it will appeal the ruling. The case stems from an incident in November 2016 in a Legco meeting. Long Hair snatched a file of papers from the desk of a government official. This is the sort of incident which, previous to the Umbrella Movement, would have been entirely disregarded or dealt with through disciplinary proceedings within Legco. It represents the intrusion of the government into areas which traditionally had been the purview of Legco and the criminalization of the behavior of elected representatives while carrying out their duties.

A month after that case was thrown out, on April 4, 2018, Long Hair was arrested and charged with assault related to an incident on April 12, 2017 outside of Legco. Long Hair is alleged to have kicked a pro-Communist Party protester who, he claims, was attacking elderly people. The case has yet to go to trial.

Avery Ng

- **charges:** *1) assaulting police officer, 2) disclosing identity of a person under investigation by the Independent Commission Against Corruption, 3) inciting unlawful assembly*
- **outcomes:** *1) found guilty of assaulting an officer and sentenced to three weeks in prison; on bail pending appeal in October 2018; 2) on May 11, found guilty on all three counts of disclosing identity of a person under ICAC investigation, sentencing at a yet-to-be-determined date; 3) trial proper to begin 15 May*

Avery Ng is right behind his League of Social Democrats party fellows Long Hair and Raphael Wong, with three cases against him (they both have four).

In October 2017, he was convicted of assaulting a police officer and sentenced to three weeks in prison. On Legco election day in September 2016, he went to the polling station where the at-the-time Chief Executive Leung Chun-ying voted. Outside, he threw a tuna sandwich at Leung. It missed and instead, allegedly, hit a police officer. In Hong Kong, this case is derisively referred to as the "tuna fish sandwich assault". It follows another infamous case in which a woman was convicted of having assaulted a police officer with her breast. He is out on bail pending an appeal scheduled for October 2018.

On May 11, he was convicted on all three counts of disclosing the identity of a person under ICAC investigation. After the media reported in April 2016 on a potential conflict of interest involving Permanent Secretary for Home Affairs Betty Fung Ching Suk-yee related to her exchanging properties with a tycoon and benefitting from the price difference, Ng reported her to the ICAC. Speaking to reporters afterwards, he said he could not disclose anything but hoped Fung would give a public explanation. He also mentioned the case on social media. It was for this he was arrested and charged in April 2017, one year after the supposed offense.

He is one of nine on trial in the Liaison Office 9 case (see above) over a protest at that location on November 6, 2016. The government successfully appealed to change the initial charges against him from two counts of inciting disorderly conduct to two counts of inciting unlawful assembly. The trial proper is scheduled to begin on July 9.

Kenneth Leung

- **charges:** *defamation*
- **outcome:** *trial yet to be held*

In March 2016, then Chief Executive Leung Chun-ying sued Kenneth Leung for defamation. Kenneth Leung is a Legco member representing the Accountancy functional constituency and the vice-chair of a pro-democracy group called Professional Commons. At the time of the Umbrella Movement in 2014, a controversy erupted over the CE receiving a HK$50-million payment from a company called UGL which was taking over another company of which Leung was a director. Leung said he received the payment before becoming CE and therefore was not required to declare it. But much about the affair remains to be disclosed. Before walking into a Legco select committee meeting investigating the matter, Kenneth Leung said the CE might be under investigation by Hong Kong or foreign tax authorities. It is for these remarks Leung Chun-ying brought the defamation lawsuit. It is the first time a Chief Executive has sued a Legco member for defamation. There has been no recent word of the progress of the lawsuit, which is yet to go to trial.

Note: Appended to the original article was a table with an overview of all of the cases against pro-democracy leaders brought by the Hong Kong government since the 2014 Umbrella Movement. It can be found online in its most up-to-date version under "Regularly updated overview of trials of Hong Kong pro-democracy leaders and activists" at https://medium.com/@KongTsungGan/regularly-updated-overview-of-trials-of-hong-kong-pro-democracy-leaders-and-activists-66ad3a0bbda9

June 4 and the need for solidarity between all peoples who oppose one-party dictatorship in China

June 4, 2018

In the last three years, I've been repeatedly asked the same two questions by a multitude of journalists.

The first question is: What do you think of the fact that many Hong Kong student unions are not participating in the candlelight vigil?[1]

The second question is: Why do you think the number of people taking part in June 4 commemorative events is declining?

When I was asked these questions, I had the suspicion the journalists already had determined their narrative and just wanted to plug my sound bite into it.

So, in the interest of disrupting that narrative, let me take the occasion of the 29th anniversary of the 1989 pro-democracy demonstrations in China and the June 4 massacre to answer those questions directly.

Question #1: What do you think of the fact that many Hong Kong student unions are not participating in the candlelight vigil?

Answering this question requires providing a bit of background. Between the 20th anniversary of June 4 in 2009 and the 25th in 2014, the dominant media narrative focused on how more young people than ever were joining and it was becoming cool to go to the candlelight vigil with a group of friends. This was all the more striking, given they had not yet even been born at the time of the events of 1989.

Then the Umbrella Movement happened. Various localist forces emerged out of it with momentum. Young people in particular were attracted to localist ideas, which focused on defending Hong Kong and asserting a separate Hong Kong identity if not a separate Hong Kong state entirely. Due above all to localist influence, many student unions held referenda in early 2016 to disaffiliate themselves from Hong Kong Federation of Students, which had ever since 1989 been a staunchly pro-democracy body committed to commemorating June 4. Localists also won elections to leadership positions in the student unions. From 2015 onward, student unions announced that they would not participate in the candlelight vigil. Some organized alternative events. This year, for the first time, except for the Polytechnic University student union,[2] it appears they are holding no alternative events.

To paraphrase the student union argument against participating in the June 4 candlelight vigil: Its organizer, whose full name is the Hong Kong Alliance in Support of Patriotic and Democratic Movements in China, advocates "patriotism". It essentially views Hong Kong people as Chinese people. It calls on the Communist Party to "vindicate" June 4, as if we are all petitioners on bended knee pleading to the emperor, the very emperor who committed the atrocity, for justice. These views are old-fashioned; at the very least, HK Alliance should consider revising them, but instead, it just does the same old thing year after year. It is backward-looking rather than forward-looking, impervious to change, and resistant to cooperating with people who have new ideas. And anyway, Hong Kong people should focus on Hong Kong. It's up to the Chinese people to sort out their own problems, and we in Hong Kong have no particular responsibility to help them. Our focus as Hong Kong people should be on defending Hong Kong and asserting a separate Hong Kong identity, not on saving China, or anywhere else for that matter.

I actually agree with many of these criticisms to one degree or another, but to publicly emphasize them and to prioritize them before unity and solidarity are mistakes that play into the hands of our common adversary.

I have little time for "patriotism" anywhere — I'm a humanist, patriotic to human beings — and given how Communist Party propaganda has attempted to equate the Party with the nation and manipulate jingoistic nationalism, "patriotism" is a particularly sullied concept in China. But it's important to understand why Hong Kong Alliance originally chose its full name: It wanted to counteract Party propaganda by asserting that being pro-democracy does not mean being anti-China; in fact, just the opposite: it means having a vision for China that goes far beyond, and is a great improvement on, Communist Party dictatorship. If it were up to me, I'd drop all mention of "patriotism", but I understand why Hong Kong Alliance retains the idea, and to me, it isn't a sticking point in participating in June 4 events, which I do not only due to a personal connection to the events of 1989 I won't go into here but also because I believe in the overarching objective of remembering what happened that year, among other reasons to fight against the Party's constant attempts to whitewash and rewrite history, which include scrubbing out the fact that it's killed far more Chinese people than all the "enemies of China" combined, many times over. Actually, the number killed on June 4 pales in comparison to the number of victims of many other previous atrocities, from the genocide against political enemies right after coming to power in 1949 to the genocide against Tibetans in the years after the invasion of Tibet to the anti-rightist campaign, to Mao's Great Famine of the late fifties and early sixties, to the Cultural Revolution and so on, up to 1989 and beyond. June 4 is significant because it is one of the Party's biggest single massacres of Chinese citizens, and the most recent. Commemorating it is also a way of remembering that the Communist Party has always been a criminal regime that will stop at nothing to defend its monopoly on power, indeed has destroyed tens of millions of lives in order to do so. Who needs that kind of "patriotism"?

It's important for Hong Kong people to know and remember that history, if for no other reason than to fully understand exactly what we are up against. June 4 is not only Chinese history; it is also Hong Kong history. Anyone old enough to have been there will tell you it had a profound impact on Hong Kong, and it continues to. The handover of Hong Kong had already been decided by the UK and China when 1989 came around. In the massacre's aftermath, there was an exodus from Hong Kong, mostly of people with the means and connections to procure foreign passports and property. Just as 1989 casts a long shadow over China today—it's not an exaggeration to say China is still in its post-'89 period of zero political reform alongside massive economic and social change—, it casts a long shadow over Hong Kong too: In the early days of the Umbrella Movement, there was a pervasive fear that the Party could do to Hong Kong what it did to the demonstrators of 1989. Recently, young pro-democracy activist Agnes Chow revealed that during the Umbrella Movement, she conceded to pressure by her parents and stepped down as spokesperson of Scholarism.[3] They feared a Chinese military crackdown and wanted her to leave the city entirely.

Such moments reveal how alive the memory of June 4 is in Hong Kong, at a very visceral level.

To know 1989 is to know Hong Kong history, to understand Hong Kong's place in history, and to understand Hong Kong's relationship with China. At a time when the Hong Kong government is attempting to scrub references to June 4 from the secondary history curriculum,[4] it's all the more important to promote its memory. The Amnesia Machine which is the Communist Party[5] is coming to Hong Kong, and remembering June 4 is an important way to counteract it.

Not only that, but remembering June 4 is a particular accomplishment of Hong Kong people. Whatever criticisms I might have of Hong Kong Alliance, it has lead the struggle to preserve that memory. Nowhere else in the world that I can think of do so many people commemorate a political event of this nature (pro-democracy demonstrations and regime-perpetrated massacre) every year as we do here. And, as many have pointed out, Hong Kong is the only place under Communist Party control where this can be done. This is a terrible thorn in the Party's side, to be constantly reminded of what it spends massive resources getting the Chinese people to forget. Why would you want to remove that thorn?

You can tell the commemoration has an effect when Party officials and Hong Kong allies make the idiotic assertion, as they have recently, that calling for the end of one-party dictatorship is against the law.[6] The logic is so twisted as to invite ridicule. The Communist Party in China has always existed entirely *above* and *outside of* the law. Where would you go to find its party registration? What mechanisms exist to hold the Party legally accountable? Just to take the situation of Hong Kong, there is no recourse to appeal decisions made about the city by the National People's Congress Standing Committee, a supposedly legislative entity. The Party has its own extralegal disciplinary and detention system, shuanggui. The army actually answers to the Party, not the state. The Party's rule is by its very nature arbitrary, and now it has tried to cement its lawlessness in the constitution, which it itself ignores whenever it so pleases. (When was the last time you heard it invoke people's right to freedom of expression, which is supposedly guaranteed in the PRC constitution?) Invoking "the law" to defend and disguise its own lawlessness has been a distinguishing feature of the regime in recent years. In China, there is no real distinction between "the law" and the Party; which is to say, there is no rule of law, only rule of Party.

To commemorate June 4 in Hong Kong is an act of resistance: we refuse to forget, we refuse to let the Party have its way with China, we refuse to let it have its way with Hong Kong. Of course, in itself, it is insufficient; many other acts of resistance must be undertaken to have an impact, and I will be the first to argue that we members of the resistance can improve a lot in that area. But that does not mean that to remember is unimportant; just the opposite.

Beyond that, commemorating June 4 is an act of solidarity; solidarity with those who fought for democracy in China all those years ago, with those who were killed by the Party for doing so, and, by extension, with those who down through the 29 years since then have continued to do so, like the Charter 08[7] signatories, like Liu Xiaobo, like the 709 rights lawyers,[8] and the thousands of mostly unsung others.

In Hong Kong, solidarity is not a selfless gesture; it is a gesture of enlightened self-interest. We know from first-hand experience how hard it is to fight for democracy, human rights and freedom against the biggest, most powerful dictatorship in the world. And those people in China are fighting for the very same things against the very same adversary. We should support them, just as they should support us. The mutual support is mutually beneficial. Of course, we must stay focused on defending Hong Kong and asserting a separate Hong Kong identity, but that is not mutually exclusive or even in tension with showing solidarity with people in China; in fact, just the opposite—the two acts complement one another. If we want people elsewhere to have solidarity with us, we should have solidarity with others.

In fact, our solidarity should be even broader than that, extending not only to those who have fought for democracy, human rights and freedom in China in the past and those who continue to do so today, but to all under Party control and influence who are doing so. That includes Taiwanese, Tibetans, Uighurs, and Southern Mongolians. We all have common aspirations. We all have a common adversary.

Working together to overturn one-party dictatorship is surely a better strategy than ignoring one another or pretending we have nothing in common. Since the Umbrella Movement, there has been greater recognition of the importance of this than before, including by localists, and there have been more efforts to reach out to, first and foremost, Taiwanese, and, to a lesser extent, also Tibetans. That is precisely why the Party threw such a tantrum when a moderate, mild-mannered guy like Benny Tai went to Taiwan and uttered the word "independence". Working together works. We should not exclude people in mainland China from this network; we should reach out to them, and commemorating June 4 is one small but symbolically important part of that work.

In defending Hong Kong, asserting Hong Kong identity, and working toward democracy and self-determination, we should have an expansive view, and we should situate our struggle within the wider context of China, Asia and the world. When engaged in the struggle, it can become very easy to develop a kind of tunnel vision—the rest of the world fades away and all we can see is ourselves. We must work to counteract that tendency and act towards others elsewhere, especially those fighting for the values and ideals we hold dear, with compassion and solidarity.

Ironically for a regime that spends so much propaganda effort on remembering the historical humiliations of imperialist incursions into China by Japan and Western powers, the Communist Party is as imperialist as previous Chinese dynasties. Under the Party, China has more outstanding territorial disputes with neighbors than any other country in the world. On top of that, it claims dominion over a wide expanse of contested territory at its peripheries—Taiwan, Hong Kong, Tibet, Xinjiang, Southern Mongolia. The people in those places have very different ideas from those of the Party of what their political status and relationship to Beijing should be. Above all else, all peoples have the right of self-determination, and this includes mainland Chinese, the Han majority, who are denied that right just as much as Tibetans and Hong Kong people. Commemorating June 4 is part of the campaign for self-determination of all peoples under Communist Party control and influence.

Question #2: Why do you think the number of people taking part in June 4 commemorative events is declining?

I sometimes think journalists who ask this question are suffering from the same sort of historical amnesia that commemoration of June 4 is meant to counteract.

In 2014, the 25th anniversary of June 4, only four years ago, the largest crowd ever, upwards of 200,000, turned out for the candlelight vigil. And that is just a few more people than turned out in 2012, the 23rd anniversary, a non-round year. That is nothing short of remarkable, attesting to the extent to which the memory of June 4 is still alive in Hong Kong people and is being passed down from one generation to the next. (Note: The 200,000 of 2014 is actually my own estimate. Hong Kong Alliance estimated 180,000, but that takes into account only the number of people who were able to enter Victoria Park. In fact, the park was so full, approximately twenty thousand people marked the vigil right outside the park, mostly on the west side, along Great George Street stretching up to the Causeway Bay MTR entrance.)

Since 2014, turnouts have been lower, but all turnouts since 2009 have been higher than any year before then. We are actually in a period of historically high turnouts, and have been for nearly a decade now. The vigil was reinvigorated by the 20th anniversary. The turnouts from 2015 on have been low only compared to the immense turnout on the 25th anniversary, but this fits with the "wave" pattern of highest turnouts in round years and dips in non-round years.

It's true that since the 25th anniversary, events in Hong Kong such as the Umbrella Movement and the rise of localism have transformed the political situation, but the true test of whether or not there may be a historically downward trajectory in participation rates for June 4 commemorative activities is next year's 30th anniversary, another round year. Maybe there will be, but it's too soon to say, and until then, the accurate story line is the *increase* in turnouts from 2009 on as compared to the many years before that. Media fixation on student unions not participating and counter-factual declines in turnout lacks perspective and is a misleading distortion of the full picture; I don't think this is down to bias as much as just plain lazy, ill-informed journalism.

The larger issue is the media stereotype of the pro-democracy movement as beleaguered and in decline. Sure we've got our problems, but it doesn't take much of a shift in perspective to see just the opposite: years of persistence and resilience under adverse conditions and in the face of the intense hostility of an implacable dictatorship. That indeed is what the candlelight vigil represents.

Justice it ain't: The Mong Kok "riot" trials

June 18, 2018

A review of Hong Kong government prosecutions of protesters for the police-protester clashes in Mong Kok at Chinese New Year, 8 to 9 February 2016

On Monday, June 11, Edward Leung, Lo Kin-man and Wong Ka-kui were sentenced to, respectively, six years, seven years, and three years and six months in prison, following their conviction for "riot" on Friday, May 18.[1] (Leung had previously plead guilty to assaulting a police officer in the same case.) The six-year and seven-year sentences are the longest yet out of the 25 related to the police-protester violence in Mong Kok, Hong Kong on the night of 8 to 9 February 2016. Cumulatively, the 25 defendants have been sentenced to 71 years, 1 month and 21 days in prison. Of those, 18 have been convicted of "riot" and sentenced to 67 years and 6 months.

On Thursday, May 31, in the largest "riot" trial, a judge sentenced nine of ten defendants to prison.[2] The heaviest sentence of four years and three months was given to Mo Jia-tao, who was 17, a minor, at the time of the incident. A 73-year-old (also reported to be 72[3]) was sentenced to three years and five months, and an autistic man got two years and four months. This last sentence was imposed against the advice of probation officers, who said community service was more appropriate. The nine were sentenced to overall 31 years and one month in prison.

With these sentences, most of the trials related to that night of violence in 2016 have concluded. Three defendants, including Leung, will be retried on counts on which the jury could not reach a verdict, and two defendants will go on trial in November. This, therefore, is a good moment to step back and analyze what has occurred.

Why "riot" is, in this case, a loaded term

The event to which these trials are related has been variously referred to as a "riot", the "Fishball Revolution", "clashes" and "civil unrest". I find "police-protester violence" or "clashes" to be the most appropriate terms.

The term "riot" was politicized by the Hong Kong government immediately after the event. It used this designation to stamp its definitive judgement on the event, to block calls for an independent inquiry into police actions on the night and to preemptively stigmatize the protesters, effectively declaring that the police were entirely in the right, the protesters entirely in the wrong. Riots occurred in Hong Kong in 1956, 1966 and 1967, and in each case the government conducted an inquiry and published a report. The government has refused to do so in relation to 2016. The term "riot" was quickly adopted by pro-Communist Hong Kong media as a blanket description of what had occurred. "Riot" is a specific (and highly problematic) offense in the Hong Kong Crimes Ordinance, and using the term may imply the view that those who participated are liable to prosecution for that offense. "Riot" also has the connotation of out-of-control violence involving destruction of property, but in fact, virtually all of the protester violence targeted police. There was no looting, there was minimal destruction of private property (only one protester was charged with an offense related to that—arson for setting a taxi on fire), and there was almost no targeting of private property. For these reasons, the term "riot" is misleading, simplistic, politically biased and best avoided.

"Fishball Revolution" is a term that tends to be used by supporters of the protesters, sometimes ironically. It refers to the fact that the protesters originally came out that night to support Chinese New Year hawkers, who may or may not have been selling fishballs, and who were accosted by Food and Environmental Hygiene Department officers and police officers. The term is hyperbolic: whatever occurred that night, a revolution it was not.

"Unrest" seems a bit abstract and distant for what after all was a discrete event occurring over the course of a single night. "Police-protester violence" or "clashes" puts the focus most squarely on what most definitely occurred: a night-long fight between police and protesters.

The trial of Edward Leung

The just-concluded trial was the highest profile of the Mong Kok cases because one of the six defendants was Edward Leung Tin-kei. At the time of the clashes, Leung was a leader of localist group Hong Kong Indigenous. He then ran for the Legislative Council in a by-election held the very same month, February 2016. While finishing third, with about 15 percent of the vote, he did well enough that he was expected to win a seat in the city-wide Legco elections of September. But he was arbitrarily disqualified from running by an administrative official at the behest of the Hong Kong government, on grounds that since he supported independence for Hong Kong, he could not be expected to uphold the Basic Law, a duty of Legco members; this, in spite of the fact that he had been allowed to run seven months previously and, in his application for candidacy, had forsworn independence advocacy and promised to uphold the Basic Law. To protest this abuse of his rights, he filed an election petition at the Hong Kong High Court, which to this day, a year and a half later, still has not been heard.

Not only is Leung probably the best-known localist leader in Hong Kong, he was also charged with "inciting riot", the first person to stand trial for that offense. In effect, the Hong Kong government was alleging that he was one of the main instigators. His fellow leader of Hong Kong Indigenous, Ray Wong Toi-yeung, was also charged with "inciting riot", but he has absconded, whereabouts unknown, and a warrant has been issued for his arrest.

"Inciting riot" was only one of the charges Leung faced. The others were two counts of riot and a count of assaulting a police officer. He plead guilty to the latter charge, was found guilty of one count of "riot", and the jury couldn't reach a verdict on the other count. He was acquitted of "inciting riot". The government has since announced that it will re-try Leung on the one riot count.

There were originally ten charged in this trial. Besides Wong, one other, Li Tung-sing, absconded. Two who are charged with "conspiracy to riot" as well as "riot", Yung Wai-yip and Yuen Chi-Kui, will be tried separately in a trial currently scheduled to begin 8 November. Of the five others who stood trial with Leung, Wong Ka-kui plead guilty to riot; Lo Kin-man was found guilty of riot; Lam Lun-hing was acquitted of three counts of riot; the jury reached no verdict in the "riot" charges against Lee Nok-man and Lam Ngo-hin; and Lam Ngo-hin was acquitted of unlawful assembly.

Of the twelve counts brought against the six defendants in the case, only four resulted in conviction and Leung was acquitted of the most serious charge against him, incitement, meaning the government has thus far failed to get any conviction related to "inciting" or organizing the protest. While the sentences of seven, six and three years four months are shockingly heavy, this trial was by far the worst result yet for the Hong Kong government in its three dozen or so prosecutions related to the Mong Kok police-protester clashes.

The only clear difference between this case and the others was that it was held at the High Court and it was a trial by jury, whereas judges issued the verdicts in the other trials. Was the government's case simply worse, or does the result perhaps also indicate that juries tend to be more lenient than judges, at least when it comes to "riot" charges? By contrast, the 31 May sentencing of 10 concluded the government's most successful case against Mong Kok defendants, with all ten convicted and sentenced to heavy prison terms.

An overview and analysis of results

Originally, 90 people were arrested in connection with the police-protester clashes, and 51 were charged. Charges were dropped against 20 due to lack of evidence, leaving 31 to prosecute. Six were later arrested or charged with additional counts.

Of the 31 trials completed so far, 25 defendants have been convicted on 34 counts. These include 21 for "riot", one for arson, five for assaulting a police officer, one for disorderly conduct, one for resisting arrest, and two for criminal damage. Eight defendants have been acquitted on 10 counts. These include five for "riot", three for assaulting an officer, one for unlawful assembly, and one for "inciting riot". In addition, a jury reached no verdict on three counts.

That's a whopping 75 percent conviction rate, compared to about 50 percent for all criminal prosecutions,[4] and about 40 percent for Umbrella Movement-related prosecutions.[5]

Looking just at prosecutions on "riot" charges, 21 out of 26, or 80 percent, have resulted in convictions.

Sentences for the 25 sentenced so far have been harsh, totaling, as noted above, 71 years, one month and 21 days. Only one conviction has resulted in a non-custodial sentence. All others were sentenced to prison, with the shortest sentence being 21 days and the longest seven years. Eighteen of those convicted of "riot" have been sentenced to, cumulatively, 67 years and six months: six to three-to-four years each; five to three-year terms each; three to two-to-three years each; two to four-to-five years each; ; one to seven years; one to six years; one was sentenced to a training centre and another to juvenile detention.

By comparison, only five demonstrators out of approximately 100 convicted for the Umbrella Movement got prison sentences,[6] and these amounted to, in all, 20 months in length. Eight police officers were sentenced to a total of 14 years and three months in prison for assaulting Umbrella Movement demonstrators.

From this, it can be concluded that Hong Kong judges take a very dim view of protester violence, dimmer than in the past. The average prison term for those convicted of "riot" is 3.75 years. The 1956 riots were much more serious, resulting in 59 deaths, but prison sentences for "riot" ranged from seven months to two years.[7]

In many of the cases, the violence committed by the defendants seemed not terribly serious. Amongst those convicted of "riot" and sentenced to three years in prison, three threw bottles and other objects at police, one held a glass bottle in his hand, and one threw bricks at police. One of the longest sentences, four years and nine months, was for "riot" and arson. It involved throwing burning objects at a taxi and setting it on fire. One of the shortest "riot" sentences—two years and 10 months—was for throwing part of a brick at police and shaking a signpost so as to loosen bricks in the pavement that could be used by others.

It also appears that judges have made a big distinction between merely committing violence and doing so as part of a riot. This can be seen by comparing those convicted of violent offenses but not "riot" to those convicted of "riot", which is defined as committing "a breach of the peace" in an unlawful assembly. (Public Order Ordinance, Cap 245, Part IV, article 19) Four were convicted of violent offenses such as assaulting an officer and received sentences totaling one year and 21 days. One defendant threw two water bottles at police. Another threw a rubbish bin in the street. Yet another punched an officer in the chest. And the fourth hit an officer in the knee with a thrown brick. It is unclear why those prosecuted for committing violent offenses at Mong Kok were not charged with "riot" like the others. As noted, those convicted of "riot" got on average 3.75 years in prison each.

Based on this comparison, it seems that the harsh sentences for "riot" have as much if not more to do with being present at an unlawful assembly where a breach of the peace has been committed as with any actual discrete act of violence perpetrated by the defendant.

The Public Order Ordinance needs reform but instead the Hong Kong government is doubling down on its use

This raises many questions about the legitimacy of the "riot" charge, which comes under the Public Order Ordinance, a set of laws on assembly that have been repeatedly criticized by the United Nations Human Rights Committee,[8] Human Rights Watch,[9] Hong Kong Watch[10] and former Hong Kong governor Chris Patten[11] as failing to meet international standards, possibly facilitating excessive restrictions on freedom of assembly, and open to abuse by police and prosecutors. In regard to "riot", the bar is set very low, for all that needs to have occurred is commission of a "breach of the peace" in an unlawful assembly. A breach of the peace could be as little as shouting loudly; in other words, it is not even equivalent to commission of an act of violence.

Many pro-democracy demonstrators have also been convicted under POO, and thirteen have received lengthy prison terms (12 to 13 months and one to eight months) for the nonviolent offense of unlawful assembly.[12]

In all of these cases, if there is evidence the defendant has committed a recognizable criminal offense, he should be tried for the discrete act that he is alleged to have committed and not for acts committed by others which the defendant had nothing to do with. In the specific cases of the Mong Kok police-protester violence prosecutions, while a protester may be charged with, for example, assault for throwing bricks or water bottles, it is much more problematic to charge the same protester with "riot". In the May 31 sentencing hearing, the judge said the 10 defendants bore "collective liability" for the "riot" on top of what each of them had done individually.[13] This is a troubling concept, especially given that none were convicted of "inciting riot" or otherwise organizing it, and no evidence was introduced that they were even coordinating their actions or in any way conspiring to "riot", but within the scope of the current vague wording of the "riot" offense, the judge apparently felt justified in considering "collective liability" part of the offense, yet another indication of the need for its revision or abolition.

While numerous human rights experts have pointed out that it is more than high time for the POO to be reformed, the Hong Kong government is instead doubling down on its use in prosecuting demonstrators, and doing so more aggressively than ever.

The lack of police accountability for its actions during the Umbrella Movement has been compounded by its similar lack in the Mong Kok police-protester violence

The Mong Kok "riot" trials should be viewed in the wider context of the event to which they are related and this particular moment in Hong Kong history. The clashes between Hong Kong police and citizens that night were the worst that had occurred since 1967. For the first time in living memory, a police officer discharged his pistol at a protest,[14] bringing Hong Kong closer than ever to its first protest-related fatality since the 1960s.

In light of the clashes' magnitude and gravity—something about which there was wide consensus in Hong Kong society across the political spectrum—the Hong Kong government should have called for an independent inquiry to determine just what happened, who was to blame, and what the underlying causes were, but instead it immediately brushed off the suggestion, rejecting calls for an inquiry less than a week after the occurrence.[15] It was determined from the start to simply label the events a "riot", to place all blame on the protesters and shield the police and government officials from any accountability. (Chief Executive Carrie Lam recently reiterated the government's refusal to authorize an independent investigation.)[16]

This is in contrast to not only previous Hong Kong government inquiries into the riots of 1956, 1966 and 1967, as mentioned above, but also, for example, the inquiry into the riots in England in 2011 by an independent panel set up by the UK government.[17]

Hong Kong actually has a Commissions of Inquiry Ordinance that lays out how this is to occur.[18] Recent commissions looked into the fatal ferry accident of 2012 and excessive lead found in drinking water in 2015. Was the police-protester violence of 2016 not at least as important as those matters, and of just as great if not greater public interest?

Just to take a single example of the consequences of this refusal to get to the bottom of what happened in a meticulous and impartial manner: In the case of the police officer who shot his gun into the air twice, the police said they would conduct an investigation. Then, a few days later, the police concluded the officer was justified in doing so, as he believed he was defending imperiled colleagues.[19] Later, the officer was presented with an official commendation for the act.[20] Such a process ridicules the whole notion of a proper impartial investigation and could actually have the effect of giving greater license to police officers to use firearms at demonstrations.

Apart from the question of whether or not the officer was justified in firing his gun, other relevant questions would include: How did it ever get to the point that the officer apparently felt he had no other recourse than to fire his gun into the air in one of the most densely populated parts of the city? How had the police allowed the situation to get so out of control that by that point the officer apparently believed his colleagues to be in real danger? Does that not reflect poorly on how the police handled the occasion? If so, what did the police do wrong; how could they have handled it better? Did the police take appropriate crowd control measures? Did they handle the demonstrators in an unjustifiably aggressive or provocative manner, as reported by many? Did they do enough to protect the rights of all involved? What are the guidelines for use of live fire, in particular at demonstrations, and do they need to be revisited and perhaps revised? (The police say they have such guidelines, but they refuse to divulge them to the public or even to Legco members, rendering public oversight impossible.)[21] What had motivated the protesters to, in some cases, attack police, given that the original "spark"— FEHD and police officers trying to prevent hawkers from selling their wares—doesn't seem sufficient motivation? Many defendants in the "riot" trials have testified that their primary motivation was anger at the police for violence inflicted upon demonstrators at the Umbrella Movement. This does seem to be a widespread sentiment, and, if so, how should that affect police policy regarding policing of demonstrations? Does it reflect a need for greater police accountability, and if so, how can that be achieved?

It is astounding that in one of the more important events to have occurred in the last few years in the city, an event of landmark historical significance, the government has decided that it is not important to look deeper into the matter and try to get to the bottom of it. Instead, it simply labels the incident a "riot", cracks down on the "rioters" through prosecutions, and moves on as if everything else is fine.

The Hong Kong government has attempted to draw the attention of the media and the people away from these questions and issues by the long parade of prosecutions of "rioters". And to quite a large extent, this seems to have been successful. It played on the accurate view that a large number of Hong Kong people, including myself, deplore violence, and then distracted people from the high probability that the police were at least as responsible for the violence of that night as the protesters. So whenever we discuss the prosecutions related to that night's events, we should always remember the context, the many unanswered questions, and the fact that the unelected government has shielded itself and the police force from any form of accountability.

As for what actually happened that night, the account that Edward Leung gave when taking the stand in his own defense at his trial[22] is close to that which circulates widely in opposition circles: FEHD officers approached hawkers in Mong Kok and demanded that they cease selling their wares since they had no license to do so. It was unclear why they felt the need to "enforce the law" so aggressively that evening, since Chinese New Year has traditionally been a time when grey areas in the application of the law were allowed to prevail, and the previous year, the FEHD took no such action. Some people come out and hawk traditional foods at that time of year and no other. It would not be cost effective for them to go through the long, arduous procedures needed to procure the relevant hawking licenses. Through social media, calls went out to come and defend the hawkers. This role had been performed by Hong Kong Indigenous and other groups the year before as well,[23] and that time, the holiday passed without major conflict, even though it was closer to the Umbrella Movement than 2016 was. As demonstrators gathered, FEHD officials called in the police for back-up. The police acted in an aggressive manner, similar to that employed to clear the Mong Kok occupation during the Umbrella Movement in November 2014 and to keep the streets of Mong Kok clear of demonstrators in the aftermath. That involved using significant and unjustifiable force such as the systematic aiming of batons at demonstrators' heads. But at Chinese New Year 2016, police were unprepared for the eventuality that demonstrators might stand up to their aggressive behavior, and the situation quickly escalated to physical confrontation.

If nothing else, the policing that evening appears ham-handed and not very well attuned to the situation. The lesson the police had learned from the Umbrella Movement clearance of the Mong Kok occupation was that it was important to be uniformly and consistently tough on demonstrators, to send them a clear message of what would be tolerated and what not. At the time of the Umbrella Movement and the Mong Kok "gao wu" demonstrations in the aftermath of the Mong Kok occupation, police had sufficient numbers on the streets to employ that strategy, but they did not on the evening in question. They simply assumed the demonstrators would be cowed and disperse, and when they did not, the police had no back-up plan.

Beyond that, it is important to remember that there has been almost no accountability for police actions during the Umbrella Movement either. There again, as with the Mong Kok violence, there were calls for an independent investigation into police actions; in particular, the eight-hour-long tear gas attacks on unarmed, nonviolent Hong Kong citizens on 28 September 2014, which were arguably the number one trigger of the Umbrella Movement, as Hong Kong people rose up in outrage.

To this day, the only information we have from police about the decision-making and the command responsibility for that action is an interview given to *South China Morning Post* by an anonymous police superintendent saying it was entirely his responsibility.[24] This account is hardly credible, falling far short of addressing the matter (just for starters: while I don't believe for a second he was solely responsible for ordering the initial attacks, even if that were the case, he certainly couldn't have ordered all on his own the tear gas attacks that continued for eight hours) and far from the kind of impartial investigation that needed to occur.

Throughout the Umbrella Movement, on numerous occasions, the police used force disproportionately, including in the clearance of Mong Kok. I can still very clearly hear in my memory the loud haunting, sickening THWACK! of police batons landing first on the umbrellas and then on the hardhats of demonstrators who were sitting in front of police lines. Later, police would say that the fact that demonstrators came "armed" with protective devices such as umbrellas (against pepperspray) and hardhats (against baton blows) was a sign they intended trouble. No, it was a sign they simply intended to protect themselves from the police violence they by then knew full well to expect, violence that was endorsed and in all likelihood also ordered by the government.

The lack of police accountability for actions during the Umbrella Movement left festering wounds which were an important precipitator of protester actions on the night of the Mong Kok clashes. People remember. And now, the lack of investigation of police actions during the Umbrella

Movement is followed by lack of investigation of police actions in Mong Kok that night, and the government tries to act as if the parade of prosecutions of "rioters" is sufficient response to the worst police-protester violence in half a century. People remember all of this as well. The wounds do not go away but fester. Langston Hughes' famous poem, written about African-Americans' struggle for equal rights in the U.S., comes to mind:

What happens to a dream deferred?

Does it dry up
like a raisin in the sun?
Or fester like a sore—
And then run?
Does it stink like rotten meat?
Or crust and sugar over—
like a syrupy sweet?

Maybe it just sags
like a heavy load.

Or does it explode?

In the newspaper, I read that the police themselves say the relations with Hong Kong people have now recovered since the Umbrella Movement,[25] and I just have to laugh: Who are they kidding? Police refer to a survey they supposedly commissioned in January this year as evidence, but that survey, if it does exist, is not publicly available. What is, is HKUPOP's regular survey on the popularity of Hong Kong disciplinary forces and the Hong Kong PLA Garrison, the most recent of which was conducted in December 2017.[26] It shows very little change in police unpopularity from November 2015 (about a year after the Umbrella Movement). The police are still the second most unpopular disciplinary force out of 10. The only one that does worse is the PLA Garrison (which is not a disciplinary but an occupying force). Indeed, that the police do only slightly better than the PLA should tell you something. They have a "satisfaction rating" of 64.1 versus the PLA's 63.3. And that 64.1 has gone up less than two points from the 62.4 of November 2015. Instead of complacency, such results should give the police cause for concern.

Rather than a blossoming love fest between the police and the people of Hong Kong, what has occurred is that official Hong Kong—the Hong Kong of the unelected government and the unaccountable police force, the Hong Kong of the continued, indefinite refusal to fulfill the promise of universal suffrage—continues down one path while the Hong Kong of a good many of its people who want justice, democracy and real autonomy, who want a government and a police force that recognize the people as the boss, that recognize they work for the people and should implement the people's will rather than regard them as underlings to be "policed", continues down another path. The paths are diverging ever further apart. What becomes of that widening gap remains to be seen, but it is politically unsustainable and will probably lead to increased repression.

The police's lesson learnt from the Umbrella Movement and the Mong Kok clashes is that it has to be tougher on demonstrators. Toward that end, it's invested tens of millions of dollars in new "crowd control" water cannon vehicles, the first of which has just been delivered.[27] I doubt many Hong Kong people are thinking, *Just what we need!* The government's lesson learnt is that it has to be harder on the pro-democracy movement and all political opposition, resulting in the most widespread crackdown since the handover, in the form of dozens of prosecutions, disqualifications from Legco, and barring of candidates from running for office on political grounds, among other means.

The people's lesson learnt is there is no justice in Hong Kong under Communist rule.

It is true that eight police officers were eventually tried and convicted for assaulting demonstrators in the Umbrella Movement. And it is true that those eight officers have been sentenced to more prison time than all Umbrella Movement protesters put together. But it is as if the government and police are using the prosecutions related to the Mong Kok clashes to take revenge on that fact. And it's important to remember that the prosecutions of those officers came about against the will of the police force, which tried to prevent them from occurring. It is only due to the tireless efforts of activists in pursuit of justice that the officers were prosecuted at all. Not only that, but what all eight officers had in common was that they were caught on video committing those acts. It appears the only chance of ever holding police accountable for violence inflicted on demonstrators is to have those actions captured on video.

But even then, accountability only applies to individual officers. Their convictions are far from what is meant by the term "police accountability". While the police have protested loudly against the convictions, showing that they are hardly impartial when it comes to the enforcement of the law, the top officers have allowed these individual frontline officers to be the fall guys, sacrificing them rather than taking responsibility themselves for systematic policies in which these officers played their part. These leaders hide behind their indignance at the convictions in the cowardly way of those who are confident they will never themselves face accountability for their actions.

The police force has been morally corrupted by its use as the guard dog of the regime. Its position is more precarious than at any time since the early 1970s when the force was perceived as so corrupt that nothing short of the creation of the Independent Commission Against Corruption could address it. Now, we don't have that kind of corruption; we have moral corruption, a corruption of purpose.

It is hard to think of a single case involving the regime and its allies that the police has adequately addressed, whether the kidnappings and abductions to the mainland of Lee Bo and Xiao Jianhua by Communist agents, the attacks on Umbrella Movement demonstrators by triad-related thugs, or pro-Communist Legco member Junius Ho's threatening pronouncement that independence advocates should be "killed mercilessly".

The Hong Kong Bar Association usually sticks quite narrowly to issuing statements on legal matters, but in its submission to the Hong Kong government as part of the upcoming Universal Periodic Review of Hong Kong and China at the UN Human Rights Council, it dedicates a full four paragraphs to the police's "increasing [deployment of] more restrict *[sic]* crowd control measures which had an impact on citizens' exercising their right to freedom of assembly". It also notes that in spite of the fact there is a pattern of judges having acquitted defendants of protest-related charges and criticizing police for making false accusations under oath, "those police officers subject to such criticisms continue to serve on the police force with impunity".[28]

Remember this context when regarding the prosecutions of young people who are now being sent to prison for years for throwing bricks and bottles at police in Mong Kok on a single night.

Repercussions and implications of the Mong Kok prosecutions

Far from blindly supporting the protesters that evening, I abhor violence of any kind. I believe the struggle for democracy, self-determination and justice must remain entirely nonviolent. I understand the anger and frustration that motivated the protesters, I feel it myself, but those motivations do not justify their violent acts, which were not only morally unacceptable but strategically idiotic, catastrophically so.

The protester attacks on police provided the government with its best opportunity to decimate localist groups through prosecutions, and it has proceeded to do so. At the time of Chinese New Year 2016, localism was on the rise, and represented, especially to many young people, an alternative to the traditional pan-democrats which many were coming to regard as naïve, weak and ineffectual.

Just a few weeks after the clashes, Edward Leung placed third in a Legco by-election and appeared to be on track to securing a seat in Legco in the city-wide elections of September (though, as it turned out, he was arbitrarily barred from running in that contest). Civic Passion won one seat in that election, and Youngspiration (with Baggio Leung stepping in to replace the disqualified Leung) two. Flash forward two years, and Hong Kong Indigenous and Youngspiration are all but moribund, and Civic Passion isn't doing much better.

Localism still exists and is still influential, again especially among young people, but it has gone underground and, apart from localist-dominated university student unions, has virtually no visible institutional presence. While there are various reasons for this (the disqualifications of Baggio Leung and Yau Wai-ching from Legco; the introduction of a new law criminalizing "insulting" the PRC anthem; the prosecution of Cheng Chung-tai; the Communist Party and Hong Kong government crackdown on independence advocacy and intimidating attempts to extend their influence on university campuses), surely the situation would look much different now if protesters had not attacked police with bricks and bottles at Chinese New Year 2016.

The prosecutions of protesters on "riot" charges also emboldened the government to go after nonviolent pro-democracy protesters more aggressively, appealing the community service sentences of 16 nonviolent protesters and procuring lengthy prison sentences as well as harsher future sentencing guidelines for convicted protesters. (Three of those prison sentences were subsequently overturned by the Court of Final Appeal, which will also hear the appeal of the 13 others in September.) The government was able to do this by dangling the specters of "violence" and "disorder" in front of judges ruling on the cases of defendants who were not convicted of violent crimes or even disorderly conduct. This prosecution tactic seems to have had a hypnotizing effect, as attested to by the harsher sentencing guidelines for those convicted of nonviolent crimes committed at protests where some violence may occur. They are to be held responsible for that violence, though they themselves were not involved in it, surely running counter to a principle of jurisprudence that the individual should be held accountable for his own actions, not others'.

Hong Kong judges are not particularly streetwise. They exist in their own version of the ivory tower, swimming in their own social circles, insulated from how ordinary Hong Kong people live. They also tend to be rather conservative. This leaves them susceptible to government narratives about what is happening on the street that may bear little resemblance to reality. And the higher up you go in the judiciary, the more this is the case. The government has taken advantage of this to drive the story that Hong Kong is somehow on the verge of "chaos", "disorder", "lawlessness" and "violence", and it is incumbent upon judges to "do something about this" through "deterrent" sentencing and harsher sentencing guidelines. The Mong Kok police-protester violence of Chinese New Year 2016 made it much easier for prosecutors to sell this hackneyed tale to gullible judges.

Regime opponents can be forgiven for thinking that the High Court in particular does not have much sympathy with their cause. Of all the cases against pro-democracy leaders and activists and Mong Kok "rioters" tried in the last two years, the High Court has decided in favor of the government in every case but one. It has disqualified six democratically elected pro-democracy Legco members. It has upheld the barring on political grounds of National Party leader Andy Chan from running for Legco. Upon government appeal of lower court sentences of community service, it has sentenced 16 pro-democracy protesters to prison for six to thirteen months for the nonviolent offense of unlawful assembly. It has found liable of contempt of court all 20 of those thusfar tried in relation to the November 2014 police clearance of the Mong Kok occupation during the Umbrella Movement and sentenced two of them to prison. (Fifteen more are on trial right now.) So far, that's 43 decisions in favor of the government, three in favor of the opposition. And even those three—Joshua Wong, Nathan Law, and Alex Chow—were initially sentenced to prison by the High Court's Court of Appeal and only had their sentences overturned by the Court of Final Appeal, which nevertheless upheld the Court of Appeal's harsher sentencing guidelines for protesters issued in the case. And that CFA decision, not least in its timing, had a suspiciously political smell to it, coming days after the three had been nominated for the Nobel Peace Prize—the government didn't want their prison martyrdom to increase the chances of them winning. The message is that the High Court is inclined to side with authority and the status quo and not persuaded by rights-based arguments.

In summary, the most immediate repercussions of the Mong Kok violence are dozens of imprisonments, the decimation of the localist movement, heightened Party and Hong Kong government resolve to attack political enemies, a harsher judicial climate for protesters, and continued and arguably increased insulation from accountability of the Hong Kong government and police force.

Not least significant, the "riot" trials have highlighted the substantial and growing gap between law and justice in Hong Kong. While some of the "riot" defendants may have committed crimes for which they should be held liable in a court of law, the larger issues behind the event, including police accountability and unenacted political reform that is required by law, continue to go entirely unaddressed. As Baggio Leung, another pro-democracy activist who has faced the courts, said, "One cannot look to the courts for justice in a place without democracy."

Note: Appended to the original article was a table, "Prosecutions related to Mong Kok violence between demonstrators and police on the night of 8 to 9 February 2016". It can be found online at https://medium.com/@KongTsungGan/justice-it-aint-the-mong-kok-riot-trials-b89431806663

The power of the peripheries

June 25, 2018

Over the past decade, major uprisings in Tibet, East Turkestan, Taiwan and Hong Kong have challenged Chinese Communist hegemony.

. . . following on my previous article about June 4, which stressed the need for solidarity and cooperation between all peoples opposed to one-party dictatorship in China.

Everything is, as they say, a matter of perspective. And of relation, of one to an other, to others.

Hong Kong is a small place.

As a city in its own right, its 7.3 million people make Hong Kong the 46th biggest city in the world by population, and the 104th biggest country in the world, bigger than 129 others.

But there are ten Chinese cities bigger than Hong Kong, including three in Guangdong alone, Shenzhen, Dongguan and Guangzhou. And of course, the country that contains them has 1.4 billion people, compared to which Hong Kong is little more than a speck hanging off a spit of land on its southeastern corner, a unique and special speck, but a speck nonetheless.

In terms of land area too, Hong Kong is small, dwarfed by the other contested territories on China's peripheries.

Tibet is enormous. Its total area, comprising the traditional three provinces of U-Tsang, Amdo and Kham, is 2.5 million square kilometers, making it the tenth biggest country in the world, just behind India, Argentina and Kazakhstan. China invaded Tibet in 1950, and in 1965, established the Tibet Autonomous Region, a misnomer if there ever was one. It comprises 1.2 million square kilometers, less than half the size of traditional Tibet, and more Tibetans live outside the TAR than inside it.

Xinjiang, whose full name is Xinjiang Uighur Autonomous Region, another misnomer, or East Turkestan to those who don't accept Chinese rule there, is also huge — 1.6 million square kilometers. (I prefer to avoid the term "Xinjiang" since it is inherently colonial, meaning in Chinese "new frontier", clearly from the Chinese perspective. It is used here solely to designate the XUAR, the entity set up by the Communist Party in 1955.)

China would look a lot different without Tibet and Xinjiang, which together make up about 42 percent of the area under the rule of the Communist regime.

Even Taiwan is many times bigger than Hong Kong: nearly 36,000 square kilometers versus Hong Kong's approximately 2,700 square kilometers, only 1,000 of which is land, the rest being water.

In terms of population, these peripheries are closer in size: Taiwan has 23.5 million people, Hong Kong 7. 3 million. There are 11 to 15 million Uighurs and 6 million Tibetans.

Altogether, they add up to about 51.8 million people at most. While this would make for a largish country (27th in the world, sandwiched between Burma and South Korea), it's again a drop in the bucket compared to China's 1.4 billion, amounting to something like 3 percent of its overall population.

In these shifting perspectives on population and area, these peripheries, Hong Kong, Tibet, East Turkestan and Taiwan, appear now tiny and now immense (well, except for Hong Kong).

But in terms of the challenges they have posed to Communist Party rule, especially in the last decade, the peoples of the peripheries have an importance disproportionate to their numbers.

Ten years of uprisings

It all started in 2008, the year of the Beijing Olympics, lest we forget — it already seems so long ago. In March, protests broke out across the Tibetan plateau and continued for about two weeks. It was the largest uprising of Tibetans since 1959, and it occurred across a very wide geographical area, encompassing nearly every part of Tibet, including areas traditionally considered both restive and quiet. These were followed in April by pro-Tibet protests along the global route of the Olympic torch relay that repeatedly disrupted the torch's progress and forced organizers to change the route to avoid protesters.

In the following year, 2009, the first post-uprising Tibetan self-immolation occurred. Since then, upwards of 150 Tibetans have self-immolated, the number peaking in 2012 with 86 documented cases. (In 2010, there were 4; 2011, 14; 2013, 28; 2014, 11; 2015, 7; 2016, 3; 2017, 4; and so far in 2018, 1). The self-immolators' most frequent calls have been for "freedom for Tibet" and the return of the Dalai Lama. This type of protest occurring so regularly over such a long period of time—nearly a decade now—is unprecedented anywhere in the world.

In 2009, the year after the protests across the Tibetan plateau, violence broke out in Urumqi, the capital of Xinjiang, with Uighurs attacking and murdering Hans, the majority group in China, and Hans and Chinese security forces responding with reprisals that included murder, torture, executions and mass disappearances that to this day have not been explained. This set off a pattern of Uighur resistance and Chinese crackdown. China's repressive measures are taken in the name of "counter-terrorism". It appears there have been one or two incidents that could be classified as terrorism, in that they were indiscriminate attacks on civilians, and there have been several other violent attacks on security forces which appear to have had a political motivation, but these are all very difficult to verify and investigate due to restricted access to the region and the closed nature of the government. At any rate, the Chinese government's repression is excessive, disproportionate and directed at Uighurs as an ethnic group, and we are currently in the crackdown's harshest phase yet by far. Hundreds of thousands of Uighurs are estimated to have been detained in political re-education camps since April 2017, entirely outside of any judicial process and for indefinite periods of time. A series of other "security" measures[1] have lead to Xinjiang being one of the most repressive places on earth, especially for Uighurs.[2] (Tibet also ranks among the least free places in the world and has for years.)[3]

In both Tibet and Xinjiang, grassroots efforts by Tibetans and Uighurs to promote their language, culture and religion have been met with harsh reprisals, largely because they are regarded by the regime as attempts to strengthen a sense of separate identity outside of government control. The two figures who perhaps best represent both the revival and the repression are Ilham Tohti and Tashi Wangchuk.[4] Both hold what would elsewhere be considered moderate political views. Ilham has said he stands for promotion of better understanding between Uighurs and Hans. Tashi is an advocate for the Tibetan language. Both have explicitly stated they are against independence for, respectively, Uighurs and Tibetans. Nevertheless, Ilham has been sentenced to life in prison for "separatism" and Tashi Wangchuk to five years for "inciting separatism".

In March 2014, the Sunflower Movement broke out in Taiwan, protesting against the Kuomintang government's attempt to force through a trade pact with mainland China that protesters said would undermine Taiwan's sovereignty and give China undue political influence. The movement resulted in the pact being shelved. The Kuomintang was defeated in the next general elections in 2016 by the traditionally pro-independence Democratic Progressive Party. Not surprisingly, Taiwan being the only periphery not under Communist control and the only one that is democratic, it is the only place where protests have succeeded in achieving their primary objectives. Indeed, the Sunflower Movement is an important milestone in the history of Taiwan's on-going democratization.

Later that same year, in September, the Umbrella Movement was triggered in Hong Kong by the police's eight-hour teargas attack on nonviolent demonstrators and lead to 79 days of street occupations involving an estimated 1.2 million people in three central areas of the city . The protesters opposed an attempt by the Party to impose fake universal suffrage on the city. They eventually succeeded in defeating that effort, but Hong Kong is no closer to the genuine universal suffrage promised it by the regime in the city's Basic Law. As in Tibet and Xinjiang, the Party's main reaction to protest in Hong Kong has been crackdown, but since it doesn't have direct control over the territory, it cannot use the same repressive means as in those regions, instead resorting to prosecutions of hundreds of pro-democracy leaders and activists, disqualifications of six democratically elected representatives to the Legislative Council, barring of other candidates from running for Legco on political grounds, greater restrictions on a variety of rights such as the right to hold elected office, the right to vote, and the right to freedom of assembly, and stepped-up attempts to mainlandize Hong Kong, which include imposition of an anthem law, the transfer of Hong Kong territory to mainland jurisdiction at the express rail terminus, and efforts to exert greater political control over education and the judiciary.

This decade of history is one all Hong Kong people, Taiwanese, Tibetans and Uighurs should know. Many know their own people's history but too little of the others'. Knowing this history should make us all more aware of our common values of freedom and human rights and our common objectives of self-determination and democracy. It should make us proud of our shared histories of resistance. And it should inoculate us against any illusions about our common adversary, the Communist Party.

The Communist Party is imperialist to the core

The dynamic of imposition and resistance on the peripheries makes clear the imperialist nature of the Communist regime. It claims sovereignty over large swaths of territory without regard to the political desires of the peoples who live there. They are not ruled by force, not consent. Their consent has never been asked for or obtained, let alone freely given. Indeed, whenever they attempt to assert their political desires, they are met with repression.

(Of course, on that latter note, the same can be said of the Han people themselves. The only thing that makes them different from the peoples of the peripheries is that the Communist regime has not subjected them to colonization, just to dictatorship. Han people who assert their rights and demand democracy and other freedoms are as much oppressed and as much our allies as any other peoples of the peripheries.)

Not long after the Communist Party rose to power, it invaded Tibet. The 13th Dalai Lama had declared independence in 1913, and at the time of the invasion, Tibet acted as an independent state in virtually every respect. After occupying Tibet in 1950, the regime forced upon the Tibetan government the infamous "Seventeen Point Agreement for the Peaceful Liberation of Tibet" in 1951. An uneasy co-existence between the Dalai Lama and the Communist Party obtained through much of the fifties but began unraveling towards the end of the decade as China imposed "reforms" in borderland areas it did not consider part of Tibet proper. Tibetans resisted and thousands fled en masse to Lhasa, where, in 1959, acting on rumors that the Party intended to kidnap the Dalai Lama, Tibetans rose up and were crushed. The Dalai Lama fled to India, where he has remained ever since, and China proceeded to do with Tibet what it had intended to do all along, swallow it whole.

In East Turkestan, the situation was more fluid at the time of the Communist Party's ascent to power. The Kuomintang's Republic of China had crushed the establishment of the first East Turkistan Republic in 1934. This was followed by a Soviet invasion and then a ten-year period of rule by the warlord Sheng Shicai (who among other things, executed Mao Zedong's brother after inviting him there as a guest). While the Qing Dynasty had always exercised influence over the region, it was only in 1884 that it declared Xinjiang a province and essentially incorporated it into the empire. The Communist Party took over Xinjiang in 1949 and created the Xinjiang Uighur Autonomous Region in 1955. The arising of a separate modern Uighur identity began a century ago, but arguably nothing has done more to both threaten and reinforce it than Communist oppression.

Hong Kong was given to China by the United Kingdom in 1997, in what the Party calls its "return to the motherland". Indeed, the "return" was the Party's birthday gift to itself, occurring on July 1, the anniversary of the founding of the Party, and the "return" featured prominently in regime propaganda about the fulfillment of its promise to re-establish sovereignty over all of what it considered China. The handover occurred without any participation of the Hong Kong people who have never formally given their consent in any way to the territory's current status as a Special Administrative Region of the People's Republic of China. The Sino-British Declaration was an agreement solely between the Party and the UK, and the Basic Law was promulgated by the Party and imposed upon Hong Kong.

Taiwan exists as a separate entity and to all intents and purposes functions as an independent country. The Communist Party threatens forcible "reunification". Taiwan's modern history is very different from that of mainland China, with direct rule by Japan preceding the Kuomintang dictatorship. Especially since the beginning of democratization in the late eighties, a separate identity and political culture have flourished. In this respect, Taiwan acts as a kind of model for the other peripheries which have not had the opportunity to develop independently. The Party abhors that model and seeks to undermine it; indeed, nothing is a greater affront to the Party than Taiwan's de facto independence, precisely because it is such a clear expression of the will of Taiwan's people.

Chinese Communist imperialism is a great irony since the Party has always staked its claim to legitimacy on its anti-imperialist ideology and its ability to regain and exert full sovereignty over China. The catch is that its idea of "China" is very different from that of the peoples of the peripheries. It has down through the years stoked nationalism by railing against the humiliations inflicted upon China by Western and Japanese imperialists while at the same time imposing its will upon Tibet, Xinjiang and Hong Kong and attempting to do so upon Taiwan.

While our adversary is clearly the Party, not Chinese people, we shouldn't be under any illusions that if China were suddenly to become a democracy, the peripheries would necessarily be so much better off. Chinese people have been so subjected to nationalistic Party propaganda without any alternative perspectives for so long in a country under strict imposition of censorship, especially in regard to "sensitive" issues such as these, that they have largely imbibed the Party's view. Even after the fall of the Party, it would take a long time for them to develop a more accurate understanding of China's relations with the peripheries, if they ever did.

In this historical period when Uighurs, Tibetans and Hong Kong people do not have the power to determine our own political status, we need to continue to assert our separate identity and our right of self-determination. This is much easier for Hong Kong people to do because of our semi-autonomy. The repression in Xinjiang and Tibet is so harsh and pervasive as to render public assertion of separate identity dangerous if not all but impossible, especially in any sustained and fully articulated manner. In those places, "keeping hope alive" must take much subtler forms.

Peoples of the peripheries, unite!

Not only do we peripheral peoples need to more fully recognize our common goals and values of self-determination, freedom, democracy and human rights, we also need to share information and ideas and learn more about each other; we need to get better at communicating with one another, strategizing, coordinating and organizing together; we need to recognize our power and develop it. Above all, we must show solidarity with one another, a substantive solidarity that can come about only through mutual understanding. This is just beginning to happen.

The best connections are between Taiwanese and Hong Kong people. Even in their case, ties only really began to develop after the Sunflower and Umbrella Movements, and it is only in this post-movement period that their common purpose has been fully recognized. The Party finds the developing relations threatening, as witnessed in its lashing out against Benny Tai for daring to mention the word "independence" while on a visit to Taiwan,[5] or in the pattern of politically active Taiwanese being denied entry into supposedly autonomous Hong Kong.[6]

Chinese, Tibetan and Uighur exile communities, especially in London and Washington, have been cooperating with one another for more than a decade. They turn out for each other's events on, for example, March 10 (Tibetan Uprising Day) and June 4 (Tiananmen Massacre) and often hold solidarity protests.

Among more progressive and youthful exile Tibetans, the importance of better understanding and communication has also been recognized. The Tibetan Youth Congress recently hosted a pan-Asian conference in Delhi, which included participants from Hong Kong and Taiwan. Its communiqué calls for "the government of China to take immediate action to ensure the freedom, human rights and self-determination for the people of Tibet, Southern Mongolia, Hong Kong" (though strikingly, the Uighurs aren't mentioned) and states that "inspirations drawn from the Sunflower Movement, Umbrella Revolution and other resistance movements around the world have motivated a new generation of activism."[7]

In early June, Students for a Free Tibet was the main organizer of the 2nd Tibet, Hong Kong, Taiwan Roundtable Conference on Freedom, Democracy and Self-Determination held in Washington, DC.[8] The first was held in Taiwan last year. (Again, strikingly, there was no Uighur involvement apart from a single participant on a panel discussion open to the public.)

These are newer initiatives, both organized by exile Tibetan youth groups who were inspired by the Sunflower and Umbrella Movements and reached out to Hong Kong and Taiwan activists.

Other events have been going on for some time, like Initiative for China's regularly held Interethnic/Interfaith Leadership Conference and the Tibet Office of Taiwan's annual international conference on Tibet,[9] both of which bring together activists from mainland China, Tibet, Taiwan and Hong Kong.

These are positive initiatives. They need to be stepped up and become less ad hoc, more representative, and more formalized. A coalition with a standing secretariat would be an appropriate goal: The Self-Determination Coalition of the Hong Kong, Taiwanese, Tibetan and Uighur Peoples.

There are challenges. Uighurs have to be more involved. Due to repression, cooperation with people inside Tibet and Xinjiang is virtually impossible these days. In light of that, exile groups have to be careful not to drag the agenda in a direction which does not consider the views and interests of the people inside, itself a challenge given how difficult it is to gauge opinion under totalitarian control. Uighurs, Tibetans, Taiwanese and Hong Kong people must show solidarity with those inside, support them in their actions, publicize abuses committed against them, and lobby on their behalf, not only internationally but also in our own communities. In Hong Kong, for example, knowledge of the situation in Tibet and Xinjiang is not widespread.

The common debate: autonomy within China or independence?

Within the different peripheral communities there are similar debates about what the periphery's relationship with China should be. Some argue for some kind of co-existence within a Chinese sphere of control, often referred to as the "real autonomy" position. Others advocate out-and-out independence.

Taiwan

Unsurprisingly, the debate is most advanced in Taiwan, whose people have taken a sharp turn away from China in recent years. Recent polls suggest that around 75 percent of Taiwanese consider Taiwan and China separate countries. More than 60 percent of Taiwanese identify themselves as Taiwanese, with only 3 percent identifying themselves as Chinese (in 1991, the ratio was 17.6 percent to 25 percent). The percentage who identify as exclusively Taiwanese rises to 78 among people 29 years or younger. Support for an outright declaration of independence depends on how the question is asked. One study asked respondents if they favor independence if it would not cause the People's Republic of China to attack. Seventy-five percent of respondents said yes. Opinion polls that pose the question with no qualifications show support for a declaration of independence hovering around 50 percent. One survey asked respondents if they favor a declaration of independence even if the PRC attacks in response, to which 43 percent of those younger than 40 said yes.[10]

Tibet

Among Tibetans in exile, the Dalai Lama dominates and, some would say, suffocates the debate, even if unintentionally. In the late 1980s, he articulated the so-called Middle Way approach. It is similar to what some Hong Kong people hoped they were getting under "one country, two systems": real autonomy, a democratic Tibet with sovereignty over domestic affairs and non-political foreign affairs, with China retaining responsibility for foreign policy and maintaining a military presence. Moving to this position was a big political risk on the Dalai Lama's part. Since China's supreme leader at the time, Deng Xiaoping, had said that apart from independence, everything was up for discussion, the Dalai Lama believed his idea had some chance, but the Middle Way approach depended on goodwill from the Chinese side that was not forthcoming.

Many Tibetans regarded the Middle Way approach as a tremendous betrayal of what was rightfully theirs, independence, but they so revere the Dalai Lama that for a long time, most were willing to at least go along with the idea, even if their hearts found it hard to embrace. In decades of living and working with Tibetans in exile, I have rarely encountered anyone with genuine enthusiasm for the Middle Way approach. At most, people will say it's the most realistic. And now with negotiations entirely stalled between the Dalai Lama and the Communist Party, it is something of an open secret that the Middle Way approach is dead in the water, though the Tibetan government-in-exile still clings to it as its official position.

The 2008 uprising in Tibet promised to act as a catalyst for change. The Dalai Lama called together a conference of diaspora Tibetans in Dharamsala to re-evaluate the Middle Way approach. My impression was that he really did want new ideas. But the conference was dominated by elders who ensured that it ended up simply reiterating support for the Middle Way approach. Though the Dalai Lama was too diplomatic to say so, I think even he was disappointed.

Meanwhile, the Rangzen (freedom) movement, which explicitly calls for independence, has grown. It includes the influential Tibetan Youth Congress. A lot of Tibet support groups split the difference between the sides and simply call for "freedom" for Tibet, and indeed, that has also been the common demand of self-immolators within Tibet, along with the return of the Dalai Lama. Exactly what would ensure Tibetans' freedom, or in what it would consist, is left unclear.

Hong Kong

In Hong Kong, anyone calling for independence before the Umbrella Movement could hardly gain any traction, but since then, calls for independence have become widespread, indeed so much so that they have elicited a virulent reaction from the Communist Party and Hong Kong government. They claim it is illegal to advocate independence, though there are no laws to that effect and no one has yet been prosecuted for doing so. The regime's hostility has driven the pro-independence movement underground: At the start of the current academic year, pro-independence banners appeared anonymously on university campuses.

Others call for self-determination, by which what is most frequently meant is that Hong Kong people have the right to determine their own political status and relationship with China, in particular after the end of the 50-year "one country, two systems" period in 2047. The regime has been just as implacably opposed to this line, saying it is tantamount to calling for independence and recently barring a candidate from a party advocating self-determination from running for the Legislative Council. What it fundamentally opposes is Hong Kong people having any say at all in their future, and it is determined to do what it must to prevent that.

Its intimidation has made it difficult to gauge support for independence and self-determination, as suggested by discrepancies between polls and volatile fluctuation of survey results. To publicly declare oneself in favor of one of these positions is to run the risk of being regarded as an outlaw. A "veiled" poll conducted in 2016 found 50 percent of university students support independence, with 90 percent holding unfavorable views of the Communist Party and considering themselves Hong Kong people, not Chinese.[11] Another poll conducted in 2017 showed an all-time low in the percentage of 18-to-29-year-olds who identified as Chinese—only 3 percent versus 65 percent who said they were Hong Kongese.[12] (Across all age groups, 37 percent identified as HongKongese and 21 percent as Chinese.) A 2016 poll conducted by *Undergrad*, the Hong Kong University Student Union magazine, showed 61 percent of university students supported independence. A CUHK poll in 2016 showed 40 percent support amongst 15-to-24-year-olds and 17 percent support among all age groups.[13]

A large amount of anecdotal evidence I've collected from interviews with activists, politicians, journalists and academics shows an ever-increasing number favoring independence, often as much as anything else because it has become impossible for them to foresee, especially after the 2014 Umbrella Movement, how Hong Kong people could achieve democracy and protect their rights and liberties in any sustainable way under Communist rule.

Uighurs

While the exile Uyghur World Congress does not take an explicitly pro-independence position, it refers to Xinjiang as East Turkestan. Its symbol has the year 1933 on it, the year the first independent republic of East Turkestan was proclaimed. Both it and the Uyghur American Association explicitly advocate self-determination for Uighurs.

Party policy on the peripheries has been a miserable failure

It's worth stressing that even among regime opponents who accept being part of China in some way, no matter where they come from, there is no enthusiasm for being part of China, especially any China ruled by the Party. Rather, those who hold these positions simply regard other options such as independence as unrealistic; real autonomy under Chinese sovereignty is not the most desirable option but, they believe, the best deal they can get. But as repression in Tibet, Xinjiang and Hong Kong indicates, even that is highly unlikely, to the point of perhaps being just as unrealistic as independence.

In the cases of all of the peripheries, the debates and the political awareness of their peoples run far ahead of anything the Party intended for them. If the measure of success of the Communist Party's policies towards the peripheries is their consent to Party control, then it has failed miserably. Sixty-nine years after taking control of Xinjiang, sixty-eight years after invading Tibet, twenty-one years after the handover of Hong Kong, and having called for the "reunification" of Taiwan with the "motherland" for the entirety of its rule, rather than gradually gaining the assent of the peoples of the peripheries to Chinese rule, the Party has alienated more of them than ever.

The power of the peripheries

And in that lies our power, the power to withhold consent, the power to resist imposition and tighter control. This is no small power. It has succeeded in delegitimizing the regime, not in its heartland, among the Han, where propaganda and censorship prevail, but in the peripheries themselves and in the eyes of much of the rest of the world, at least those who are watching and paying attention to what is going on. In the last ten years, stories of the Tibetan uprising and self-immolations, the Sunflower Movement, the Umbrella Movement, and the resistance and oppression in Xinjiang have made headlines around the world.

A culture of resistance has arisen, the consolidation of which can build a solid foundation for the future. This culture says to the regime, Your claims are in dispute. It's forced the regime to show that the only way it can continue to rule is by force, not by consent, and as such, it is illegitimate, for rule by force is both legally and morally impoverished. The China of the Communist Party is not a sustainable construct because it exists only through massive imposition and therefore can only continue by massive repression. To this the peripheries attest.

The power of the peripheries is the power of the powerless, a term coined by Vaclav Havel in his seminal essay of the same name back in 1978.[14] Havel wrote it only a year after Charter 77[15] was published in Soviet-era Czechoslovakia. Charter 77 was the precursor to China's own Charter 08,[16] for which the Communist Party made Liu Xiaobo pay with his life.

Havel was concerned with the question of how to contend with a regime that appeared omnipotent. His answer was that even the most powerful regime can only maintain its grip through the consent of the ruled, even if this consent consists of little more than passive resignation and going through the motions. If the ruled withdraw their consent, the regime's monopoly on power is unsustainable. It may not fall tomorrow or even in the near future, but its fate is sealed.

Perhaps the most famous term from Havel's essay is "living in truth". The idea behind it is that regimes such as the dictatorships of the Soviet Union and eastern Europe as well as the Chinese Communist Party maintain their grip by enforcing lies, by blanketing the society with lies, by making all of public life and politics little more than one big systemic lie. People can choose to not believe the lies in private, but as long as they continue to go along with them in public, they help to reinforce the lie and therefore also the power of the regime. Once people refuse to go along with the lie, starting in very small ways in their daily lives, they begin to "live in truth" and the regime's power begins to unravel.

Across the peripheries, many examples of this "living in truth" can be seen, both when people overtly stand up and confront the regime and when they take what may appear to be quieter and more understated measures having to do with reinforcing and protecting their culture, their religion, their language, their sense of separate identity.

To resist, to refuse, to reject, and to "live in truth", constructing to the extent possible the culture and society we wish to see through our interactions with others and our political, cultural and economic actions—each of us must decide the degree to which we can do this and the most appropriate means.

The point is that the part of a human being, and of a people, that yearns for freedom, truth and dignity can never be fully repressed, and if we take that part and cultivate it, both individually in our own lives and collectively, we are also cultivating the power to withstand the power of the regime and to eventually strive toward our positive goals of self-determination, freedom, human rights and democracy.

The conventional wisdom is that because of our smallness, we are almost entirely dependent on what happens in the realms of power, first and foremost within the Party, and then, if the regime were ever to change, among the Han majority. According to this wisdom, there is almost no chance that Tibet will ever be free, nor for that matter the Uighurs or Hong Kong people. The regime is simply too strong and will never allow it.

But that wisdom, such as it is, can be flipped: our very peripherality gives us some advantages and opportunities that those closer to the center of power may not have or of which they may not avail themselves. As we defend ourselves from power, imposition, control and colonialism, we are also constructing the cultures of post-totalitarian societies and little by little realizing the state of affairs we wish to see and determining our future for ourselves.

From this perspective, the individual, and, by extension, the peripheries have only as much power as we realize within ourselves. If we believe we are powerless, then we are. Part of the regime's power derives from instilling this sense of powerlessness and, concomitantly, its own omnipotence. If we take what power we have into our own hands, it can eventually become a strength difficult to deny, especially over the long term. From this perspective, the seeming omnipotence of the regime can appear almost beside the point.

On the fourth anniversary of the Umbrella Movement, a way forward for the Hong Kong freedom struggle

September 28, 2018

September 28 marks the fourth anniversary of the start of the Umbrella Movement. Last year, I wrote an assessment of the movement and considered its impact on the politics of HK as well as publishing a book that is a comprehensive account. This year, I find the best way to commemorate what I hope will eventually become HK's national day is to look forward. Here, I suggest how the HK freedom struggle, though increasingly under siege, can proceed and prevail.

1. As it stands

Since the Umbrella Movement, HK freedom fighters have taken many initiatives. New organizations have arisen and new ideas have been articulated. The most notable are localism and calls for self-determination and independence, all of which appeal to substantial numbers, especially among young people and the most politically engaged.

At the same time, the Communist Party and Hong Kong government have carried out an unprecedented attack on the HK freedom struggle while stepping up efforts to control and mainlandize HK. These include:

- the National People's Congress Standing Committee's interpretation of the Basic Law and the subsequent disqualification of six pro-democracy Legco members;
- the barring of nine candidates from running for Legco on political grounds;

- the prosecution of 29 pro-democracy leaders in 45 different cases as well as of hundreds of other activists, leading to 14 prison sentences for pro-democracy leaders and 11 for other activists
- the extraordinarily long sentences given to those convicted of "riot" in relation to the Mong Kok police-protester clashes of 2016;
- the cross-border abductions of HK bookseller Lee Bo and mainland tycoon Xiao Jianhua;
- the express rail terminus co-location arrangement, which for the first time ever hands over HK land to mainland jurisdiction, in contravention of the Basic Law;
- the promulgation of an anthem law on the mainland and its insertion into the Basic Law, requiring HK to criminalize "insult" to the anthem; and
- the Hong Kong government's plan to ban the HK National Party on "national security" grounds for its advocacy of independence

This is an onslaught, and it's worth stressing that virtually all of those developments are unprecedented. The lesson the Party learned from the Umbrella Movement was to relentlessly double down, and its campaign ever more resembles the crackdowns routinely carried out on the mainland.

The question is, how to respond? Or, rather, how to plot the course of the freedom struggle, taking these challenges into account? In the difference of emphasis between those two questions lies an important distinction.

The attacks have put the HK freedom struggle on the defensive, and much of its work has been reactive. As we watch HK becoming more authoritarian, less free and less autonomous, a lot of time and effort has been spent on trying to prevent the worst from happening, and not enough on positively realizing our vision of a free, liberal, democratic society.

The HK freedom struggle must make a transition from defense to offense, from reactive to pro-active, from fighting to stop the worst from happening to bringing about the best.

It must unite, organize and strategize, finding new ways of working together, reaching out to more people and getting them involved, developing its vision and using it to inspire and recruit, and promoting a parallel society that circumvents Party intransigence.

Finally, it must recognize that increased sacrifice and suffering will be the inevitable price to pay for freedom and prepare itself psychologically for the long, hard road ahead.

2. The Resistance and Self-determination Council

The HK freedom struggle will play out over years and decades. There will be no easy victories and probably many defeats along the way. While most of those involved recognize this prospect, we have not sufficiently considered its implications or planned accordingly.

Important to many long-term freedom struggles over the past century has been a strong, central organization: the Indian National Congress, the African National Congress of South Africa, the Palestine Liberation Organization, to name a few of the better known. These organizations were all imperfect and some advocated violence (which I reject), but they provided their struggle with unity, continuity, purpose, a sense of direction, and leadership.

The groups, organizations and institutions that currently exist in HK are insufficient for the long-term struggle. There needs to be more collaboration on strategy, more communication, and more coordination of plans and activities.

Last year, I proposed a Resistance and Self-determination Council to address this need. The body needn't have that particular, admittedly clunky name (Hong Kong National Congress or Hong Kong Liberation Organization might sound snappier!); the point is, whatever the name, its function would be to bring the disparate groups of the freedom struggle together to maximize their power and effectiveness.

Remember that our adversary has infinitely greater resources at its disposal, including nearly limitless amounts of money, the largest political organization in the world, a massive security apparatus and a huge military, not to mention propaganda, censorship, and a ruthlessly Leninist will to power.

In the face of that, it is essential to unify and act in a coordinated manner. That certainly doesn't mean we must always agree or have the exact same objectives. It means we must recognize each other as allies who share the same general vision and goals as well as a common adversary.

The council would be made up of all groups in the freedom struggle that wish to participate, from moderate pan-democratic political parties to self-determinationist and pro-independence parties, to civil society organizations working for democracy and human rights.

The reason I call the body the Resistance and Self-determination Council is that the key words, "resistance" and "self-determination", correspond to the two main tasks of the freedom struggle, the defensive and constructive work it needs to do.

As for the first term, this is clearly *an era of resistance*, to which the list of attacks and infringements at the start of this article attests. A clear and widespread awareness of the need for resistance has been present ever since mid-2014 with the issuance of the Party's White Paper on Hong Kong, the OCLP referendum, the 8/31 NPCSC ruling, the student strike and occupation of Civic Square and, of course, the Umbrella Movement. This culture of resistance is a strength of the struggle, and it should be cultivated. Its purpose is to defend HK and strengthen and promote HK identity. Much power comes from resistance, and it is often easier to mobilize people to say NO than to keep them involved in the arduous on-going pursuit of the positive goal.

As I wrote a year ago, much of the disillusionment in the aftermath of the Umbrella Movement was due to a desire for quick fixes or magical solutions. We must rid ourselves of that illusion and see long-term resistance as the effective strategy that it is. In resisting, we also construct our identity, and in fortifying that, we strengthen the struggle as well. Rather than undertaken with grim determination, resistance can and should be joyful.

The resistance work of the council would consist of coordinating approaches to combating mainlandization and Party attempts to increase control, restrict rights and encroach upon autonomy. At present, there are many resistance efforts, but they can appear scattershot and unsupported by a wider strategy and network.

Under the resistance brief would also come the work of pro-democracy representatives in the Legislative Council. There's almost nothing positive that can be achieved within HK's rigged formal political system, but it is still very important to preserve veto power so as to prevent the worst from happening (fake suffrage, Article 23 "national security" legislation, etc). Legco representatives also do excellent work resisting a host of other anti-democratic measures. The Resistance and Self-determination Council would help to link their efforts to related efforts in civil society and frame them within an overall strategy.

While fortifying resistance, we should direct more of our energy toward *attaining the positive goal*, which I here designate as self-determination, though exactly what that may be would be for the members of the council to decide.

There are two reasons why I think self-determination should be the common goal.

The first has to do with recent history. Up until the Party's refusal to allow implementation of genuine universal suffrage in 2014–2015, it can be said there was an implicit contract between the Party and HK people: HK people would (grudgingly) recognize PRC sovereignty over HK in exchange for the Party (grudgingly) granting HK autonomy and democracy. But with that refusal, the Party definitively broke the contract, and all of its actions since then (again, see list above) simply serve to support that assertion. What can HK people do in response but invoke the right of self-determination? I've discussed this at length elsewhere and won't go into detail here but only emphasize that this is a basic human right of all peoples that is also guaranteed in the Basic Law (Article 39 →ICCPR, ICESCR Article 1). The council would collaboratively define what exactly self-determination means in the HK context and map out how to get there. At a bare minimum, it must involve HK people deciding the future of HK, including its political status, especially after the end of the 50-year "one country, two systems" period in 2047. (We also need corresponding slogans, hashtags and memes that succinctly state the cause and express people's desire: #2047ItsOurChoice #2047NowWeDecide, etc.)

Secondly, defining the goal as self-determination would provide a common ground to achieve unity amongst the many disparate groups of the freedom struggle, from moderate pan-democrats to localists, self-determinationists and independence advocates. Even moderate pan-democratic groups such as ReformHK have advocated self-determination,[1] with others such as ADPL and Civic Party espousing related concepts.[2] On the other end of the spectrum, independence is perhaps the most emphatic expression of self-determination, and independence advocates would have to concede to the group the necessity of self-determination being at least an intermediate stop along the way to their ultimate goal. Of course, there is a substantial gap between what the moderates call "internal self-determination", on the one hand, and full independence on the other, but the point of the council would be to mediate and debate the gap, to compromise where possible and agree to disagree where not.

And yes, moderate pan-democrats would have to sit down with independence advocates, whatever mutual suspicion there may be, including fear on the part of the pan-dems of being smeared with the pro-independence label, as has already happened to staunch moderates like Benny Tai.[3] And yes, localists and independence advocates would have to set aside some rigid, self-righteous tendencies. If the sides do not, then the future of the struggle really is a split. Of course, splintered freedom struggles can and do exist, and can and do make progress, but it is a huge liability—witness Syria's fragmented opposition. The only absolute condition of membership in the council should be an unequivocal commitment to nonviolence: Perhaps I am wrong, but I do think localist groups which in the past may have used terms like "by any means necessary" have begun to see the folly of armed uprising.

Not only does there need to be much more debate about what the HK freedom struggle's ultimate goal should be but also about the *strategy* for getting there.

To give an idea of what I mean, take this example: Both Joshua Wong and Eddie Chu advocate self-determination. Starting back in 2015, Joshua envisioned using referenda as a means to reach the goal of self-determination, with the intention of eventually holding a referendum on the post-2047 political status of HK around 2030.[4] It was an attractive idea, but the sticking point was, how in the world did he expect the Party would ever recognize such a referendum? On the other hand, after winning a seat in Legco in 2016 with the most votes ever for any Legco candidate, Eddie Chu said the self-determination movement should work through Legco.[5] He thought that within an election or two, most of the pro-democracy camp would be self-determinationist. Not long after that, the Hong Kong government initiated disqualification proceedings against six Legco members, four of whom were self-determinationist or pro-independence, and then Agnes Chow was barred from running to replace her disqualified Demosistō party fellow Nathan Law on the grounds that her party advocates self-determination. So much for the Legco path to self-determination.

In fact, the conclusion that must be reached is that there's simply no means of progress for the HK freedom struggle within the rigged political system, from which an increasing number of people and political beliefs have been barred. But that still leaves the question of, Well, then, how?

That's the sort of the strategizing the freedom struggle needs and the council would do, collectively, through debate and discussion. And in doing so, the council would become the path it was trying to find. That is to say, a probable answer to the question of how to work toward the goal of self-determination is to promote a *parallel society*, a movement that doesn't worry about getting the Party's say-so but instead concentrates on building up a strong, wide-ranging civil society outside of Party control, "liberated zones" so to speak: Instead of demanding autonomy, we create it. We psychologically secede from Communist domination with joy and pride. This leaves the question of how to attain the ultimate objective open while at the same time recognizing that it must involve strengthening the parts of HK society which already act as forces of resistance and markers of separate identity. Rather than banging our heads against the wall of the Party, for the time being we sidestep it. Of course, ultimately, a showdown is inevitable, but in the meantime, there's so much more we could do.

In his book, *The Egyptians: A Radical History of an Unfinished Revolution*, Jack Shenker characterizes Egypt today, after the re-imposition of dictatorship, as divided in two parts, which he calls Mubarak Country and Revolution Country. Mubarak Country has political power and controls the security forces and the economy. But Revolution Country is still very much alive and can be found in the many cracks and crevices of society, among activists, workers, the poor, intellectuals, writers, and musicians who elude regime attempts to extinguish them. The two "countries" have diametrically opposed visions of what Egypt should be. This sounds like HK. Here, there are also two separate "countries"—call them Communist Country and Umbrella Country. As I have noted elsewhere, "What is happening in HK now is people are thinking about the sort of society they want, the sort of society that corresponds to how they want HK to be. That cultural efflorescence is almost diametrically opposed to Party rule, which is why the Party does what it can to wipe it out." These are the roots of the parallel society that must be cultivated.

Whereas the Party can refuse to recognize referenda and block entrance to the formal political system, it can't prevent the development of a parallel society except by taking extreme measures such as a more severe crackdown on civil liberties than what we have seen up to now. Indeed, it might eventually do that, but it's up to us to make full use of the free space that still exists.

Key to the development of that parallel society is *organizing and recruiting*, reaching out to people and inviting them to join the struggle. In addition to articulation of the ultimate goal and strategizing to reach it, these should be top priorities of the council. The goal is to have a Resistance and Self-determination Committee in every HK public housing estate and neighborhood. The committees would be made up of residents of their area and linked to the council. They would carry out whatever activities they see as important and relevant in their part of town. When needed and called upon by the council, the committees can help to mobilize people in their areas, for example, for a demonstration or other activity.

Organizing of this sort is painstaking work that requires commitment and constant effort. For most groups in the freedom struggle, it would mean operating differently from how they are used to. It's not about campaigning for the next election or trying to get people to come out to the next demonstration; it's about creating a strong, long-lasting foundation. It's also about shifting the culture and the society in the direction of resistance and self-determination, about growing the movement and getting people involved.

At the moment, the freedom struggle is, to put it simply, understaffed. Meanwhile, there are many frustrated, angry and aware young people out there whose energy can be channeled toward constructive ends, as well as many others awaiting the call. There is also deep pessimism. The pessimism comes from seeing the way things are but not seeing a way out. People need to be invited into the process so that they can see that, collectively, we the people are that way out. (#WeAreTheWayOut) This helps to overcome debilitating pessimism, which can otherwise easily lapse into the fatalism, resignation and apathy that the Party is all too happy to see in HK people.

As I noted a year ago, the Umbrella Movement "did more than any other event to promote a politically conscious and active citizenship, and this especially among a huge majority of young people, upwards of 80 to 90 percent of whom are in favor of democracy and genuine autonomy. This resistance is a factor that the Party will have to contend with for years and perhaps even generations to come; indeed, it could outlast the Party itself. It is not going too far to say that the fate of HK rests on what this generation of young people decides to do."

The freedom struggle has a strong natural base. Opinion polls have for years shown upwards of two-thirds of HK people want universal suffrage and support the idea of HK becoming a democracy. Other opinion polls have shown something like one in six people identify themselves as localists. And over the last two years, still others show that anywhere from 40 to 61 percent of HK young people (classified as 18-to-29-year-olds in some polls, 15-to-24-year-olds in others) support independence. Meanwhile, fewer HK people than ever identify themselves as Chinese, 21 percent overall and only 3 percent of young people.[6] Within those numbers lies potential for the freedom struggle, but only if we tap into it.

3. The inevitability of suffering and sacrifice

Given that the HK freedom struggle will be long and hard, one of the most pressing questions HK people face is, Are we up for it?

Along the way, it will almost certainly entail much greater suffering and sacrifice than we have faced up to now.

A poorer, less developed society may have the advantage of having less to lose. The distractions and creature comforts of a consumer society like HK can act as the "opium of the masses": They're not a real way out, but they dull the pain and allow us to look away from the fact that our society's being undermined and usurped.

As a friend put it not long ago, "The commies sized us up and are convinced they've got our number. At first, they were a little bit worried, but then they saw we're just a bunch of soft kids." Is that the case? Time will tell.

Many might decide the struggle's not worth it, too painful and risky, the possibility of success too remote. An increasing number might "vote with their feet". Articles about people emigrating appear on a regular basis.[7] At just about every social occasion these days, the question arises: "Are you getting out?"

Just what might the price of struggle be?

When Joshua Wong, Nathan Law, Alex Chow, Raphael Wong and twelve others were sentenced by the High Court to longer prison sentences than ever before for nonviolent protest-related crimes, people began to get a sense of what the price might be. When Edward Leung and 25 others were sentenced to extraordinarily long prison sentences for violent crimes related to the police-protester clashes of 2016, people began to get a sense of what the price might be. Now that the HK government is in the process of banning HK National Party, the very first time any political group will be outlawed in HK, people are beginning to get a sense of what the price might be. With the evidence recently presented by Demosistō and Studentlocalism, people are beginning to see that it will involve ever more pervasive surveillance, monitoring and intimidation.[8]

More people will have to be willing to risk the prospect of prison. In the face of increasing persecution and the Party's refusal to entertain our demands, we will have to escalate: labor strikes, public housing rent strikes, boycotts, civil disobedience, even hunger strikes. None of these forms of escalation come without cost. It will become more difficult to lead ordinary lives. The burden will continue to fall disproportionately on young people, who must lead the way. Our actions may provoke a more severe crackdown. The struggle could even, at some point, entail loss of life and involve facing armed force by the Hong Kong police and Party army. It's important to remember our adversary is one of the most violent, criminal regimes in history, up there with the Nazis and Soviet Communism in terms of number of victims, and it has massacred its own people in the streets as recently as 1989.

We will have to work together and take initiatives with great deliberation and coordination so as to appropriately balance the struggle for the goal with the risks to those involved.

And throughout we must remain resolutely nonviolent.

If we decide we are not willing to pay the price—and it may indeed be a very high price to pay; we should have no illusions—, we will suffer the consequence of watching our city die before our eyes, knowing that we decided not to do what needed to be done to prevent it.

4. Lessons from Ireland

> *It is not those who inflict the most but those that can suffer the most who will conquer.*
>
> —Terence MacSwiney, Irish nationalist who died in 1920 after a 74-day hunger strike in a British prison while serving a sentence for sedition

Ireland was occupied and dominated for centuries by a much more powerful and populous neighbor. Indeed, for much of that time, Britain was among the most powerful countries in the world. Somehow, throughout it all, Ireland managed to preserve a separate identity and a desire for freedom, even as the colonizer came to so dominate the Emerald Isle that its native language was virtually extinguished, replaced by English.

In the early twentieth century, after decades of intense struggle and at a time when Britain was relatively weak, Irish republicans managed to force a stalemate: Irish home rule (ie, genuine autonomy within the UK) except for five Protestant-majority counties in the north of the island. Three decades later,

Irish home rule became the fully independent Republic of Ireland in 1949, but the five-county exception became Northern Ireland, a part of the UK. So the struggle went on, resulting eventually in the Good Friday peace agreement of 1998, which preserved Northern Ireland but ensured the rights of its Catholic minority.

Thus, by the end of the twentieth century, after eight centuries of various forms of English domination, Ireland was able for the most part to throw off its neighbor's colonialism and become a successful modern country.

But look at the suffering this entailed: war, famines, mass poverty, mass emigration, and, in the latter stages, both state and paramilitary terrorism, thousands killed, thousands imprisoned, young people dying on hunger strike.

Down through the centuries, one of the key markers of separate identity that helped to empower the resistance to colonial domination was the majority's religion, Catholicism. But Catholicism was also its own form of oppression, and in recent decades, after revelations of numerous abuses perpetrated by the Church, Ireland has begun to throw off that oppression too, legalizing divorce, same-sex marriage and, soon, abortion amidst vastly declining Church attendance. Ireland is one of the great human rights success stories of recent years.

Hong Kong and Ireland have a lot in common. Both were claimed by huge and powerful neighbors that appeared to hold them in an iron grip. Few outsiders showed solidarity with their peoples, for fear of offending their powerful oppressor. Many said there was no chance of them attaining substantial autonomy because the oppressor was just too powerful and too intent on maintaining its grip. The colonizer promoted immigration, changing the demographic makeup of the society, implanting a population loyal to the colonizer, so that it could not be so clearly discerned that most people wanted home rule/autonomy/independence. And now it looks as if HK might follow in Ireland's footsteps with mass emigration as well.

There are also important differences. Ireland was economically backward compared to Britain whereas HK is more developed than the PRC. The majority of HK's population is considered to have the same ethnic identity as the majority of the population on the mainland (Han Chinese) whereas the Irish were considered to have a separate ethnic identity from the English (though then again, in most respects, they were no more visibly distinguishable from one another than, say, a Hong Kong person of Chinese ancestry from a mainland Chinese). The English, while oppressors, also had a liberal self-image and

Ireland was less integral to their national identity whereas the Communist Party is adamantly anti-liberal, anti-democratic, Leninist, and stakes its claim to legitimacy partly on its ability to recover and maintain sovereignty over all parts of what it considers China. Hong Kong's been ruled by China for only 21 years (though previously colonized since 1842 by the British) whereas Ireland was under Britain for centuries. Over the last century, when the Irish made the most headway in their freedom struggle, British power was in decline, whereas China is becoming more powerful. But perhaps the most important difference is the amount of suffering and sacrifice the Irish endured.

From the example of Ireland and a comparison with Hong Kong, some lessons can be derived.

Lesson #1: All long-term freedom struggles undergo "low tides" and periods in which it may even appear that the oppressed have been defeated. They need to be tenacious, to sink their roots deep so as to persevere and survive through the dark years. Resistance helps to fortify a separate identity, which in turn is one of the core strengths of resistance.

Lesson #2: In the middle of the struggle, it can often be hard to say who is winning and who is losing, and what may appear a defeat at one point could end up, looking back, to be the beginning of a bigger victory. In 1981, republican prisoners in Northern Ireland went on hunger strike. Margaret Thatcher was the British prime minister at the time, and she decided to take a hardline: Let the terrorists die. And die they did, ten in all. Then the hunger strike was called off without a single demand having been met. At the time, even Irish nationalists considered it a great victory for the Iron Lady and feared that it could even lead to the demise of the cause. But the UK's victory proved Pyrrhic. The hunger strikers gained mass sympathy throughout Ireland. From prison, some ran for parliament in both the UK and the Republic of Ireland, and two won, including, most famously, Bobby Sands, who died on hunger strike while an MP. It became clear that the mass popular support could be turned into victory at the ballot box, and the republican party Sinn Fein moved into electoral politics. It is now the largest party in Northern Ireland. The British could no longer deny the nationalist cause, leading to the Good Friday Agreement of 1998, bringing peace to Ireland. True, nationalists did not achieve their ultimate aim of reuniting all of Ireland, but Catholics are no longer a systematically oppressed minority in the north, and there is a sense of popular sovereignty and a modicum of justice. The "failed" prison hunger strikes were the turning point. (The

1916 Easter Rising is another example of this dynamic of a loss becoming the start of a victory.)

Lesson #3: In cases like Ireland and Hong Kong, occupied and dominated by a must larger neighbor, the oppressed must be willing to endure, sacrifice and suffer, most likely over a long period of time, in order to prevail. In the HK freedom struggle, we must be savvy—able to apprise our situation honestly—but if we are to have a true commitment to freedom, we must never give up or become so demoralized as some have after the Umbrella Movement and during the subsequent years of persecution and mainlandization.

I used to work for Tibetan Children's Villages in India. TCV educates Tibetan exile children, many of whom fled their occupied country and, without their parents, crossed the tallest mountains in the world to get a genuinely Tibetan education under the protection of the Dalai Lama. In the TCV cafeteria, his famous message hung on the wall: "Never give up. No matter what is going on, never give up. Never give up. No matter what is going on around you, never give up."

In another context, those words might be little more than cliché, but addressed to Tibetan children who may never see their parents again and whose country is occupied, who have crossed the highest mountains in the world to simply get an education in their own language, their own religion, their own culture, and whose future as individuals and as a people is exceedingly uncertain, they're not. That precept is baked into the way that they think, the way that they feel, the way that they experience the world, the way that they see themselves, the way that they live.

If HK people make that precept a part of who we are, then we, like the Irish, like the Tibetans, may still have a chance. As long as there is resistance, there is hope.

Censorship in Hong Kong since the Umbrella Movement

This article first appeared on November 17, 2018 and was most recently updated on January 18, 2019.

Sixty-three incidents listed and categorized by type of expression, censor and victim indicate political censorship has been getting worse in HK for some time.

After a recent series of incidents—the cancellation of Chinese artist Badiucao's exhibition on 1 November after having received threats,[1] the refusal of entry to Hong Kong of *Financial Times* journalist Victor Mallet on 8 November,[2] and the cancellation of Ma Jian's 10 November Hong Kong International Literary Festival events by two different venues (one of which eventually reconsidered)[3]—, I began to think I should track incidents of censorship in Hong Kong. What follows is a list of incidents that have occurred over the past four years. I suspect it is far from exhaustive, but it is extensive enough to indicate a pattern of worsening censorship.

The list goes back to the 2014 Umbrella Movement. Of course, there was censorship before the Umbrella Movement. Especially in the months preceding the movement, as pressure built, censorship increased dramatically. For example, the postal service refused to deliver Scholarism's flyers,[4] and the Leisure and Cultural Services Department of the HK government denied use of Tamar Park to students on the climactic day of their class boycott,[5] ironically leading to them getting the idea of occupying Civic Square, thus triggering the Umbrella Movement, a classic case of censorship backfiring.

But since then, censorship in HK has become more widespread and the number of incidents has increased. Especially in regard to certain issues, the Communist Party and HK government have made a concerted effort to impose a censorship regime upon the city, frequently invoking a vaguely defined "red line" and repeating "freedom of expression is not absolute" like a mantra.

This list includes only clear, discrete instances of political censorship. That means cases in which people have been prevented from saying something, or prevented from holding an event or a public gathering or otherwise associating, or punished for clearly political reasons for doing any of the above, or because of their political opinions or expressions, or when governmental authorities have used their power to condemn political expression for the clear purposes of deterrence and intimidation.

As such, the list is by definition incomplete because censorship works, to a large extent, through creating an environment hostile to free expression and encouraging people to censor themselves: we will never know the expression that might have occurred if people felt fully free to express themselves.

Routine censorship is arguably the most pervasive and problematic. The Communist Party's Liaison Office owns at least an 80 percent market share of book distribution and retail in HK, including 51 bookstores.[6] These bookstores do not carry books politically disagreeable to the Party. A substantial portion of the media is owned by Party allies.[7] In annual reports by the Hong Kong Journalists Association, journalists have year after year reported widespread self-censorship in the media.[8] Art from the Umbrella Movement has not found a home in any official institutions in Hong Kong and instead has had to seek sanctuary abroad.[9] Police routinely declare demonstrations "unlawful", and judges have issued stricter sentencing guidelines for certain protest-related crimes, sending the signal that it is dangerous to demonstrate and you could be arrested and punished, deterring people from coming out.

The incidents of censorship itemized here are like canaries in the coal mine, bellwethers, the tip of the iceberg. One suspects and feels there is much more beneath the surface. Both systemic censorship (Party control of the book industry, for example) and discrete incidents of censorship (for example, the bookseller detentions) "ripple outward", having widespread effects that largely go unreported. Most forms of censorship never reach the surface because they are standard practice. A striking number of cases itemized below only came to light because institutions reversed initial decisions to allow an event to occur or adopted a new censorious policy.

The detention of five HK booksellers on the mainland in late 2015 is widely perceived to have sent a chill through the HK book industry. Highly reputable publishers such as Bao Pu (best known for having published Zhao Ziyang's memoir[10] and for having decided not to publish Li Peng's after Party intervention[11]) have moved their publishing operations elsewhere. The fact that so much of the book industry is controlled by the Party meant that I didn't even try to find a city-wide book distributor for my *Umbrella: A Political Tale from Hong Kong* or to get it into bookstores.

Also not included in the list are instances of restrictions on largely non-political expression. Buskers and street performers have recently been banned at Mong Kok[12] and Times Square,[13] part of wide-ranging attempts by the government and property developers to more tightly restrict the use of already inadequate public space in a crowded city. These efforts have a negative impact on the opportunity to fully exert freedom of expression and are part of the increasingly censorious environment in HK.

The inclusion of some of the items on the list may be controversial. To take one example, six newly elected pro-democracy Legislative Council members were disqualified in October 2016 for their expressions during the Legco oath-taking ceremony. They were removed from office over what they said and how they said it though they had broken no law and were not charged with a crime—a clear case of censorship.

That incident shows too how closely the right of freedom of expression is often related to other rights, such as freedom of belief and opinion, the rights to vote, to run for election, and to be elected and hold public office, and the right to participate in government. In other cases, free speech is closely linked to the rights to freedom of assembly and of association.

Likewise, the barring of candidates from running for public office on political grounds—which has become standard practice by the Electoral Affairs Commission since the September 2016 Legislative Council elections, with altogether eleven candidates barred— both punishes their previous expression of political beliefs and infringes upon their right of freedom of expression.

It's worth emphasizing that in all these cases of censure resulting in legal action being taken to punish or prevent expression, the victims' expression was not explicitly prohibited by law and the victim had broken no law and was charged with no crime. Given that Basic Law Article 39 states, "The rights and freedoms enjoyed by Hong Kong residents shall not be restricted unless as prescribed by law," governmental authorities have had to adopt "creative" means to prevent and punish political expression which is not explicitly prohibited but which they deem unacceptable.

One of the striking aspects of post-Umbrella censorship is the sheer number of means the HK government has employed to censor— disqualifications from Legco, barrings from elections, a ban on a political party, gross intimidation of the press, compelling semi-independent governmental departments and agencies and public universities to censor, use of arcane and rarely used laws, and aggressively pursuing cases in the courts with the help, in one case, of intervention by the Communist Party in the form of an "interpretation" of the Basic Law. In pursuit of its censorship aims, it has damaged rule of law, the independence of the judiciary, the civil service and academic freedom as well as compromising the only free elections HK had.

As the list below shows, it is not only governmental authorities that censor. While the HK government and the Communist Party and its agents are the censors in 42 of the 63 cases, the list of censors includes arts and cultural institutions, universities, businesses, the media, venues and events, advertisers and even, in one case, the United Nations.

Many of us censor ourselves in our daily lives, and in doing so, condition ourselves and others to do so. In regard to the "Beneath Lion Rock" episode itemized below, it was hotels and actors that decided not to cooperate with the television program, effectively censoring themselves and making it more difficult for the show to be completed. Often in the past four years, well-meaning people have warned me, "Be careful what you say." Very important ways to resist censorship are to refuse to censor ourselves and others, to check ourselves whenever we do, to support others who freely express themselves, especially if they get in trouble for doing so, and to call out those who do censor, especially if they do so from positions of power and authority.

An analysis of the cases

There are 41 entries below related to 63 different incidents of censorship. For example, the disqualification of six pro-democracy Legco members is one entry involving six cases. Other entries that contain more than one case are the detained booksellers, the censoring of election materials, the barring of election candidates (in three different entries), the censoring of the word "national" in reference to Taiwan universities in government flyers, and the censoring of independence advocacy on university campuses.

Types of expression censored

independence (22 cases), criticism of the Communist Party (16), pro-democracy (10), self-determination (7), Taiwan-related (4), anti-corruption (3), criticism of Chief Executive (2), books about China (1), foreign reporting on corruption (1)

Some of the cases are difficult to categorize. For example, why exactly was the "Countdown Machine" censored? Presumably because it coincided with the visit of Party leader Zhang Dejiang. Therefore, I classify it under "criticism of the Communist Party". Joshua Wong was barred from appearing at Asia Society before official criticism of his party Demosistō's self-determination stance really ramped up; therefore, this type of censored expression is classified as "pro-democracy". Benny Tai mentioning independence in Taiwan is one of three cases classified in two categories, "independence" and "Taiwan-related", though it could also be classified under "pro-democracy", since essentially what the government and its allies were doing was signalling to moderate pro-democracy leaders like Tai that they too are fair game. The other double-categorized cases are the Chief Executive threatening *Apple Daily* with legal action over an article about an allegedly corrupt buisness deal he was involved in, under both "criticism of Chief Executive" and "anti-corruption" and actually suing Kenneth Leung over a statement the latter made about the same deal.

Censors

HK government—29 cases, including specific agencies and departments, Electoral Affairs Commission (13), High Court (6), Leisure and Cultural Services Department (3), Chief Executive (3), Food and Environmental Hygiene Department (2), police (2), Companies Registry (1), Hong Kong Arts Development Council (1)

Communist Party and its agents—13 cases

arts and cultural institutions—5 cases, including Asia Society (2), Hong Kong Arts Development Council, M+, and Tai Kwun

universities—4 cases, including specific instances at Baptist University, Polytechnic University and Chinese University

businesses—3 cases (cinemas, hotels, a delivery service)

media—6 cases, ViuTV, TVB, RTHK, Ming Pao

venues and events—2 cases, The Annex at Nan Fung Place, Yabuli Youth Forum 2018

advertisers—1 case, Lancôme

United Nations—1 case

Direct victims

I say "direct victims" because, ultimately, all HK people are the victims.

politicians—20 cases, including Lau Siu-lai (2), Nathan Law (2), James Chan (2), Edward Yiu, Leung Kwok-hung, Baggio Leung, Yau Wai-ching, Agnes Chow, Joshua Wong, Eddie Chu (2), Edward Leung, Ventus Lau, Alice Lai, Yeung Ke-cheong, Nakade Hitsujiko, and Kenneth Leung

political parties—15 cases, including Demosistō (6), HK National Party (5), Youngspiration (3), League of Social Democrats (2)

artists and artworks—9 cases, including Denise Ho (2), Ma Jian, Badiucao, "Beneath Lion Rock", "Raise the Umbrellas", "Countdown Machine", "Ten Years", "Right and Wrong"

journalists—6 cases, including RTHK (2), Apple Daily, Sing Pao, Victor Mallet

businesses—5 cases, the Causeway Bay Books booksellers

academics and students—5 cases, including *Undergrad* magazine, Benny Tai, Billy Fung, Wang Dan

events—3 cases, Hong Kong International Literary Festival, Free Expression Week, Yabuli Youth Forum 2018

organizations—2 cases, Foreign Correspondents Club, Civil Human Rights Front

Patterns

The HK government is by far the biggest censor, doing much of the Communist Party's bidding, but the Party itself has not hesitated to involve itself directly, despite the fact that according to the "one country, two systems" principle of a "high degree of autonomy" for HK, it is not supposed to interfere. It has employed a variety of means, from the legal (unilaterally inserting an "intepretation" into the Basic Law so as to determine the outcome of a court case), to more frequent public statements by Party officials on a variety of HK cases (prohibiting those who call for an end to one-party dictatorship from running for Legco, Benny Tai, independence and self-determination advocacy, etc), to actually abducting people off the streets (HK bookseller Lee Bo).

Perhaps just as troubling as the fact that government authorities are the biggest censors is the extent to which a variety of other organizations and individuals have participated in the censorship, presumably not least due to (usually indirect) pressure from government authorities. It should be emphasized, though, that in few of the cases of non-governmental censorship has the government actively told another entity to censor. In this respect, the case of Andy Chan and the Foreign Correspondents Club is exceptional. Rather, these entities have surmised the correct political position and acted of their own accord, presumably so as to stay on the good side of the authorities.

The conclusion is that the greatest threat to freedom of expression in Hong Kong is the combination of governmental authorities and non-governmental actors practicing censorship, in turn encouraging society-wide self-censorship.

Notably, Ma Jian's case is the only one of the 63 cases in which the censor, Tai Kwun, reversed its decision in the face of public criticism.

List of incidents of political censorship

in chronological order, starting with the most recent

The following list errs on the side of caution: There had to be pretty strong and clear evidence in order for an incident to be included. All of the below incidents were reported in the media; most were reported widely. I came across many borderline cases. I found it especially difficult to evaluate reports of suspected censorship in the media, in particular having to do with removal of articles, discontinuation of regular columns and changing of editorial staff. These might have been politically motivated and censorious, or have had a censorious effect, but in many cases, that's unclear.

To give an example of some of the omissions, reported cases of censorship I have not included here are *HK01*'s publication, deletion and republication of an article on new information about the Tiananmen massacre;[14] *HK Economic Journal*'s discontinuation of Joseph Lian's column;[15] the barring of online-only media from government press conferences (finally lifted in September 2017[16]); threatening anonymous letters sent to *Hong Kong Free Press*;[17] and *SCMP*'s deletion of an opinion column linking Xi Jinping with a Singaporean investor.[18]

Delivery service SF Express refuses to send books about China and political topics

14 January 2019, ***Censorship:*** In two separate cases, delivery service SF Express refuses to send books. In one case, the sender attempts to send books from Taiwan to Hong Kong. Three books are rejected on grounds that they constituted"sensitive content".[19] The SF Express employee who rejects them explains "no books are allowed right now, especially ones about China." In the other case, SF Express refuses to send two books from Hong Kong to South Korea, telling the sender this is because the books constitute "sensitive content".[20] ***Censor:*** SF Express, a mainland-owned company with a large presence in Hong Kong. ***Outcome:*** In Taiwan, SF Express refuses to acknowledge the incident. In Hong Kong, SF Express makes no comment on the specific case. The books are not even ones generally recognized as the sort Chinese authorities would deem "sensitive" or "prohibited". It is unclear whether the refusal to send books is related to company policy of any kind, but the fact that two separate incidents are reported, along with the company's reticence, raises the question.

China spies on *Wall Street Journal* reporters in Hong Kong

7 January 2019, ***Censorship***: News emerges that in 2016 China "was surveilling the [*Wall Street Journal*] in Hong Kong at Malaysia's request, including 'full scale residence/office/device tapping, computer/phone/web data retrieval, and full operational surveillance'".[21] ***Censor:*** Chinese authorities ***Outcome:*** The news is based on notes taken by the Malaysian government and shown to *WSJ*, from a meeting with Sun Lijun, the then head of China's domestic-security force. A variety of groups have called on the Hong Kong government to investigate the report,[22] but the government has given no sign that it is or will. In the wake of the abductions from Hong Kong of Lee Bo and Xiao Jianhua by mainland agents, the Hong Kong government and police have a poor track record of getting to the bottom of reports of mainland security agents and spies operating in Hong Kong, and many people have little to no confidence that they can or will do so. While it is debatable whether spying per se constitutes censorship, in this case it is certainly a restriction on freedom of the press, especially with the news coming in the wake of the Hong Kong government's refusal to renew the visa of Victor Mallet. It has a chilling effect on the environment for foreign reporters in Hong Kong.

Independence advocacy banned from Civic Square

1 January 2019, ***Censorship:*** People with signs advocating Hong Kong independence are not allowed to enter Civic Square at government headquarters during the annual January 1 pro-democracy march.[23] This is the second time the government has attempted to bar independence advocates from the square. The first was in October 2018.[24] ***Censor***: The Hong Kong government advises protest organizers, who themselves were not independence advocates, beforehand that such expression would not be allowed[25] and reiterates its prohibition afterwards on grounds that advocating independence is against the Basic Law,[26] even though there is no statutory law prohibiting independence advocacy and people are free to propose amendments to the Basic Law at any time. ***Outcome***: A few independence advocates enter Civic Square in spite of the prohibition, managing to elude security guards who attempt to prevent them. The government warns afterwards that the protest organizer, Civil Human Rights Front, might be prevented from using Civic Square in future, pressuring CHRF to censor fellow citizens on the government's behalf.[27] The incident is a continuation of the government's draconian restrictions on the use of Civic Square since it was closed in summer 2014 and since then only partially reopened under highly restricted terms of use that the High Court has ruled unconstitutional because disproportionate and contrary to human rights law.[28] The incident is a continuation also of the government's insistence that independence advocacy is illegal and against the Basic Law, though it has never tested these assertions in a court of law.

Eddie Chu barred from running for village representative

2 December 2018, ***Censorship:*** Eddie Chu Hoi-dick is barred from running in an election for village representative in Yuen Long on grounds that he advocates self-determination and believes Hong Kong people have a right to choose independence (although he doesn't advocate that himself).[29] This is in spite of the fact that he is a sitting Legislative Council member. In fact, in the 2016 Legco election, he received more votes than any candidate ever. ***Censor:*** Electoral Affairs Commission of the Hong Kong government. ***Outcome:*** Chu becomes the eleventh candidate to be barred from running on political grounds; the second in a row, after Lau Siu-lai, to be barred from running due to self-determination advocacy even though both were allowed to run (and won) in September 2016; the first sitting Legco member to be barred from running in an election; and the first candidate to be barred from a non-Legco election. The Party and HK government are intent on excluding self-determinationists from all elections, though there is no law against advocacy of either self-determination or independence, and no court has ever ruled that advocacy of either is "against the Basic Law", as the government claims. (In fact, the right of self-determination is enshrined in Basic Law Article 39.) The "red line" is arbitrary and shifting, and elections in HK are further compromised.

Tai Kwun bars Ma Jian at Hong Kong International Literary Festival, then relents

10 November 2018, ***Censorship:*** Tai Kwun refuses use of its venue on grounds Ma Jian is too "political". Then the alternative venue, the Annex at Nan Fung Place, also refuses use. Tai Kwun backtracks and agrees to hold the two events involving Ma Jian after a public outcry.[30] ***Censor:*** Tai Kwun & the Annex at Nan Fung

Place. ***Outcome:*** The events are held, in the only clear case in Hong Kong of a censor reversing its decision, but doubt is cast over Tai Kwun's and more broadly Hong Kong public cultural institutions' commitment to freedom of expression.

Badiucao art exhibition at Free Expression Week closed after threats

2 November 2018, ***Censorship:*** Chinese artist Badiucao receives unspecified threats from Chinese authorities. He first decides not to come to HK to attend the opening of his exhibition "Gongle" for fear for his safety. Then the exhibition is cancelled entirely.[31] ***Censor:*** Chinese authorities. ***Outcome:*** The rest of Free Expression Week goes ahead as planned. The main organizer, *Hong Kong Free Press,* announces it will be bigger next year.

Lau Siu-lai barred from running for November Legislative Council by-election on political grounds

12 October 2018, ***Censorship:*** The Electoral Affairs Commission bars Lau Siu-lai from running in a Legislative Council by-election to fill a seat vacated by her disqualification in 2016. Its grounds are her previous advocacy of self-determination.[32] ***Censor:*** Electoral Affairs Commission of HK government. ***Outcome:*** Lau is the tenth candidate in all to have been banned on political grounds, preceded by six in 2016 Legco elections and three in March 2018 by-elections. She probably would have won the seat which she won in 2016, when she was not barred from running even though she advocated self-determination then, the moving goalposts a clear sign of the Party and HK government's shifting, arbitrary and hardening "red line". The only free and fair elections in HK, for Legco geographical constituencies, have been substantially compromised by political screening, leaving probably at least one-fifth of the electorate effectively disenfranchised.

Hotels refuse rooms, actors pull out of RTHK "Beneath Lion Rock" episode

October 2018, ***Censorship:*** The director reports hotels not allowing the iconic program, "Beneath Lion Rock" to book a room for shooting and actors changing their mind and declining to participate.[33] The episode is about bookseller

Lam Wing-kee's return to Hong Kong after his detention in China, and is therefore apparently considered "sensitive" by some. ***Censors:*** Hotels and actors. ***Outcome:*** The incident is an indication of creeping self-censorship within the tourism and entertainment industries. The episode is aired on RTHK.

Demosistō submission to UN Universal Periodic Review of China's human rights record removed by UN human rights office

September-November 2018, ***Censorship:*** Apparently at China's request, the Office of the United Nations High Commissioner for Human Rights removes the submissions of Demosistō and six other groups from its stakeholder summary for the UN Universal Periodic Review of China (including Hong Kong and Macau).[34] Eventually, it reinserts reference to the submissions of five of those groups, but not those of Demosistō and one other. ***Censor:*** Office of the UN High Commissioner of Human Rights, apparently at China's request. ***Outcome:*** Demosistō and the other groups were effectively excluded from the UPR, by the Office of the High Commissioner for Human Rights no less, even though that office in the past has continually stressed the importance of civil society participation. Doubt is cast on the independence and impartiality of that office, and there is growing suspicion that UN human rights mechanisms are being undermined by China.

HK National Party banned

24 September 2018, ***Censorship:*** The HK government bans HK National Party for its advocacy of independence, on grounds it endangers national security and public order. To do so, it employs a never-before-used provision in the Societies Ordinance.[35] ***Censor:*** The HK government ***Outcome:*** This is the first time ever a political group has been banned for any reason. HK National Party is appealing to the Executive Council, but its chances of success are considered exceedingly low.

Independence advocacy on university campuses

September 2018, ***Censorship:*** Baptist University removes "politically sensitive" portions of the student union president's speech from the program for the school year opening ceremony.[36] Polytechnic University removes independence-related content from the student union's Democracy Wall, sparking protests and hunger strike.[37] ***Censors:*** Baptist and Polytechnic universities. ***Outcome:*** PolyU eventually comes to an agreement with the student union to return to the previously agreed rules for the Democracy Wall. The atmosphere for freedom of expression on university campuses worsens. Independence advocacy is driven further underground.

Talk by Andy Chan, head of HK National Party, at HK Foreign Correspondents Club condemned by authorities

14 August 2018, ***Censorship:*** Communist Party and HK govt demand FCC cancel event on the ground that it would provide a platform for independence advocacy. ***Censor:*** Communist Party and HK government. ***Outcome:*** The event goes ahead as planned.[38] On 24 September, HKNP becomes the first political party ever to be banned in HK. On 5 October, news emerges that the work visa of Victor Mallet, vice-chair of FCC who hosted Chan's talk, was not renewed. He becomes the first foreign journalist effectively expelled from HK on political grounds. On 9 November, Mallet is barred from entering HK.[39]

RTHK decides not to livestream Andy Chan's talk at FCC

August 2018, ***Censorship:*** RTHK director Leung Ka-wing orders that Andy Chan's talk at the Foreign Correspondents Club not be livestreamed, saying that "the station cannot provide a platform for Hong Kong independence."[40] ***Censor:*** Leung Ka-wing, RTHK director ***Outcome:*** The broadcaster was allowed to broadcast the talk, just not stream it live. (This incident might not have been included in the list except for the fact that the director's reported reason for not allowing a livestream was clearly political and not having to do with, for example, the newsworthiness of the occasion.)

Yabuli Youth Forum 2018 tells journalists to let it vet news reports

June 2018, ***Censorship***: A forum organized by a mainland think tank tells journalists to sign a declaration giving the organisers the power to edit and approve their reporting on the event and to not report on some of the Party officials attending.[41] ***Censor:*** Yabuli Youth Forum 2018. ***Outcome:*** Journalists ignore the directive, instead publicizing the censorship attempt.

Benny Tai's speech in Taiwan condemned in orchestrated attack

April 2018, ***Censorship:*** The HK government leads a campaign against HKU law professor and former leader of Occupy Central, Benny Tai, after a speech he gave in Taiwan. The Communist Party and Party allies in HK shrilly participate in this orchestrated condemnation, falsely claiming he advocated HK independence; in fact, he merely discussed the hypothetical possibility of HK independence if China one day becomes a democracy. ***Censor:*** HK government, the Party and HK Party allies. ***Outcome:*** Though some critics call for Tai's dismissal from his professorship at Hong Kong University, HKU takes no action. Because Tai is known as a consummately moderate pro-democracy advocate in quite a traditional mold, the fact that he was singled out as an individual by the HK government for criticism over something he never even said was taken as a sign by the pro-democracy movement that in these days, the government may declare open season on anyone.

CCP emissaries say calling for an end to one-party dictatorship in China will be grounds for disqualification from Legco

March 2018, ***Censorship:*** Following changes to the Chinese constitution, HK National People's Congress delegate Tam Yiu-chung & a Party official say candidates may be barred from running for Legco if they call for an "end to one-party dictatorship", a common demand in HK. ***Censor:*** Former DAB Legco member and current NPC delegate Tam Yiu-chung and Chen Sixi, deputy director of the Liaison Office in Macau. ***Outcome:*** No one has (yet) been barred on these grounds, but the statements cast doubt on the candidacy later in the year of Lee Cheuk-yan, a leader in HK Alliance, which organizes the June 4 candlelight vigil and has always called for an end to one-party dictatorship. Lee is the replacement candidate for Lau Siu-lai, after she is barred for advocating self-determination. Lee is eventually allowed to run. This is part of a general trend of a variety of political opinions being deemed by the Party, the HK government and Party allies as unacceptable for holders of elected public office, casting a pall of censorship over politics and of uncertainty over elections. Increasingly, the suspense of these compromised elections is not who wins but which pro-democracy candidate manages to thread the needle of the acceptable.

Three candidates for March Legislative Council by-elections barred from running on political grounds

January-February 2018, ***Censorship:*** The Electoral Affairs Commission bars three candidates from Legislative Council by-elections, Agnes Chow, Ventus Lau and James Chan. Chow is barred because her party, Demosistō advocates self-determination, and Lau and Chan because of supposed independence advocacy. Chan was also barred in 2016. ***Censor:*** The Electoral Affairs Commission of the HK government. ***Outcome:*** Up to now, nine candidates in all have been barred on political grounds in 2016 and 2018 elections. Agnes Chow probably would have won a seat. She was running to replace Nathan Law, who was expelled from Legco in 2016 due to his expression during oath-taking, right after winning the election. He was allowed to run for Legco though their party advocates self-determination, but Agnes was barred on those grounds, another sign of the shifting, arbitrary and hardening "red line".

Demosistō application to register at Companies Registry rejected

January 2018, ***Censorship:*** The HK government refuses to allow Demosistō to register as a company, issuing notice nearly two years after it had applied. It usually takes the registry a matter of days to respond to an application, one of the reasons HK often bills itself as the easiest place in the world to start a business. ***Censor:*** The Companies Registry of the HK government. ***Outcome:*** Demosistō is effectively denied legal recognition, making it impossible to set up a bank account in the party's name and more difficult to accept funding. Its leader, Joshua Wong, has applied for judicial review of the decision. Some fear this is a step toward banning the party altogether. There is suspicion about the timing, with the rejection coming two years after the application and in the same month that Agnes Chow is eventually barred from running for Legco on the grounds that her party advocates self-determination.

Independence advocacy on campuses condemned by university heads

September 2017, ***Censorship:*** HK university heads issue a joint statement condemning independence advocacy after anonymous banners appear on university campuses, especially at Chinese University. University officials threaten to remove them and students vow to prevent that. ***Censors:*** HK university heads, backed by the HK government. ***Outcome:*** Independence advocacy continues but is driven underground and is often anonymous. At the start of the following academic year, more advocacy of independence occurs and there are more attempts by university authorities to prevent it. This is the first instance of university heads openly acting jointly to prohibit expression. It is considered a sign of the growing influence of the Party on universities and weakening commitment to academic freedom and freedom of expression by university leaders.

TVB suspends political satire show during Xi Jinping visit

July 2017, ***Censorship:*** Minutes before it is to air, TVB informs RTHK, producer of well-known political satire show "Headliner", that the program will be postponed. Xi Jinping is visiting Hong Kong. Liu Xiaobo and views critical of Xi Jinping's visit are in the program. TVB says the show is postponed to make way for "breaking news", but the news in question turns out to be a pre-recorded speech by... Xi Jinping, which other stations have already reported on earlier in the day. ***Censor:*** TVB. ***Outcome:*** RTHK lodges a formal complaint against TVB. The show is aired after Xi Jinping leaves town.

Joshua Wong prohibited from speaking at Asia Society Hong Kong

July 2017, ***Censorship:*** Asia Society Hong Kong prohibits Joshua Wong from speaking as part of a book launch. ***Censor:*** Asia Society Hong Kong. ***Outcome:*** Event organizer PEN Hong Kong relocates the launch to the Foreign Correspondents Club. Asia Society headquarters in New York issues a statement distancing itself from Asia Society HK and ascribing the decision to staff "error in judgment", but this is the second event Asia Society HK has cancelled for apparently political reasons.

Demosistō and League of Social Democrats members prevented from marching to flag-raising ceremony

July 1, 2017, ***Censorship:*** Demosistō and LSD members are attacked by pro-CCP thugs. Then 20 are arrested by police even though they are the victims of the attacks. They were attempting to march to the flag-raising ceremony marking the 20th anniversary of the handover where they intended to protest. Xi Jinping is in the city, and large numbers of police officers exert great effort to ensure no protester gets near him, essentially putting the area of the city around official venues under lockdown. There are many other smaller incidents that appear to unduly restrict freedom of expression. ***Censor:*** Pro-CCP thugs and the HK police. ***Outcome:*** All 20 pro-democracy protesters are released without charge. Police say they arrested the demonstrators "for their own safety". Joshua Wong unsuccessfully tries to sue the police for unlawful arrest and injuries sustained while being arrested.

National Party prevented from holding demonstration

June 30, 2017, ***Censorship:*** Police prevent the HK National Party from holding a public gathering to mark the 20th anniversary of the handover, even though the party tries to hold the gathering in two places in Tsim Sha Tsui that are far away from any venues where official commemorations are due to be held. It appears the mere fact of Xi Jinping being in the city means the National Party will not be allowed to appear anywhere in public. ***Censor:*** HK police. ***Outcome:*** The National Party eventually finds a room to meet at Baptist University, thanks to the student union there. This incident proves to be one of many steps taken by authorities to persecute the party, leading to banning the party altogether, the first time any political group has been prohibited from existing in HK.

Pro-democracy Legco member Kenneth Leung sued by CE for defamation

6 March 2017, ***Censorship***: Chief Executive Leung Chun-ying sues pro-democracy Legislative Council member Kenneth Leung for defamation over a claim Leung made that the CE is being investigated by overseas tax authorities in relation to a business deal concluded before Leung Chun-ying became CE. ***Censor:*** Chief Executive Leung Chun-ying ***Outcome:*** The case has yet to go to trial. This is the first time a CE has sued anyone for anything, though Leung threatened to sue *Apple Daily* in 2016 for defamation over claims made in regard to the same business deal.

Party agents threaten pro-CCP *Sing Pao Daily*

February 2017, ***Censorship:*** After pro-Communist Party *Sing Pao Daily* publishes articles critical of HK Chief Executive Leung Chun-ying, CE candidate Carrie Lam, Party leader Zhang Dejiang and the Liaison Office, its website is attacked and its staff receive threats. Evidence suggests the attacks and threats had to have come from Party agents. ***Censor:*** Probably Communist Party agents. ***Outcome:*** The incidents are reported to the police. The conflict is suspected to be a case of factional infighting within the Party. This is the only clear incident of a pro-CCP victim of censorship, but it is for a type of expression that is among the most commonly censored in HK, criticizing the Communist Party.

Youngspiration and National Party stalls prohibited at Victoria Park New Year fair

19 January 2017, ***Censorship***: The HK government terminates license agreements of two political parties led by young people, Youngspiration and HK National Party, for stalls at HK's biggest New Year fair, claiming they would "very likely endanger public order and public safety". ***Censor:*** The Food and Environmental Hygiene Department of the HK government. ***Outcome***: The two groups are not allowed to appear. The incident is part of a government effort to deny use of public space and participation in government-administered events to groups it considers enemies.

Six elected pro-democracy Legco members disqualified over oath-taking

November 2016-July 2017, ***Censorship:*** The HK government brings legal cases against six newly elected pro-democracy Legco members over their oath-taking upon assuming office, Baggio Leung, Yau Wai-ching, Leung Kwok-hung, Lau Siu-lai, Nathan Law and Edward Yiu. In the middle of the trial of the first two, the National People's Congress Standing Committee passes an "interpretation" of the Basic Law that virtually compels the High Court to disqualify them. ***Censor:*** The Communist Party, HK government and High Court. ***Outcome:*** Free and fair elections and the rights of voters and candidates have been significantly compromised. Lau Siu-lai is subsequently barred from running when she tries to regain her seat. Agnes Chow is barred from running when she tries to fill party fellow Nathan Law's seat. A pall is cast over expression of political opinion, in particular those advocating independence and self-determination. Baggio Leung and Yau Wai-ching lose their appeals. Leung Kwok-hung is still awaiting the High Court hearing of his appeal.

Screening of "Raise the Umbrellas" documentary cancelled at Asia Society Hong Kong

November 2016, ***Censorship:*** Asia Society Hong Kong cancels the screening of "Raise the Umbrellas", a documentary about the Umbrella Movement. ***Censor:*** Asia Society Hong Kong. ***Outcome:*** Along with cinemas dropping "Ten Years" in spite of its commercial success, this is part of a trend of venues refusing to show films related to "politically sensitive" topics. Independent HK filmmakers are increasingly left with options similar to those on the mainland: to show at universities, private screenings and international film festivals.

Billy Fung and Wang Dan's ViuTV show cancelled

October 2016, ***Censorship:*** ViuTV cancels its episode of "Travels with rivals" featuring Fung and Wang after the two appear at the Foreign Correspondents Club of Japan and discuss HK independence, even though it was ViuTV itself that arranged the event. ***Censor:*** ViuTV. ***Outcome:*** The station later apologizes for falsely accusing Fung and Wang of arranging the FCC talk themselves but reiterates "the station's stance is clear that we do not allow anyone making speeches advocating Hong Kong independence on the channel."

Chief Executive Leung Chun-ying threatens *Apple Daily* with legal action

October 2016, ***Censorship:*** Chief Executive Leung Chun-ying takes the extraordinary step of threatening pro-democracy *Apple Daily* with legal action for publishing an editorial accusing him of corruption related to a murky business deal Leung was involved in before becoming CE. This is the first time a sitting CE has ever even threatened to sue anyone. ***Censor:*** Leung Chun-ying, head of

HK government. ***Outcome:*** Leung does not eventually sue *Apple Daily*, but in March 2017 sues pro-democracy Legco member Kenneth Leung for defamation for claiming overseas tax authorities are investigating Leung in relation to the business deal. That case has yet to go to trial. After leaving office, Leung threatens to sue several others, all over alleged defamation. Arguably, the incidence of attacks on *Apple Daily* has actually declined since the period directly before and during the Umbrella Movement. In those months, Jimmy Lai, the owner of *Apple Daily*, was assaulted and had his home firebombed and his email hacked, the paper's production centre was picketed by pro-CCP protesters, and the paper had its deliveries destroyed at drop-off points around the city. The decline in attacks on *Apple Daily* may be related to its defiant resistance to attempts to muzzle it. For example, in response to Leung's threat to sue, it posted a video mocking the legal letter by putting Leung's head on Pikotaro and having him dance a version of "Pen-Pineapple-Apple-Pen".

Denise Ho's music banned on the Chinese internet

September 2016, ***Censorship:*** Chinese censors scrub Cantopop star Denise Ho's music from the internet because of her participation in the Umbrella Movement and her support for democracy in HK. ***Censor:*** Chinese internet authorities. ***Outcome:*** HK entertainers, many of whom get a significant portion of their income from the mainland, are forewarned that supporting democracy in HK will kill their careers in China. Denise Ho reorients her career and is widely supported by people in HK.

Legco election flyers of Nathan Law and Eddie Chu not approved

August 2016, ***Censorship:*** The Electoral Affairs Commission holds up approval of flyers by two Legco election candidates, Nathan Law and Eddie Chu, both of whom advocate self-determination. ***Censor:*** The Electoral Affairs Commission of HK government. ***Outcome:*** The candidates are forced to revise their flyers or face being ineligible for free postal delivery for Legco candidates. After he is elected, Nathan Law is disqualified from office over his oath-taking, and his party fellow is subsequently barred from running to fill his seat on grounds their party Demosistō advocates self-determination.

Six candidates for September 2016 Legislative Council elections barred from running on political grounds

July-August 2016, ***Censorship:*** The Electoral Affairs Commission bars six candidates from Legislative Council elections, Edward Leung, Andy Chan Ho-tin, Alice Lai Yee-man, Yeung Ke-cheong, James Chan Kwok-keung, and Nakade Hitsujiko on political grounds. ***Censor:*** The Electoral Affairs Commission of the HK government. ***Outcome:*** For first time ever, candidates are barred from running on political grounds. Edward Leung probably would have won a seat. This is the beginning of a string of barrings of up to now eleven candidates and also of the compromising of the integrity and fairness of the only free and fair elections HK had.

Lancôme cancels sponsorship of Denise Ho concert

July 2016, ***Censorship:*** Lancôme cancels a Denise Ho concert it was sponsoring after *Global Times* stokes online calls on the mainland for a boycott of her music for supporting democracy in HK. ***Censor:*** Lancôme. ***Outcome:*** In protest, Denise Ho goes ahead with a free concert on the streets of Sheung Wan. 3,000 attend. She eventually finds sponsorship from a local company for a concert that sells out 50,000 seats. Supporters protest against Lancôme at its stores. HK entertainers are forewarned to avoid speaking out on any topic which might offend the Communist Party.

"Countdown Machine" removed from the façade of International Commerce Centre

May 2016, ***Censorship:*** Hong Kong Arts Development Council cancels the "Countdown Machine" installation on the façade of the International Commerce Centre as the third-ranking Communist Party member Zhang Dejiang is scheduled to arrive in Hong Kong. The "machine" counts down the time remaining before the "one country, two systems" arrangement is due to expire in 2047. **Censor:** Hong Kong Arts Development Council, an HK government agency. ***Outcome:*** Yet another cultural and arts institution in HK is considered compromised when it comes to its stance on freedom of expression on "politically sensitive" issues. A year later, the same building, ICC, displays this (uncensored) message on its façade: "Enthusiastically celebrate the 20th anniversary of Hong Kong's return to the motherland."

Ming Pao editor sacked after publication of Panama Papers

April 2016, ***Censorship:*** Editor Keung Kwok-yuen, is fired after *Ming Pao* publishes articles about the major global leak of the Panama Papers, which show HK to be a major conduit for wealthy Chinese to get their money out of China as well as the biggest hub in the world for a variety of shell companies which appear to have as their main purpose to launder money from elsewhere. ***Censor:*** *Ming Pao*. Reporters say the decision was taken by Malaysian chief editor Chong Tien Siong, who is seen as pro-CCP. ***Outcome:*** Protests of hundreds against the action and a statement denouncing it from seven HK journalists organizations including *Ming Pao*'s own staff association. *Ming Pao* is also seen by many to have declined as a leading and authoritative voice in HK journalism. It is doubtful *Ming Pao* will collaborate in further ICIJ coalition investigations. (ICIJ's local partner for Panama Papers was *HK01*.) In February 2014, *Ming Pao* editor Kevin Lau was nearly chopped to death in a street attack in broad daylight. This happened weeks after ICIJ published "Leaked records reveal offshore holdings of China's elite", a report on which *Ming Pao* did collaborate. Lau's attackers were brought to trial and eventually given long prison sentences, but it was never discovered who ordered the attack or why. HK already suffers from a paucity of investigative reporting on corruption and the finance industry, and this case will certainly not do anything to encourage more; if anything, the opposite. In Hong Kong, almost no investigative journalism is produced as a result of the Panama Papers revelations in which HK featured prominently.

HK government removes "national" from names of three Taiwan universities in its ads for cultural events

March 2016, ***Censorship:*** The Leisure and Cultural Services Department deletes "national" from the names of Taiwan universities in three separate cases of leaflets advertising LCSD-sponsored events involving people from those universities. ***Censor:*** The Leisure and Cultural Services Department of the HK government. ***Outcome:*** There have been no reports since then of similar occurrences. Perhaps it was an overly worried bureaucrat, though the fact that it happens in three separate cases suggests an order was handed down.

"Ten Years", dystopian film about HK 10 years from now, dropped by cinemas

Early 2016, ***Censorship:*** Though "Ten Years" is wildly popular, outcompeting even the new Star Wars movie at the box office, & awarded "Best Film" at HK Film Awards, HK cinemas stop showing the film after it is criticized by Party-run media in China. ***Censor:*** HK cinemas. ***Outcome:*** Dozens of free public screenings are arranged throughout the city. Party allies in the film industry call for reform in film awards. HK filmmakers get the message that "edgy" films won't be shown in cinemas.

Five booksellers from Causeway Bay Bookstore detained in China

30 December 2015, ***Censorship:*** Five booksellers from Causeway Bay Bookstore specializing in publishing and selling books "banned" in China are detained on the mainland. One, Gui Minhai, is abducted from Thailand and another, Lee Bo, from off the streets of HK. ***Censor:*** Party agents. ***Outcome:*** Four of the five are eventually released. Gui Minhai is still in detention. Lam Wing-kee disobeys Party orders and speaks out about his detention when he returns to HK. The incidents are widely regarded as having decimated the "banned book" business in HK and even those not specializing in that genre have been known to have closed down or moved their business away from HK. The incidents cast a chill over book publishing and for the first time give HK citizens the feeling that anyone could be snatched from the streets and spirited across the border. The HK police investigation into Lee Bo's abduction is closed without identifying any suspects or finding that any crimes have been committed.

M+ museum exhibition of contemporary Chinese art

December 2015, ***Censorship:*** The name of a touring art exhibition is changed when it comes to Hong Kong, from "Right and Wrong" to "M+ Sigg Collection: Four Decades of Chinese Contemporary Art", apparently for fear of a negative reaction by the authorities to the more strident original title. ***Censor:*** M+ museum, a governmental institution. ***Outcome:*** While apparently minor, and while "controversial" artists such as Ai Weiwei are still included in the show, the decision fuels on-going worries about the independence and courage of a new major cultural institution even before it opens.

CE criticizes student union magazine in policy address

January 2015, ***Censorship:*** Chief Executive Leung Chun-ying criticizes *Undergrad*, the magazine of the Hong Kong University student union, in his annual policy address for "fallacies" related to a book it published called *Hong Kong Nationalism* and a cover story called "Hong Kong people deciding their own fate". This is extraordinary: never before has a CE used a policy address to single out a student publication or organization for criticism. It comes less than a month after the end of the Umbrella Movement, in which students played a major role. ***Censor:*** Chief Executive Leung Chun-ying ***Outcome:*** No direct action has been taken against *Undergrad*, but in retrospect, this is the clarion call for attempts to more tightly restrict academic freedom and control universities as well as to attack political speech deemed unacceptable by the Party and HK government.

Endnotes

Some thoughts on the Hong Kong anti-parallel trade demonstrations

1 Population Policy Strategies and Initiatives, Chief Secretary for Administration's Office, January 2015, p3, https://www.hkpopulation.gov.hk/public_engagement/pdf/PPbooklet2015_ENG.pdf

2 "Interview: Ian Rowen", Brian Hioe, New Bloom, March 7, 2015, https://newbloommag.net/2015/03/07/interview-ian-rowen/

Six months after the Umbrella Movement began, where is the Hong Kong pro-democracy movement?

1 Varsity, March 2015, http://varsity.com.cuhk.edu.hk/index.php/category/periscope/march-2015-civic-awakening/

What would it take to succeed? The Hong Kong pro-democracy movement through the lens of nonviolent civil resistance theory and in global context

1 "Hong Kong Democracy Activist- Benny Tai", HARDtalk, 31 March 2015, https://www.bbc.co.uk/programmes/p02ml673

2 "An expert explains how Hong Kong's protesters could actually win", Zack Beauchamp, Vox, October 2, 2014, https://www.vox.com/2014/10/2/6883313/hong-kong-protest-win

3 "Reform proposal to be tabled soon", Hong Kong Information Services Department, April 9, 2015, http://www.news.gov.hk/en/categories/admin/html/2015/04/20150409_182507.shtml

4 "How the Umbrella Revolution Could Win", Jay Ulfelder, Dart-Throwing Chimp, 1 October 2014, https://dartthrowingchimp.wordpress.com/2014/10/01/how-the-umbrella-revolution-could-win/

5 黃之鋒戴GoPro請願遭便衣警攬跌，蘋果日報, 25 April 2015, https://hk.news.appledaily.com/local/realtime/article/20150425/53672704

A brief encounter with the Hong Kong police

1 "Overview of Legal Cases Related to the HK Umbrella Revolution", Kong Tsung-gan, April 21, 2015, https://medium.com/@KongTsungGan/overview-of-legal-cases-related-to-the-hk-umbrella-revolution-7734adecdb0

2 The six-monthly report on Hong Kong, 1 July to 31 December 2014, Deposited in Parliament by the Secretary of State for Foreign and Commonwealth Affairs, February 2015, p11, https://assets.publishing.service.gov.uk/government/uploads/system/uploads/attachment_data/file/415938/Hong_Kong_Six_Monthly_Report_July-Dec_2014.pdf

3 "Overview of Legal Cases Related to the HK Umbrella Revolution", Kong Tsung-gan, April 21, 2015, https://medium.com/@KongTsungGan/overview-of-legal-cases-related-to-the-hk-umbrella-revolution-7734adecdb0

4 "Protesters Say Public Order Ordinance Restricts Their Rights", Simpson Cheung, *South China Morning Post*, 10 November 2012, https://www.scmp.com/news/hong-kong/article/1078885/protesters-say-public-order-ordinance-restricts-their-rights

5 "China: Hong Kong Political Reform Proposal a Farce", Human Rights Watch, April 22, 2015, https://www.hrw.org/news/2015/04/22/china-hong-kong-political-reform-proposal-farce

26 years on, we still live in the shadow of June 4, 1989

1 "On the 26th Anniversary of Tian'anmen Massacre, an Open Letter to Fellow Students in Mainland China", a group of overseas Chinese students, letter penned by Gu Yi, China Change, May 27, 2015, https://chinachange.org/2015/05/27/on-the-26th-anniversary-of-tiananmen-massacre-an-open-letter-to-fellow-students-in-mainland-china/

2 Censorship and Conscience: Foreign Authors and the Challenge of Chinese Censorship, PEN America, May 20, 2015, https://pen.org/research-resources/censorship-and-conscience/

3 "Leading U.S. retailer launches 'special section' for China-themed books", Wang Fan, Zhou Xiaozheng, Xinhua, May 26, 2015, http://www.xinhuanet.com//english/2015-05/27/c_134274189.htm

4 "At mødes eller ikke mødes med Dalai Lama", Louise Grønkjær, Martin Gøttske, Information, 7 February 2015, https://www.information.dk/udland/2015/02/moedes-moedes-dalai-lama

A tribute to all of the people of the Hong Kong pro-democracy movement on the occasion of the defeat of the Communist Party's fake suffrage proposal (because it's not often these days that someone stares down the dictator)

1 "20150617 Dennis Kwok's Speech against the Constitutional Reform Proposal", Dennis Kwok, June 17, 2015, https://www.youtube.com/watch?v=pVzFgP1gweQ

2 "Five July 1 rally groups denied licences for fund-raising on street", Joyce Ng, *South China Morning Post*, 26 June 2015, https://www.scmp.com/print/news/hong-kong/politics/article/1826576/five-july-1-rally-groups-denied-licences-fund-raising-street

3 "There are 391,277 young people aged 18 to 30 not registered as voters. Dateline is 2 July." Real HK News, 24 June 2015, https://www.facebook.com/realhknews/posts/1711461532414800

4 "Hong Kong ranks low in global indices on democracy, political rights and income inequality… and it's getting worse", Kong Tsung-gan, May 8, 2015, https://medium.com/@KongTsungGan/hong-kong-ranks-low-in-global-indices-on-democracy-political-rights-and-income-equality-7f381f9c4777

Commentary on Joshua Wong's essay on the next phase of the Hong Kong pro-democracy movement

1 "Collected articles on Hong Kong self-determination", Joshua Wong, Jeffrey Ngo, Commissioner Song Zhe and the Office of the Foreign Ministry of the People's Republic of China in Hong Kong, https://medium.com/@KongTsungGan/collected-articles-on-hong-kong-self-determination-2711991e744f

2 "The next phase of the democracy movement: A referendum on on constitutional reform and sustainable democratic self-governance", Joshua Wong, August 2, 2015, translation by Lucas Tse, Lewis Ho and Kong Tsung-gan, https://medium.com/@KongTsungGan/the-next-phase-of-the-democracy-movement-a-referendum-on-constitutional-reform-and-sustainable-b66c164842b7

Hong Kong one year after the start of the Umbrella Movement: Injustice and a complete lack of accountability

1 "Applications made for Occupy anniversary rallies", RTHK, 12 September 2015, http://news.rthk.hk/rthk/en/component/k2/1210962-20150912.htm

2 "Hong Kong police target 'principal instigators' after all sites cleared", Samuel Chan, Alan Yu, Joyce Ng, *South China Morning Post*, 16 December 2014, https://www.scmp.com/news/hong-kong/article/1663105/hong-kong-police-target-occupy-central-instigators-after-all-sites?page=all

3 "I've no regrets about the tear gas, says top police officer who ordered its use", Lana Lam, Clifford Lo, *South China Morning Post*, 5 October, 2014, https://www.scmp.com/news/hong-kong/article/1609835/ive-no-regrets-about-tear-gas-says-top-police-officer-who-ordered-its?page=all

4 "LC Urgent Q1: Strict police guidelines for the use of force", Hong Kong government press releases, October 15, 2014, https://www.info.gov.hk/gia/general/201410/15/P201410150734.htm

5 "Police launch internal review of how they handled Occupy Central protests", Niall Fraser, *South China Morning Post*, 15 March 2015, https://www.scmp.com/news/hong-kong/article/1737998/police-launch-internal-review-how-they-handled-occupy-central?page=all

6 "Basic Principles on the Use of Force and Firearms by Law Enforcement Officials", Eighth United Nations Congress on the Prevention of Crime and the Treatment of Offenders, Office of the High Commissioner for Human Rights, https://www.ohchr.org/EN/ProfessionalInterest/Pages/UseOfForceAndFirearms.aspx

7 "Use of Force- Guidelines for Implementation of the UN Basic Principles on the Use of Force and Firearms by Law Enforcement Officials", Amnesty International, 9 February 2015, http://www.amnestyusa.org/research/reports/use-of-force-guidelines-for-implementation-of-the-un-basic-principles-on-the-use-of-force-and-firear

8 "Was it Lawful for the Police to Use Tear Gas on Protesters in Hong Kong?" Simon Young, HKU Legal Scholarship Blog, September 29, 2014, http://researchblog.law.hku.hk/2014/09/legal-authority-for-police-to-use-tear.html

9 "'My expat friends think Hong Kong is great': Police watchdog chief chides 'negative and unconstructive' Hongkongers", Samuel Chan, *South China Morning Post*, 24 September 2015, https://www.scmp.com/print/news/hong-kong/law-crime/article/1860939/my-expat-friends-think-hong-kong-great-police-watchdog

11 "Statement of the Hong Kong Bar Association on the Use of Force by Hong Kong Police at Harcourt Road on 28 September 2014", Hong Kong Bar Association, 29 September 2014, https://hkba.org/sites/default/files/20140929-Press_Statement_of_HKBA_29_September_2014.pdf

12 "Message to all HKU students and staff by HKU President and Vice-Chancellor Professor Peter Mathieson", Press Releases, The University of Hong Kong, 30 September 2014, https://www.hku.hk/press/press-releases/detail/11745.html

13 "OCCUPY CENTRAL- DAY TWO: Full report of the day's events", *South China Morning Post*, 29 September 2014, https://www.scmp.com/news/hong-kong/article/1603762/live-severe-disruption-expected-day-dawns-occupied-hong-kong?page=all

14 "Hong Kong's young umbrella revolution", Angus Grigg, Financial Review, September 30, 2014, https://www.afr.com/news/policy/foreign-affairs/hong-kongs-young-umbrella-revolution-20140929-jl4nt

15 "Protesters Occupy Hong Kong; Police Use Tear Gas, Pepper Spray", Radio Free Asia, September 28, 2014, https://www.rfa.org/english/news/china/teargas-09282014163548.html

16 "OCCUPY CENTRAL- DAY TWO: Full report of the day's events", *South China Morning Post*, 29 September 2014, https://www.scmp.com/news/hong-kong/article/1603762/live-severe-disruption-expected-day-dawns-occupied-hong-kong?page=all

17 "Teachers join students' boycott as Occupy Central continues", Young Post, September 29, 2014 https://yp.scmp.com/news/hong-kong/article/91140/teachers-join-students%E2%80%99-class-boycott-occupy-central-continues

18 "From students to company bosses, Hongkongers show support for Occupy Central", Phila Siu, Joyce Ng, Timmy Sung, Tony Cheung, Chris Lau, *South China Morning Post*, 30 September 2014, https://www.scmp.com/print/news/hong-kong/article/1604157/students-company-bosses-hongkongers-show-support-occupy-central?page=all

19 Ibid.

20 Ibid.

21 Ibid.

22 Ibid.

23 "HKUPOP releases popularity figures of Hong Kong disciplinary forces and the PLA Hong Kong Garrison", Public Opinion Programme, The University of Hong Kong, June 11, 2015, https://www.hkupop.hku.hk/english/release/release1264.html

24 "Zhang Xiaoming's controversial speech on Hong Kong governance: full text", *South China Morning Post*, 16 September 2015, https://www.scmp.com/news/hong-kong/politics/article/1858484/zhang-xiaomings-controversial-speech-hong-kong-governance

25 "U.N. rights watchdog calls for open elections in Hong Kong", Stephanie Nebehay, *Reuters*, October 23, 2014, https://www.*Reuters*.com/article/us-hongkong-china-un/u-n-rights-watchdog-calls-for-open-elections-in-hong-kong-idUSKCN0IC18V20141023

26 "Overview of Legal Cases Related to the Hong Kong Umbrella Revolution", Kong Tsung-gan, April 21, 2015, https://medium.com/@KongTsungGan/overview-of-legal-cases-related-to-the-hk-umbrella-revolution-7734adecdb0

Advocating independence for Hong Kong is neither illegal nor against the Basic Law

1 "Occupy co-founder Benny Tai calls on Hongkongers to defy 'sugar-coated authoritarianism'", Kimmy Chung, *South China Morning Post*, 16 September 2017, https://www.scmp.com/news/hong-kong/politics/article/2111483/occupy-co-founder-benny-tai-calls-hongkongers-defy-sugar

2 "Response from Students' Unions of Higher Institutions towards the Joint Statement by Heads of Universities", CUSU Facebook page, 16 September 2017, https://m.facebook.com/story.php?story_fbid=1590570134338723&id=416069858455429&__tn__=%2As%2As-R

3 "CUHK independence action 'may amount to sedition'", RTHK, 16 September 2017, http://news.rthk.hk/rthk/en/component/k2/1352597-20170906.htm

4 "Don't be naïve and test the law with Hong Kong independence slogans, former Bar Association chairwoman says", Kimmy Chung, *South China Morning Post*, 16 September 2017, https://www.scmp.com/news/hong-kong/politics/article/2111477/dont-be-naive-and-test-law-hong-kong-independence-slogans

5 "Theories of Secession", Allen Buchanan, Philosophy & Public Affairs, Vol. 26, No. 1 (Winter, 1997), pp. 31-61, https://www.jstor.org/stable/2961910

Three years on, the fallout from the Umbrella Movement determines the politics of Hong Kong today

1 Tweet by Kong Tsung-gan, 20 August 2017, https://twitter.com/KongTsungGan/status/899227463200395264

2 "'Morale boost': Politicians and activists speak of renewed solidarity at Sunday's march over protester jailings", Karen Cheung, *Hong Kong Free Press*, 21 August 2017, https://www.hongkongfp.com/2017/08/21/morale-boost-politicians-activists-speak-renewed-solidarity-sundays-march-protester-jailings/

3 "A turn to localism? Civic Party launches 10th anniversary manifesto", Kris Cheng, *Hong Kong Free Press*, 16 March 2016, https://www.hongkongfp.com/2016/03/16/a-turn-to-localism-civic-party-launches-10th-anniversary-manifesto/

4 "Pro-democracy ADPL party calls for self-determination in 30th anniversary manifesto", Kris Cheng, *Hong Kong Free Press*, 8 June 2016, https://www.hongkongfp.com/2016/06/08/pro-democracy-adpl-party-calls-for-self-determination-in-30th-anniversary-manifesto/

5 "Election Results, 2016 Legislative Council Election", https://www.elections.gov.hk/legco2016/eng/results.html?1539831076617

Mainlandization: An overview of Communist Party attempts to control and assimilate Hong Kong

1 "We get it, CY ... One Belt, One Road gets record-breaking 48 mentions in policy address", Gary Cheung, *South China Morning Post*, 13 January 2016, https://www.scmp.com/news/hong-kong/politics/article/1901017/we-get-it-cy-one-belt-one-road-gets-record-breaking-48

2 "Hong Kong gov't bans two political groups from selling goods at New Year fair citing safety concerns", Ellie Ng, *Hong Kong Free Press*, 19 January 2017, https://www.hongkongfp.com/2017/01/19/hogn-kong-govt-bans-two-political-groups-from-selling-goods-at-new-year-fair-citing-safety-concerns/

3 "Taiwan controversy after gov't dept. asks theatre company to amend promotional material", Kris Cheng, *Hong Kong Free Press*, 21 March 2016, https://www.hongkongfp.com/2016/03/21/taiwan-controversy-after-govt-dept-asks-theatre-company-to-amend-promo-material/

4 "HKU poll: Only 3.1% of young Hongkongers identify as Chinese, marking 20 year low", Kris Cheng, *Hong Kong Free Press*, 21 June 2017, https://www.hongkongfp.com/2017/06/21/hku-poll-3-1-young-hongkongers-identify-chinese-marking-20-year-low/

5 Population Policy Strategies and Initiatives, Chief Secretary for Administration's Office, January 2015, p3, https://www.hkpopulation.gov.hk/public_engagement/pdf/PPbooklet2015_ENG.pdf

6 "Hong Kong Tycoons Visit Beijing as Students Boycott Classes", Te-ping Chen, Isabella Steger, *Wall Street Journal*, September 22, 2014, https://www.wsj.com/articles/hong-kong-tycoons-visit-beijing-as-student-boycott-starts-1411366778

7 "Beijing to take a more active role in Hong Kong's affairs, hints Xi Jinping", Joyce Ng, Ng Kang-chung, *South China Morning Post*, 22 September 2014, https://www.scmp.com/news/hong-kong/article/1597637/beijing-take-more-active-role-hong-kongs-affairs-hints-xi-jinping

8 "HKGCC Supports Implementation of Universal Suffrage for the Chief Executive Election", Hong Kong General Chamber of Commerce, 31 August 2014, http://www.chamber.org.hk/en/media/press-releases_detail.aspx?ID=3531

9 "Business chambers condemn Occupy Central in newspaper ads", Gary Cheung, *South China Morning Post*, 11 June 2014, https://www.scmp.com/news/hong-kong/article/1529895/business-chambers-condemn-occupy-central-newspaper-ads

10 "Now Advising China's State Firms: The Communist Party", Gregory Stuart Hunter, Steven Russolillo, *Wall Street Journal*, August 14, 2017, https://www.wsj.com/articles/now-advising-chinas-state-firms-the-communist-party-1502703005

11 "Special Report: The mainland's colonization of Hong Kong's economy", Clare Baldwin, Yimou Lee, Clare Jim, *Reuters*, December 31, 2017, https://www.*Reuters*.com/article/us-hongkong-china-economy-specialreport-idUSKBN0K901320141231

12 "Hong Kong's biggest landowners usurped by mainland developers", Peggy Sito, Viola Zhou, Summer Zhen, Jennifer Li, *South China Morning Post*, 28 February 2017, https://www.scmp.com/property/hong-kong-china/article/2074808/hong-kongs-biggest-landowners-usurped-mainland-developers

13 "20 Years After Handover, China Looms Ever Larger over Hong Kong Markets", Steve Russolillo, *Wall Street Journal*, June 28, 2017, https://www.wsj.com/articles/defying-expectations-china-looms-large-over-hong-kong-markets-1498702872

14 Ibid.

15 "I Won't Make Jesus Bow Down to Xi Jinping", Derek Lam, *New York Times*, August 23, 2017, https://www.nytimes.com/2017/08/23/opinion/derek-lam-xi-jinping-jesus.html

16 "HK13.8m buys 'successful future' calligraphy by Beijing's top representative in Hong Kong", Fanny Fung, *South China Morning Post*, 16 April 2014, https://www.scmp.com/news/hong-kong/article/1483750/hk138m-bid-successful-future-calligraphy-beijings-top-representative

17 "Money in Politics with Chinese Characteristics", *The Real Hong Kong News*, 31 May 2014, https://therealnewshk.wordpress.com/2014/05/04/money-in-politics-with-chinese-characteristics/

18 "Students told to leave Tamar; pro-Beijing group to use park", EJ Insight, September 25, 2014, http://www.ejinsight.com/20140925-students-told-to-leave-tamar-pro-beijing-group-to-use-park/

19 "有參加遊行人士不清楚遊行目的", I-Cable News, 17 August, 2015, http://cable-news.i-cable.com/ci/videopage/news/439427/%E5%8D%B3%E6%99%82%E6%96%B0%E8%81%9E/%E6%9C%89%E5%8F%83%E5%8A%A0%E9%81%8A%E8%A1%8C%E4%BA%BA%E5%A3%AB%E4%B8%8D%E6%B8%85%E6%A5%9A%E9%81%8A%E8%A1%8C%E7%9B%AE%E7%9A%84

20 "In Pictures: Best foot forward: Hong Kong's military-style youth groups", AFP, *Hong Kong Free Press*, 19 June 2017, https://www.hongkongfp.com/2017/06/19/pictures-best-foot-forward-hong-kongs-military-style-youth-groups/

21 Two Systems Under Siege: Beijing Turns the Screws on Hong Kong Media: 2017 Annual Report", Hong Kong Journalists Association, July 2017, https://www.hkja.org.hk/ebook/e_Annual_report_2017/mobile/index.html

22 "Threatened Harbor: Encroachments on Press Freedom in Hong Kong", PEN America, January 16, 2015, https://pen.org/research-resources/threatened-harbor/

23 "Wang & Fung: Tensions between China and Hong Kong and update report in the semi-autonomous territory", FCCJ Channel, Foreign Correspondents Club of Japan, October 17, 2016, https://www.youtube.com/watch?v=fQSJz7sROCQ

24 "Shameless: Activists slam ViuTV after channel cancels reality show over pro-independence speech", Kris Cheng, *Hong Kong Free Press*, 20 October 2016, https://www.hongkongfp.com/2016/10/20/shamless-activists-slam-viutv-channel-cancels-reality-show-pro-independence-speech/

25 "Chinese media mogul revealed as owner of Hong Kong broadcaster TVB, in potential regulatory breach", Kris Cheng, *Hong Kong Free Press*, 11 May 2017, https://www.hongkongfp.com/2017/05/11/chinese-media-mogul-revealed-owner-hong-kong-broadcaster-tvb-potential-regulatory-breach/

26 "中聯辦操控三聯中華商務",蘋果日報,8 April 2015, https://hk.news.appledaily.com/local/daily/article/20150408/19104025

27 "中聯辦掌控聯合出版集團擁三大書局兼壟斷發行　議員指涉違《基本法》", 蘋果日報, 9 April 2015, https://hk.news.appledaily.com/local/daily/article/20150409/19106286

28 "Creeping censorship in Hong Kong: How China controls sale of sensitive books", Ilaria Maria Sala, *The Guardian*, 19 May 2015, https://www.theguardian.com/world/2015/may/19/censorship-in-hong-kong-how-china-controls-sale-of-sensitive-books

29 "Hong Kong book giant in censorship row after returning books to 'pro-democracy' publisher", Jeffie Lam, *South China Morning Post*, 8 March 2015 https://www.scmp.com/news/hong-kong/article/1732853/beijing-criticised-publication-new-series-anti-occupy-books

30 "Basic Law violation seen as LOCPG tightens grip on HK publishers", Betsy Tse EJ Insight, 9 April 2015, http://www.ejinsight.com/20150409-basic-law-violation-seen-as-locpg-tightens-grip-on-hk-publishers/

31 "Unsafe harbour? Academic freedom in Hong Kong", David Matthews, *Times Higher Education*, September 10, 2015, https://www.timeshighereducation.com/features/academic-freedom-in-hong-kong-unsafe-harbour

32 "2015 Policy Address", Leung Chun-ying, January 14, 2015, https://www.policyaddress.gov.hk/2015/eng/

33 "Hong Kong Leader Singles Out College Magazine for Helping Cause 'Anarchy'", Isabella Steger, *Wall Street Journal*, January 14, 2015, https://blogs.wsj.com/chinarealtime/2015/01/14/hong-kong-leader-singles-out-college-magazine-for-helping-cause-anarchy/

34 "HKU governing body to discuss donations accepted by Occupy leader Benny Tai", Joyce Ng, *South China Morning Post*, 22 May 2015, https://www.scmp.com/news/hong-kong/politics/article/1806254/universitys-governing-body-discuss-donations-accepted-occupy. See also "HKU Council rejects audit report on Benny Tai donations", EJ Insight, March 26, 2015, http://www.ejinsight.com/20150326-hku-council-rejects-audit-report-on-benny-tai-donations/

35 "HKU 'satisfied' over donations from Benny Tai Yiu-ting", Peter So, Shirley Zhao, *South China Morning Post*, 31 December 2014, https://www.scmp.com/news/hong-kong/article/1671601/hku-satisfied-over-occupy-donations-benny-tai-yiu-ting

36 "CY ally Arthur Li appointed HKU council chairman amid strong opposition", Kris Cheng, *Hong Kong Free Press*, 31 December 2015, https://www.hongkongfp.com/2015/12/31/cy-ally-arthur-li-appointed-hku-council-chairman-amid-strong-opposition/

37 "'One country, two systems' guarantees HK prosperity", Xinhua, 30 June 2007, http://www.chinadaily.com.cn/china/2007-06/30/content_5424310.htm

38 "Demosisto party slams gov't teaching materials on Chinese national identity", Jun Pang, *Hong Kong Free Press*, 2 September 2017, https://www.hongkongfp.com/2017/09/02/demosisto-party-slams-govt-teaching-materials-chinese-national-identity/

39 "Mother tongue squeezed out of the Chinese classroom in Cantonese-speaking Hong Kong", Yuen Chan, *Hong Kong Free Press*, 22 July 2015, https://www.hongkongfp.com/2015/07/22/mother-tongue-squeezed-out-of-the-chinese-classroom-in-cantonese-speaking-hong-kong/

40 "It's no more efficient than Cantonese but Putonghua still the long-term objective for Hong Kong schools", Shirley Zhao, *South China Morning Post*, 27 June 2016, https://www.scmp.com/news/hong-kong/education-community/article/1982327/its-no-more-efficient-cantonese-putonghua-still

41 "In translation: The Occupy sentence review- why Hong Kong's appeals court jailed Joshua Wong, Nathan Law & Alex Chow", Karen Cheung, *Hong Kong Free Press*, 18 August 2017, https://www.hongkongfp.com/2017/08/18/translation-occupy-sentence-review-hong-kongs-appeal-court-jailed-joshua-wong-nathan-law-alex-chow/

Hong Kong's right of self-determination: The only way left?

1 "Theories of Secession", Allen Buchanan, *Philosophy & Public Affairs*, Vol. 26, No. 1 (Winter, 1997), pp. 31-61, https://www.jstor.org/stable/2961910

2 "The next phase of the democracy movement: A referendum on on constitutional reform and sustainable democratic self-governance", Joshua Wong, August 2, 2015, translation by Lucas Tse, Lewis Ho and Kong Tsung-gan, https://medium.com/@KongTsungGan/the-next-phase-of-the-democracy-movement-a-referendum-on-constitutional-reform-and-sustainable-b66c164842b7

3 "Our Manifesto", Demosistō, https://www.demosisto.hk/about?lang=en

4 "Let Hongkongers decide city's future after 2047, pro-democracy figures say", Karen Cheung, *Hong Kong Free Press*, 21 April 2016, https://www.hongkongfp.com/2016/04/21/65478/. For the full text, see 香港前途決議文, 香港革新論 ，https://www.facebook.com/reformhk/photos/a.477369359107299.1073741828.477063762471192/587284284782472/?-type=3&theater

5 "Pro-democracy ADPL party calls for self-determination in 30th anniversary manifesto", Kris Cheng, *Hong Kong Free Press*, 8 June 2016, https://www.hongkongfp.com/2016/06/08/pro-democracy-adpl-party-calls-for-self-determination-in-30th-anniversary-manifesto/

6 "Founded for Hong Kong: Local, autonomous and pluralistic: The Civic Party Tenth Anniversary Manifesto", Civic Party, https://www.civicparty.hk/?q=en/node/7026

7 "Self-Determination in Hong Kong is a Non-Issue", Song Zhe, *Wall Street Journal*, October 18, 2016, https://www.wsj.com/articles/self-determination-in-hong-kong-is-a-non-issue-1476807740

8 "Collected articles on Hong Kong self-determination", Kong Tsung-gan, https://medium.com/@KongTsungGan/collected-articles-on-hong-kong-self-determination-2711991e744f

9 "Reclaiming our right to self-determination in post-Umbrella Hong Kong", Joshua Wong, Jeffrey Ngo, World Policy, 14 October 2016, https://worldpolicy.org/2016/10/14/reclaiming-our-right-to-self-determination-in-post-umbrella-hong-kong/

10 "West Papua independence petition is rebuffed at UN", Ben Doherty, Kate Lamb, *The Guardian*, 30 September 2017, https://www.theguardian.com/world/2017/sep/30/west-papua-independence-petition-is-rebuffed-at-un

11 "Eddie Chu- Hong Kong Self-Determination", Foreign Correspondents Club of Hong Kong, 11 October 2016, https://www.youtube.com/watch?v=xeObX1guJmk

12 《香港革新論II》導論：從世界思考香港前途, 方志恒, InMedia, https://www.inmediahk.net/node/1051492

Booing the Party anthem means our souls have not been harmonized

1 "Video: Hong Kong football fans boo Chinese national anthem once again during Bahrain friendly", Kris Cheng, *Hong Kong Free Press*, 9 November 2017, https://www.hongkongfp.com/2017/11/09/just-hong-kong-football-fans-boo-chinese-national-anthem-bahrain-friendly/

2 《撐起雨傘》, Hong Kong Flyer 香港飛行頻道, October 4, 2014, https://www.youtube.com/watch?v=kEyG46wL-UE

3 "Soweto Gospel Choir - Nkosi Sikelel", Panellctp Traditional Gospel Music, July 3, 2011, https://www.youtube.com/watch?v=tTtINHRja4k

4 "Insult Laws: Insulting to Press Freedom: A Guide to Evolution of Insult Laws in 2010", Patti McCracken, Freedom House, World Press Freedom Committee, https://freedomhouse.org/sites/default/files/Insult%20Law%20Report.pdf

5 German Criminal Code, Section 90a: Defamation of the State and its Symbols, http://www.gesetze-im-internet.de/englisch_stgb/englisch_stgb.html

6 The Prevention of Insults to National Honour Act, 1971, https://web.archive.org/web/20170123231821/http://mha.nic.in/sites/upload_files/mha/files/pdf/Prevention_Insults_National_Honour_Act1971.pdf

7 National Anthem Act 1968 (Revised 1989), http://www.commonlii.org/my/legis/consol_act/naa19681989229/

8 Singapore Arms and Flag and National Anthem Act, Article 14, https://sso.agc.gov.sg/SL/SAFNAA1959-R1

9 "Insult Laws: Insulting to Press Freedom: A Guide to Evolution of Insult Laws in 2010", Patti McCracken, Freedom House, World Press Freedom Committee, https://freedomhouse.org/sites/default/files/Insult%20Law%20Report.pdf

10 Ibid.

11 "President mandates standing for national anthem and respecting flag", Mada Masr, May 31, 2014, https://madamasr.com/en/2014/05/31/news/u/president-mandates-standing-for-national-anthem-and-respecting-flag/

12 Freedom in the World Report 2017: Populists and Autocrats: The Dual Threat to Global Democracy, Freedom House, https://freedomhouse.org/report/freedom-world/freedom-world-2017

13 "Sitting and standing during the national anthem", Mshari Al Thaydi, Al Arabiya, 11 September 2016, http://english.alarabiya.net/en/views/news/middle-east/2016/09/10/Sitting-and-standing-during-the-national-anthem.html

14 "Philippines May Get New Law: Sing National Anthem with Spirit or Face Prison Time", Daniel Victor, *New York Times*, June 27, 2017 https://www.nytimes.com/2017/06/27/world/asia/philippines-may-get-new-law-sing-national-anthem-with-spirit-or-face-prison-time.html?_r=0

15 "Could Mocking Russia's National Anthem Soon Land You in Jail?", Damien Sharkov, Newsweek, July 21, 2016, https://www.newsweek.com/could-mocking-russia-national-anthem-land-you-jail-482665

16 "National anthem must be played before movies in theatres, rules Supreme Court", Utkarsh Anand, The Indian Express, December 1, 2016, https://indianexpress.com/article/india/india-news-india/national-anthem-national-flag-supreme-court-theater-4402827/

17 "Why should Japan's teachers have to sing the national anthem?", Alex Marshall, *The Guardian*, 20 October 2012, https://www.theguardian.com/commentisfree/2012/oct/20/no-harmony-singing-japan-national-anthem

18 "Does the United States or other countries compel national anthem etiquette?", Scott Bomboy, Constitution Daily, National Constitution Center, August 31, 2016, https://constitutioncenter.org/blog/does-the-united-states-or-other-countries-compel-national-anthem-etiquette

19 "No arrests for failing to stand for anthem", RTHK, 5 November 2017, http://news.rthk.hk/rthk/en/component/k2/1363106-20171105.htm

20 "Explainer: National Anthem Law, New Criminal Law Amendment, and Their Implications for Hong Kong", Changhao Wei, NPC Observer, October 31, 2017, https://npcobserver.com/2017/10/31/explainer-national-anthem-law-new-criminal-law-amendment-and-their-implications-for-hong-kong/

21 "Sex Pistols – God Save the Queen", Sex Pistols Official, https://www.youtube.com/watch?v=yqrAPOZxgzU

22 " God Save the Queen 7" vinyl released, Monday, October 8, 2007", JohnLydon.com, http://www.johnlydon.com/press/pistols.html

23 "King of Norway reigns on Facebook after diversity speech", Nicole Puglise, Jon Henley, *The Guardian*, 7 September 2016, https://www.theguardian.com/world/2016/sep/06/king-harald-norway-diversity-speech

24 "More Hongkongers now living below poverty line, labour and welfare chief says", Phila Siu, *South China Morning Post*, 6 November 2017, https://www.scmp.com/news/hong-kong/community/article/2118491/more-hongkongers-now-living-below-poverty-line-labour-and

25 "Poverty and Income Inequality Increase in Norway", The Nordic Page, November 15, 2017, https://www.tnp.no/norway/economy/poverty-income-inequality-increase-norway

26 "National anthem of Norway (lyrics)", Dhiaga Tiarna, March 12, 2012, https://www.youtube.com/watch?v=VRS6cbLOrPQ

27 "Maria Mena – Mitt Lille Land (Fra Oslo Domkirke Juli 30, 2011) med lyrics", Mary Ann Arceo, August 2, 2011, https://www.youtube.com/watch?v=tOQAVXLKq2A

28 "Subtitled speech by Prime Minister Jens Stoltenberg to the victims of the 2011 Norway attacks", SimianP, July 24, 2011, https://www.youtube.com/watch?v=80Pbd9UvZuY

The disqualification of Agnes

1 "Pro-democracy ADPL party calls for self-determination in 30th anniversary manifesto", Kris Cheng, *Hong Kong Free Press*, 8 June 2016, https://www.hongkongfp.com/2016/06/08/pro-democracy-adpl-party-calls-for-self-determination-in-30th-anniversary-manifesto/

2 "Let Hongkongers decide city's future after 2047, pro-democracy figures say", Karen Cheung, *Hong Kong Free Press*, 21 April 2016, https://www.hongkongfp.com/2016/04/21/65478/

3 Most of Joshua Wong and Jeffrey Ngo's articles on self-determination, along with rebuttals by the Communist Party, can be found at "Collected articles on Hong Kong self-determination", Kong Tsung-gan, https://medium.com/@KongTsungGan/collected-articles-on-hong-kong-self-determination-2711991e744f

4 "Interview: Pro-democracy election candidate Agnes Chow: who is she and why does she want your vote?", Jason Y. Ng, *Hong Kong Free Press*, 25 January, 2018, https://www.hongkongfp.com/2018/01/25/interview-pro-democracy-election-candidate-agnes-chow-want-vote/

5 "About Us", Demosistō, https://www.demosisto.hk/?lang=en

6 "Democratic self-determination – Demosistō's roadmap for the self-determination of the Hong Kong people", Demosistō, https://www.demosisto.hk/article/details/46

7 "Justice Sec Teresa Cheng gave legal advice to gov't over banning of candidates from legislative by-election", Kris Cheng, *Hong Kong Free Press*, 29 January 2018, https://www.hongkongfp.com/2018/01/29/justice-sec-teresa-cheng-gave-legal-advice-govt-banning-candidates-legislative-election/

8 "Eddie Chu- Hong Kong Self-Determination", Foreign Correspondents Club of Hong Kong, 11 October 2016, https://www.youtube.com/watch?v=xeObX1guJmk

Why Joshua, Nathan, Alex and the Umbrella Movement would be an excellent choice for the Nobel Peace Prize

1 "Bipartisan group of lawmakers nominates Hong Kong's pro-democracy Umbrella Movement for the Nobel Peace Prize", Congressional-Executive Committee on China, February 1, 2018, https://www.cecc.gov/media-center/press-releases/bipartisan-group-of-lawmakers-nominates-hong-kong%E2%80%99s-pro-democracy

2 "In full: Hong Kong pro-democracy activists 'honoured' by Nobel Peace Prize nomination", AFP, *Hong Kong Free Press*, 3 February 2018, https://www.hongkongfp.com/2018/02/03/full-hong-kong-pro-democracy-activists-honoured-nobel-peace-prize-nomination/

3 "Democracy Index 2017", The Economist Intelligence Unit, https://www.eiu.com/topic/democracy-index

4 "Freedom in the World: Democracy in Crisis", Freedom House, https://freedomhouse.org/report/freedom-world/freedom-world-2018

5 "All Nobel Peace Prizes", The Nobel Prize, https://www.nobelprize.org/prizes/lists/all-nobel-peace-prizes/

6 "Did Oslo Kowtow to Beijing? A ChinaFile Conversation", ChinaFile, December 21, 2016, http://www.chinafile.com/conversation/did-oslo-kowtow-beijing

7 "This grey summer, we've lost something of ourselves. We are frightened into silence.", Harald Stanghelle, Aftenposten, 18 August 2017, translated by Kong Tsung-gan, https://medium.com/@KongTsungGan/this-grey-summer-weve-lost-something-of-ourselves-we-are-frightened-into-silence-6b5377ffd9d6

8 "挪威諾貝爾委員會主席 Berit Reiss-Anderson —2017.7.19 8PM 【劉曉波頭七追思會】 "MEMORIAL FOR LIU XIAOBO"", HK Alliance, July 19, 2017, https://www.youtube.com/watch?v=OJiEiOTU-5s

"China rebukes 'meddling' US congressmen over Nobel Peace Prize nomination for Hong Kong's Joshua Wong", Tony Cheung, Catherine Wong, *South China Morning Post*, 2 February 2018, https://www.scmp.com/news/hong-kong/politics/article/2131749/china-rebukes-meddling-us-congressmen-over-joshua-wong-nobel

Has independence become the secret dream in many hearts?

1 "Submission by Human Rights Watch to the UN Human Rights Committee on the implementation of the ICCPR in the Hong Kong Special Administration Region, China", Sophie Richardson, Human Rights Watch, drafts/www2.ohchr.org/english/bodies/hrc/docs/ngos/humanrightswatch-hongkong.docx

2 "Concluding observations on the third periodic report of Hong Kong, China", United Nations Human Rights Committee, 11-28 March 2013, http://www2.ohchr.org/english/bodies/hrc/docs/co/ccpr-c-chn-hkg-co-3_en.doc

3 "Advocating independence for Hong Kong is neither illegal nor against the Basic Law", Kong Tsung-gan, https://medium.com/@KongTsungGan/advocating-independence-for-hong-kong-is-neither-illegal-nor-against-the-basic-law-10ae49a5d9bb

4 Photos of police filming independence advocates at the January 1, 2018 march, Kong Tsung-gan, https://twitter.com/KongTsungGan/status/948013961047240704

5 Excerpt about Hong Kong from Benny Tai's speech in Taiwan, 戴耀廷:台灣演講!【我們正面對一個挑戰，我們的自由在一步一步的倒退、減少】, 香港事, April 1, 2018 https://www.youtube.com/watch?v=0nuBj2UVenM

6 "Response by HKSAR Government to media enquiries", Press Releases, The Government of the Hong Kong Special Administration Region, March 30, 2018, https://www.info.gov.hk/gia/general/201803/30/P2018033000690.htm

7 "Eddie Chu- Hong Kong Self-Determination", Foreign Correspondents Club of Hong Kong, 11 October 2016, https://www.youtube.com/watch?v=xeObX1guJmk

8 "Benny Tai has always supported independence", RTHK, 9 April 2018, http://news.rthk.hk/rthk/en/component/k2/1390140-20180409.htm

Turning Hong Kong's Legislative Council into a mini-National People's Congress

1 "Legislature passes controversial house rule changes taking powers from lawmakers", Kris Cheng, *Hong Kong Free Press*, 15 December 2017, https://www.hongkongfp.com/2017/12/15/legislature-passes-controversial-house-rule-amendments-taking-powers-lawmakers/

2 "Six-monthly report on Hong Kong: July to December 2017", Foreign and Commonwealth Office, 15 March 2018, https://www.gov.uk/government/publications/six-monthly-report-on-hong-kong-july-to-december-2017

3 "Hong Kong Special Administrative Region (SAR) 2017 Report", European Commission, 24 April 2018, http://europa.eu/rapid/press-release_IP-18-3502_en.htm

4 Tweet by Joshua Wong in response to the European Commission report, 25 April 2018, https://twitter.com/joshuawongcf/status/989362390129983488

Criminalizing the opposition in Hong Kong

1 "A January of discontent: Hong Kong's crackdown on pro-democracy activists gathers pace", Kong Tsung-gan, *Hong Kong Free Press*, 7 January 2018, https://www.hongkongfp.com/2018/01/07/january-discontent-hong-kongs-crackdown-pro-democracy-activists-gathers-pace/

2 "Overview of prosecutions and lawsuits brought by the Hong Kong governments against pro-democracy leaders", Kong Tsung-gan, last updated 13 April 2018, https://medium.com/@KongTsungGan/overview-of-prosecutions-and-lawsuits-brought-by-hong-kong-government-against-pro-democracy-leaders-b5fdf0b6ec0e

3 "Regularly updated overview of trials of Hong Kong pro-democracy leaders and activists", Kong Tsung-gan, last updated 18 October 2018, https://medium.com/@KongTsungGan/regularly-updated-overview-of-trials-of-hong-kong-pro-democracy-leaders-and-activists-66ad3a0bbda9

4 "Hong Kong activist Avery Ng convicted of disclosing details of corruption probe, faces up to a year in prison", Ellie Ng, *Hong Kong Free Press*, 11 May 2018, https://www.hongkongfp.com/2018/05/11/just-hong-kong-activist-avery-ng-convicted-disclosing-details-corruption-probe-faces-year-prison/

5 "Ousted lawmakers Yau Wai-ching and Baggio Leung guilty of unlawful assembly after chaotic scene in legislature", Ellie Ng, *Hong Kong Free Press*, 11 May 2018, https://www.hongkongfp.com/2018/05/11/just-ousted-lawmakers-yau-wai-ching-baggio-leung-guilty-unlawful-assembly-chaotic-scene-legislature/

6 "Arrests, prosecutions, convictions and sentences related to Hong Kong pro-democracy demonstrations from 11 June 2014 to 18 June 2015", Kong Tsung-gan, February 24, 2017, https://medium.com/@KongTsungGan/arrests-prosecutions-and-convictions-related-to-hk-pro-democracy-demonstrations-from-1-1-june-2014-c15be1e6be00

7 "LCQ11: Arrests and prosecutions in relaton to public order events", Secretary for Security, Mr. Lai Tung-kwok, March 2, 2016, https://www.info.gov.hk/gia/general/201603/02/P201603020641.htm

8 "Overview of prosecutions and lawsuits brought by the Hong Kong governments against pro-democracy leaders", Kong Tsung-gan, last updated 13 April 2018, https://medium.com/@KongTsungGan/overview-of-prosecutions-and-lawsuits-brought-by-hong-kong-government-against-pro-democracy-leaders-b5fdf0b6ec0e

9 "A January of discontent: Hong Kong's crackdown on pro-democracy activists gathers pace", Kong Tsung-gan, *Hong Kong Free Press*, 7 January 2018, https://www.hongkongfp.com/2018/01/07/january-discontent-hong-kongs-crackdown-pro-democracy-activists-gathers-pace/

10 "The unprecedented Hong Kong government crackdown on the pr-democracy movement continues apace, and January is set to be its busiest month yet", Kong Tsung-gan, last updated 29 May 2018, https://medium.com/@KongTsungGan/the-unprecedented-hong-kong-government-crackdown-on-the-pro-democracy-movement-continues-apace-and-f2cda6ed36aa

11 "Democrat Ted Hui arrested over phone snatching incident, as pro-Beijing lawmaker seeks to oust him", Karen Cheung, *Hong Kong Free Press*, 5 May 2018, https://www.hongkongfp.com/2018/05/05/just-democrat-ted-hui-arrested-phone-snatching-incident-pro-beijing-lawmaker-seeks-oust/

12 "Magistrates' 50% conviction rate is 'shockingly low', blasts former Hong Kong DPP", Paul Benedict Lee, *Hong Kong Free Press*, 8 July 2015, https://www.hongkongfp.com/2015/07/08/former-prosecutor-calls-magistrates-50-3-conviction-rate-shockingly-low/

13 "Rule of Law Index 2017-2018", World Justice Project, http://data.worldjusticeproject.org/#groups/HKG

14 "Hong Kong Special Administrative Region (SAR) 2017 Report", European Commission, 24 April 2018, http://europa.eu/rapid/press-release_IP-18-3502_en.htm

15 "Six-monthly report on Hong Kong: July to December 2017", Foreign and Commonwealth Office, 15 March 2018, https://www.gov.uk/government/publications/six-monthly-report-on-hong-kong-july-to-december-2017

16 "Statement of the Hong Kong Bar Association on the Decision of the NPCSC of 27 December 2017 on the co-operation agreement between the mainland and the HKSAR on the establishment of the port at the West Kowloon station of the Guangzhou-Shenzhen-Hong Kong express rail link for implementing co-location arrangement", Hong Kong Bar Association, 28 December 2017, https://hkba.org/sites/default/files/20171228%20-%20Bar%20Co-Location%20Arrangement%20Statement%20%28English%29%20FINAL_0.pdf

17 "Statement of the Hong Kong Bar Association on Disqualification", Hong Kong Bar Association, 14 February 2018. https://hkba.org/sites/default/files/20180214%20-%20%20Statement%20of%20the%20Bar%20Association%20on%20Disqualification%20%28SW%29%20%28WK%29%20%28LL%29%20%2814%20Feb%29%20English%20version%20at%201522.pdf

18 "Pro-democracy activist Agnes Chow files petition over decision to ban her from Hong Kong by-election", Kris Cheng, *Hong Kong Free Press*, 8 May 2018, https://www.hongkongfp.com/2018/05/08/pro-democracy-activist-agnes-chow-files-petition-decision-ban-hong-kong-election/

19 "Activist Joshua Wong files legal challenge against Hong Kong Companies Registry for denying registration for his party", *Hong Kong Free Press*, 18 April 2018, https://www.hongkongfp.com/2018/04/18/activist-joshua-wong-files-legal-challenge-hong-kong-companies-registry-denying-registration-party/

20 Tweet by Kong Tsung-gan, 20 August 2017, https://twitter.com/KongTsungGan/status/899227463200395264

21 For a full account of the Mong Kok clearance, excerpted from my book, Umbrella: A Political Tale from Hong Kong, see "The clearance of the Mong Kok occupation on 25 and 26 November 2014, Hong Kong Umbrella Movement", Kong Tsung-gan, October 13, 2017, https://medium.com/@KongTsungGan/the-clearance-of-the-mong-kok-occupation-on-25-and-26-november-2014-hong-kong-umbrella-movement-1fbf9592b42a

22 "3 months jail for activist who ignored court order during Occupy Mong Kok protest camp clearance", Ellie Ng, *Hong Kong Free Press*, 30 March 2017, https://www.hongkongfp.com/2017/03/30/3-months-jail-for-activist-who-ignored-court-order-during-occupy-mong-kok-protest-camp-clearance/

23 "Activists arrested in their homes for alleged participation in unlawful assembly last year", Kris Cheng, *Hong Kong Free Press*, 11 January 2017, https://www.hongkongfp.com/2017/01/11/activists-arrested-in-their-homes-for-alleged-participation-in-unlawful-assembly-last-year/

June 4 and the need for solidarity between all peoples who oppose one-party dictatorship in China

1 "8 Hong Kong student unions will not attend June 4 vigil to commemorate Tiananmen Massacre", Ellie Ng, *Hong Kong Free Press*, https://www.hongkongfp.com/2018/05/19/8-hong-kong-university-student-unions-will-not-attend-june-4-vigil-commemorate-tiananmen-massacre/

2 "June 4 splits students, Poly U plans street stall", RTHK, 30 May 2018, http://news.rthk.hk/rthk/en/component/k2/1398947-20180530.htm

3 "Interview: Pro-democracy election candidate Agnes Chow: who is she and why does she want your vote?", Jason Y. Ng, *Hong Kong Free Press*, 25 January, 2018, https://www.hongkongfp.com/2018/01/25/interview-pro-democracy-election-candidate-agnes-chow-want-vote/

4 "1967 leftist riots and 1989 Tiananmen massacre excluded from Hong Kong's revised history curriculum", Catherine Lai, *Hong Kong Free Press*, 31 October 2017, https://www.hongkongfp.com/2017/10/31/1967-leftist-riots-1989-tiananmen-massacre-excluded-hong-kongs-revised-history-curriculum/

5 "Rewriting history in the People's Republic of Amnesia and Beyond", Louisa Lim, The Conversation, May 28, 2018 https://theconversation.com/rewriting-history-in-the-peoples-republic-of-amnesia-and-beyond-90014

6 "Those calling for end to 'one-party dictatorship' probably cannot run for legislature, Beijing official says", Kris Cheng, *Hong Kong Free Press*, 25 April 2018, https://www.hongkongfp.com/2018/04/25/calling-end-one-party-dictatorship-probably-cannot-run-legco-seats-says-beijing-official/

7 "In full: Charter 08- Liu Xiaobo's pro-democracy manifesto for China that lead to his jailing", Human Rights in China, *Hong Kong Free Press*, 14 July 2017, https://www.hongkongfp.com/2017/07/14/full-charter-08-liu-xiaobos-pro-democracy-manifesto-china-led-jailing/

8 China lawyer crackdown, *Hong Kong Free Press*, https://www.hongkongfp.com/china-lawyer-crackdown/

Justice it ain't: The Mong Kok "riot" trials

1 "Localist Edward Leung sentenced to six years in jail for his participation in Mong Kok unrest", Karen Cheung, *Hong Kong Free Press*, 11 June 2018, https://www.hongkongfp.com/2018/06/11/localist-edward-leung-sentenced-six-years-jail-mong-kok-unrest-participation/, See also "Hong Kong localist Edward Leung convicted of rioting over Mong Kok unrest", Karen Cheung, *Hong Kong Free Press*, 18 May 2018, https://www.hongkongfp.com/2018/05/18/breaking-hong-kong-localist-edward-leung-convicted-rioting-mong-kok-unrest/

2 "19-year-old Mong Kok protester sentenced to over 4 years in prison for rioting", Karen Cheung, *Hong Kong Free Press*, 31 May 2018, https://www.hongkongfp.com/2018/05/31/19-year-old-mong-kok-protester-sentenced-4-years-prison-rioting/

3 "Nine more jailed over 2016 Mong Kok riots", RTHK, 31 May 2018, http://news.rthk.hk/rthk/en/component/k2/1399217-20180531.htm

4 "Magistrates' 50% conviction rate is 'shockingly low', blasts former Hong Kong DPP", Paul Benedict Lee, *Hong Kong Free Press*, 8 July 2015, https://www.hongkongfp.com/2015/07/08/former-prosecutor-calls-magistrates-50-3-conviction-rate-shockingly-low/

5 "Criminalizing the opposition in Hong Kong", Kong Tsung-gan, https://medium.com/@KongTsungGan/criminalizing-the-opposition-in-hong-kong-1ea873033a6c

6 Ibid.

7 "The Modern Era 1945-1967", Hong Kong Police Force, https://www.police.gov.hk/info/doc/history/chapter02_en.pdf

8 "Concluding observations on the third periodic report of Hong Kong, China", United Nations Human Rights Committee, 11-28 March 2013, http://www2.ohchr.org/english/bodies/hrc/docs/co/ccpr-c-chn-hkg-co-3_en.doc

9 "Submission by Human Rights Watch to the UN Human Rights Committee on the implementation of the ICCPR in the Hong Kong Special Administration Region, China", Sophie Richardson, Human Rights Watch, drafts/www2.ohchr.org/english/bodies/hrc/docs/ngos/humanrightswatch-hongkong.docx

10 "The Hong Kong Watch view on the conviction of Edward Leung to 'rioting' charges", Hong Kong Watch, May 18, 2018, https://www.hongkongwatch.org/all-posts/2018/5/18/the-hong-kong-watch-view-on-the-conviction-of-edward-leung-to-rioting-charges

11 "Ex-governor Chris Patten calls Public Order Ordinance 'vague', 'open to abuse' following Edward Leung riot sentencing", Holmes Chan, *Hong Kong Free Press*, 11 June 2018, https://www.hongkongfp.com/2018/06/11/ex-governor-chris-patten-calls-public-order-ordinance-vague-open-abuse-following-edward-leung-sentencing/

12 After this article was written, the thirteen had their 13-month prison sentences overturned by the Court of Final Appeal in September 2018 and replaced by new sentences of time already served, which in most of their cases amounted to about 100 days in prison, although in three cases, about six months.

13 "Nine more jailed over 2016 Mong Kok riots", RTHK, 31 May 2018, http://news.rthk.hk/rthk/en/component/k2/1399217-20180531.htm

14 "Live warning shots fired during Mong Kok unrest, 9.2.15", *Hong Kong Free Press*, https://www.youtube.com/watch?time_continue=127&v=nqSotqe6dTc

15 "Hong Kong Government Rejects Calls for Inquiry into 'Fishball Riot'", Radio Free Asia, 15 February 2016, https://www.rfa.org/english/news/china/riots-hk-02152016151608.html

16 "No gov't investigation into Mong Kok unrest following sentencing of localist Edward Leung, says Hong Kong leader", Holmes Chan, *Hong Kong Free Press*, 13 June 2018, https://www.hongkongfp.com/2018/06/13/no-govt-investigation-mong-kok-unrest-following-sentencing-localist-edward-leung-says-hong-kong-leader/

17 "2011 riots inquiry recommendations ignored by government, says Lammy", Vikram Dodd, *The Guardian*, 29 March 2013, https://www.theguardian.com/uk/2013/mar/29/2011-riots-panel-proposals-unimplemented

18 "Cap.86 Commissions of Inquiry Ordinance", Hong Kong E-Legislation, https://www.elegislation.gov.hk/hk/cap86?xpid=ID_1438403567964_004

19 'Officer did not violate orders by firing into air, police probe concludes", Karen Cheung, *Hong Kong Free Press*, 12 February 2016, https://www.hongkongfp.com/2016/02/12/officer-did-not-violate-orders-by-firing-into-air-police-probe-concludes/

20 "Policeman, who opened fire during CNY Mong Kok riot, to be awarded for 'devotion to duty'", Coconuts Hong Kong, August 10, 2016, https://coconuts.co/hongkong/news/policeman-who-fired-live-bullets-during-cny-mong-kok-riot-be-awarded-devotion-duty/

21 "Hong Kong police urged to reveal guidelines on use of force to the public", Jeffie Lam, *South China Morning Post*, 22 June 2016, https://www.scmp.com/news/hong-kong/politics/article/1979367/hong-kong-police-urged-reveal-guidelines-use-force-public

22 "Hong Kong localist Edward Leung tells Mong Kok riot trial he acted out of duty to protect hawkers and crowds", Jasmine Siu, *South China Morning Post*, 18 April 2018, https://www.scmp.com/news/hong-kong/law-crime/article/2142162/hong-kong-localist-edward-wong-tells-mong-kok-riot-trial-he

23 "Activists gather to defends New Year's street hawkers from Kweilin Street 'cleanup'", Thomas Chan, Coconuts Hong Kong, February 19, 2015, https://coconuts.co/hongkong/news/activists-gather-defend-new-years-hawkers-kweilin-street-cleanup/

24 "I've no regrets about the tear gas, says top police officer who ordered its use", Lana Lam, Clifford Lo, *South China Morning Post*, 5 October 2014, https://coconuts.co/hongkong/news/activists-gather-defend-new-years-hawkers-kweilin-street-cleanup/

25 "Confidence in Hong Kong police restored after low of 2014 Occupy protests, retiring assistant chief Steve Hui says", Clifford Lo, *South China Morning Post*, 21 May 2018, https://www.scmp.com/news/hong-kong/hong-kong-law-and-crime/article/2146935/public-confidence-hong-kong-police-has

26 "HKUPOP release popularity figures of Hong Kong disciplinary forces and the PLA Hong Garrison and the PSI", Hong Kong Public Opinion Programme, The University of Hong Kong, December 5, 2017, https://www.hkupop.hku.hk/english/release/release1504.html

27 "First police water cannon arrives in Hong Kong", RTHK, 23 May 2018, http://news.rthk.hk/rthk/en/component/k2/1397614-20180523.htm

28 "Comments of The Hong Kong Bar Association on the Outline of the Third Report of The Hong Kong Special Administrative Region for the United Nations Human Rights Council Universal Periodic Review", Hong Kong Bar Association, 7 May 2018, https://hkba.org/sites/default/files/Human%20Rights%20-%20Third%20Report%20of%20HKSAR%20for%20United%20Nations%20Human%20Rights%20Council..5.18%20%28webpage%29.pdf

The power of the peripheries

1 "China: Big Data Fuels Crackdown in Minority Region", Human Rights Watch, February 26, 2018, https://www.hrw.org/news/2018/02/26/china-big-data-fuels-crackdown-minority-region

2 "What Really Happens in China's 'Re-education' Camps", Rian Thum, *New York Times*, May 15, 2018, https://www.nytimes.com/2018/05/15/opinion/china-re-education-camps.html

3 "Report: Tibet Remains Among Least Free Places in World", Free Tibet, January 17, 2018, https://freetibet.org/news-media/na/report-tibet-remains-among-least-free-places-world

4 See "China Wants You to Forget Ilham Tohti: Uyghur Critic Two Years into Life Sentence Should Be Freed", Sophie Richardson, Human Rights Watch, https://www.hrw.org/news/2016/09/20/china-wants-you-forget-ilham-tohti, and "A Tibetan Tried to Save His Language. China Handed Him Five Years in Prison", Chris Buckley, *New York Times*, May 22, 2018, https://www.nytimes.com/2018/05/22/world/asia/tibetan-activist-tashi-wangchuk-sentenced.html

5 "Interview: Labelled a threat to China, Hong Kong law scholar Benny Tai says Beijing is trying to brainwash Hongkongers", Kris Cheng, *Hong Kong Free Press*, 12 April 2018, https://www.hongkongfp.com/2018/04/12/interview-labelled-threat-china-hong-kong-law-scholar-benny-tai-says-beijing-trying-brainwash-hongkongers/

6 "Expanding 'blacklist': Taiwanese scholars say Hong Kong visa applications rejected", AFP, 22 December 2017, https://www.hongkongfp.com/2017/12/22/expanding-blacklist-taiwanese-scholars-say-hong-kong-visa-applications-rejected/

7 "Joint Statement 'International Youth Conference 2018'", Tibetan Youth Congress, https://www.tibetanyouthcongress.org/2018/05/joint-statement-international-conference/

8 "2nd Tibet, Hong Kong, Taiwan Roundtable Conference on Freedom, Democracy and Self-Determination", Students for a Free Tibet, https://www.studentsforafreetibet.org/2ndtthkconferencexi/

9 "Taiwan International Conference on Tibet iterates Middle Way", Tibet Post, 8 November 2017, http://www.thetibetpost.com/en/news/international/5805-taiwan-international-conference-on-tibet-iterates-support-for-middle-way

10 "The Taiwanese See Themselves as Taiwanese, not Chinese", Fang-Yu Chen, Wei-ting Yen, Austin Horng-en Wang, Brian Hioe, Washington Post, January 2, 2017, https://www.washingtonpost.com/news/monkey-cage/wp/2017/01/02/yes-taiwan-wants-one-china-but-which-china-does-it-want/?noredirect=on&utm_term=.49c2e5c51256

11 "Nearly 40 per cent of Hong Kong students in 'veiled' poll support violent protests", Kimmy Chung, *South China Morning Post*, 2 October 2017, https://www.scmp.com/news/hong-kong/politics/article/2113646/nearly-40-cent-hong-kong-students-veiled-poll-support

12 "HKU poll: Only 3.1% of young HongKongers identify as Chinese, marking 20 year low", Kris Cheng, *Hong Kong Free Press*, 21 June 2017, https://www.hongkongfp.com/2017/06/21/hku-poll-3-1-young-hongkongers-identify-chinese-marking-20-year-low/

13 "One in six support Hong Kong independence from China: poll", *Reuters*, July 25, 2016, https://www.*Reuters*.com/article/us-hongkong-china-survey-idUSKCN1050GT

14 "The Power of the Powerless", Vaclav Havel, International Journal of Politics, 1979, International Center on Nonviolent Conflict, https://www.nonviolent-conflict.org/resource/the-power-of-the-powerless/

15 "Declaration of Charter 77", 1 January 1977, https://ktwop.files.wordpress.com/2011/12/charter-77-declaration.pdf

16 "In full: Charter 08- Liu Xiaobo's pro-democracy manifesto for China that lead to his jailing", Human Rights in China, *Hong Kong Free Press*, 14 July 2017, https://www.hongkongfp.com/2017/07/14/full-charter-08-liu-xiaobos-pro-democracy-manifesto-china-led-jailing/

On the fourth anniversary of the Umbrella Movement, a way forward for the Hong Kong freedom struggle

1 "Let Hongkongers decide city's future after 2047, pro-democracy figures say", Karen Cheung, *Hong Kong Free Press*, 21 April 2016, https://www.hongkongfp.com/2016/04/21/65478/

2 "Pro-democracy ADPL party calls for self-determination in 30th anniversary manifesto", Kris Cheng, *Hong Kong Free Press*, 8 June 2016, https://www.hongkongfp.com/2016/06/08/pro-democracy-adpl-party-calls-for-self-determination-in-30th-anniversary-manifesto/. See also "A turn to localism? Civic Party launches 10th anniversary manifesto", Kris Cheng, *Hong Kong Free Press*, 16 March 2016, https://www.hongkongfp.com/2016/03/16/a-turn-to-localism-civic-party-launches-10th-anniversary-manifesto/

3 "I heard Benny Tai's independence remarks and approved gov't statement condemning him, says Chief Exec. Carrie Lam", *Hong Kong Free Press*, 6 April 2018, https://www.hongkongfp.com/2018/04/06/i-heard-benny-tais-independence-remarks-approved-govt-statement-condemning-says-chief-exec-carrie-lam/

4 "The next phase of the democracy movement: A referendum on on constitutional reform and sustainable democratic self-governance", Joshua Wong, August 2, 2015, translation by Lucas Tse, Lewis Ho and Kong Tsung-gan, https://medium.com/@KongTsungGan/the-next-phase-of-the-democracy-movement-a-referendum-on-constitutional-reform-and-sustainable-b66c164842b7

5 "Eddie Chu- Hong Kong Self-Determination", Foreign Correspondents Club of Hong Kong, 11 October 2016, https://www.youtube.com/watch?v=xeObX1guJmk

6 "HKU poll: Only 3.1% of young Hongkongers identify as Chinese, marking 20 year low", Kris Cheng, *Hong Kong Free Press*, 21 June 2017, https://www.hongkongfp.com/2017/06/21/hku-poll-3-1-young-hongkongers-identify-chinese-marking-20-year-low/

7 See "Young professionals are leaving Hong Kong in droves in search of better lives where family, friends and fun comes first", Rachel Leung, David Vetter, South Chna Morning Post, 18 August 2018, https://www.scmp.com/news/hong-kong/politics/article/2160161/young-professionals-are-leaving-hong-kong-droves-search, and "Hong Kong's doctors and nurses head for Australia, Canada and Britain, as 24,300 residents emigrate in 2017", Emily Tsang, *South China Morning Post*, 24 February 2018, https://www.scmp.com/news/hong-kong/community/article/2134561/hong-kongs-doctors-and-nurses-head-new-lives-australia

8 See "Hong Kong pro-democracy group says two members detained and questioned during travel to mainland", Kris Cheng, *Hong Kong Free Press*, 27 August 2018, https://www.hongkongfp.com/2018/08/27/hong-kong-pro-democracy-group-says-two-members-detained-questioned-travel-mainland/, and "Hong Kong pro-independence group says members' families 'warned' by mainland authorities", Kris Cheng, *Hong Kong Free Press*, 3 September 2018, https://www.hongkongfp.com/2018/09/03/hong-kong-pro-independence-student-group-says-members-families-warned-mainland-authorities/,

and "Political surveillance in Hong Kong", Kong Tsung-gan, https://medium.com/@KongTsungGan/political-surveillance-in-hong-kong-4044fe88c6c0

Censorship in Hong Kong since the Umbrella Movement

1 "Chinese dissident Badiucao's Hong Kong show cancelled over 'threats'", BBC, 3 November 2018, https://www.bbc.com/news/world-asia-china-46080408

2 "Senior Financial Times journalist Victor Mallet barred from entering Hong Kong", Tom Grundy, *Hong Kong Free Press*, 9 November 2018, https://www.hongkongfp.com/2018/11/09/just-senior-financial-times-journalist-victor-mallet-banned-entering-hong-kong/

3 "In U-turn, Hong Kong art space Tai Kwun says it will host dissident author Ma Jian's event", Holmes Chan, *Hong Kong Free Press*, 9 November 2018, https://www.hongkongfp.com/2018/11/09/breaking-u-turn-hong-kong-art-space-tai-kwun-says-will-host-dissident-author-ma-jians-event/

4 "Hongkong Post criticized for refusing to send democracy activists' fliers", Jeffie Lam, *South China Morning Post*, 28 August 2014, https://www.scmp.com/news/hong-kong/article/1581295/hongkong-post-criticised-refusing-send-democracy-activists-fliers

5 "Students told to leave Tamar; pro-Beijing group to use park", EJ Insight, September 25, 2014, http://www.ejinsight.com/20140925-students-told-to-leave-tamar-pro-beijing-group-to-use-park/

6 "Mainlandization: How the Communist Party works to control and assimilate Hong Kong", Kong Tsung-gan, *Hong Kong Free Press*, 15 October 2018, https://www.hongkongfp.com/2017/10/15/mainlandization-communist-party-works-control-assimilate-hong-kong/

7 Ibid.

8 Annual reports, Hong Kong Journalists Association, https://www.hkja.org.hk/en/hkjas-news/publications/annual-report/

9 "Disappearing act: What happened to the art from Hong Kong's Umbrella Movement?", Laura Mannering, AFP/*Hong Kong Free Press*, 29 September 2018, https://www.hongkongfp.com/2018/09/29/disappearing-act-happened-art-hong-kongs-umbrella-movement/

10 "Bao Pu Discusses Zhao Ziyang's Memoir", Sky Canaves, *Wall Street Journal*, June 4, 2009, https://blogs.wsj.com/chinarealtime/2009/06/04/bao-pu-discusses-zhao-ziyangs-memoirs/

11 "Exclusive: Publication of China crackdown memoirs halted", Benjamin Kang Lim, *Reuters*, June 19, 2010, https://www.*Reuters*.com/article/us-china-tiananmen-memoirs/exclusive-publication-of-china-crackdown-memoirs-halted-idUSTRE65I0NY20100619

12 "The closure of Mong Kok's pedestrian zone exposes one of Hong Kong's dirty little secrets", Tim Hamlett, *Hong Kong Free Press*, 5 August 2018, https://www.hongkongfp.com/2018/08/05/closure-mong-koks-pedestrian-zone-exposes-one-hong-kongs-dirty-little-secrets/

13 "Buskers to be temporarily banned from Hong Kong piazza, court rules", Holmes Chan, *Hong Kong Free Press*, 8 October 2018, https://www.hongkongfp.com/2018/10/08/buskers-temporarily-banned-times-square-piazza-hong-kong-court-rules/

14 "News outlet HK01 rejects watchdog's concerns over 'self-censorship' of declassified Tiananmen Massacre report", Elson Tong, *Hong Kong Free Press*, 28 December 2017,

https://www.hongkongfp.com/2017/12/28/news-outlet-hk01-rejects-watchdogs-concerns-self-censorship-declassified-tiananmen-massacre-report/

15 "HK Economic Journal should restore outspoken writers column, says letter from employees", Gene Lin, *Hong Kong Free Press*, 2 August 2016, https://www.hongkongfp.com/2016/08/02/hk-economic-journal-restore-outspoken-writers-column-says-letter-employees/

16 "On-line media to be admitted to government media events", The Government of the Hong Kong Administrative Region Press Releases, September 19, 2017, https://www.info.gov.hk/gia/general/201709/19/P2017091900332.htm?fontSize=1

17 "Police launch investigation after threatening letters sent to *Hong Kong Free Press* staff", *Hong Kong Free Press*, 4 October 2017, https://www.hongkongfp.com/2017/10/04/police-launch-investigation-threatening-letters-sent-hong-kong-free-press-staff/

18 "*South China Morning Post* removes letter linking Xi Jinping with Singaporean investor", Tom Grundy, *Hong Kong Free Press*, 21 July 2017, https://www.hongkongfp.com/2017/07/21/south-china-morning-post-removes-article-linking-chinese-president-xi-jinping-singaporean-investor/

19 "Taiwan delivery service refuses to send books to Hong Kong due to Chinese censorship, writer claims", Holmes Chan, *Hong Kong Free Press*, 14 January 2019, https://www.hongkongfp.com/2019/01/14/taiwan-delivery-service-refused-send-books-hong-kong-due-chinese-censorship-writer-claims/

20 "Scholar claims courier service SF Express reufsed to deliver his book related to Hong Kong Umbrella Movement", Holmes Chan, *Hong Kong Free Press*, 18 January 2019, https://www.hongkongfp.com/2019/01/18/scholar-claims-courier-service-sf-express-refused-deliver-book-related-hong-kong-umbrella-movement/

21 "WSJ Investigation: China Offered to Bail Out Troubled Malaysian Fund in Return for Deals", Tom Wright and Bradley Hope, *Wall Street Journal*, January 7, 2019, https://www.wsj.com/articles/how-china-flexes-its-political-muscle-to-expand-power-overseas-11546890449

22 "China Spies on International Media in Hong Kong. Will Hong Kong Authorities Investigate?", Maya Wang, Human Rights Watch, January 9, 2019, https://www.hrw.org/news/2019/01/09/china-spies-international-media-hong-kong

23 "Scuffle at New Year's Day rally as man carrying Hong Kong independence banner enters gov't protest hotspot", Holmes Chan, *Hong Kong Free Press*, 2 January 2019, https://www.hongkongfp.com/2019/01/02/scuffle-new-years-day-rally-man-carrying-hong-kong-independence-banner-enters-govt-protest-hotspot/

24 "Separatist slogans not permitted at Hong Kong gov't headquarters protest site, says Chief Exec.", Kris Cheng, *Hong Kong Free Press*, 2 October 2018, https://www.hongkongfp.com/2018/10/02/separatist-slogans-not-permitted-hong-kong-govt-headquarters-protest-site-says-chief-exec/

25 "Democrats set to rally outside Hong Kong gov't HQ, as pro-independence groups barred from forecourt", *Hong Kong Free Press*, 1 January 2019, https://www.hongkongfp.com/2019/01/01/democrats-set-rally-outside-hong-kong-govt-hq-pro-independence-groups-barred-forecourt/

26 "HKSARG reiterates its zero tolerance on HK independence", The Government of the Hong Kong Special Administrative Region Press Releases, January 1, 2019, https://www.info.gov.hk/gia/general/201901/01/P2019010101012.htm

27 "March organizer could be banned from 'Civic Square' over 'failure to stop separatist' display at forecourt of Hong Kong government headquarters", Danny Mok, Tony Cheung,

South China Morning Post, 3 January 2019, https://www.scmp.com/news/hong-kong/politics/article/2180466/march-organiser-could-be-banned-civic-square-over-failure

28 "Gov't move to restrict access to protest hotspot 'Civic Square' was unconstitutional, court rules", Holmes Chan, *Hong Kong Free Press*, 20 November 2018, https://www.hongkongfp.com/2018/11/20/govt-move-close-off-protest-hotspot-civic-square-unconstitutional-hong-kong-court-rules/

29 "Hong Kong bans pro-democracy lawmaker Eddie Chu from running in village election" Tom Grundy, *Hong Kong Free Press*, 2 December 2018, https://www.hongkongfp.com/2018/12/02/breaking-hong-kong-govt-bans-lawmaker-eddie-chu-entering-village-election-race/

30 "In U-turn, Hong Kong art space Tai Kwun says it will host dissident author Ma Jian's event", Holmes Chan, *Hong Kong Free Press*, 9 November 2018, https://www.hongkongfp.com/2018/11/09/breaking-u-turn-hong-kong-art-space-tai-kwun-says-will-host-dissident-author-ma-jians-event/

31 "Statement: Free Express Week 'Badiucao' art exhibition", *Hong Kong Free Press*, 2 November 2018, https://www.hongkongfp.com/2018/11/02/statement-free-expression-week-badiucao-art-exhibition/

32 "Hong Kong bans democrat Lau Siu-lai from standing in legislative by-election", Holmes Chan, *Hong Kong Free Press*, 12 October 2018, https://www.hongkongfp.com/2018/10/12/breaking-hong-kong-bans-democrat-lau-siu-lai-standing-kowloon-west-election/

33 "RTHK to air docudrama based on 'abducted' bookseller's return to Hong Kong", Kris Cheng, *Hong Kong Free Press*, 18 October 2018, https://www.hongkongfp.com/2018/10/18/rthk-air-docudrama-based-abducted-booksellers-return-hong-kong/

34 "Joint Press Statement: China UPR: Civil Society Deeply Concerned by Removal of Key Stakeholder Information by the UN Office of the High Commissioner for Human Rights for Upcoming Universal Periodic Review of China", Human Rights Watch, November 5, 2018, https://www.hrw.org/news/2018/11/05/joint-press-statement-china-upr

35 "Pro-independence party officially banned by Hong Kong gov't in historic move restricting freedom of assembly", Kris Cheng, *Hong Kong Free Press*, 24 September 2018, https://www.hongkongfp.com/2018/09/24/breaking-pro-independence-party-officially-banned-hong-kong-govt-historic-move-restricting-freedom-assembly/

36 "Student leader accuses Baptist University of removing anti-China remarks from his speech", Holmes Chan, *Hong Kong Free Press*, 5 September 2018, https://www.hongkongfp.com/2018/09/05/student-leader-accuses-baptist-university-removing-anti-china-remarks-speech/

37 "Polytechnic University students end hunger strike after school backs down in censorship row", Holmes Chan, *Hong Kong Free Press*, 8 October 2018, https://www.hongkongfp.com/2018/10/08/polytechnic-university-students-end-hunger-strike-school-backs-censorship-row/

38 Video: In full – Activist Andy Chan says Hong Kong independence is the only path to democracy at press club talk", *Hong Kong Free Press*, 14 August 2018, https://www.hongkongfp.com/2018/08/14/video-full-activist-andy-chan-says-hong-kong-independence-path-democracy-press-club-talk/

39 "Senior Financial Times journalist Victor Mallet banned from entering Hong Kong", Tom Grundy, *Hong Kong Free Press*, 9 November 2018, https://www.hongkongfp.com/2018/11/09/just-senior-financial-times-journalist-victor-mallet-banned-entering-hong-kong/

40 "Journalists Assoc. expresses 'extreme regret' over RTHK's ban on livestreaming pro-independence activist's talk", *Hong Kong Free Press*, 10 August 2018, https://www.hongkongfp.com/2018/08/10/journalists-assoc-expresses-extreme-regret-rthks-ban-live-streaming-pro-independence-activists-talk/

41 "Chinese forum event attended by Hong Kong ex-leader CY Leung tries to censor local media", Holmes Chan, *Hong Kong Free Press*, 25 June 2018, https://www.hongkongfp.com/2018/06/25/chinese-forum-event-attended-hong-kong-ex-leader-cy-leung-tries-censor-local-media/

42 "I'm behind condemnation of Benny Tai: Carrie Lam", RTHK, 6 April 2018, http://news.rthk.hk/rthk/en/component/k2/1389767-20180406.htm

43 "Benny Tai a threat to the country, warns official", RTHK, 11 April 2018, http://news.rthk.hk/rthk/en/component/k2/1390637-20180411.htm

44 "Benny Tai accused of turning Hong Kong's streets into 'rivers of blood' by pro-Beijing lawmakers during heated independence debate", Kimmy Cheung, South China Moring Post, 24 May 2018, https://www.scmp.com/news/hong-kong/politics/article/2147591/benny-tai-accused-turning-hong-kongs-streets-rivers-blood

45 "Response by Hong Kong SAR Government to media enquiries", The Government of the Hong Kong Special Administrative Region Press Releases, March 30, 2018, https://www.info.gov.hk/gia/general/201803/30/P2018033000690.htm

46 "Hongkongers may be barred from elections over 'end one-party dictatorship' slogans, says top Beijing delegate", Kris Cheng, *Hong Kong Free Press*, 20 March 2018, https://www.hongkongfp.com/2018/03/20/hongkongers-may-barred-elections-end-one-party-dictatorship-slogan-says-top-beijing-delegate/

47 "Advocates of ending 'one-party dictatorship' cannot serve in Hong Kong legislature, says Chinese official in Macau", Kris Cheng, *Hong Kong Free Press*, 20 March 2018, https://www.hongkongfp.com/2018/03/20/advocates-ending-one-party-dictatorship-cannot-serve-hong-kong-legislature-says-chinese-official-macau/

48 "Hong Kong ban on pro-democracy election hopeful Agnes Chow 'illegal and groundless', party says", Tom Grundy and Kris Cheng, *Hong Kong Free Press*, 27 January 2018, https://www.hongkongfp.com/2018/01/27/breaking-hong-kong-ban-pro-democracy-election-hopeful-agnes-chow-illegal-groundless-party-says/

49 "Hong Kong bars another citizen from standing in March by-election", Kris Cheng, *Hong Kong Free Press*, 31 March 2018, https://www.hongkongfp.com/2018/01/31/breaking-hong-kong-govt-bars-another-citizen-standing-march-election/

50 "James Chan third citizen to be barred from election by Hong Kong government over political beliefs", Kris Cheng, *Hong Kong Free Press*, 1 February 2018, https://www.hongkongfp.com/2018/02/01/just-james-chan-third-citizen-barred-election-hong-kong-govt-political-beliefs/

51 "Activist Joshua Wong files legal challenge against Hong Kong Companies Registry for denying registration for his party", *Hong Kong Free Press*, 18 April 2018, https://www.hongkongfp.com/2018/04/18/activist-joshua-wong-files-legal-challenge-hong-kong-companies-registry-denying-registration-party/

52 "Statement by Heads of Universities", University of Hong Kong, 15 September 2017, https://www.hku.hk/press/news_detail_16811.html

53 "TVB accused of self-censorship over sudden suspension of political satire show during Xi Jinping's visit", Ellie Ng, *Hong Kong Free Press*, 5 July 2017, https://www.hongkongfp.com/2017/07/05/tvb-accused-self-censorship-sudden-suspension-political-satire-show-xi-jinpings-visit/

54 "Asia Society faces backlash as Joshua Wong demands explanation over 'blocked' book launch", Elson Tong, *Hong Kong Free Press*, 6 July 2017, https://www.hongkongfp.com/2017/07/06/asia-society-faces-backlash-joshua-wong-demands-explanation-blocked-book-launch/

55 "US Asia Society HQ blames Hong Kong centre for 'error in judgment' over Joshua Wong ban", Elson Tong, *Hong Kong Free Press*, 7 July 2017, https://www.hongkongfp.com/2017/07/07/us-asia-society-hq-blames-hong-kong-centre-error-judgement-joshua-wong-ban/

56 "HK20: Joshua Wong among 20 activists taken away by police after scuffle with pro-Beijing group", Kris Cheng, *Hong Kong Free Press*, 1 July 2017, https://www.hongkongfp.com/2017/07/01/hk20-joshua-wong-among-20-activists-taken-away-police-scuffle-pro-beijing-group/

57 "Hong Kong democracy activists struggle to be heard under Pres. Xi Jinping security lockdown", Ellie Ng, *Hong Kong Free Press*, 3 July 2017, https://www.hongkongfp.com/2017/07/03/hk20-hong-kong-democracy-activists-struggle-make-voices-heard-pres-xi-jinpings-visit/

58 "Democracy activist Joshua Wong loses case over police use of handcuffs; says courts should clarify law", Holmes Chan, *Hong Kong Free Press*, 5 July 2018, https://www.hongkongfp.com/2018/07/05/democracy-activist-joshua-wong-loses-case-police-use-handcuffs-says-courts-clarify-law/

59 "Pro-independence party's Handover eve vigil relocated to Baptist University due to heavy police presence", Elson Tong, *Hong Kong Free Press*, 1 July 2017, https://www.hongkongfp.com/2017/07/01/pro-independence-partys-handover-eve-vigil-relocated-baptist-university-due-heavy-police-presence/

60 "Chief Exec. CY Leung sues pro-democracy lawmaker for defamation, in a first for Hong Kong", Kris Cheng, *Hong Kong Free Press*, 6 March 2017, https://www.hongkongfp.com/2017/03/06/chief-exec-cy-leung-sues-pro-democracy-lawmaker-for-defamation-in-a-first-for-hong-kong/

61 "Pro-Beijing, anti-CY Leung paper Sing Pao says management has received 'serious threats', website attacked", Elson Tong, *Hong Kong Free Press*, 22 February 2017, https://www.hongkongfp.com/2017/02/22/pro-beijing-anti-cy-leung-paper-sing-pao-says-management-received-serious-threats-website-attacked/

62 "Red paint, stalking: Pro-Beijing paper comes escalated violence 'aimed at silencing dissent'", Ellie Ng, *Hong Kong Free Press*, 27 February 2017, https://www.hongkongfp.com/2017/02/27/red-paint-stalking-pro-beijing-newspaper-condemns-escalated-violence-aimed-silencing-dissent/

63 "Hong Kong gov't bans two political groups from selling merchandise at New Year fair citing safety concerns", Ellie Ng, *Hong Kong Free Press*, 19 January 2017, https://www.hongkongfp.com/2017/01/19/hogn-kong-govt-bans-two-political-groups-from-selling-goods-at-new-year-fair-citing-safety-concerns/

64 "Asia Society Hong Kong cancels screening of Umbrella protest film amid political concerns", Catherine Lai, *Hong Kong Free Press*, 13 November 2016, https://www.hongkongfp.com/2016/11/13/asia-society-hong-kong-cancels-screening-umbrella-protest-film-amid-political-concerns/

65 "'Shameless': Activists slam ViuTV after channel cancels reality show over pro-independence speech", Kris Cheng, *Hong Kong Free Press*, 20 October 2016, https://www.hongkongfp.com/2016/10/20/shamless-activists-slam-viutv-channel-cancels-reality-show-pro-independence-speech/

66 "Wang & Fung: Tensions between China and Hong Kong and update report in the semi-autonomous territory", 日本外国特派員協会 会見映像 オフィシャルサイト FCCJchannel, October 17, 2016, https://www.youtube.com/watch?v=fQSJz7sROCQ

67 "ViuTV apologises to reality show guests after Hong Kong independence row", Kris Cheng, *Hong Kong Free Press*, 22 October 2016, https://www.hongkongfp.com/2016/10/22/viutv-privately-apologises-to-former-student-leader-after-hong-kong-independence-row/

68 "CY Leung denies his legal threats against Apple Daily affect Hong Kong's press freedom", Ellie Ng, *Hong Kong Free Press*, 4 October 2016, https://www.hongkongfp.com/2016/10/04/cy-leung-denies-his-legal-threats-against-apple-daily-affect-hong-kongs-press-freedom/

69 不滿籲追究UGL事件向《蘋果》發律師信 689斥社論阻競選連任, Apple Daily, 30 September 2016, https://hk.news.appledaily.com/local/realtime/article/20160930/55711548

70 "China's censors scrubbed a Hong Kong pop star's music from the internet because she supports democracy", Josh Horwitz, Quartz, September 22, 2016, https://qz.com/788121/chinas-censors-scrubbed-a-hong-kong-popstar-activist-denise-hos-music-from-the-internet/

71 "Election mailouts under censorship as fourth candidate barred from running", Kris Cheng, *Hong Kong Free Press*, 2 August 2016, https://www.hongkongfp.com/2016/08/02/election-mailouts-censorship-fourth-candidate-barred-running/

72 "Edward Leung of Hong Kong Indigenous barred from LegCo election", Kris Cheng, *Hong Kong Free Press*, 2 August 2016, https://www.hongkongfp.com/2016/08/02/breaking-edward-leung-hong-kong-indigenous-barred-legco-election/

73 "Hong Kong bans pro-independence National Party from running for election", Kris Cheng, *Hong Kong Free Press*, 30 July 2016, https://www.hongkongfp.com/2016/07/30/breaking-hong-kong-bans-pro-independence-national-party-from-running-for-election/

74 "Election mailouts under censorship as fourth candidate barred from running", Kris Cheng, *Hong Kong Free Press*, 2 August 2016, https://www.hongkongfp.com/2016/08/02/election-mailouts-censorship-fourth-candidate-barred-running/

75 "Localist candidate who explicitly rejects Basic Law barred from LegCo election" Kris Cheng, *Hong Kong Free Press*, 1 August 2016, https://www.hongkongfp.com/2016/08/01/localist-candidate-explicitly-rejects-basic-law-barred-legco-election/

76 "Edward Leung of Hong Kong Indigenous barred from LegCo election", Kris Cheng, *Hong Kong Free Press*, 2 August 2016, https://www.hongkongfp.com/2016/08/02/breaking-edward-leung-hong-kong-indigenous-barred-legco-election/

77 "Another pro-independence candidate barred from running in LegCo elections", Kris Cheng, *Hong Kong Free Press*, 2 August 2016, https://www.hongkongfp.com/2016/08/02/another-pro-independence-candidate-barred-running-legco-election/

78 "Lancome scraps Hong Kong concert with Denise Ho; online backlash over move to distance itself from pro-democracy star", Raymond Yeung, *South China Morning Post*, 5 June 2016, https://www.scmp.com/news/hong-kong/politics/article/1966367/lancome-scraps-hong-kong-concert-denise-ho-online-backlash

79 "In pictures: 3,000 fans and supporters attend Denise Ho concert after controversial Lancome cancellation", Gene Lin, *Hong Kong Free Press*, 20 June 2016, https://www.hongkongfp.com/2016/06/20/in-pictures-3000-fans-and-supporters-attend-denise-ho-concert-after-controversial-lancome-cancellation/

80 "'Ungrounded, unjustified and arbitrary': Artists slam removal of ICC protest art", Karen Cheung, *Hong Kong Free Press*, 25 May 2016, https://www.hongkongfp.com/2016/05/25/

ungrounded-unjustified-and-arbitrary-artists-slam-removal-of-icc-protest-art/

81 "Hundreds join protests over sacking of Ming Pao editor", AFP, *Hong Kong Free Press*, 2 May 2016, https://www.hongkongfp.com/2016/05/02/hundreds-join-protest-sacking-ming-pao-editor/

82 "Leaked records reveal offshore holdings of China's elite", International Consortium of Investigative Journalists, https://www.icij.org/investigations/offshore/leaked-records-reveal-offshore-holdings-of-chinas-elite/

83 "More accusations of censorship emerge as gov't dodges questions over Taiwan controversy", Kris Cheng, *Hong Kong Free Press*, 23 March 2016, https://www.hongkongfp.com/2016/03/23/more-accusations-of-censorship-emerge-as-govt-dodges-questions-over-taiwan-controversy/

84 "Hong Kong's popular, lucrative horror movie about Beijing has disappeared from theaters", Heather Timmons, Quartz, February 17, 2016, https://qz.com/615831/the-most-successful-movie-made-in-hong-kong-in-years-has-been-pulled-from-theaters/

85 "Dystopian film about Hong Kong in 2025 touches nerve with Beijing", Clare Baldwin, *Reuters*, March 27, 2016, https://www.*Reuters*.com/article/us-china-film-tenyears-idUSKCN0WJ0F2

86 "In Hong Kong, Fears for an Art Museum", Amy Qin, *New York Times*, December 25, 2015, https://www.nytimes.com/2015/12/26/arts/international/in-hong-kong-fears-for-an-art-museum.html?module=inline

87 "The 2015 Policy Address", https://www.policyaddress.gov.hk/2015/eng/pdf/PA2015.pdf

Made in the USA
Columbia, SC
07 September 2019